To Laura & [illegible]
with love from [illegible]

SOCIAL ECONOMICS: AN ALTERNATIVE THEORY
Volume 1: Building Anew on Marshall's Principles

Social Economics: An Alternative Theory

Volume 1
Building Anew on Marshall's Principles

Neva R. Goodwin

St. Martin's Press   New York

First published in the United States of America in 1991

Printed in Hong Kong

ISBN 0–312–05780–6

Library of Congress Cataloging-in-Publication Data
Goodwin, Neva R.
Social economics: an alternative theory/Neva R. Goodwin
p.   cm.
Includes bibliographical references and index.
Contents: v. 1. Building anew on Marshall's Principles.
ISBN 0–312–05780–6 (v. 1)
1. Neoclassical school of economics.   2. Welfare economics.
3. Economics—Social aspects.   4. Marshall, Alfred, 1842–1924.
Principles of economics.   I. Title.
HB98.2.G66   1991
330.15′56—dc20   90–20763
                                                             CIP

To **David** and **Miranda**, with much love, and some apologies for the times when this work has claimed too much of my attention.

Contents

Contents   xiii

List of Figures

Preface

This book is addressed, first of all, to economists. Nevertheless, it should be noted that *Social Economics: An Alternative Theory* has been written with more than one audience in mind. In particular, while Parts I, II, and III are all basic to the formulation of the proposed alternative system of economic theory, social economics, it may be that a non-economist, focusing on the methodology of the social sciences, might wish to go directly to Part II; while a confirmed neoclassical economist, curious about what this book can say that is new about that paradigm, may wish to begin with Part III.

In the economic area, this book will take up some topics central to neoclassical economics. Neoclassical economics itself, as a system of economic theory, will also be discussed. More space, however, will be given to the economic issues which are insufficiently addressed by either neoclassical or Marxian economics.

More broadly, a number of issues will be examined which are of concern for the social sciences in general. It is therefore hoped that this book will also find readers among non-economists who have a stake in other social sciences.

Subjects of public policy will not be addressed directly; however, some of the motivation for the book comes from the perception that economic systems (both capitalist and communist), and the social realities that accompany them, have been changing faster than theory has been able to keep up. (This motivation is most openly expressed at the end of Chapter 4). The book represents, in part, an attempt to project the beginnings of a system of economic theory that will be appropriate to contemporary realities.

The first two Parts of the book, then, are designed to be read by economists and also by other individuals interested in the social sciences and their interactions with the real world. Hence an effort has been made to communicate in a language which is not specialised to one discipline. Relatively few technical terms have been used; where they appear, they are explained in the notes.

A few sections are likely to be of less interest to non-economists: these include the second half of Chapter 1 (following 'Some Examples of "What is asked" Beyond What Existing Systems of Economic Theory Can Answer') and some parts of Chapters 6 and 7. The whole of Part III is more specialised, and terminology that has been developed for the discipline of economics is used more freely there, without concessions to the general reader. Warnings are posted at the beginning of Part III, for the non-economist who wishes to venture into it.

How each reader perceives this book will depend upon many things; perhaps chief among them will be whether the reader's focus is on what the book includes, or on what it leaves out. When I, the author, look at it from the latter perspective, I become discouraged; a very large project has been opened here, and only a small fraction of what it projects is accomplished in this work. It is my hope, therefore, that you, the reader, will focus upon what is offered here; and, where your thinking runs on to what else is needed in social economics, that you will not despair of its appearing in later work on the subject.

NEVA R. GOODWIN

Acknowledgements

I have many people to thank for their kindness, patience, and substantive contributions to this book.

Paul Streeten has given hours to reading a series of drafts, distilling his responses into most valuable reactions and suggestions. He has been an intellectual guide and a highly valued friend. Mohan Rao likewise gave me the benefit of much time and excellent advice at a critical stage; he and Paul Streeten each read at least two complete drafts – an heroic task.

Harvey Leibenstein, Kathleen Langley and Jeffrey James also were kind enough to read an early draft in its entirety (twice the length of the present book!), and I am grateful to each of them for their time and useful comments.

Pankaj Tandon gave a careful reading to Part III, which benefited much from his suggestions. Robert Dorfman spared not his criticism, and the book is the better for the three chapters withdrawn on his friendly advice. Ashoka Mody suggested a reorganization of Part I for which I am very grateful. The arguments I have had with Peter Doeringer along the way have done us both good. Robert Bishop made helpful comments on an early outline. Lee Halprin gave a close reading and detailed suggestions on material which will appear partly in this volume, partly in the next. Barbara Brandt kindly read and responded to a late draft of the full manuscript.

I was fortunate to participate for three years in an interdisciplinary discussion group which studied and applied the approach of discourse analysis in a variety of contexts. Members of the group who read parts of the manuscript, and provided useful feedback, included Robert Solow, S. M. Miller, Harriet Ritvo, Peter Buck, Paul Fideler, James Paradis, and William Gamson. (It was at the insistence of the last of these, that I spell out precisely what I was doing in Part III, that caused me to sit down and write Chapters 6 through 10 of the present book.)

Robert Cohen, philosopher and physicist, gave me encouragement through some perplexities in Part II. I benefited from a Summer 1989 visit to the World Institute for Development Research in Helsinki, where I was able to present my work on Chapter 11 and to receive especially helpful comments from Martha Nussbaum and Uskali Mäki.

Joshua Lederberg, ranging far from his own field, has been kind in bringing pertinent bibliographical references to my attention.

I am truly grateful for the assistance of all these individuals as well as others with whom I have discussed many of the ideas of this book over the course of several years. The most fruitful discussions are not always the ones in which there is most agreement. Since I have only sometimes, but not always, been won over to a different viewpoint, it must be said that no one but myself is to blame for errors of emphasis, omission or commission which remain.

I would like to acknowledge with warm gratitude the liberating assistance of my housekeeper, Eliane Chieregato.

My husband, Bruce Mazlish, has provided the ideal combination of intellectual stimulus, wide knowledge, and a fresh point of view on a great range of subjects. His willingness to read drafts as they appear and to share his own ideas, as well as his kind and loving emotional support, are treasures about which I can only say: if everyone had so good a friend, what a splendid world this would be!

NEVA R. GOODWIN

Part I
Introduction to Social Economics

1 The Field of Economics and Systems of Theory Therein

Our subject is economics. Let us consider the possibility that neoclassical and Marxian economics – the two dominant systems for pursuing this subject – do not exhaust the possibilities of the field. This book will propose the outlines for a third alternative (in Part I). It will then provide the details for a few of the elements suggested in the initial outline.

A diagram will be helpful for conceptualising our subject (see Figure 1.1):

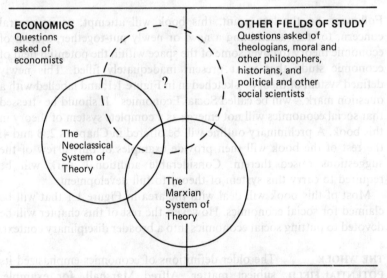

ECONOMICS
Questions asked of economists

OTHER FIELDS OF STUDY
Questions asked of theologians, moral and other philosophers, historians, and political and other social scientists

The Neoclassical System of Theory

The Marxian System of Theory

Figure 1.1 Some systems of economic (and other) theory; their relations to the field of economics and to other fields of study

The picture drawn here gives the outline of one field of study, Economics (on the left), and suggests the presence of other adjacent fields of study, which are lumped together on the right. Within economics we see part of the space that is roughly defined by the 'questions asked of economists' occupied by the neoclassical system of economic theory, and another part occupied by the Marxian system of theory, with some overlap between the two. The schema is used to illustrate a few important points:

- Two terms are brought to the fore here: *field of study*, and *system of theory*. Economics, philosophy, political science, etc., are examples of the former (which may also be called *disciplines*); neoclassical economics and Marxian theory of the latter (which may also be called *paradigms*).
- While a system of theory is conceived of as a lesser set than a field of study, it is possible for a system of theory to overlap some of the space of more than one field; Marxian theory, for example, is shown as so doing.
- Neither neoclassical economics alone, nor neoclassical and Marxian theory together, cover all of the potential field of study defined as 'economics'.

Following on the last point, this book will attempt, as its central concern, to start assembling a new, or newly put-together, system of economic theory to cover some of the space within the potential field of economic study that is at present inadequately filled. This newly defined system of theory – sketched in in Figure 1.1, and labelled with a question mark – will be called Social Economics.[1] It should be stressed that social economics will not emerge as a complete system of theory in this book. A preliminary outline will be offered in Chapters 2, 3 and 4; the rest of the book will then provide examples of only a few of the suggestions raised therein. Considerable additional work will be required to carry this system of theory to full development.

Most of this book will deal with the area in Figure 1.1 that will be claimed for social economics. However, the rest of this chapter will be devoted to putting social economics into a broader disciplinary context.

THE WHOLE POTENTIAL FIELD OF ECONOMICS   The older definitions of economics emphasized its subject matter. Alfred Marshall, for example, defined 'political economy or economics' by saying that 'it is on the one side a study of wealth; and on the other, and more important side, a study of man.'[2]

The definition which became popular in the 1940s is that economics: 'is the science which studies human behavior as a relationship between ends and scarce means which have alternative uses.'[3]

Samuelson and Nordhaus give almost the same words as these for the leading modern definition. However, the working definition which they urge the student of economics to keep in mind is that this discipline is employed to study: '*What* is produced, *how*, and *for whom*.'[4]

One thing which all these definitions have in common is an assumption: that the author is speaking for the whole field of economics. Figure 1.1 contains the implicit suggestion that it is also valid, and may in fact be common, for an economist to speak for something less than this whole field. Formal definitions such as those given by Robbins or by Samuelson and Nordhaus are appropriately applied to neoclassical economics as a particular system of economic theory. For the content of the whole field of economics Marshall's broader statement, or the 'working definition' of Samuelson and Nordhaus may be more appropriate approximations.

In addition to definitions by content, there exist also definitions emphasising the *approach* of economics, saying (with some justification) that any statement of content that is broad enough to define the whole potential field of economics could also be applied equally well to other social sciences. However, if the criticism of content-definitions is that they are too broad, approach-definitions may be too narrow.[5] I will attempt a different cut at the problem, one that will make three overlapping approximations to a definition of 'the field of economics'. None of the three alone is sufficient, but all of them together may adequately define the fuzzy set we are after.

As the first part of this alternative, let us consider that a field of knowledge may be generated teleologically, in response to the uses to which it will be put. This results in a definition of economics as:

that field of knowledge which attempts to answer

(a) the questions that are asked of economists; and
(b) the questions which economists ask of the material they observe.

The approach to be taken in this book will lean strongly towards application; *social economics will be developed first of all in order to serve as policy economics*. Hence, in this definition, part (a) will be emphasised.

Even the two parts, (a) and (b) together, are still not enough, however, to outline the field. If we were to go no further than this, each economist would then simply carve out his or her subset that would be defined by questions which come from people whom s/he respects, and which define areas that s/he finds of particular interest. An example in my own case will be seen later in this chapter: because Alfred Marshall's work occupied a place of special importance in the history of economic thought, and because his questions define areas of particular interest to me, Marshall's questions to the field of economics will be used as a starting point in this book.

Looking for a second approach to give boundaries to the questions asked of and by economists, I will draw on the formulation of a leading group in the search for alternative systems of economic theory. Paul Ekins, as spokesman for this group, refers to *economy, ecology, society* and *ethics* as the four critical points of reference for an understanding of 'the essential components of human life' which 'interact indivisibly in a single system'.[6] He uses a metaphor for this 'single system' wherein the four points are set in three dimensional space to define an equilateral tetrahedron, as shown in Figure 1.2.

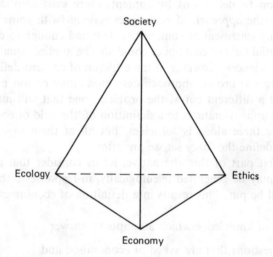

Figure 1.2 The interrelation of economy, ecology, society and ethics*

* **Note**: While our understanding – especially our formal understanding – of such a set of subjects as those described in Figure 1.2 must depend upon some kind of subdivision into areas of concentration, there is nevertheless no single cut at the world which will permanently remain as the best way to view a particular area. Systems of theory, as well as the larger category, fields of study, will, over time, use up the major advantages to be had from particular approaches to self-definition, and will invite newcomers to say, 'Here is a better way of ordering the subjects of our concern'. The new ways may not be better in the long view of history, but at a particular time they may open up possibilities not available to the older paradigms; and those fresher possibilities may at that time have more scope for new learning than the older ones, when most of what was to be seen under their pool of light has been worked through.

As drawn in Figure 1.2, each point is connected to each of the other points. Neoclassical economics goes out a little way along the line from 'economics' towards 'society', less towards 'ethics' and 'ecology'. The set of alternative systems of economic theory that Ekins describes under the umbrella term, 'the living economy', may go much farther towards all three. If social economics is to be one of the examples of 'the living economy' (neither conception is yet far enough developed so that one can define their relationship with certainty), it would probably stay a little closer to the economic focus than is permitted under the 'living economy' umbrella of alternatives.

Taking the skeletal frame for 'the essential components of human life' as thus outlined, I would propose to elaborate on the metaphor by saying that the centre, or core, of the tetrahedron contains the *goals* that are common to all the areas of the social sciences suggested by the four points. Those common goals may be summed up under the single word, *welfare*. The meaning of this term will be discussed in the next chapter, and its application considered in Chapter 3; for now I will simply define it in terms of four principal elements:

- survival
- happiness
- self-actualization
- moral/spiritual development.

$\left.\right\}$ WELFARE: principal elements

Welfare, with its four elements, are what will be described in Chapter 2 as 'primary goals'. It is only as we look to the level of secondary goals (ideals that are not ends in themselves, but that are seen as good because they will lead to the primary goals) that we begin to move towards the 'economics' corner of the tetrahedron in a way that will help us to say what it is that defines the field of economic study as something different from other fields. Until the next chapter, when a more detailed definition of the *secondary goals* of economics will be proposed, they will simply be listed as:

- consumption
- sustainability/health
- hope
- 'enhancing activities'
- economic justice.

$\left.\right\}$ WELFARE: secondary goals

Note that some of these secondary goals may also be secondary (or even primary) goals for other fields in the social sciences. It is only as a *cluster* of goals that these five elements are to be understood as helping to define the field of economics.

It should also be noted that neoclassical economics – representing not the whole field of economics, but one system of theory therein – does not particularly orient toward all of the secondary goals just mentioned. Instead, as will be argued later, it concentrates so largely upon the first one (to do with increasing consumption possibilities) that this often becomes *the* primary goal in neoclassical economic thinking. (This subject will receive more attention in *Social Economics, Volume 2*.) Similarly, in another system of theory, the Marxian, a concept of justice (perhaps more appropriately called 'social justice', as distinct from the definition I will propose) is elevated to a primary position.

One reason for attempting to assemble a new paradigm, social economics, is the belief that *goals are, themselves, an attribute of the field of economics which has been insufficiently recognised and discussed in both of the now-dominant paradigms.* Another reason is the above-mentioned perception of limitations in the goals of the two now dominant paradigms; neither deals with as broad a definition of human welfare as may be appropriate to the system of economic theory that is needed for the changed and changing circumstances of the late twentieth and early twenty-first centuries.

Returning to the broader field of economics, we now have three propositions which may be used together in approaching its definition:

- The field of economics is generated in part out of curiosity, and in part teleologically. It responds to issues which economists deem of interest or – more to the point for social economics – it is a response to the practical uses to which it will be put, via the questions that are asked of economists.
- Economics is one of four defining elements of an area of human concerns which includes, as the other three reference points, ecology, society and ethics.
- While sharing the *primary goal* of human welfare (understood to include survival, happiness, self actualization, and moral/spiritual development) with these other areas of human concern, there are a set of *secondary goals* (consumption, sustainability/health, hope, 'enhancing activities' and economic justice) which, as a set, mark out a territory that is of special economic concern.

Social economics is not proposed to be used *instead of* the existing dominant paradigms (neoclassical and Marxian economics), but rather as something additional, that can be used alongside of them. It should be able to cover those parts of the total field where the existing paradigms are not at their strongest.

There is a story, especially popular among economists, about the Near-Eastern fool-savant, Nasruddin, which provides a useful metaphor for the subject at hand. One night Nasruddin's neighbours found him on his hands and knees under a street lamp. He explained that he was hunting for his house key, and the neighbours joined to help him. When, after a while, the search had yielded no success, a neighbour asked,

'Are you sure you dropped your key here?'
'Oh no, further up the street.'
'Then why are you looking here?' they all asked. Nasruddin answered, 'Because this is where the light is.'

Given one, very dominant, paradigm in Western, capitalist economics, account has often not been taken of where the key was dropped: the search goes on under the brightest pool of light. There is a need, within the total field of economics, for one or more additional pools of illumination which will cover areas within the whole potential field of economics where neither the neoclassical nor the Marxian lamps reach very well.

SOME EXAMPLES OF 'WHAT IS ASKED', BEYOND WHAT EXISTING SYSTEMS OF ECONOMIC THEORY CAN ANSWER There are economic questions – especially questions which probe the subtler issues *behind* the setting of prices and quantities, or which look forward to their *effects* – which do not receive good answers from the neoclassical system of theory. Most importantly, issues keep arising which have to do with the reason why we care about prices and quantities, production and allocation – issues, that is to say, regarding human welfare. These are issues of what will, in this book, be referred to as 'human value' (as opposed to 'economic value', a concept which has been captured by the neoclassical economists and defined as synonymous with *price*). The remainder of this chapter will give a few examples of such questions, and will suggest – quite impressionistically, as an introduction to the main subjects of the book – that the existing paradigms are well suited to dealing with some kind of questions, but not, for example, these:

Subject to what limitations is the price of anything [i.e., its economic value] a measure of its desirability [i.e., its human value]?

How far is the industrial efficiency of any class impaired by the insufficiency of its income?

How far would an increase of the income of any class, if once effected, be likely to sustain itself through its effects in increasing their efficiency and earning power?[7]

These questions have to do with the feedback loop which connects the *end results* of production and distribution (summarised as 'social welfare', or disaggregated into the welfare of separately defined groups in society) with the *processes* of production and distribution. The father of neoclassical economics, Alfred Marshall (Marshall will also be cited as the father of social economics) followed up on the questions just quoted by 'taking it for granted that a more equitable distribution of wealth is to be desired', and then asking:

How far would this justify changes in the institutions of property, or limitations of free enterprise even when they would be likely to diminish the aggregate of wealth?

How far could this be done without injustice, and without slackening the energies of the leaders of progress? (ibid.)

Note the apparent mingling of normative and positive questions here: 'How far would this *justify* . . .' implies a normative position; 'How far *could* . . .' sounds more positive. A similar admixture may be found in the further questions:

Ought we to rest content with the existing forms of division of labour?

Is it necessary that large numbers of the people should be exclusively occupied with work that has no elevating character?

Is it possible to educate gradually among the great mass of workers a new capacity for the higher kinds of work; and in particular for undertaking co-operatively the management of the business in which they are themselves employed? (ibid., p. 35.)

There is a more neutral, or positive, sound to the last collection of questions that will be presented at this point:

How far does economic freedom [Marshall means a system which is operated by the invisible hand of market interactions determined by self-interested rationality] tend of its own action to build up combinations and monopolies, and what are their effects?

How are the various classes of society likely to be affected by
[economic freedom] in the long run;

what will be the intermediate effects while its ultimate results are
being worked out;

and, account being taken of the time over which they will spread,
what is the relative importance of these two classes of ultimate and
intermediate effects? (ibid., p. 34.)

How this last set of questions is answered has been, for most of this
century, the justification for the choice between capitalist versus
socialist or communist economic systems (with the choice of economic
system usually determining the prevailing system of economic theory –
although good arguments can also be made to say that the causality
runs the other way).

The quotations from Marshall's *Principles* that we have just seen are
useful examples of the range of questions that define the whole
potential field of economics, including some of those which tend to lead
outside of the area most effectively illuminated by the neoclassical
system of theory.

What are the areas that are, in fact, most effectively covered by
neoclassical economics? Any detailed attempt to answer that question
is bound to provoke arguments. As a starting-point for thought I will
suggest my own list of the core elements of content and approach
where the neoclassical illumination is most helpful.

I suggest that the pool of light shed by neoclassical economics most
effectively encompasses:

– behaviour that may be understood as atomistic; that is 'rational' in
  the sense of maximising, self-interested, and instrumental; that is
  characterized by 'infinite greed' and by stable, consistent
  preferences; and that is chiefly motivated by economic gain or a
  close approximation thereto;
– where choices are to be made particularly concerning the allocation
  of money, among items that can be made to conform to
  quantitative terms, on the basis of adequate and accurate
  knowledge of how economic behaviour will contribute to an
  individual's welfare, and under conditions of scarcity;
– where the aggregation of micro elements can be simply made,
  because the theory of the atomistic cases is applicable to the
  aggregation thereof, and where social welfare (including the
  welfare of future societies) can be achieved by maximisation of
  individual welfare;

- in the context of markets which may be approximately described by all the conditions required for perfect competition, resulting in 'consumer sovereignty', and where efficiency is highly valued as especially important to maximisation of consumer welfare;
- within a political/economic/cultural system sufficiently 'capitalistic' so that there are many distinct owners of things, and where 'owning' and 'having' are essential value assumptions;
- where change may be most usefully understood at the margin, or formalised as a sequence of iterations, but where equilibrium states are of more significance than the changes between them;
- and where all of the aspects mentioned here may be given a formal representation, with the appearance of precision; and it is possible to maintain the ideal of a purely positive science.

Virtually every neoclassical economist who reads this list will find some elements to object to. 'Infinite greed' is the first element that is likely to raise strong objections from some, but others may say 'I do not assume the motive of economic gain', or 'my paradigm does not require a premise of capitalism', etc. Such readers are asked to remember that the list overlaps, but is not intended to be identical with, the assumptions actually made by the field or by any individual economist: its point is, rather, to describe what are the conditions of the world under which the neoclassical paradigm is most useful and applicable.

Against this backdrop, let us return to the illustrative questions quoted from Alfred Marshall. The 'marginalising' qualities of these questions (that is, the qualities which put them on or outside of the margin of the neoclassical pool of light) will be discussed as issues of *content* and issues of *approach*.

SOME ISSUES OF CONTENT THAT ARE LEFT OUT OF EXISTING POOLS OF ECONOMIC ILLUMINATION

There are many economic topics which cannot be well accommodated within the neoclassical paradigm. By no means all of them are mentioned in the questions just quoted from Alfred Marshall, but some of the major ones are raised.

A   Some content issues scanted by neoclassical economics

A1 Neoclassical economics has left issues of *class* largely to the Marxian paradigm. In part there may be a simple history-of-science reason for this; like siblings tacitly agreeing not to strive in one another's areas of excellence, neoclassical economics has tended to avoid the ground claimed by the

Marxians. A more substantive reason, however, is in the way that the neoclassical methodology is served by keeping to a minimum the characteristics ascribed to its actors. It deals with 'entrepreneurs' and 'heads of households' and 'employers' and 'employees', but it has a hard time dealing with these entities when they are laid on another grid which would define them in terms, e.g., of class or race or gender – grids which would require the recognition of still other descriptors more familiar to the field of sociology than to the neoclassical system of economic theory.

A2   Marshall contrasts the *existing forms* of division of labour with the possibility that workers might attain a *new capacity* for 'higher kinds of work'. He stresses here, as important subject-matter for the field, the welfare of the people who are producing the goods and services. To the questions of 'what is produced, how, and for whom', he would add – perhaps as a priority – questions about the effect of the work upon the worker.

Neoclassical economics would not make the contrast just cited, for several reasons. An important one is that it is a system of theory which is kept coherent in part by operating via a single point of view. The point of view of neoclassical economics is that of the consumer; not the consumer as a whole person (one who will be affected by what is consumed, just as the worker is affected by what s/he produces) but as one whose welfare only relates to the *getting* (not the *using*) of consumption goods.

A3   In contrast to the tone and content of Marshall's questions, neoclassical economics is rarely found asking, 'what if things were different from what they are?' Methodologically, it has chosen to *accept as given* a number of essential issues.

For instance, the neoclassical economist assumes that utility functions and welfare functions will be given exogenously to the field; it does not look at how activities of economic importance may change the real interpretations of welfare and happiness which are supposed to be approximated by these functions.

Moreover, the most rigorous method of defining a desirable welfare change in the neoclassical system is the concept of a Pareto optimum.[8] The moves which are permitted by this approach are stringently restricted by the initial distribution of resources.

In taking resource distributions and welfare functions as given, many issues of change are marginalised.

A4   Similar to the foregoing is a problem in fitting to the neoclassical paradigm Marshall's question about the relative importance of the 'ultimate versus the intermediate' effects of economic freedom. The neoclassical methodological emphasis upon equilibrium does not ask whether the ultimate effect is the *important* one; it merely seeks to define that ultimate, equilibrium state. The transitional, intermediate states tend to be much messier; they are less easily presented with what has become the standard for rigour in neoclassical economics, and they therefore have little place in the content of this system.

B   Some content   *B1* The issue of class is obviously one that is dealt
issues   with at length in the Marxian system. Much of
scanted by   what needs to be said about that subject is said
Marxian   therein; and indeed, the subject will not recur as
economics   such as an important theme in this book. However,
                       as will be noted later, there is a need, somewhere in
the field of economics, for issues of class to be raised *in conjunction with* some of the other divisions in human society that are not so much emphasised in the Marxian system.

B2   Marxian economics gives more weight than does neoclassical economics to the welfare of the worker; but the two systems are alike in adopting only one of these points of view without recognising (a) that *point of view* is one of the critical defining features of a system of theory, and (b) that most people are *both* workers and consumers. Without glossing over the real conflicts between these two points of view, there is need for a system which can deal with human welfare in a more complete way than now exists in either dominant paradigm.

B3   The Marxian paradigm sheds light on some important, large issues in long-term, economic change. The materialist dialectic, the recognition of economic and class-related sources for economic and technological change, and the neomarxian contribution to the idea of hegemony, are examples of contributions to the understanding of major changes in economic systems. In addition to combining these with the neoclassical examination of the movement between equilibrium states, there remains a need for additional elements in our understanding of the industrial and post-industrial evolution of human economic options and choices.

B4 The future remains inadequately represented in both of the dominant systems of theory. This is a serious defect within the field of economics, which attempts to balance competing claims upon the uses of resources; for we, or our children, may pay dearly when the claims of the future are left out of these equations.

SOME ISSUES OF APPROACH THAT ARE LEFT OUT OF EXISTING POOLS OF ECONOMIC ILLUMINATION

A Neoclassical

Neoclassical economics defines success in its own area (i.e., those acts or qualities which are rewarded by status, publication, salary, etc.) in terms of certain 'scientific values' which are widely understood to be (but which, I will argue, may not be) necessarily inherent to the best work in the field. The more closely an economist's work appears to be aligned with these values, the more likely s/he is to achieve success within the profession. Ideas, also, are successful (gain recognition and currency) to the extent that they are compatible with these values. The 'scientific values' in question include:

A5 *Rigour*: this is a difficult word to define, being often used and seldom discussed. It includes a high value on internal consistency and particular kinds of logic; in practice it gives relatively little value to fact or empirical observation; and it tends to evaluate methods of argument according to the difficulty of the mathematics employed. The more difficult the math, the more persuasive the argument. Economic analysis which relies more heavily on other analytic techniques than on mathematics is devalued.

A6 The use of *ideal descriptions* as heuristic devices and as bases for modelling: here the analogy is often made to physics where, for example, the ideal of a frictionless state, or of a perfect vacuum, are useful concepts for the understanding of certain physical interactions.

A7 The idea of *value-neutrality*; the goal of having a science wherein the arguments and the results are based only on fact and reason (or on assumption and reason), with no influence upon them of any human values. This is, apparently, an issue of approach, but it has an impact upon content which is of great significance. Among the subjects raised in the quotations by Marshall, the positivist (or 'value-neutral') approach marginalises, for example:

- The welfare issues which are raised in such questions as that
relating 'the industrial efficiency of any class' to 'the insufficiency
of its income'; or those speculating on the 'existing forms of
division of labour'. Also, 'insufficiency', 'work that has no
elevating character', and 'the higher kinds of work', are value-
laden words or phrases which would be discouraged within the
neoclassical approach.
- Marshall's inquiry into the relation between 'economic' and
'human' values ('Subject to what limitations is the price of
anything a measure of its desirability?') is the question least well
able to be accommodated within the approach of neoclassical
economics. The significance of this question is to ask what
importance we should attach to prices, which are a major part of
the subject of the field of economics. The problem of why this
meta-question can no longer fit into neoclassical economics, and
the detective trail that shows how Marshall himself was
instrumental in removing it from the neoclassical approach, will
be the subject of Part III of this book.
- The question of how far an assumption 'that a more equitable
distribution of wealth is to be desired . . . would justify changes in
the institutions of property, or limitations of free enterprise.' Only
a value can *justify* something. The 'rigorous', 'value-neutral'
approach of neoclassical economics can show a mathematical
equality or inequality between two things, producing formulae
which may be taken outside of the formal neoclassical paradigm
and used to justify actions; but questions about justification as
such are not likely to be presented in formal neoclassical
economics. (A similar discussion would show that the issue of
how far such changes could be taken 'without injustice' is also
discordant with the neoclassical approach.)
- Marshall's stress upon economic freedom was not quite the same
as the modern neoclassical economist's emphasis upon competition. As may be seen from the last set of his questions that we
quoted, Marshall recognised that market freedom could result in
anti-competitive 'combinations and monopolies'. This fact is, of
course, also recognised by the modern neoclassicists. However, this
has become complicated in the context of a system of theory which
formally eschews normative positions while having informally
become associated with a strong normative commitment both to
economic freedom (esp. from government meddling) and to
competition, as two ideals. There are strong reasons why, even in

the writings of sophisticated economists, the ideals of *laissez-faire* and of free trade are not infrequently conflated, with the conflict between these ideals conveniently ignored. Informally, neoclassical economists are uncomfortable about recognising a conflict between two ideals. Formally, they feel hesitant about taking what, for Marshall, was a natural step: to ask, what *should* be done about the anti-competitive results of economic freedom? When Marshall asked that question, he was led to a favourite topic: 'co-operative business'. The idea of competition plays an important role in both the content and the approach of neoclassical economics; the idea of cooperation, as an important alternative, has little room in this system of theory.

B Marxian Are all of the issues just listed, as being ill fitted to the neoclassical economic approach – especially its positivist bent – adequately illuminated by the Marxian pool of light? Some adherents of that system would say Yes. Some counter arguments will be included in the rest of this section.

Regarding the ways or the extent that the 'scientific values' of neoclassical economics may also be seen as limitations upon Marxian economics, the following may be said:

B5 Rigour: the Marxian paradigm makes claims to being 'scientific' that are at least as sweeping as the neoclassical claims. Marx's own support for this was in his verbal logic. His modern successors often employ a more mathematical logic, similar to that of the neoclassicists, since the latter have succeeded in imposing upon the whole field of economics the impression that their own is the only true version of rigour.

B6 Ideal descriptions: the two paradigms have a similar limitation, related to the different ways in which both posit ideal states of the world. The ideal of communism, as a political goal of the Marxian system, looks, and in some ways is, very different from the ideals of equilibrium, perfectly competitive markets, and Rational Economic Man which the neoclassical system holds up as simplifications expediently adopted for the sake of modelling. However, in both cases the ideal states are what lie in the central focus of their pools of light, while the *transitional processes* leading out of the real here and now (towards the ideal states or not, as the case may be) often go on in the dark.

There is also an effect of the fact that, as the conditions of the real world approach their ideal states, these two paradigms are better able to make useful positive statements about the world; this fact tends to create a normative bias, even in the neoclassical system, in favour of bringing about the ideal conditions (such as competition).

Later we will reconsider the implicit assumption that the use of ideals, or ideal cases, in the social sciences is roughly equivalent to the way ideals are employed in physics. The latter may be understood as limit cases, of a particular kind: they are the limits to functions which are continuous all the way out to the limit. Going from normal friction, to much reduced friction, to 'almost no friction', to the limit case of 'zero friction', is a smooth process with no phase-shifts or discontinuous jumps. The question needs to be raised whether the attainment of either the Marxian ideals of communism, or such neoclassical ideals as general equilibrium, perfect competition, and Rational Economic Man, would not, in fact, involve such changes in the nature of reality as we know it that the attainment of these limits would imply a discontinuity. When that is the case, then the analogy to the use of limit cases as 'ideals' in physics is a poor one. (This issue will be explored at greater length in Chapter 11.)

While the approach of focusing the light of analysis upon such limits has been used extensively in the existing systems of economic theory (for the good reason that this is the easier thing to do), the alternative – of concentrating upon the process of change, rather than upon its idealized end-points – remains to be developed.

B7 Value-neutrality: Marx's own highly emotive, polemical style kept human values so central to his writing that it is still more difficult for Marxian than for neoclassical economists to claim value-neutrality. However, that polemical style is not the only, and may well not be the best, way of dealing with human values in the human sciences. Certainly 'justice' and 'injustice' are words frequently used therein, especially with reference to classes. The perspective of class is, however, so widely used in Marx's own writings that it tends to obscure other grids that could be laid upon a human society. When people are necessarily seen as either capitalists or proletarians, it is hard to perceive other important distinctions, as between the rural and the urban poor; between blue- and white-collar workers; between males and females; between present and future generations; etc. Economic justice is required, in daily life, in conflicts between a far more subtle and shifting array of interests, interest groups, and points of view than were recognized by Marx.

The foregoing observations are as far as this book will go to suggest why the existence of the Marxian paradigm does not cover all of the field left out of neoclassical economics. Most of the comparisons from here on will be made to the neoclassical paradigm.

Notes

1. This is not a wholly new name. It would, perhaps, have been ideal to start with a name that had no prior associations, but none such occurred which were meaningful; and *social economics* seems particularly apt: it emphasises the place of economics as a social science, and stresses, too, the fact that humans are social beings.

   Existing uses of this name are, by and large, compatible with the system of theory which this author would like to define; but this project will not be limited by, or act as though under obligation to accept, all of the associations which others may have to 'social economics'.

2. Alfred Marshall, *Principles of Economics*, 1st to 8th edns, p. 1.

   There will be many more occasions to quote from Alfred Marshall's *Principles of Economics*. When not otherwise stated, the edition referred to will be the 8th edn, first printed in 1920 by Macmillan, and reprinted in 1982 by Porcupine Press, Philadelphia. Henceforth all references to the eighth editiion will be cited simply as *Principles*. When other editions are used, the particular source will be noted.

3. Lionel Robbins, *An Essay on the Nature and Significance of Economic Science* 2nd edn (Macmillan, London, 1948) p. 16.

4. See the introductory chapter to *Economics* by Paul A. Samuelson and William D. Nordhaus; 12th edn, (McGraw-Hill, New York, 1985) p. 13.

5. See, for example, Gary Becker, *The Economic Approach to Human Behavior* (University of Chicago Press) 1976. He specifies: 'The combined assumptions of maximizing behavior, market equilibrium, and stable preferences, form the heart of the economic approach as I see it' (p. 5.)

6. The passages in quotation marks are from 'Central Concerns of Living Economics'; app: to the *Living Economy Network Mailing* 1, January 1989; from the office of Paul Ekins, School of Peace Studies, University of Bradford. The outlines of the tetrahedron of Figure 1.2 were described to me by Ekins in a conversation in April 1989.

7. *Principles*, pp. 33–4. As Marshall's long sentences and paragraphs are sometimes taxing to follow, some liberty has been taken here, and in the sets of quotations immediately following, in breaking them down into more readable chunks.

8. For a succinct and insightful statement on the reason why neoclassical economics is drawn to Pareto optimisation – and the consequences of this approach – see the quotation from Talbot Page on p. 84, below.
   (A Pareto improvement is a change which benefits at least one person, and harms none: a Pareto optimum is a situation which cannot be changed in any way that is a Pareto improvement. Note that redistribution from the rich to the poor is not a Pareto improvement; the rich lose. In fact there are relatively few changes which are Pareto improvements; while a situation described as a Pareto optimum may be far from optimal by other criteria.)

2 A Projection of the Goals and Methods of Social Economics

This book is an introduction to social economics; a fuller development of the subject will require time, effort, and exposition by many hands comparable to that which has been afforded to the neoclassical and Marxian systems. At this stage we can, however, consider the question: *What will a fully developed system of social economics ultimately look like?* It clarifies this question to think about it from the perspective of teaching/learning: What would a student, who went to school to learn about social economics, be taught?

The organising principle of Chapters 2–4 is an effort to show how the key elements of social economics could fall into courses. One might, for example, structure a curriculum as follows:

NOTES FOR A SOCIAL ECONOMICS CURRICULUM

I Supply and demand

An important portion of the curriculum would revisit neoclassical economic perceptions of price and quantity adjustments with respect to domestic and international trade and consumption; to money; and to factors of production. However, accepting the intersection of demand and supply as the major determinant of price, more attention will be paid to the issues which, in turn, determine supply and demand. Neoclassical economics considers only the determinants that are defined as integral to the production function of the firm and the utility function of the individual. These functions are normally kept simple enough to permit mathematical or mathematics-like modelling and manipulation. Important issues which are generally left out (in part, at least, because their complexity is such that they are not best treated within the methodologies now popular in mainstream economics) include

A: power, coercion, and many aspects of regulation
B: definitions of individual, group and class identity
C: values, in the sense of assumptions of 'what matters'
D: perceptions, beliefs, and fashions of thought

The social economist will then address different ways of studying things that are supplied and demanded that may receive a fresh understanding from this system of theory: for example, stressing the *differences* among factors of production; giving serious attention to *non-monetised* or *non-market* aspects of the economy (e.g., the domestic and government sectors); and emphasising *quantity (or other) adjustments* where price is not the only, or the most important, constraint faced by producers and consumers. (*These issues of supply and demand will not be further explored, as such, in this volume, however, they will be implicit in, and will receive support from, much of the argument of the book.*)

The social economics curriculum would diverge further from the standard neoclassical curriculum in consideration of such areas as the following:

Social Economics, vol. 1, Chapter 2:

II	**Normative issues in economics**	A	The goals of the field
		B	The responsibility of the professional
		C	Values as part of the subject matter of the field

III	**Tools and methods**	A	The use of assumptions
		B	Judgment
		C	Issues of accounting

Social Economics, vol. 1, Chapter 3:

IV	**Welfare as the primary goal and subject of economics**	A	The assessment of welfare
		B	Identification of all actors; internalisation of externalities
		C	Conflicts between the individual and society

V	**Development and change**	A	Industrialisation
		B	Consumerism
		C	Ecological side-effects
		D	Issues of autonomy, control and dependence
		E	The meaning of well-being after successful industrialisation

VI	**Production**	A	Technology
		B	Work
		C	Productivity analyses

Social Economics, vol. 1, Chapter 4:

VII	**Issues of human psychology**	*A*	Altruism
		B	Trust
		C	Incentives and motivations
		D	Learning; fashions and fads; familiarity and strangeness
		E	Activities
VIII	**Human groupings and inter-actions**	*A*	Aggregation issues
		B	Institutions, including governments
IX	**Economic systems**	*A*	Macro and global economics
		B	A third alternative;; system and theory

This is an outline – indeed, it is but an early and incomplete draft of an outline – of a project which will be fleshed out a little more in the rest of Part I; then the rest of this book will go into detail in just a few of these areas.

The largest part of this book, Part II, will be devoted to addressing some of the issues that arise in a consideration of Section III, 'Tools and methods'; especially what is involved in the incorporation of *judgment* within the recognised tools of a social science; and how to anticipate when the realisticness[1] of *assumptions* will matter. Some groundwork will also be laid (in Part III) for dealing with Section IIC, 'Values as part of the subject matter of the field of economics'. A broader look at Section II, 'Normative issues in economics', and at some aspects of Section VI, 'Production' is planned for *Social Economics*, Volume 2.

As this project develops, in this book and in future work, it will become increasingly obvious in what ways the outline above is far from being a complete curriculum. Even the relatively small part of the outline which will be dealt with at length in this volume is glaringly incomplete: for example, much more will need to be said, in later work, about tools and methods.

Even while assuming that other headings as well as subheadings will come to the fore as the system of theory is developed, I will go on, in the remainder of Chapter 2, and in Chapters 3 and 4, to provide a sampling of the topics that would come under the headings just suggested, discussing one or a few items under each, by way of illustrating some of the qualities, emphases and approaches that are needed in an alternative system of economic theory.

II Normative issues in economics Neoclassical economics, since the time of Alfred Marshall, has tried to deal with human values in a purely positive fashion, by dealing nonjudgmentally, unselectively, with what people actually want. Here it has failed, for it has emphasised instead the *things* that *consumers* want, ignoring the *activities* that matter to people (especially to people as workers), and normatively imposing the resultant vision in its image of a welfare optimum.

There are in fact a number of ways in which human values can be dealt with positively – as long as it is recognised (1) that there are normative issues involved as well; and (2) that the attempt to emphasise the positive never effectively gets rid of the normative. The methodology of social economics will include:

– A positive recognition of the fact that the future is likely to be different from the present, including the possibility that future wishes and even future needs may not be identical to present ones.
– A positive recognition that economic actions taken today may influence human values of the future.
– A positive recognition of a wider range of human wishes and needs than is taken account of in the neoclassical paradigm:

   ● including activities;
   ● discriminating between needs and wants;
   ● and operating from the point of view of workers as well as of consumers.

– And finally, a positive recognition that human values are an integral part of economics, not only as subjectmatter, but also as something which each economist brings along as part of his/her own personal attributes – as part, that is, of the analyser, who is as critical to analysis as are the techniques of analysis. In particular, the *point of view* adopted by systems of economic theory, or by individuals practicing within those systems, has a normative, not a positive, derivation.

(Many of these issues will be relevant to some or all of the other topics of these three chapters.)

IIA The goals   All social sciences contain some notion of human
    of the field   welfare which forms or informs the goals attached
                to each system of theory. Beyond this statement,
generalisations become increasingly hazardous, as the goals held by
individuals are, ultimately, the basis for – and yet are not necessarily
identical with – the goals of the social sciences practiced by those
individuals. Nevertheless, a few generalisations will be attempted here
regarding the goals of neoclassical economics; then the proposed goals
for social economics will be outlined.

When Samuelson and Nordhaus say that: 'Among many definitions,
the leading one today defines economics thus: *Economics is the study of
how we choose to use scarce productive resources that have alternative
uses to produce commodities of various kinds*' (Samuelson and
Nordhaus, 1985, p. 13), they are paving the way for neoclassical
economics to be the science which shows how to be *efficient*, with the
goal of *maximising consumption possibilities*. Formal statements in
neoclassical economics do not usually put the maximisation of
consumption, or even of consumption possibilities, up front as the
goal. However, it is very common to find consumption casually slipped
in as a proxy for utility; and it *is* claimed, up front, that utility is what is
to be maximised.

The improvement of consumption possibilities is a noble goal; any
system of economic theory which ignored it could have only a minor
place in the field. Given the inadequacy of consumption possibilities
faced by a majority of the five-billion-plus human beings on this planet,
to increase consumption possibilities, at least for part of the human
population, must be a high priority for any economic system, and for
any system of economic theory. However, the concept of *maximising*
includes no indicator of 'enough', or 'too much'; nor does it sufficiently
draw attention to the trade-offs that may be involved: when you get
more of one thing, you may be doing harm somewhere else.

Social economics, while recognising the *temporal* priority of
consumption for those whose basic needs are not met, must take care
not to accept consumption as the goal of the first *logical* priority.
Consumption is the need that has to be satisfied first, but once it is
satisfied it is often felt that it is not sufficient as an end in itself; it is
then looked upon as a means to some other end. (Hence the distinction
which is drawn, for example, in the philanthropic profession, between
'what makes life possible' and 'what makes life worthwhile'.)

Some sophisticated modern economists have emphasised that there
is a 'state of being' goal which is the justification for the secondary

'having' goal – even while less careful work in the neoclassical paradigm has conflated the two. In the best neoclassical work consumption is 'only' a means to the end of utility. The weakness here is that utility is under-defined. This weakness has three principal effects: 1) it encourages the use of 'having' as a proxy for the desired state of 'being'; 2) there is nothing either in the concept of utility as a state of 'being', or in consumption, as a matter of 'getting or having', to draw our attention to the importance of 'doing'; and 3) little or no attention is paid to the cases where more consumption actually decreases the utility of the consumer or of other members of society.

Given these problems, it seems advisable to summarise the final goals of social economics by the use of the word, *welfare*, in place of *utility*. It will not be possible – or perhaps even desirable – to provide anything like a complete definition for so large a concept, but we will try at least to give some more specifics than have been offered for 'utility'.

Let us begin with the question: welfare *for whom*? The answer suggested here will be that the relevant concern is with *the welfare of all living human beings and of all those who will exist in the future*. Consideration will also be included for *the welfare of the global ecosystem*. (Whether this is included because it is essential to human welfare, or because it is a final value in itself, is a question which, fortunately, does not need to be answered here. Either reason is sufficient for this discussion.)

To add specificity to the concept of the 'final goal' or 'end-in-itself' of welfare, it can be understood as having four principal aspects – where each aspect may also be understood as a 'final goal'. They are:

- survival
- happiness
- self-actualisation   WELFARE: principal elements
- moral/spiritual development.

The first of these stands apart from the others, in that 'survival' is perceived as an end-in-itself when it is in doubt, but when it is comfortably assured, not only does it tend to fall out of consciousness, but unhappy people may feel (and sometimes act upon this feeling) that survival alone is not a sufficient primary goal.[2]

The second element, 'happiness', is in effect identical with the single final goal in most Utilitarian philosophy. Many criticisms of that stream of thought have made it clear that 'happiness' is pallid when not linked with some idea of human potential – the third term. The fourth term is intended to suggest that it is meaningful and important to think of human life in moral/spiritual terms of 'better' and 'worse', as well as in hedonistic terms of 'more or less happy'.

What secondary goals will be most effective for the achievement of our final goals? For those neoclassical economists who assume consumption as *the* final goal, efficiency need not be questioned as the secondary goal appropriate to maximise consumption. Some more specific goals, such as specialisation in production, or free trade, may then also be suggested (and argued over) as additional (logically lower-level) goals in the neoclassical system, instrumental to the efficiency which is instrumental to consumption.

By contrast, social economics will stress that consumption is not a *primary* goal which is necessarily to be *maximised*, but rather it is a *secondary* goal which is to be *balanced* with several other secondary goals, all of them to be aligned together towards a broader conception of welfare. What other secondary goals might we then cite, along with consumption? We can now begin to cluster secondary goals which promote one or more of the four elements of welfare (some will also promote other secondary goals) – recognising that, in a system with quadric (as opposed to unitarian) final goals, there are likely to be conflicts (e.g., between things that appear to promote happiness at the expense of spiritual development, or vice versa.) For the purposes of a system of economic theory, it is probably most practical simply to assume that some of these conflicts are unresolvable.[3] The critical secondary goals proposed for the field of economics are:

- consumption;
- sustainability/health
- hope
- 'enhancing activities'
- economic justice.

WELFARE: secondary goals

IIA 1 A general increase in the **consumption** possibilities for humankind depends upon efficiency, and upon technological progress (including some kinds of specialisation), which are, therefore, tertiary goals. As such, efficiency and technological progress must be balanced against other primary, secondary and tertiary goals with which they may conflict, so that what will finally be recommended by social economists will not be every efficiency, or every kind of technological progress, but procedures which are ecologically, socially, and humanely sound. With that said, it remains true that productivity increases achieved through efficiency and technological progress are of enormous importance. This is a subset of the concerns of social economics – but it is a subset of such significance that it well merits an entire system of economic theory where these goals have top priority. Fortunately, such a system already exists, in neoclassical economics.

A *targeted* increase in the consumption possibilities of those who most need it involves an additional set of considerations. These will be discussed under IIA 5, below; they may be summed up as goals of equity.

If all of the equity goals could be achieved, we would find that the productivity goals would take on a very different appearance. For example, there is, in fact, enough food produced in the world today so that the food needs of all human beings could be met – supposing perfectly equal distribution. When productivity goals conflict with sustainability goals (as they are increasingly recognised to do), pressure may build up to emphasise distribution over production in addressing basic consumption needs.

IIA 2 The idea of **sustainability** starts with a view of the total resource base (material, human, technological) as the link between present and future possibilities for achieving human welfare. It stresses that increased productivity of inputs of labour and materials should be based as much as possible upon more inputs of information and of inert capital per unit of output.

An example is the requirement for increasing productivity of land. This was emphasised in the time of the classical economists (and earlier); in today's terms it may be seen as, primarily, a function of three things: population growth; achievement of basic needs; and distribution. Because there are likely to be ecological limits to the sustainable growth of output-per-hectare, it is critically important to bring these three things into a balance which will be decreasingly dependent upon continued growth of land productivity.

A key indicator of sustainability is **health**. In the context of the goal of sustainability, individual health must be linked to an even broader notion of societal health. Here we take as a goal not only the health (mental and physical, near- and long-term) of individual human beings; but also the sustainable productivity of the systems within which they are embedded. This approach recognises the structural interrelationships of an array of systems in which human societies participate, so that societal health depends upon (and therefore, as a goal, includes) the health of systems of social relationships and global and local market systems; of biological systems; of local and distant soils; of plants, and animals; and, ultimately, of all people, everywhere.

A healthy system is characterised, among other things, by informational feedback loops which reinforce actions that contribute to the general health of the system, and discourage those which harm it. Given the webs of interrelationships, actions which help one sub-system at the expense of another are not regarded as likely to be the most constructive. (The concept of 'healthy competition' remains, however, a valid one for some uses.)

IIA 3 The inclusion of '**hope**' as a secondary goal is perhaps biased by the era or the culture in which this is written; it refers to the idea of 'progress' which is an integral part of cultures affected by the Industrial Revolution. The shift to the less specific 'hope' arises from a recognition that unending *material* progress, in which every generation has access to more consumption goods per capita than the generation before, may not continue, monotonically,[4] to contribute to the welfare goals of happiness, self-actualisation, or moral or spiritual development; 'well-being is not the same as well-having'.[5] Unending material progress may even be counterproductive in terms of the species' survival, and it may encounter impassable limits. These may be temporary, but they may last for longer or shorter periods. Alternatively, material progress, as we have known it, may be transformed into a much more pronounced cycle of booms and busts, in which increased consumption is only possible for the generations on the upswing, after a population collapse. Given the anguish that would accompany the 'busts' in such cycles, they represent one of the least desirable scenarios. Another possible type of scenario is one which has suffered two decades of unpopularity, but which may return for serious consideration by the end of this century: the steady state concept.

The idea of 'hope' is what was felt to be missing from earlier steady state thinking. Not enough attention was paid (even if the lack of attention was in the readers and listeners, rather than in the formulaters of the ideas) to ways in which people could continue to hope for progressive improvement of the human lot – even if in some absolute terms, for people who had reached a certain level of affluence, *material* consumption were to level out. Here is where it is critical, for advanced modern societies, that emphasis shifts to include *doing* as of equal importance to *having*: ecological and resource constraints are not so likely to limit progressive welfare improvement which is linked to 'activities' as they are to limit that version of 'progress' which depends upon expanding material consumption.

IIA   4 '**Enhancing activities**' is a term that will be used here to refer to things people do – or the aspects of things people do – that are not merely a drain on human energy, but that are in some way a benefit for the doer. 'Human capital' is a term which refers to the *product* of such activities; the activities themselves have no more general name, in existing economics, than 'human capital enhancement', or, perhaps, 'non-alienating work'. The first of these refers only to the activity as a means to an end; the second is a double negative. There are very few economists (Alfred Marshall and Tibor Scitovsky are the most outstanding examples – see Chapter 4, Sections VIID and VIIE) who have given activities a place within what may be analysed as the goals of economics.

Two examples of enhancing activities are education and work. The first of these is among the areas in which it is possible to conceive of virtually limitless 'progress'. This has two aspects. (a) On the supply side, one of the uses for education is to enhance productivity. For more and more people this already means enhanced ability to produce services such as health care, information, or education, rather than material goods. (b) On the demand side, to the extent that we wish to purchase (and that we benefit from purchasing) an increasing proportion of services (including education) in our 'market basket' of household consumption, wealth will circulate with as much welfare-enhancement (and with less danger to the sustainability of our systems) through the production of such services as it might through the production of goods.

With these points in mind, neoclassical economists have defined education as part consumption, part production. Social economics, moving away from the dichotomy where everything must be listed under one of these two categories, will stress that education is an important means to the end of production, but is also important as an *activity* – a category which may also be something very like an end in itself.

Much of what was said about education applies also to work. In the neoclassical paradigm work is understood as a means to the end of consumption: in the social economics paradigm it is recognised that it can, and often does, have additional value to the worker as an activity in itself.

IIA 5 **Economic justice**: This term may be defined and employed in a manner which has simultaneously an ethical and a practical content. As a first approximation let us define it as a goal in which *those who reap the rewards (of particular economic activities) pay the costs.* The first obvious point is, of course, that this is no more achievable than perfect competition. Like perfect competition in the neoclassical paradigm, however, in social economics 'economic justice' is a secondary goal which is useful as a reference point, to sharpen our thinking and to guide our emphasis. (The consequences of defining this concept as is done here obviously lead to the subject of externalities, a subject which will be dealt with at several points further on.)

Although improvements in the distribution of material goods are easiest to effect in times of material growth, they are even more critical to basic welfare (starting from the satisfaction of basic needs) when the total consumption possibilities of a society are *not* growing. It is extremely difficult, at this moment, to predict how the interplay of human ingenuity and ecological constraints will come out, even a few decades hence; new hopes for cheap energy sources arise at the same time as we discover how dearly the system is paying for past and present uses of energy as well as for past and present deployments of chemical and other material resources. Among the scenarios that must be considered is the possibility that, in order to sustain the viability of the human ecosystem, it may be necessary to halt the growth of the aggregate consumption of the rich countries; one of the most unpleasant scenarios would be a necessary halt to the growth of the aggregate consumption of the entire human population.

IIB The responsibility of the professional   It is normally assumed that the education of doctors, lawyers, and certified public accountants will impart not only knowledge and information, but also a code of ethical standards. There would seem to be equally good reasons to require that policy analysts and policy advisers should also subscribe to a code of ethics for their professions, whether they were trained in the area of 'economic policy', 'social policy', or whatever.

Much is demanded of economics today. It is increasingly recognised that there are economic aspects to virtually every social problem, and economists are asked to elucidate these aspects, and to assist in addressing the problems with which they are connected. At the same time, the increasingly academic system of neoclassical economics is evolving on a progressively narrowing path, limiting ever more the scope of its formal application. In part this is the result of a commendable honesty. Given the type of formalisation which economics has adopted (starting with tentative assays early in this century, then emerging as a major defining feature in the 1940s, with Samuelson's *Foundations of Economic Analysis*), it has been important to delineate precisely the area within which such formalisation can operate. Hence among neoclassicists there has appeared a growing gap between theoretic/academic economics, on the one hand, and applied/empirical economics on the other.

I have stressed the 'applied' aspect of the field of economics, not only identifying social economics with that aspect, but also suggesting that much 'theoretical' economics should be judged on the basis of its ultimate usefulness in application. To the extent that any education in the broad field of economics may result in individuals using their training to assist in the making of economic policy, then there is a responsibility which requires some conscious attention to an ethical code. Without further discussion of how this might apply to other systems of economic theory, suggestions will here be put forth as to how one might go about formulating such a code for social economics.

IIB 1 First, every social economist should give some thought to the goals of the field. Are the ones outlined in this chapter sufficient? Should there be additions? Deletions? Changes in emphasis or priority? How is the individual to relate them with his/her personal value system?

IIB 2 Second, the social economist should be prepared, whenever attempting to answer a question in a real-world situation, to take responsibility for examining that question. At the very least, the social economist should probe what it is that the questioner really wants to know: is the question, as posed, adequate, or should it be reformulated? (See Chapter 9 for further discussion of this issue.)

IIB 3 Third, the social economist should be able and willing to access other information and skills than his or her own. Very often, the questions asked of economists go beyond the wisdom or knowledge of any single person. Knowing whom else to ask or to call in is often as valued as (and may be more valuable than) giving a partial answer.

IIB 4 Fourth, the social economist should take responsibility for knowing and understanding the basic methodology involved when an economist 'does' economics. If economists today take little of such responsibility, they are hardly to be blamed for this: there has not been much written or taught along these lines. As a move toward correcting this imbalance, these issues will make up the bulk of Part II of this book.

IIC Values as   If we accept that human motivations, built in part
part of the   upon human values, are a critical part of the content
subject   of economics in particular, and the social sciences in
matter of   general, we must consider the possibility that human
the field   values play a much larger role in the social than in the
natural sciences. The values of the human beings pursuing any science are, in reality, never irrelevant; but they become significant in a special way in the social sciences because this area must also take human values as a part of its content; that is, as among its objects of study.

Much confusion has entered the field of economics through the overloading of one word (*value*) with two theoretical roles and two meanings. The two meanings of value are: (a) the one claimed by economics: 'exchange value, or price'; and (b) the one upon which that overt economic value depends: 'what people think things are really worth.' (Meaning (b) in turn is related to – but is not philosophically or logically identical with – the neoclassical concept of *utility*; it is more closely related to the term *welfare* as it is proposed to be used in social economics.) Both meanings, (a) and (b), are highly variable, depending upon circumstances, but the first is strictly relative, depending upon an interaction of all the effective demands of all the economic actors in the society. The second, along with its relation to the relative matter of wants, has also some anchoring in needs which may be psychic, if not economic, absolutes.[6] The overt theoretical role played by (a) 'value as price' is to express the relationships between all goods and services in a society, as perceived, at the margin, by all consumers and producers in the society. Economic theory continues to maintain an additional, normally unacknowledged, role played by (b) 'human value': implicit in the proposition that 'individual preferences matter' is the fact that human values are a part of the content of economic studies.

Some of the confusions caused by these double uses can be cleared up by social economics if it employs two distinct and well-defined terms:

- *price*, to mean exchange value (nothing is gained by saying 'exchange value' when we mean price; it only confuses the issue); and

–   *human value*, to mean 'what people think something is worth' (or 'value in use'; the latter term should probably be abandoned, as many of the things which have human value do not strike the casual observer as being 'used').

III Tools and methods   The important questions asked about complex economic realities probe issues of growth, change and disequilibrium; property ownership, production and distribution; surplus generation and allocation; the relationships between economic growth, human needs and satisfactions; the impacts of humans upon their environment; the point of view of economics; and manifold aspects of human nature, including those which permit trust, seek activity, and operate outside competition. Aspects of all of these require a different theory beyond what is now available. Such a different theory will require different tools. Much that is important within it will not be amenable to the tools of neoclassical economics.

Great resourcefulness has been expended in seeking out a truly and usefully dynamic methodology, including ways of representing within our models successive time periods (the familiar $t_0, t_1, t_2 \ldots t_n$), shocks (random or systematic, exogenous or endogenous) and iterative changes. Yet the formal power of neoclassical economics still rests in the static mode. Having tried to go beyond this by all of the most plausible avenues within the range of what is thinkable, it may now be time to try thinking the unthinkable.

The suggestion here is that we reverse what has become a monotonic direction of change in fashions of economic methodology, wherein economists of both dominant paradigms seem only able to ratchet up to ever more sophisticated and difficult mathematical techniques and methods.

When the existing tools and techniques are used as a first approximation, in the more 'elementary stages' of our thinking – when they are employed in a context in which they are recognised as (often metaphorical) aids, as Marshall said, 'to give definiteness to our ideas' – when our highly symbolic tools and techniques are kept in their proper place, subordinate to judgment and life experience – then they do not run much danger of causing us to 'diverge from the actual facts of life'.[7] However, ever-more sophisticated mathematics may not be the road on which we will draw nearer to our goal of dealing 'scientifically' with the empirical, dynamic, disequilibrium issues of greatest importance. In proposing social economics as an alternative way of understanding economic phenomena, it will make sense to leave to neoclassical economics the gains from those of its models which do not fit the social economics approach, while using a different approach to pick up different insights and understandings with a different usefulness.

What are the alternatives? A few suggestions will be made in the remainder of this chapter; more will be found in Part II. This is only a small beginning of a very large task. Neoclassical economists have had a hundred years to bring their methodologies to their current state; those who would compete for space in the field of economics will have to expect to spend much time in developing their own methods.

IIIA The use of There is a significant area (that which is well
 assumptions illuminated by the neoclassical pool of light)
wherein economic understanding can be based upon the rather minimalist caricature of human behaviour which arises from the essential axioms adopted by neoclassical economics. At the beginning of the next chapter we will see examples from five areas where issues of practical importance to economics are cast in the shade by the neoclassical assumptions about human beings as 'rational economic men'. Other examples of especially problematical assumptions include the rarely-expressed but often-held assumption that the satisfaction of preferences is the same thing as the maximisation of utility – which is, in turn, assumed to be the same thing as the maximisation of welfare. This is based upon (probably unconscious and unexamined) assumptions about information: i.e., people know what will make them happy; they know what, in the long as well as the short run, is 'good for them'.

A quite different class of problematical assumption is that which says that markets can represent the values of a society in the long run as well as in the short. Here the problems are, at a conscious level (thanks to Kenneth Arrow[8]) well known. It is known how stringent are the requirements for this assumption to be valid – so stringent that, in fact, we cannot expect that these requirements ever will be met in reality. What is problematical here is that the stringent requirements are not brought up again on every occasion when an economist makes the assumption that the future can be and is represented in current markets. Since we know that, under certain conditions this theoretically *could* be the case, too often it is assumed – without mentioning the tiresome necessary conditions – that it *is* the case.

On its essential subject, human nature, the core axioms of neoclassical economics have proven to be well-chosen; it is unlikely that any other equally minimal set could achieve so much. Nevertheless, some questions occur:

– Assuming that, as economists, our principal concern is about how the choices and actions of individuals combine with the choices and actions of others to result in 'what is produced, how, and for whom', and that, as economists, we will rarely be concerned with Ms Smith or Mr Chang in themselves – why might we sometimes want a more realistic understanding of how individuals make choices and undertake actions of economic significance?
– Given that a system of theory is built, essentially, upon a base of psychological axioms, and given that those axioms only accord with actual human behaviour some, not all of the time, then when can we expect our 'unrealistic assumptions' to run us into trouble?

These constitute the reverse side of the questions that ask:

– Using a limited approximation to human psychology as a basis for understanding economic activity, how far can we spin out our theories before the limitations of the original assumptions will interrupt the usefulness of conclusions derived within this system?
– Can we predict, from the limitations of the original assumptions, the character and scope of the pool of light that will be cast by the theories based upon them?

These questions have not previously (to my knowledge) been formulated in this manner, and therefore we do not possess even the beginning of the generalisations which would guide us to their answers. The groundwork for establishing such generalisations will be laid in Chapters 11 and 12. My preliminary hypothesis is that

there is a finite set of understandings that can be achieved by any social science which is built upon assumptions that simplify drastically from the subject matter.

This hypothesis generates the following description:

In the early days of the development of a social science, imaginative researchers can keep discovering nearly virgin tracts of territory which are amenable to explication by a system built upon the said unrealistic assumptions. As the paradigm matures, the area that was most suitable for this approach has all been exhaustively worked. Researchers find themselves reworking the same areas, with diminishing hope of having anything importantly new to show for it; while the edges of the charted land are no longer hopeful frontiers, but areas of diminishing marginal returns to further investigation.[9]

This metaphor may be helpful in understanding the way that a social science progresses – slowing down when it has used up the area most suitable for the application of one set of assumptions and techniques, then taking on a new burst of energy when new assumptions and/or techniques are introduced. It does not, however, give us a way of predicting when or where, in the evolution of a system of theory, the limitations built into the original assumptions can be expected to become serious constraints. Nor does it give answers to meta-questions concerning the way in which assumptions are employed. For instance:
–   Are there a variety of possible ways of employing the assumptions we make?
–   How is one to distinguish between consequences flowing from the manner in which assumptions are employed versus consequences from the initial choice of assumptions?

The process of addressing these questions is likely to bring us to some equally knotty meta-questions on the development and application of techniques. There may also be limits to the uses of particular techniques; even more probable are limits to the uses of particular techniques in conjunction with particular assumptions.

It is to be hoped that a standpoint from which it will be possible to formulate more 'judgeable', if not 'testable', generalisations on these subject will emerge as we bring into play an alternative paradigm which will enable us to observe how the illumination from the neoclassical system of economic theory covers some, but not all, of the issues of importance to the broader potential field of economic studies.

IIIB   Judgment   With regard to the techniques of social economics, the most general proposal to be made in this book is that, in putting somewhat less emphasis upon the formal techniques (such as mathematical modelling) which are so characteristic of neoclassical economics, social economics will be putting relatively more weight upon less formal characteristics of the practitioners of this system. Especially, we will dwell upon the characteristic which will be referred to as 'judgment'.

Related issues will repeatedly appear in this book under a variety of names, such as 'credibility', 'trust', or 'persuasion'. Judgment will also be seen to be related to sociology-of-science issues of certification that arises with the following questions:

–   If social economic analysis is more obviously to depend upon the judgment of the analyst than does neoclassical economic analysis, how will the clients and users of social economics know which is the best work?
–   How will they know which social economist to listen to?
–   How can we ensure that the field builds upon the best work done to date, rather than on inferior work?

The first answer to all of this is that it is not the comparison to neoclassical economics that makes this proposed emphasis in economic methods look problematical. That is to say, in most neoclassical economic analysis, too, judgment is ultimately a major factor, even when it is not emphasised.

It is essential to understand this point. There is nothing inherent to the techniques *per se* which are employed by neoclassical economists that assures that the answers they generate will be correct. Instead, the correctness of the answer depends upon judgment at several points:

–   Where any empirical facts are used, judgment is critically required for *the selection of which facts to include in the model*, and which ones to leave out. The selection of different categories of facts, or of different facts within categories, will often result in different models with different answers.
–   Models, including the assumptions upon which they depend, even when they are thought of as pure theory, are still, at some remove, intended as pictures of the real world. E.g., a model of expenditure patterns may claim that individuals do, or do not, care about the welfare (i.e., the consumption – generally used in these models as the proxy for welfare) of their descendants. The resulting model, compared to other models of expenditure patterns, is judged to 'work' more or less well as it is more or less able to predict how macro fluctuations in consumption move in relation to GNP growth, business cycles, etc. Given the relatively short time periods over which such predictions generally remain stable, *the choice of*

> which model to use (*as, indeed, of which variables to test*; e.g., perhaps there is something which is more relevant than, or which is a critical determinant of, concern for future generations) is also, ultimately, a matter of judgment and persuasion, not of 'proof'.

– Different techniques applied to what appear to be the same materials are likely to produce different results. (NB: the choice of technique usually imposes some restrictions upon the selection or interpretation of the variables, facts, or other 'materials' on which they work). There tends to be a strong bias in favour of the newest techniques (which are often the ones that fewest other individuals are competent to judge critically); but in fact it is a matter of judgment which is *the most appropriate technique for the analysis of a particular subject.*

– Finally, judgment is required for *the reading, evaluation, interpretation and application of the results*[10] which are produced from any analysis.

What does 'judgment' mean, as used in these examples? Webster's *Third International Dictionary* has it as 'The mental or intellectual process of forming an opinion or evaluation by discerning and comparing.... The wise or just exercise of this capacity.... Discernment, discretion.' (Compressing this to 'judgment is discernment, which is the process of discerning' one is reminded that dictionaries are, in the end, self-referential closed systems.) The critical quality which I intend to include in the use of this word is the discretion to know when to ask, 'what is important here?' and the discernment to come up with a 'good' answer to that question. (That question will recur from time to time throughout this book; in its most general form it is the question, 'what matters?') Judgment is also concerned with the ranking of priorities – assessing what matters more, and most, in given situations.

A reliance upon quantitative or mathematical techniques cannot, in fact, save the social scientist from also relying (whether covertly or openly) upon judgment. Judgment must, in any case, make the first and last decisions: of what facts and simplifications, models, assumptions and techniques to employ; and of how to interpret and evaluate the results.

Some economists have striven to give to their discipline the appearance of being able to offer *techniques* (which depend upon the abstraction, 'science') *in place of judgment* (which depends upon the character of individual human beings). This is false. Those who believe that an academic certification of economists which attests only to techniques, ignoring judgment, can produce reliably credible analysts of any aspects of reality, are misled. Social economics, in admitting to the need for judgment in its practitioners, will not be creating a new problem; it will just be admitting the existence of an old one.

What, then, can we do about the problem? The answers that can be given will not be entirely satisfactory, especially to those who seek certainty. This does not excuse us, however, from ignoring those answers that do exist. They may be summarised as follows:

IIIB 1 An emphasis on judgment reveals the imperative that social economics must be defined with respect to how it is taught as well as with respect to the content and methods of its analysis.

The teaching of judgment, on the face of it, is an exceedingly difficult thing. Before becoming too discouraged on this point, however, we should note that, if we cannot describe how judgment is *directly taught*, we can nevertheless think constructively about how it is *learned*. (See IIIB 2.)

IIIB 2 Most often judgment is formed inductively by doing things. This suggests an emphasis upon hands-on experiential approaches such as field-work type apprenticeships. The case method of teaching also is likely to have a useful application here.

IIIB 3 Factual knowledge can exist without much judgment; it is harder for the reverse to be true. Attention to the empirical side of whatever areas an individual studies will be supportive of, if not supplying the sufficient condition for, the development of judgment. Judgment must be honed by bringing it to bear on facts of the real world.

IIIB 4 Many sophisticated and 'powerful' techniques and tools of statistics, econometrics, linear programming, etc. are now available to social scientists. Attention needs to be paid to the problems which arise when a non-verbal language is employed for exploring and communicating facts and perceptions in the social sciences. Judgment in this area can be both promoted and assisted by the techniques of critical analysis and appraisal of contemporary and/or older economic texts which will be described in Part II of this book.

IIIB 5 Excessive narrowness mitigates against judgment, in ruling out of the field some of the things that should be evaluated, compared, and weighed for importance. The opposite, too, can become a danger; attempting to weigh and compare too many things, one might become paralysed. Clearly, experience is important here; the human mind can adapt to increased levels of complexity, at least when the increases are made by appropriate increments.

The education of a social economist, then, should stress context, training the student to ask such questions as, 'What can I learn about the subject at hand by seeing it in the next larger frame of reference?' or, 'In this context, what are the most important questions? What data are most pertinent? What should I be looking for?'

IIIB 6 Economics cannot be its own context. For fullest development of judgment – including, importantly, the ability to judge when one is outside of one's own competence, and to know what other kind of assistance to seek – it may be desirable that the design of an advanced degree in social economics include a year or so of coursework in adjacent social sciences. It cannot be expected that each social economist will be an expert in all of the relevant related fields, including business and labour management; human ecology/environmental studies; sociology; anthropology; sociobiology; psychology; logic; moral philosophy; agronomy and nutrition; comparative cultures; cultural and social history; etc., etc. However, there would be an important synergy of overlapping and complementary approaches and skills if each social economist had some expertise in at least one of these fields.

One useful approach to the teaching of social economics might be a requirement that any student who takes social economics as his/her major study should also adopt as a 'minor' another discipline such as one of those just listed. Another approach would be to think about what training would be required to prepare the social scientist to participate constructively in multidisciplinary teams. (For further reason to value such training, see IIB 3, above, and Chapter 9, below; especially 'The Social Responsibility of the Social Scientist: Getting the Questions Right')

IIIB 7 If judgment is defined, after the fact, as the quality which results in 'correct' analysis and 'right' answers to real world situations and problems, then there is little evidence to support what is, however, frequently assumed: that judgment – being 'right' – is positively correlated with exceptional intelligence. Good judgment may, however, be positively correlated with the *combination* of intelligence with deep intellectual honesty. This is a relatively rare combination, for 'deep intellectual honesty', as I mean that phrase, requires two things: self-knowledge, constantly probed, plus humility.[11] For obvious reasons, the second requirement, humility, tends to be negatively correlated with high intelligence.

What are the educational inputs which can make the best of intelligence in young people by combining it with deep intellectual honesty? Later chapters of this book (especially Chapters 10, 11 and 12) will emphasise the philosophical position of realism, which (1) accepts that there is a real world outside of our heads ('world realism') and (2) holds up an ideal of 'truth' whereby it is understood that representations of that real world should attempt to communicate about it as accurately as possible ('truth realism').[12] Thus understood, the philosophical position of realism deserve to be discussed and thought about in the education of social scientists. Some people will not be able to subscribe to it, having a deep conviction that there is no such thing as truth; they may adhere to strict relativism, subjectivism, etc. Most people, however, are likely to find that the principles of realism are in fact the ones on which they have instinctively been acting, at least some of the time.

Serious discussion of realism should be helpful in emphasising the importance of treating empirical facts with respect – in contrast to the disrespect which they are commonly accorded in much of graduate economics training today. This is the first step in promoting deep intellectual honesty. The second step is to stress that, if we are serious about trying to achieve accuracy in apprehending and communicating about reality, the first reality which we must know concerns ourselves – our ways of perceiving, of learning, of communicating. Techniques for enhancing this area of knowledge, and then for using it in social science communication, are proposed throughout Part II.

For help in acquiring that most elusive aspect of deep intellectual honesty – humility – I can only suggest some ways to begin. Humility is related to respect for other people, including those whose mental activities one regards as less quick, sharp, logical, or whatever, than one's own. Such respect can, in fact, be promoted in the classroom, by teachers who are not afraid to recognise the possibility that any student, on being exposed to material which is familiar to the teacher, may observe something new, or may see an old fact in a new light. It can also be promoted by encouraging students to work in groups, in projects so structured that every individual's contribution to a group effort is of value to the whole.

IIIC Issues of   Accounting systems are methods for counting up
      accounting   what matters to us – what 'counts'. If we find we
                     are interested in things that previously did not seem
to count so much, we will need new systems to account for them. One
description of the recent history of 'indicators proliferating to challenge
GNP' reads as a description of new concepts of welfare as they have
entered the economic profession in successive waves over the last thirty
years:

> Many of these new indicators were developed in the 1960s, and
> began deducting some of the social costs of urbanisation, congestion,
> crime, traffic delays, etc., from 'gross' GNP, thus arriving at slightly
> more sober assessments which drew attention to the 'bads' as well as
> the 'goods' of industrialisation. They included the Measure of
> Economic Welfare, proposed by William Nordhaus and James
> Tobin, 1971. Japan's Net National Welfare (Japan Economic
> Council, 1973) also deducts some kinds of environmental damage
> and depletion of the Earth's natural 'capital'.
> The debate was joined by such development economists as Irma
> Adelman and Cynthia Taft Morris (1973) and others, who focused
> on the propensity for income disparities to increase right along with
> GNP in developing countries, leading to the by now familiar
> widening gap between rich and poor, both within and between
> nations. Such debates and new indicators were fostered by the more
> fundamental and encompassing works of Barbara Ward (1966) and
> her study of the economics of *Spaceship Earth* and similar paradigm-
> shifting efforts by Kenneth Boulding in *Beyond Economics* (1968)
> and the work of Sweden's Gunnar and Alva Myrdal to name a few.
> David Morris of the Overseas Development Council (1980) joined in
> with the Physical Quality of Life Indicator) (PQLI), which shifted
> attention to new measures of success in maintaining the quality of
> life in livable environments, housing, health-care, education, as well
> as money-denominated income. During the same period the United
> Nations Environment Programme developed the Basic Human
> Needs (BHN) indicator (McHale, 1979), which shifted attention to
> measuring how these broader indicators of quality of life affected all
> income groups, and particularly focussed on measuring the success
> of a nation's economic policy by how well it met the basic human
> needs of its poorest citizens.[13]

This chapter began with a discussion of the goals of social economics; the accounting systems that will be most useful to this system of theory will be those that count up the things that are particularly important to know about if we are to strive toward these goals. Some of the types of indicators just listed will obviously be the ones of choice in relation to particular aspects of welfare. Others remain to be developed.[14]

IIIC 1 Social economists must be able to use, and know the appropriate application for, a multiplicity of indicators and accounting measures.

Standard national income and product accounts, including such familiar measures as GNP (Gross National Product), NNP and NDP (Net National and Net Domestic Product), etc., are useful indicators that can be drawn upon to enhance our understanding of some of what is happening in the economic sphere of life. As economists, citizens or policy-makers, we should not expect our accounting systems to tell us everything at once: to be useful, they have to make a distillation and abstraction from the world. One set of accounts will be useful in one context, another in another. We run into trouble, however, when we unthinkingly accept the accounting system that happens to lie most readily at hand as the answer to the question we happen to be asking – or when, with a little more sophistication, we restructure our questions so that they will be answerable by the accounts that are available. The first of these errors distorts our understanding; the second limits progress in achieving new knowledge and understanding.

With more careful analytical attention paid to the idea of 'welfare' than has been given to the neoclassical notion of 'utility', it should become evident that one of the conclusions of social economics must be that *there is no single indicator that can summarise all aspects of welfare*. A 'bottom line' is meaningful when one has added and subtracted income and expense figures, for example, for a year's activity in a business. There is no meaningful 'bottom line' that can compare, e.g, the welfare of a child who has been well-nourished but has had no education, with the welfare of an undernourished child who has, however, had access to a good school.

IIIC 2 Systems of accounting will be determined by beliefs as to what things are most important to count.

An example of the kind of accounting system which may be sought for the uses of social economics would be one that, in order better to capture long-term values, would explicitly account for 'stocks' in addition to the 'flows' which are more commonly the subjects of the NIPAs. This approach would be particularly sympathetic to concerns for 'sustainability' – a concept which is only now beginning to be adopted from the realm of ecology into that of economics. It would begin with an accounting of all the physical resources actually available to a region, nation, or other area of interest. It might also have a separate accounting for a more speculative list of 'resources potentially available' (e.g., young children who, if not malnourished, mal-educated, and mal-socialised, could be expected to become productive workers). These 'stocks' would represent the wealth of the area. The flow-accounting would then operate in terms of additions to and subtractions from the stocks of actual and/or potential wealth.

An example of the way in which such a system would sharpen our observations is the issue of what have been called 'defensive expenditures'. These are expenditures which are called for only as a result of 'bads' generated by the patterns of production and/or consumption in a society: e.g., the cost of restoring a river to its original condition after it has been polluted by some production process; or the cost of medical care necessitated by unhealthy patterns of work or consumption. Under most current accounting practices, the renewed health of a river, an alcoholic, or a stress patient, is viewed as a 'new' product, ignoring the fact that the 'old' product (the original, pre-industrial state of the river, or earlier good health of the patient) had been used as an *apparently* free factor in production or consumption. Hence the 'defensive expenditure' required to produce a state of ecological, economic or individual health is often counted as a net gain to GNP. Of course renewed health *is* a gain to welfare – after the fact of ill-health has been accepted; but the sort of stock-accounting suggested here would recognise that the original state of health was not a free good, and would assign a cost to using it up.[15]

Searching for a starting place for these considerations, social economists will be assisted by ecological writings, where, in particular, audits of energy efficiency are sometimes made; it is possible, for example, to find how many calories of all kinds of energy are required in order to put some (often lesser) number of calories on the table in front of the American consumer.[16]

The extreme neoclassical position assumes that any true or relevant notion of 'value' we might attach to inputs and outputs is reflected in prices, and that calculation of 'values' not weighted by prices is irrelevant to economic considerations. They argue that if farmers and middlemen make economic choices which result in a technological system that employs more fossil fuel calories to produce food-on-the-table than it finally provides in usable calories of food to the consumer, then those choices must be economically rational.

The social economics view suggests that people may be more influenced by fashions, misinformation and ignorance than is currently accepted among neoclassical economic theorists (see section VIID, below). It also stresses the frequency with which some costs (e.g., those which will have to be borne by people in the future, and those currently borne by individuals and groups whose situation is not felt economically by the decision-makers) fail to be accounted for within existing market systems and the theory that describes and guides them. An example of such failure is the fact that, while many things which the market used to treat as free goods have ceased to be free, this change was generally not anticipated as a 'future cost' to be represented in the (then) 'present prices'. Another problem has been the conflation of the idea of 'free' with 'unlimited'. For example, the time which a parent spends in socialising his/her child, though 'free', is not unlimited, and may, indeed, be relatively quite scarce.

A partial list of issues that need to be considered in choosing 'what to count' include:

IIIC 2a **Long versus short run**. As in the examples just given, a longer-term perspective can show us that some things which have been thought of as 'free' in fact have an associated cost.

Also, 'the conventional neoclassical concept for managing time, the discounting of future benefits-and-costs streams, leads to what has been termed a 'dictatorship' of the present generation (Page, 1977). Discounting can make molehills out of even the biggest mountains. At the usual positive discount rates reflecting the opportunity cost of money, almost any income stream past 20 or 30 years is discounted into irrelevancy'.[17] Yet to the people who will be alive and counting their resources in 20 or 30 years, the values of those resources, and of their income streams, will not be irrelevant: they will be just as real and important to them as the current benefits are to us now.

IIIC 2b **Permanent versus temporary**. Again, this is a distinction which has particular relevance to a stock-accounting system; the point is to inject a more meaningful notion of time into our measurement of costs and benefits. If some component of the stock of wealth (e.g., the resource base) is damaged, how long-lasting are the effects? The answer obviously has meaning for the size of the cost associated with the activity.

IIIC 2c **Costs versus benefits; social versus private costs and benefits**. What is a cost in one place in society may be a benefit in another. For example, alcohol manufacturers and private clinics benefit from alcoholism, while to society as a whole the costs of this abuse are generally regarded as outweighing the benefits. As suggested earlier, an important thrust of social economics will be the correct allocation of costs and benefits – making sure that social costs which can be traced to their roots in private activity are effectively identified with that activity. ('The entity that reaps the benefits should pay the costs.') Accounting systems can play an important role both in the detective work related to this effort, and in clarifying and making known its results.

IIIC 2d **Micro versus macro**: Different things are important, and have to be treated differently, depending on the level of consideration. In particular, what appears as a cost on a micro level may be a benefit at a higher level of aggregation – and yet again a cost at a still more macro level. It is essential to be able to know which level of aggregation is the most appropriate for different uses, even while retaining an awareness that the level receiving one's focused attention is embedded in complex social economic subjects at various levels of aggregation.

IIIC 2e **Needs versus wants**: This is an issue for accounting which especially addresses consumption as an input to welfare. It is also an issue which may be used to evaluate accounting systems. We could, for example, ask: 'to what extent do our accounting systems measure a society's ability to meet basic individual and social needs?' It will immediately be objected that it is 'unfair' to apply such a standard to GNP: this was not what it was designed to measure. That is true; and if our question were, 'how good a measure is GNP?' the 'fair' way to answer that query would, obviously, be to ask, 'how well does it measure what it was designed to measure?' (essentially, aggregate effective demand[18]). However, the initial question, regarding the performance of our systems by the standard of measuring basic needs satisfaction, is still important. By asking it, we may provide the motivation for development or refinement of accounting systems that can more directly address it.

IIIC 3 **Different tools and techniques are often needed when accounting for things that can be measured or counted versus for things that are essentially unquantifiable.**

Several obvious points in this regard have been made already.

– The welfare of a society is importantly influenced by the totality of its productive output. GNP accounting has been criticised for *seeming* to give summary figures on what is produced, while in fact omitting most of the productive activities that do not come ready-quantified with a wage; e.g., 'informal sector' activities. (Again, it should be stressed that this criticism stems from an unfair demand that the GNP serve as a measure for subjects it was not designed to measure.)

– The rash of unproductive money-making schemes which have plagued the world's economies in the 1980s (including currency arbitrage, playing interest-rate differentials, and other forms of speculating and of paper entrepreneurship) have made it clear as it rarely has been before, how *non*-identical are money and wealth: even more, how exchanges involving money can be entirely disassociated from welfare production.

The fact that some things lend themselves to quantification more readily than others has stood in the way of creating accounting systems which account for what is most important, instead of what can most readily be counted. Imagination will have to be used to find ways, for example, of employing inequalities where equalities cannot be specified. For example, there may be places where ordinal listings will be of use (in a sense, that is what is being done when a population is divided into income-level quartiles or quintiles); or, where it is impossible to assign hard numbers, yet watershed characteristics may be found such that groups can be described as being in some sense 'greater than, or less than, X'.

Another approach may include a willingness to measure by different yardsticks than the ones we are used to (e.g., for some purposes tons or kilowatts are more useful than price). What may sometimes break the log-jam on this problem will be acceptance of low levels of aggregation. We may, for example, sometimes have to be content with separate figures on tons of wheat and kilowatts of energy, recognising that, for certain purposes, there is no meaningful bottom line which will aggregate these things together.

Just to give one further example of the kinds of imaginative thinking which are being employed by many individuals concerned to find solutions to these problems, I will quote once again from the anthology of alternative economic approaches collected by Paul Ekins. This is from an essay on 'Making the Informal Economy Visible' by David Ross:

> to compare the real net benefits to society, or the level of human activity between formal and informal activities on the basis of the dollar value of final output alone, is erroneous and biased in favour of showing a greater contribution by the formal economy. Therefore, there is a need to look for a better indicator of levels of activity in the different sectors. The one proposed here is 'time-activity' (numbers of persons multiplied by hours spent at economic activity).... Time-activity measures will not represent a dollar value measure of a nation's output, but will show the distribution of human effort among the different formal and informal sectors (Ekins, 1986, p. 162).

*   *   *

What should be evident here is that accounting is not the dull, dry science normally thought of; it not only reflects our assumptions and world-views; it also helps to shape them. As has been suggested earlier, one of the most urgent needs for societies of the future is to assign costs correctly (often by internalising externalities; see Section IIIB, above). Accounting methods can play a crucial role in this.

The examples of creative approaches to accounting for 'what matters' which have been given in this section are only a beginning. They are intended to stimulate optimism as well as imagination in seeking for alternative tools and methods for the use of social economics. The useful tools will undoubtedly include some that are very 'high-tech'; but it is to be hoped that they will be developed in a context where they will be judged by their results, in terms of explanatory power and as a useful basis for action, rather than in a context which will reward 'rigour' and 'power' in techniques for their own sake.

Notes

1. This subject will be explored in Chapter 11: there it will be seen that it is important to distinguish between 'realisticness' and 'realism'; hence the use of the former word in spite of its odd sound. See also the discussion of 'world realism' and 'truth realism' on p.42 and p.162.

2. It might be thought that something like physical well-being ought to be included with survival ('what is life without health?'). I prefer to keep it at the level of secondary goals (see, p. 28), under 'health' (but also, to some extent, implied in 'consumption'), where it is a means to the ends-in-themselves of happiness, self-actualisation, and moral/spiritual development.

3. In basing itself upon the unitarian principles of Utilitarianism, neoclassical economics has (usually) managed to avoid irresolvable final-goal conflicts. It has thus maintained its claim to consistency, as one of the chief 'scientific' values; but this has been at a significant cost in terms of limiting the meaning of the goal of neoclassical economics.

   There is an important issue here which can best be understood as an issue of character, or personality. There are no logical grounds for the choice of final (or 'primary') goals, or 'basis values' (see Chapter 14 for discussion of this point) – those goals, or values, which provide the motivation for all other goals or values. Nor is there a *logical* reason to choose a single final goal rather than some multiplicity thereof. However, there are practical reasons why certain personalities will find a strong appeal in the reduction of all possible final goals to a single one. Some persons find an aesthetic appeal in the tidiness of a unitary goal. It is simpler. (Occam's razor, in this case – as in many other cases where it is too readily employed – is a principle which has no bearing on the 'rightness' of the choice; it simply opts for what is neater, easier to handle). There is also a methodological advantage in adoption of a single, simple goal: it makes maximisation possible. Above all, a unitary goal eliminates (in theory) the discomfort which for some personalities may be intolerable, of choices among ultimate goals which have to be handed over to judgment, because they have no absolute logical basis.

4. This word may be employed more often in economics than in other social sciences. A monotonic change is one in which the direction of change is never reversed. For example, a monotonically increasing function could appear on a graph as sometimes slanting up to the right, and sometimes flat, but never slanting down to the right.

5. Sandra S. Batie, 'Sustainable Development: Challenges to the Profession of Agricultural Economics', Presidential Address, AAEA Summer Meeting 1989, Baton Rouge, La., p. 4. The author cites Wolfgang Sachs, 'A Critique of Ecology: The Virtue of Enoughness', *New Perspectives Quarterly* (1989) in connection with this phrase.

6. See also the discussion on 'basis values' in the first section of Chapter 14, below.

7. All of the phrases just quoted are Marshall's (from *Principles*, pp. 381–2.) The full quotation is in Chapter 3, n. 5, below.

8. See, for example, Kenneth Arrow, 'An Extension of the Basic Theorems of Classical Welfare Economics' (in J.Neyman (ed.) *Proceedings of the*

Second Berkeley Symposium on Mathematical Statistics and Probability (University of California Press, Berkeley, Calif., 1951).

9. The hypothesis just put forward, if accurate, would explain the situation which Paul Streeten has described thus:

> The social sciences, particularly economics, have experienced growing specialization and growing emphasis on elegant techniques that have come at the expense of realism and relevance to the policy questions of the day. 'Excellence' is defined by the standards evolved within each discipline, and the criteria for professional advancement depend largely upon agility within the established intellectual technologies.
>
> As a result, these disciplines have tended to 'overgraze' these territories of knowledge that are defined as important by the discipline, while neglecting those areas of emerging policy concerns where the social returns are often higher. Similarly, they have often failed to adapt their methodologies to the character of the policy problems that need to be solved. For example, the increasingly sophisticated mathematical techniques used in economics have not yielded correspondingly more accurate analyses of the real world, or better predictions, as they have in the natural sciences. (Paul P. Streeten, 'Reflections on the Role of the University and the Developing Countries', *World Development*, vol. 16, no. 5, May 1988.)

For another comment, dealing again with the exhaustion or obsolescence of a paradigm, see the quotation from Sir John Hicks at the end of Chapter 18 of this book.

10. The sociologist, S. M. Miller, claims that if one reads only the tables without the text in an article stressing econometrics, approximately 50 per cent of the time one will come to the opposite conclusion about the meaning of the tables than that intended by the author. (Personal communication, May 1987.) This is an interesting experiment to make in one's own reading.

11. The basis for 'deep intellectual honesty', as thus defined, is evidently pre-intellectual, or pre-cognitive.

12. I follow Uskali Mäki in this way of subdividing the philosophical position, 'realism'. See the quotation from Mäki on p. 162.

13. Hazel Henderson, 'TOES, 1985', quoted in Paul Ekins (ed.) *The Living Economy* (Routledge and Kegan Paul, London, 1986) p. 36.

14. Some more recent publications which carry this subject forward, especially in the area of natural resource accounting, and which also provide excellent bibliographies, are (1) Ernst Lutz and Salah El Serafy, *Environmental and Resource Accounting: An Overview*, The World Bank Policy Planning and Research Staff, Environmental Department Working Paper No. 6, June 1988; and (2) Robert Repetto, William Magrath, Michael Wells, Christine Beer and Fabrizio Rossini, *Wasting Assets: Natural Resources in the National Income Accounts*, A World Resources Institute Report, 1989. (Other relevant works by these authors are also listed in the Bibliography).

In a somewhat different vein, Thomas Michael Power's *The Economic Pursuit of Quality* (M. E. Sharpe, Armonk, New York and London, 1988)

52 *Introduction to Social Economics*

provides (especially in Chapter 6) a collection of imaginative and
suggestive approaches to the evaluation, for the purposes of practical
discussion and information, of things whose 'true value' we may assume
to be immeasurable. Building on all of the foregoing, Herman E. Daly
and John B. Cobb, Jr. have suggested additional approaches in Chapter 3
of *For The Common Good: Redirecting the Economy Toward Community,
the Environment, and a Sustainable Future* (Beacon Press, Boston MA,
1989).

A more wide-ranging approach to social accounting is taken by
Richard Estes; see, e.g., *The Social Progress of Nations* (Praeger
Publishers, New York, 1984). See also Roefie Hueting, *New Scarcity
and Economic Growth: More Welfare Through Less Production?* tr. Trevor
Preston (North-Holland Publishing Company, Amsterdam, 1980).

15. It may be that, in the record of environmental impact statements which
has been assembled over the last two decades, there is a rich vein of
material to be mined for an approach such as that suggested here.

16. A well-known example of such energy accounting may be found in Gerald
Leach, *Energy and Food Production* (IPC Science and Technology Press
for the International Institute for Environment and Development,
Guildford, 1976). For a good overview on history and current research
in this field see Cutler J. Cleveland, 'Biophysical Economics: Historical
Perspective and Current Research Trends' in *Ecological Modelling*, 38
(1987) pp. 47–73; (Elsevier Science Publishers, Amsterdam).

17. Batie, 1989, p. 18.

18. 'Effective demand' is a term whose special meaning within economics
should be made clear to the non-economist. It means 'what people are
both willing and able to pay for'. Often when economists use the word
'demand' they mean 'effective demand'.

3 Welfare, Production, Development and Change; A Projection for Social Economics

Among the interesting and important issues that should lie within the domain of economics one might cite the following examples (some of them issues of central concern to neoclassical or Marxian economics, some not):

- the role of prices (including taxes) in affecting human behaviour
- the role of human behaviour and attitudes in determining prices
- the various contributions of production to human welfare
- the various contributions of consumption to human welfare
- the ways in which the welfare of people as consumers is linked to, and simultaneously in tension with, the welfare of people as workers/producers.

IV   Welfare as the primary goal and subject of economics   The common theme in the concerns just mentioned is welfare. A somewhat philosophical definition of that concept was proposed in the last chapter. We will now turn to some of the issues with which economics must wrestle if it is to be a science which accepts and responds to the goal of contributing to human welfare.

IVA   The assessment of welfare   In comparison to neoclassical economics, which often uses as a touchstone the question, 'what is produced, how, and for whom?', social economics (more like the Marxian paradigm in this respect) will be informed by a question which will accompany all of its analysis: 'who gains and who loses?' (This is one form of the more general attempt to *identify all the actors*; see below.) In comparison to the neoclassical paradigm, which adopts efficiency as the desired characteristic of any means to any end, the social economics paradigm

53

will adopt, first, a search for positive sum games. Secondly, where win-win (Pareto-optimal, positive-sum-game) situations are not available, the rule will be, *ceteris paribus*, to give a degree of preference to those changes wherein the number of winners is larger and/or the number of losers smaller. An additional rule for assessing changes will come from the Rawlsian approach, where changes which promote equality (increasing the welfare of the least fortunate members of a group or society) are preferred over other types of changes.

These three guidelines – preferring (a) win-win games, (b) an increased number of winners, and (c) equalising welfare improvements – may at times be in internal conflict. No simple method is proposed for finding the right balance between them, but examples of such conflicts, and of balances which have been found, will be topics for study and discussion in the practice and teaching of social economics.

Utilitarian utility maximisation and Rawlsian max-min principles have an advantage, here, in apparently providing simpler rules. In actual application, however, neither of these is simple, either, although the Rawlsian problem of identifying the worst-off group and raising their welfare is not so horrendous as the identification, quantification and aggregation problems implicit in the Utilitarian rule if it were ever actually to be applied. (It is almost impossible to find examples of where this actually has been applied, except where consumption is used as the proxy for utility.)

In recognition of the fact that maximising implies an endless, and endlessly expensive, search for all alternatives, the proposed social economics approach assumes that, even for Utilitarians or Rawlsians, all welfare rules ultimately have to be applied in a satisficing manner.[1] Given this assumption, a first exercise in any real world application of social economics will be *a preliminary definition of what is satisfactory*. Such a definition should be realistic, and will therefore be demanding.

A neoclassical economist may claim to have maximised a social *welfare* function when in fact s/he has done nothing more than show on a graph how a society can rise to the highest *aggregate consumption levels*, given a small and not necessarily realistic set of assumptions. The social economist will need to look at the affected groups in the society and (without using the neoclassical dodge of hypothesising that the winners *could* compensate the losers) s/he will keep searching for strategies that do a better job of increasing winnings, decreasing losses.

The Utilitarian and Rawlsian rules are made to appear 'do-able' by the fact that the satisfactory point is precisely determined (as long as the theory remains on paper) as a calculable maximum. The social economics search for positive-sum games, for equalising welfare improvements, and for ways of increasing the number of winners, will give no illusion that the 'best' solution has definitively been found; but *it will propose ways of defining 'better', for as long as successive users wish to keep trying to improve their strategies.*

IVB Identification of all actors; internalisation of externalities The social economics emphasis upon winners and losers will require special attention to defining who are the actors – whose interests may be affected by any particular move. An important aspect of this will be *the conscious attempt to identify interests that may not be represented, or adequately represented, in markets*: e.g., the interests of the future; of those who lack purchasing power; and of those who will be affected, positively or negatively, by externalities.[2]

Externalities are so termed because they are external to the market trading process, but they are not external to the ecological process. Indeed, they are integral and fundamental. From a sustainable development perspective, externalities are the ultimate physical output of the economic process . . . . Therefore, maximizing economic output is seen as maximizing externalities as well. However, like neoclassical economists, sustainable development advocates also perceive that externalities arise from institutional failure; current property rights neither provide incentives to protect the environment nor to protect the rights of minority cultures (Batie, 1989, p. 21).

If there is a single problem which can be described as the most urgent for all market economies of the future, it is this: to discover how far it is possible to go in 'internalising the externalities' – *to insert into the cost and profit accounting of individual or institutional actors the costs and benefits to society or to other individuals which result from their actions.*

This is an idea which is not infrequently espoused by neoclassical economists; however, much about the neoclassical paradigm – especially its reification of the free market ideal – makes it hostile to the kind of meddling with markets that would likely be necessary in order to put the idea into practice. As an example of the thorny problems which we might encounter in such practice, let us consider something which has had a special appeal for many of the economists upon whom social economics will especially draw, starting with Alfred

Marshall. That is, workers' cooperatives, as a means of fostering important values in production which go beyond the profit motive.

Marshall indicated that simply to make cooperation able to compete in a competitive world was not enough: the 'great evil of our present system', he said, was manifest in the maldistribution of wealth and income, providing, on the one hand, the wrong kind of incentive to elicit socially optimum actions; and resulting, on the other hand, in both envy and poverty.[3] The issue was how to link causally the benefits which an economic actor or institution confers on its environment and the benefits which it derives from the environment. In the cooperatives example, the need is for some way of making the positive externalities of workers' cooperatives show up internally, as economic viability. *How* to do this is a practical issue of the highest priority: it is an example of what may be the single greatest challenge to economists of the 1990s and the early twenty-first century.

Much time and thought will be required to outline and then develop in theory (let alone in practice) a programme which will combine internalisation of externalities with the concept of economic justice suggested in Chapter 2. To show the kinds of directions in which such a programme might be developed, a few of the questions and answers which it could evoke are illustrated here.

Q.: Isn't there an asymmetry in saying 'Those who reap the (presumably private) rewards pay the (presumably social) costs'? Isn't that what government is for, to deal with social costs?

A.: There is no reason to assume that all rewards are always private, all costs public; but in a case where this happens to be so, it is particularly critical to be sure that the costs and benefits come home to the same actor(s), so that the comparison can be made as a basis for rational decision-making. In the reverse case, too, if it is the public that is reaping all the benefits of an activity, it makes sense that it be the public (probably, though not necessarily, via a government) that bears the cost.

Q.: Why isn't normal cost-benefit analysis adequate for this?

A.: Consider two 'bundles'; a bundle of rewards, both social and private, accruing from some particular economic activity; and a bundle of costs, both social and private, attached to the same activity. A normal cost-benefit analysis would say that, when these have all been added up, the activity should not be undertaken if the costs outweigh the benefits; and they should be undertaken in the opposite case. However, if you are an individual or group who is exposed only to the costs, while some other entity reaps all the benefits, you may not agree with that cost-benefit analysis.

The first step is to get the costs and benefits felt in the same places. At the same time we have to ask, who will actually make the cost-benefit analysis, and on what basis? Too often it is made by an actor who confronts only a small part of one bundle (the cost bundle, let us say), along with a large part of the other. To this actor, the activity is worthwhile. What we want to do is to make sure that the whole of both bundles are taken into account together.

Q.: What about the aggregation problem, and incomparability of utilities among individuals? How can you sum up the costs and benefits?

A.: Very often you cannot; but that does not mean you cannot try to get them assigned to the same actor. That, in fact, is the advantage of this approach over hypothesising about when the winner could compensate the loser. To do the latter – even to model it with precision – you have to be able to quantify winnings and losings. If the same person is actually *bearing* both the costs and the benefits, quantification is not needed: every individual possesses, in what is often called 'intuition', a function that is far better at performing the kind of judgments called for in many cost-benefit analyses than anything that can be defined as an algorithm or programmed into a computer.

Q.: That's all very well, but suppose the end result of this 'intuitive' process is the judgment, by the firm that is confronted with, say, the full cost of its polluting activity, that it should go out of business; how do you then allocate the cost of the loss of those consumption goods and those jobs? In the end you'll find yourself having to compare incomparables: things like the value of clean water (not as an end in itself, but as a means to some more generalised notion of welfare) versus the welfare value of jobs creation and output of consumer goods.

A.: Now you're emphasising the social benefits from the activity. Fair enough. The first cut at that evaluation, on the consumption side, comes from neoclassical analysis, which shows (via marginal

analysis and consumer surplus) that the 'value' of a thing to its
purchasers is equal to or greater than the price at which it is
actually sold. Social economists would then muddy those waters by
pointing out that there may be unrepresented would-be consumers
who value the thing very highly, but the value of money is so high
to them (because they have little of it), that they cannot make the
purchase. These people are already out of the market; more will get
pushed out if the clean-up bill raises the price of the product. A lot
more work needs to be done in this theoretical area.

The next social good which you say is threatened is jobs. That is
a benefit accruing especially to the particular workers who hold
them: if society at large asks that those who receive the benefit from
a polluting activity should pay its costs, the point here would be to
make a fair allocation of those costs among the final users of the
product (consumers), the owners of the business, and the workers.
The last group is the one to whom it often seems least fair to bring
home the costs of this activity: one could say, however, as a start,
that if a polluting industry has been an especially profitable one,
permitting unusually high wages and benefits to the workers, then
it would not be unreasonable to reduce the attractiveness of those
particular jobs in the course of allocating the costs of clean-up.

On the harder question, where actual job loss is at issue, we'll
have to specify our assumptions before we can even begin to
address this. Just to show the direction in which such a social
economics analysis would go, here are a few of the questions that
would be asked on the way to assessing this social good:

- What is the probability that the company actually will go out
  of business when the private beneficiary is forced to bear the
  social costs?
- What is the opportunity cost of these jobs – i.e. what other
  jobs, or welfare schemes, are available for such displaced
  workers to fall back on? How do the alternatives compare, in
  terms of the workers' welfare, with the existing employment
  situation?
- What are the dynamic possibilities for creating something new
  to replace this polluting industry? Could such a fresh start
  create an opportunity for the creation of better jobs? (And, not
  only *could* this happen, but *would* it?)
- As compared with alternative opportunities, real or probable,
  are there special social benefits connected with the activity in

question? If that can be shown, then it is the society which reaps at least some of the benefits, and (to return to your original question) then it is the society which should bear the costs associated with those benefits. If 'the society' decides (the mechanism through which such an amorphous thing as a society 'decides' something is always problematical, of course; I don't mean just to take that for granted) that this cost-benefit analysis comes out unfavorably, then it will decide to do without the costs and the benefits.

It should be evident that the proposed social economic emphasis upon welfare does not result in an easy, rosy view of economic realities. It requires a positive effort to identify, as specifically as possible, all the relevant actors, and to trace the generation of costs and benefits to their source; and it is associated with a normative goal of allocating costs to the actors who have received the rewards generated along with those costs.[4] Both the positive and the normative aspects just described will uncover conflicts and bring to light, if not create, tensions.

IVC Conflicts   Consumption as well as production has externa-
between the   lities – costs or benefits to someone else that are
individual   not automatically reflected as market-imposed
and society   costs or benefits to the consumers or producers
                 from whom they flow. These issues become
emotional ones in part because they exacerbate a source of unease with which modern, especially Western societies, have hardly even tried to come to grips. This is the conflict between individual and societal goals and interests. This conflict is thrown into sharper relief when it is presented through other than modern eyes. As I will often find it useful to do, I will describe one aspect of this issue as it appeared to Alfred Marshall, a hundred years ago.

Marshall's goals for society may be traced to a point of view wherein society is to be made good in order to support (through the eradication of poverty and other means) what may be summed up as the spiritual development of individuals. He did not stop to consider seriously the possibility of a real conflict between the short-term spiritual development of a particular individual – e.g., a woman who wants to expand her horizons and enlarge her personal independence through participation in marketed (as opposed to household) production – versus society's long-term needs; e.g., for the maintenance or upgrading of moral values in society and of aesthetic, sanitary, educational and nutritional standards in homes.

Marshall's way of ignoring such a possible conflict was, in his discussions of women, strongly to counsel their continued devotion to a traditional role which was geared to the above-mentioned societal needs. He was shortsighted in being unable to conceive of a world in which the personal goals of women with regard to education and work might take precedence over the care of homes and children. He did, however, supply one thing which is seriously missing from today's imperfect resolution of these individual/societal conflicts: that is, a strong emphasis on the *importance* of the contributions traditionally made by mothers and housewives.

The modern dilemma in this area may be defined as the failure of markets to force society to return, to the providers of these essential contributions, benefits equal to those which they conferred on their environment. Women were bearing the costs; society was reaping the benefits; the situation was an unstable one to which many modern women have responded by leaving their traditional roles.

The cost to society of progress on the front of individual women's needs often falls most heavily, in the present, upon young children. Inadequate care for their moral and practical early socialisation is the basis for society's future problems, in the form of unhappy people, antisocial behaviour, poor learning skills, and foregone productivity. What is overlooked by the neoclassical paradigm, viewing 'society' as nothing more than a collection of individuals tied together through markets, is the fact that neither the future health of society nor the present needs of young children are directly or adequately represented in markets. One reason for this oversight has been the unspoken assumption that, when markets fail, government must step into the breach; that there is no other alternative. The idea (and, where it has been tried, the reality) of government supplying those domestic services which individuals are not supplying is, indeed, very unappealing.

Looking from a modern perspective, it seems that, while the women's movement has achieved significant (though incomplete) progress in enabling women to compete in areas of work traditionally reserved for men, it has, if anything, gone backwards in recognising the dignity and the true value of the kinds of work traditionally performed by women. Society has as critical a need as ever for this work; but it has not yet recognised its value by rewarding it with the status and pay that would make it comparable to work performed outside the home.

The need for social economics, in this regard, is to add Marshall's appreciation for societal needs that have not yet been adequately represented in markets to the modern recognition of the unfairness of relying upon women's personal sacrifices as the solution to these needs. The starting point for thus going beyond both Marshall and his heirs must be the recognition of genuine conflicts between individual's needs and the long-term needs of society. Until there is courageous, full recognition of the unpleasant fact of such a conflict, the prospects for its resolution remain poor.

Beyond such recognition, the next step must be a more sophisticated policy analysis than that depending upon a simplistic either-or ('either free market or totalitarian government') approach. In fact, we know better than that; there is a growing body of experience with the ways in which governments, rather than stepping in to do the jobs needed by society, can create incentives which, at best, make those jobs desirable to individuals on a fair and equitable basis. (*Not*, that is, by decreasing other opportunities so that the needed job remains as the least bad out of a bad set of options.)

V Development and change   Social economics will use its understanding of the behaviours of individuals and of institutions (see Chapter 4, below) as a basis upon which to build to a dynamic view of societies undergoing processes of change and development. It will seek to identify and understand the economic forces which may be seen to have been at work, especially since the inception of the Industrial Revolution, to create the winds of change that continue, ever more powerfully, to blow through all contemporary societies.

If the criterion of importance which one chooses is the well-being of all the human citizens of this planet, development is the most important subject in economics today. 'The high theme of economic progress' (as Marshall called it[5]) is a theme which, today, is most overtly and centrally to be found in the subdiscipline known as development economics. This is unfortunate – not because development economics is messier, less rigorously structured than most of the rest of the field (it is, but precisely because it has continued, more than most of mainstream neoclassical economics, to deal with messy, real-world problems of growth and change) – but because it has been left to a subdiscipline to grapple with subjects that should be of central importance to the whole field.

The understanding of 'development' may be enlarged – and social economics will attempt so to enlarge it – to take in all the processes of economic change that have gone on, since the mid-eighteenth century, in each country once it was touched by the Industrial Revolution. Walt Rostow's 'stages of development' concept has been largely abandoned as too simple and too ethnocentric; it turned out to be false, and offensive, for the so-called 'developed' nations to see their situation as simply the most advanced stage in a sequence in which all others would necessarily follow. It should now be possible to divorce a larger view of development from Rostow's single track simplification. In particular, social economics will look at the major common themes of development with which all regions of the world are struggling, such as:

A. *Industrialisation*, with its special meanings for education and health, as well as for the nature and organisation of work, and for the distribution of power and of resources.
B. *Consumerism*, with its impact not only on motivations to produce, but also on cultural, spiritual and political aspects of human existence.
C. The *ecological side-effects* of, e.g., population growth, technology, consumption choices and modern methods of industrial and agricultural production.
D. *Issues of autonomy, control and dependence*, raising the question: What economic, social, or other welfare difference does it make when production and consumption activities are divided into specialised sub-activities, and/or take place at widely separated geographic locations?
E. As and where development is 'successful', a new context arises for more metaphysical, but not less important, problems of *the definition of well-being*. These highlight concerns for the macro-adjustment of supply and demand as they are mediated by distributional issues.

V A Industrial-   It is important to recognise that different people
isation   attach different meanings to the terms: **Industrial Revolution**, **modernisation**, **Westernisation**, **development**, **progress**, and **growth**. Taking any two of these terms, it is possible to find someone who will maintain that one of them refers to something which s/he regards as 'bad', while the other one is 'good'; and also to find someone else who will take the opposite side. (I had thought that the most improbable of all would be to find someone who

was 'pro-growth', but 'anti-development'; but I have just discovered someone – a serious and respected economist – who takes that position.) It is also, of course, possible to find individuals who are opposed to any kind of change at all; and the one thing all of these words have in common is that they all refer to change.

In seeking, then, a common language with which we can converse about economic realities and their history, I would propose the following statements and definitions.

– The **Industrial Revolution** started roughly two hundred years ago, in Great Britain and Western Europe, and has spread until, today, there are few parts of the world where it has not begun.

Although different facets and phases of the Industrial Revolution can be identified, it is descriptively most useful to understand much of the change, modernisation, development, and growth that is taking place in any part of the world as still part of the same long historical process called the Industrial Revolution.

It is also useful to understand some kinds of change evident in the world today (including some very localised changes, and some that are widespread) as *reactions* to aspects of the Industrial Revolution which meet with resentment or resistance.

– **Westernisation** is a word which has often become associated, and confused, with many of the others listed above, because so many of the processes of the Industrial Revolution were transmitted or imposed from the West to the East. (By a common convention this terminology, in this context, is understood to include transmission from the North to the South.) The most useful understanding of the concept of Westernisation is a cultural one. By this definition, Westernisation occurs when cultural, social, religious, etc. elements, which are indigenous to the West are transmitted to other cultures. This most often does, but need not necessarily, come along with elements that are especially associated with the Industrial Revolution itself, rather than with any particular culture. To give two examples: (1) Individualism is deeply ingrained in the culture of Western humanism; it *also* is of relevance to industrial behaviour, but its first meaning is a cultural one. When individualism spreads in the 'East' due to 'Western' influences, this is appropriately seen as an aspect of Westernisation. (2) 'Time-clock work ethics', on the other hand, while they may often be learned from the West, are something which have been necessary to most cultures that have accepted the Industrial Revolution, as a part of industrialisation *per se*.

- **Modernisation** may be broader and less pointed than Westernisation; it has to do with casting aside some aspect of the old order (technology, at the least; values and customs, if it is to penetrate more deeply), in favour of technologies, values and customs of more recent popularity.

- **Progress** is the most overtly normative of all these words; it might be defined as a modernisation process of which the speaker approves (unless it is being cited sarcastically, in ironic quote marks).

- **Growth** implies 'more' or 'bigger'. It often takes on the special meaning of 'more output (GNP) per capita'. It could mean 'more of the same' (growth without development), or it could mean 'more of something new' (growth with modernisation).

- The view of **development** employed here is one which, while not proposing that 'development' means something quite as undetermined as 'change', nevertheless stresses that it is not something which only goes on in places which are at some 'early' or 'undeveloped' phase vis-à-vis the Industrial Revolution. Potentially, at least, it may include all of the other terms emphasised here. This is, however, for many people, the essential question: *must* development imply growth *and* industrialisation *and* modernisation *and* Westernisation? Also, might it imply other important aspects which are not part of the list of industrialisation-related words?

My summary definition of 'development', in view of all the foregoing, is this: it is a type of change that is unidirectional (i.e., not circular); it includes some set of what is meant by the words, 'growth', 'industrialisation', 'modernisation' and 'Westernisation'; however, in each setting it will occur with different mixtures of these four types of change. Because of the unidirectional, 'moving-into-the-future' meaning of development, the single one of these other four concepts which must *always*, in some form, accompany development is 'modernisation' – as long as we understand that word to have an evolving meaning; because what is 'modern' in 1990 is quite different from what was modern in 1940 – or what will be modern in 2040.[6]

I would add one further observation: there can be no major change, of the kind associated with the word 'development', that does not entail significant cost and distress. It may be worth it to some or most (rarely all) of those involved. It may also be the case that any relatively 'change-free' alternative that we can imagine would entail at least equal cost and distress. At the same time, those involved in projecting, guiding, or planning change need to work to spread the burdens of change as fairly as possible, and to help those most hurt by it. Again, the role of government is implicitly invoked, and with it the questions asked earlier: Are our only options *markets* or *governments*? What other institutions or procedures might we call on?

VB   Consumerism   Consumerism may be regarded as an aspect of either modernisation, or development, or Westernisation – although it can also arise through other channels. Only a few aspects of this very large subject will be discussed here.

The simplest economic models have portrayed consumption as though it is a benefit which must be weighed against only one cost, and that one a cost borne entirely by the consumer, in the form of the price required to purchase the consumption good. More sophisticated approaches must account for other costs, e.g.:

VB 1   Environmental harm which occurs during production, consumption, and/or disposal of goods.

VB 2   Costs of utilisation of resources which may be increasingly transferred to the consumer in, for example, the nuisance-value of recycling and disposal.

VB 3   Harm to the consumer which may occur not only through consumption of, e.g., addictive drugs and alcohol, but also through ingestion of a variety of other substances (artery-clogging, cancer-inducing, hormone- or pesticide-laced foods etc.); perhaps through exposure to media (mind-rotting, violence-stimulating); and perhaps through other patterns of consumption which have an addictive, numbing, or dis-informing effect.

Regarding the third type of cost, especially where there are serious issues of addiction or of ignorance involved, the neoclassical solutions of raising the cost of the addictive substance, or lowering the cost of the healthy but unknown alternative, do not adequately deal with the welfare issues. Price is an important motivator; these are good examples of cases where it is overwhelmed by other motivators.

Many instances of the first type of cost (environmental harm) can be loaded onto price, and we may expect to see this occurring more in the future – though, again, this will not just happen by itself, through the automatic action of markets; it will require some kinds of active (often governmental) interventions in markets and pricing.

By contrast, the example given in point VB 2 is one where the principle, 's/he who reaps the benefit should bear the cost', is translated into other than price terms, i.e., into 'nuisance value'. Communist societies have generally chosen to allocate scarce items which are regarded as requisites, or rights (especially such basic needs as food, shelter, clothing and medical care) via the nuisance value of quantity rations, queues, etc., rather than via price. Welfare states have done the same on a less generalised basis, often with a two-tier system where those who could not afford private education, medical care, or housing may (under variously more or less stringent systems of means-testing, etc.) receive state-supplied versions of the same, often of lower quality, and with more nuisance costs attached.

We face a likelihood of increased pressures for market economies to use non-price rationing, just at the time when command economies are opening up to the market. There are several reasons for such pressure in the market economies, including the rapidly mounting costs (along with growing capabilities) of health care; the prospect of scarcities in such basic requirements as drinkable water; and the collective suffering caused by pollution of such public goods as breathable air. On the last two environmental issues, the underlying logic is that it is difficult, if not impossible, to calculate the harm that is done by each increment of consumption (or production for consumption) of polluting items; attempts to translate that harm into market prices might be devastating to small consumers (the poor) before it deters the large (rich) consumers; and the conclusion is likely to be that there are areas where consumption must be limited, but not solely by the price mechanism.

Thus market economies, which already possess sizeable pockets of non-price distribution in public sector involvement in health, education, housing, etc. (as well as in the domestic or informal sectors), seem likely to face more, not less, significant areas where economic theory will have to pay attention to quotas, nuisance values, and other quantity restrictions. Increasingly, 'fair' distribution will become an issue of approximately equal concern to all kinds of economic systems. The two now dominant paradigms each have different useful things to say about this issue, but more theoretical attention is still called for.

One further example may be given of issues regarding consumption which require new attention. This may be put in terms of the question: how much of the demand for consumption is endogenous to the field of economics?

Traditionally, such issues as cross-elasticities (e.g, demand for small cars may go up when the price of petrol rises, but down when motorcycles are improved or made cheaper) have been considered to reside squarely within the neoclassical paradigm, while tastes have been regarded as exogenous. Neomarxian thinking, by contrast, has portrayed the ruling classes as manipulating the tastes and perceptions of the masses so that the latter would play the desired economic and political roles – including the role of mass consumers. While the division of societies into a very few classes may be too simplistic, it is nevertheless important to explore further the insight that consumer tastes are affected in some ways that are endogenous to the economic system. As will be discussed later (see Section VII D in Chapter 4, below), our educational systems, formal and informal, inevitably play an important part in shaping the character of human beings as economic actors – as consumers and as producers.

It is not only the case that an economic system is shaped by an educational system; the reverse is also true. Such an observation may give rise to disquieting visions of an Orwellian manipulative society. However, it is too late to think that we can escape all of the implications of this vision by ignoring them; many of them are already with us. The question is whether manipulation is to be left solely to Madison Avenue, or whether other forces will attempt to weigh in as well (as, increasingly, anti-smoking, anti-alcohol, and other forces of 'the new Victorianism' are doing). This is not a purely economic question, but it has important implications for our understanding of some important economic issues.

VC Ecological side-effects   To talk about this aspect of development is to open the subject of the long-run impact of development.
The economic behaviour of modern Man leaves an increasingly long-lasting imprint upon the natural world. You and I, reader and writer, will most likely not be alive in three score years and ten; but the patterns of consumption and production – and, underlying

these, the patterns of human reproduction – in which we now participate are affecting the same ecosystem that will provide the basis for the economic behaviour and the economic possibilities of those who will take our places as long as the human race survives. *Human ecology is the repository of the set of options that will be available to humans in the future.*

Whether we adopt human welfare, or utility, or economic justice, or any other goal as our primary one, we must also confront the decision: are we interested in welfare, utility or justice only for people now living, perhaps only during this year, or this electoral term? Or do we take these ideas seriously with respect to the longer run: current lifetimes; the next generations; or many human generations? These are not decisions to be taken lightly, or made by default, for they will make a significant difference, not only in economic practice, but also in economic theory.

Neoclassical economics stresses that wants, and the means to their satisfaction, are always to be understood and modelled within a context of scarcity. An emphasis upon ecological side-effects also brings to the fore a notion of scarcity, but it has important differences from the neoclassical view of this subject.

The neoclassical view of resource scarcity is that it is a constraint in the short run which can, and in all likelihood will, be pushed back, in the long run, by the application of new technology. New opportunities will yield growth in desires (this is as close as the model comes to admitting endogeneity of tastes), and that same growth will bring us up against a new set of constraints; but no absolute limits are expected to be encountered.

The ecological perspective is less optimistic about the human ability to overcome all resource constraints. Yes, we may be able to go on far beyond the foreseeable future, substituting more common resources for those which become scarce; but our very use of resources – the 'throughput' of production and consumption – imposes a strain, not just upon our reserves of any single mineral or gas, but upon the whole ecosystem. The ultimate constraint is the ability of the biosphere to absorb the products (summarised as 'pollution') of the ever greater numbers of human beings, responsible for ever greater amounts of throughput per capita.

Referring back to the first approach taken (in Chapter 1) to the definition of the field of economics – via the questions that are asked of it – it is noteworthy that an economics which embraces the ecological view finds that the larger challenge to our discipline posed by the sustainable development theme is the reconsideration of *questions that neoclassical economists have tended to neglect.* What are the fundamental causes and dynamics of economic growth in society? What are the relationships between economic growth, natural resources, environmental quality, and human welfare? Is discounting an appropriate means of analyzing resource use in the future? Do resources other than the human mind matter? What are the distributional implications of policies? (Batie, 1989, p. 29; italics added).

The quotation above is from the 1989 address by the President of the American Agricultural Economic Association. Her paper continues with an examination of where these issues fit into our existing paradigms; it is worth quoting a long passage:

These questions are not new to economics. The physiocrats believed natural resources were the fundamental force empowering economic growth and that human societies should live in harmony with the laws of nature (Oser and Blanchfield). The marginalists were preoccupied with questions relating to human welfare distribution and social reform (Cooter and Rappoport). However, the sustainability concept is not a mere resurrection of old classical themes. New concepts from ecology, non-equilibrium thermodynamics, and mathematical catastrophe-theory are strongly influencing perceptions. While these same influences are modifying some contemporary economics perspectives, a coherent, comprehensive integrated model of economic and environmental interaction does not yet exist (Barbier). Precious few models incorporate assumptions that are appropriate for the investigation of the sustainability of economic development (Norgaard, 1985). Even the institutional school, which has long been interested in the role of institutions in achieving change (Klein), has tended to emphasise institutions apart from nature (Norgaard, 1985).

The traditional assumptions of the neoclassical model were adopted to facilitate all investigation of market transactions. The basic assumptions of the neoclassical framework do not fit the natural world. *Nor do the main questions of inquiry of the neoclassicalists require such a fit.* The assumptions of divisible resources that can be owned, the concept of a continuum of reversible stable equilibriums, and the neglect of feedback from the natural world to economic systems within the neoclassical model make powerful predictors of many economic system responses (Norgaard, 1985). These assumptions, however, are inappropriate for many of the questions asked by sustainable development advocates (ibid., p. 30; italics added).

VD Issues of   Increasing globalisation of trade and commerce
autonomy,   have brought increasing awareness of the ways in
control and   which individuals are dependent upon impersonal
dependence   market forces. A typical example of one type of
reaction engendered by this growing awareness is the following comment from a writer who is particularly concerned with issues of unemployment:

> I have observed how, unless a local economy contains a wide range of varied, locally owned and controlled businesses, it stands at the mercy both of the international trade-winds, which can destroy a mono-crop economy overnight, and of the policy-makers in Tokyo or New York, who can close down a local branch without ever even knowing properly where it is. The experience of powerlessness is devastating (Guy Dauncey, 'A New Local Economic Order', in Ekins, 1986, pp. 264–5).

What, in the context of the globalisation of trade and commerce, does it mean when, e.g., a starving people grow tea to export, rather than food that they could eat? There are two most probable explanations:

1 The pressure of population, or declining soil fertility, has brought about a situation such that the area cannot, with available technologies, compete in food production with the import price for food; in the extreme, it may actually be unable to produce enough food for local self-sufficiency.

2 The alternative type of explanation suggests that the ownership of productive assets and/or the investment policies that have been pursued on the local, national, and/or international level, have resulted in a situation wherein tea plantations are more profitable, from the point of view of those who decide how investments are to be allocated, than the production of food for local consumption.

Arguments over these issues, on the abstract level, resemble the story of the blind men disputing the nature of the elephant. They go on endlessly, because the proponents of each side focus on only one of the explanatory descriptions.

- Those favouring local independence cite cases where reason 2 is predominant; they then argue that patterns of ownership and government policies are arbitrary and should be a focus for change. They often point out cases where those who reap the rewards are *not* bearing the costs of the investment decisions.
- By contrast, proponents of the economic concept of the 'gains from trade' cite explanation 1, and say that situations such as the tea-growing case do not arise out of arbitrary decisions, but represent the outcome of efficient markets; and that attempts to go against this reality would be counterproductive.

In fact, one may observe that dependence and powerlessness have also been experienced, with a comparable range of impacts, in relation to capricious or uncaring *local* centres of power or resource control. However, the deeper, more significant point is that the movement towards localisation of economic power and action (related to E. F. Schumacher's 'Small is Beautiful' concept) includes some often under-appreciated aspects of economic rationality.

Large corporations have extensively explored the economies of large scale, at the same time as their growth has also been impelled by other logics of bigness (quirks of the financial markets, and of tax and other legislation; bargaining power *vis-à-vis* governments, customers and subcontractors; etc.) which have nothing to do with productive efficiency. The logics of smallness include, on the one hand, efficiencies of information, trust, transportation and other elements that affect transactions costs; and, on the other hand, a strong appeal to other values than efficiency as defined by profit.

Again, bigness and smallness each have their benefits, in terms of efficiencies as well as other values, and each have their costs. Economic justice – the situation in which those who reap the benefits pay the costs – may often be best served by 'big-small partnerships'. Examples would span the range from the political (e.g., 'top-down to bottom-up' relationships, such as the government of the city of Rio de Janeiro acting in concert with the grassroots organisers of the *favelas*) to the economic (e.g., a multinational company acting with local suppliers of inputs, including labour, to maintain a healthy local economy). In each case such partnerships work when the big and the small discover that common interests (i.e., costs and benefits felt in common) are significant enough that they are also willing to pool the benefits or costs that had been accruing to only one side or the other.

Issues of autonomy and control go outside of the economic sphere, into basic questions of the distribution of power; but they circle back in, returning to the requirement that market systems (where they are the predominant framework for exchange and production) be designed so as to internalise both positive and negative externalities.

VE The meaning of well-being after successful industrialisation   It is not uncommon to find an advanced industrial economy facing, on the one hand, a situation of inadequate access to food, shelter, and education in a large fraction of its population; along with, on the other hand, insufficient (effective) demand in the society as a whole. The problem of effective macro demand smaller than potential macro supply may be manifest either as open unemployment of factors, or in disguised human unemployment, including the absorption of great numbers of people in unproductive or non-welfare-enhancing or 'defensive' activities (from the military to substance abuse clinics to the creation of artificial wants through advertising). Such situations leave us to wonder what problems we would encounter in an economy in which people only purchased things which (by some plausible definition) added to their true happiness and well-being, and in which there was no need for military expenditures. Could an economy like that of the USA make the necessary changes to absorb, *in such a way as to provide the necessities now 'ineffectively' demanded by those whose basic needs are insufficiently met*, the hundreds of millions of people whose present jobs would thereby disappear? How could the resources released from waste creation and military insecurity be diverted to the uses of childcare, medical care, education and the provision of basic needs for all? These questions should, and perhaps one day will, pose *the* great macro problems for 'post-industrial' societies.[7]

VI Production   Welfare issues relating to consumption and production, and the positive and negative externalities of consumption and production, have been raised at several points. Now we will take another look at the subject of production as a process, stressing particularly the theoretical need for conceptual disaggregation of factors.

The social economics view of production will treat separately land (in the literal sense of the word), labour, capital, technology, and material inputs. Within these categories it will note the important practical and conceptual differences between, for example, energy and other material inputs; or different aspects of land, with different economic meanings for different purposes: e.g., soil quality, geographic location, relation to water resources, and so on.

VIA Technology   The history of economic thought will figure in many places in the development and teaching of social economics. A little knowledge of the evolution of economic thinking with respect to factors of production provides a good example of the usefulness of the understanding to be gained therefrom.

In the classical economic view, partly rooted in the land-based theory of value of the Physiocrats, agriculture was the productive activity of first consideration, and here the essential trade-off was perceived to be between two inputs: land and labour. It was thought that the productivity of one of these inputs could only be enhanced by adding more of the other. Since both were characterised by diminishing marginal returns, the factor whose use was increased would suffer a productivity decline. Hence the pessimism of such classical economists as Malthus and Ricardo.

As the classical framework was also applied to non-agricultural production, the term 'capitalism' came into use, and capital was increasingly perceived to be another input of prime significance. Reluctant to abandon the simplicity of a two-input model, economists sometimes described capital as 'congealed labour', or regarded it as the super-category under which land was to be included. At other times, however, the useful distinction between rent and other types of returns on capital investments was brought to the fore.

The classical economists, by and large, did not identify capital closely enough with machinery and other aspects of technology so as to loosen the limitations of the land/labour trade-off on the perception of opportunities for productivity growth. As the Industrial Revolution continued, however, the importance of technology has increasingly been recognised as an explanation for continued growth of output. Even in agriculture the premises for the pessimism of classical economics seemed to be refuted as it turned out to be possible to apply technological inputs in such a way as to simultaneously enhance the productivity of *both* land *and* labour.

While there have continued to be 'Malthusian pessimists' who proclaim that we are about to run up against some global system of diminishing marginal returns such that technological progress will come to an end, a brighter view is offered by the 'technological optimists' who insist, instead, that the ingenuity of humankind will continue to find technological inputs that can maintain the momentum of ever greater productivity of all critical factors.

If we unbundle our understanding of the various types of inputs, it may be that both the Malthusian pessimists and the technological optimists will be found to be correct. A set of distinctions among 'technological inputs to agriculture' which may make sense of the debate between the optimists and the pessimists is one which labels two subsets of technological inputs thus:

- '*mm*' (for mostly material inputs) is the group of technological resources whose limitations, with declining marginal returns, we have begun to see;
- '*ii*' (for the information-intensive, immaterial inputs) is the group of technological resources that appear to retain significant potential to enhance the productivity, and reduce the intensity of use, of most or all other factors.[8]

A conceptual unbundling of the inputs to production should lead to a better understanding of hidden as well as obvious costs and benefits of each of them. Technology, as just suggested, can be roughly divided according to whether its inputs are more materials intensive versus those technologies that increasingly replace materials with invisible inputs such as information. Among the material inputs, special attention is needed to distinguish between those that are renewable easily and soon; those that may be regenerated with difficulty, or only over a long time period; and those that are to all intents and purposes non-renewable. Also, the distinction needs to be made between technologies that release more, or less, pollutants as compared to those currently in use.

It is becoming increasingly evident that technological choices are dependent upon the capacity of the natural environment to absorb the demands made upon it in the course of production and consumption. When markets are working well, they translate harmful short- and long-term environmental strains into higher costs and prices. When this translation does not occur, or occurs inefficiently, or too late, we may describe the situation as one of market failure. Such market failures may be serious enough that partially or fully non-market solutions are required, with special ingenuity required in those situations where there is no simple way to 'internalise the externalities'.

The subject of technology is one wherein the ecological view, upon which the social economics approach will draw, becomes especially prominent. The ecological view often leads to a 'conservationist' approach which may be summarised in the idea, 'what you inherit from nature is likely to be the best you will have – try to preserve it intact.' This leads to an emphasis on, for example, the recycling of plant wastes as humus. By comparison, the 'technological fix' approach says: 'don't worry about what you use up, you can always replace it.' In the instance of agricultural recycling, the technological optimists tend to view chemical additives as perfect substitutes for organic matter, while the conservationists stress the complexity of ecological interactions, and the difficulty of understanding what it is that one is trying to replace. More broadly, the ecological view also stresses the importance of not abandoning knowledge of traditional patterns of human resource use before discovering the values which are presumed to be represented in their endurance.

It is useful to note that, while there are ideological value biases and preferences underlying these different approaches (ranging from unconscious beliefs regarding the inherent goodness or badness of human nature, to personality traits which find change more or less frightening or exciting or fun), they also contain significant reference to empirical content. A social economist may not be qualified to judge under what circumstances chemical additives are, or are not, adequate substitutes for organic matter, but s/he will have some tools which will be useful in the debate. The social economics approach to the topics mentioned here would be to attempt to ascertain which aspect(s) of human welfare are being emphasised; then, in light of the goals, consider the prospective losses as well as gains (who will be hurt as well as who benefited), even if the losers include some non-paying, non-voting group such as future generations. This will lead to an inquiry into the relative immediate costs of the proposed action, and a search for ways of making probabilistic estimates regarding their longer term costs (accounting issues again).

VIB Work A disaggregated approach to factor analysis would include an awareness of the biases and bases for such approaches as the ecological, 'technological optimist', neoclassical and social economics positions just cited. The need for disaggregation is even more evident when we turn to a consideration of the input to production which is directly supplied by human beings.

Human labour is so different, in so many ways, from capital, energy, other materials, land and technology, that much understanding is sacrificed when we accept the convenience of classifying them together. Just to give one, important example: human labour is self-motivating. The worker does not act automatically or passively on commands or suggestions, but transforms them, both cognitively and motivationally, into his/her own programme for action.[9]

It should be emphasised, again, that social economics is oriented to an applied, and particularly a public, policy concern. It is anticipated that governments and other public institutions will increasingly recognise their responsibility for long-term as well as short-term welfare; and that the key link between present and future welfare is to be found in the concept of sustainability, which expresses the 'eco-eco' (economic-ecological) relationship. One way that this responsibility will be expressed will be through tax policies; it will imply recognition, e.g., of the fact that, where income taxes are the chief source of revenue for a government, the effect is discrimination against labour as compared to capital, land, and other material factors of production. This creates an incentive to replace labour with energy and materials.

Technology choices are critically important both in deciding how much employment of labour shall be associated with a given output, and also for deciding the nature of the work that will be available. Capitalist systems in general have few ways of formally taking these values into account. Labour employment is a result of other decisions that have nothing to do with work, particularly decisions about output (whose goal is consumption, not work) which are, in turn, largely (though not exclusively) regulated by perceptions of opportunities for profit. As governments become increasingly sophisticated in their recognition of these social effects, new mechanisms will need to be sought to counteract the possibly welfare-reducing effects of existing tax and other policies.

Neoclassical economics deals with profits as a bottom-line construct: the result of a calculation, after the returns from a productive activity have come in, of the difference between costs and revenues. Marxian economics probes more deeply into the generation of profits, claiming that they come out of a surplus which can (in that paradigm) only be generated by labour. While not adopting such a 'labour theory of value', it is proposed that social economics reconsider some aspects of the relationship between labour and profits.

Specifically, let us start with the concept of 'slack' – a word which has been used to describe conditions that allow workers to operate below the 'maximum effort level'. It has been noted (by Leibenstein and others) that it is virtually impossible even to define the maximum effort level; no matter how hard you are working, it is almost always possible to find some increase of pressure that will persuade you to work a little harder. (The limit might be called the heart-attack level.) If prison-camp conditions are taken (as an example, with regard to physical labour) as an approximation to 'the maximum effort level', it becomes evident that, except under the most extreme conditions, some slack exists in any productive activity.

Slack is, I would contend, one translation of a 'surplus' when the latter is defined as *revenue generated above the minimum necessary to keep a production process going.* This definition sounds like economic profit as described in the neoclassical paradigm, but an important difference is implied: that *the presence of surplus may be felt, and its benefits captured, at different points in the production process – not only at the end, in the form of profit.* The existence of slack, in this model, may be understood as equivalent to the possibility for workers (including managers) to allocate some surplus to themselves (in the form of amenities above bare necessity, time for cracking jokes and thinking about other things than work, etc.) before it emerges in the profit line.

When, with this concept of 'surplus' in mind, we look at the transformation of materials into outputs desirable to human beings, we have a new way of appreciating that production is not just a long stream of means to a single, final pair of ends: the consumer's utility from the product, and the owner's utility from the profits. Other goods, as well as bads (including increases as well as reductions in entropy, to use the 'biophysical economics' perspective), are being created all along the way. A 'take-off' from the surplus in the form of 'slack' is only one of these.

VIC Productivity analysis   The concepts suggested in the foregoing section will be elaborated in *Social Economics*, volume 2.

So, too, it must be understood that this initial overview of some issues which need a different kind of attention than that given by the neoclassical and Marxian paradigms is not intended to list all the areas calling for attention. Only a single additional aspect of productivity – one that refers us back to the methodological issue of 'accounting' – will be mentioned here; a more complete survey will have to await later work.

We often encounter estimates of labour productivity. In the simplest terms, a society's statistics on output per person indicate the possibilities for consumption per person. Rising labour productivity is a necessary (though not sufficient) basis for rising average wages. Similarly, land productivity, which is often calculated, has a special meaning because rising land productivity is essential to feed growing populations with essentially static land resources. We may also find estimates of the productivity of financial capital (or, as is sometimes calculated, of foreign exchange), which may be seen as proxies for measuring the productivity of other scarce resources. By comparison, figures on the productivity of material resources are relatively hard to find. The least common of all (because it is so hard to perform) is a total factor productivity analysis.

The point to be made here is that productivity analysis on any one factor alone should be regarded as something approaching dangerous knowledge, in that it can be extremely misleading, and is often misused. As Robert Dorfman puts it, 'single factor productivity analysis implicitly treats all other factors as free goods'.[10] That tendency must be reversed if we are to find ways of internalising externalities.

One reason, again, for doing the latter is to make bridges between the short and the long run. Similarly, a promising effect of the social economic approach to the study of production, putting it into the ecological perspective which has been suggested in the last two chapters, may be a softening of the lines between 'micro' and 'macro' (and, too, 'global') analyses; for, by seeing production as embedded in an ecosystem which is, ultimately, part of a global network of interrelationships, what had been the micro analysis of the theory of the firm becomes part of an understanding which stretches much further, both temporally and spatially.

Notes

1. A concept introduced by the economist Herbert Simon, 'to satisfice' means to seek a solution which will meet a predetermined 'satisfactory' standard. Once such a satisfactory solution has been found, the search ends. The contrast is with maximising, wherein all alternatives are considered, and the best is chosen. For Simon's trenchant analysis of why maximising is usually impossible, see 'A Behavioral Model of Rational Choice' in H. S. Simon, *Models of Man* (Wiley, New York, 1957).

   For another alternative to maximising, 'matching' (a concept from experimental psychology), see Chapter 17, n. 10.
2. Externalities are costs and benefits to some set of the system as a whole (the whole ecosystem; the human race; the society in which the activity is

embedded; or some subsets or individuals within that society) that are not automatically reflected as market-imposed costs and benefits to the consumers or producers from whom they originate.

3. Alfred Marshall, 'Co-operation', in A. C. Pigou (ed.) *Memorials of Alfred Marshall* (Kelley & Millman, New York) p. 238.
Henceforth this book will be cited simply as *Memorials*. Cf. also, for example, *Principles*, pp. 495 and 201.

4. The neoclassical approach, emphasising the idea of 'compensating the losers', has tended towards allocating *benefits* to the actors who have borne the *costs*. Sometimes this will be the more practical way to go; but in general it seems less likely actually to happen, and carries with it more problems of moral hazard, than the social economics suggestion just put forth.

   We will see an example, in the next section, where the neoclassical response to the feminist issue is to say that, since women have traditionally borne certain societal costs, they should now reap equalising benefits in the form of equal access to a male lifestyle. By contrast, the approach I am suggesting proposes that, since society has long reaped the benefits of traditional women's work, ways should now be found to allocate the costs of those services more evenly through society.

5. 'The theory of stable equilibrium of normal demand and supply helps indeed to give definiteness to our ideas; and in its elementary stages it does not diverge from the actual facts of life, so far as to prevent its giving a fairly trustworthy picture of the chief methods of action of the strongest and most persistent group of economic forces. But when pushed to its more remote and intricate logical consequences, it slips away from the conditions of real life. In fact we are here verging on the high theme of economic progress; and here therefore it is especially needful to remember that economic problems are imperfectly presented when they are treated as problems of statical equilibrium, and not of organic growth' (A. Marshall, *Principles*, pp. 381–2).

6. Herman Daly makes a simpler distinction:

   By 'growth' I mean quantitative increase in the scale of the physical dimensions of the economy; i.e., the rate of flow of matter and energy through the economy (from the environment as raw material and back to the environment as waste), and the stock of human bodies and artifacts. By 'development' I mean the qualitative improvement in the structure, design, and composition of physical stocks and flows, that result from greater knowledge, both of technique *and of purpose* (Herman E. Daly, 'The Economic Growth Debate: What Some Economists Have Learned But Many Have Not'; *Journal of Environmental Economics and Management*, 14, 323–36 (1987)).

   Daly's distinctions between growth and development bear an interesting similarity to my growth and development 'mm' and 'ii' techniques for expanding productivity; see Section VIA, below.

   For a suggestive articulation of how these definitions are relevant to our understanding of contemporary events, see Bruce Mazlish, 'The

Breakdown of Connections and Modern Development', in *Global Commons: Site of Peril, Source of Hope*, a special issue of *World Development* (ed. N. R. Goodwin; forthcoming, 1991.)

7. These issues are expanded in 'Equity to the Rescue of Efficiency' (Goodwin, forthcoming).

8. This thinking is expanded in 'Lessons for the World from U.S. Agriculture: Unbundling Technology', N. Goodwin, forthcoming in *Global Commons: Site of Danger, Source of Hope* (a special issue of *World Development*, 1991).

9. Ecologists are likely to note that the material world, too, is responsive, not purely passive, and that we do better to understand our place in the ecosystem as a set of relationships composed of multitudinous, multidirectional interactions than to think in terms of a one-way imposition of order by Man on his/her environment. Nevertheless, the human-to-human relationships which take place in the workplace are qualitatively different from interactions among other factors of production.

10. Personal communication, January 1989.

4 Individuals and Institutions in Social Economics

This chapter will conclude the sampling of topics which are given as examples of social economics as a system of theory. As we look at some of the micro issues of human psychology which social economics must consider, it is worth beginning with the reminder that there is more than one body of knowledge which can be drawn upon to aid in an economic understanding of human behaviour; e.g., the various branches of psychology, as well as existing syntheses especially intended for use in the field of economics (cf. the work of George Katona, or Amitai Etzioni). As social economics develops there might come to be a standard (though, it is to be hoped, always evolving) set of understandings in this area – but nothing that could be so simply summarised as the statement that 'Rational economic man maximises his perceived self-interest'.

VII Issues of human psychology In looking at micro-level behavior we need to remind ourselves that, in fact, neither neoclassical economics, nor any other imaginable system of theory that would obviously belong in the field of economics, is much concerned with tracing the behaviour of any one particular individual. The neoclassical system is concerned with economic outcomes which are the result of aggregated individual behaviours, especially in the intersections of the purchasing behaviours and the producing/selling behaviours which create prices. In order for the neoclassical system of theory to be 'correct' (i.e., to make good predictions and accurate descriptions of this level of activity), it is not necessary for the psychosocial axioms of the system to be realistic, but only for the outcomes to be the same as they would be *if* these axioms *were* realistic.

Often this parsimonious approach yields useful insights. Neoclassical economics has developed tools well adapted to model a micro-economic picture

-   in which individual actors are understood to behave atomistically, minimising the interaction effects among them;
-   where these individuals may be simplistically understood as rationally self-interested, with 'rational behaviour' understood as *maximising* and *instrumental*;
-   where economic gain may be understood as at least a reasonable proxy for most significant motivations, and prices adequately reflect the most important and relevant human desires and satisfactions;
-   and where all significant actors are willy-nilly competitive.

However, in part because of what has been lost in this set of simplifications, the neoclassical system diminishes in power and relevance

-   as the focus shifts from a micro picture of individual interactions to a macro picture of societies operating as complex whole organisms;
-   where cooperative behaviours have an economic significance;
-   as we try to understand changes in these organisms over time;
-   as our concern focuses on values other than prices which are used in defining some notions of welfare;
-   as we try to relate some real future with the real present (both of these being disequilibrium realities);
-   or as we try to make certain necessary translations between reality and theory and back again.

Unfortunately, the neoclassical paradigm contains no way of predicting when its insights will be seriously off, or why; and those occasions are sometimes of great economic significance. This is why there is need for a companion/alternative to the neoclassical paradigm which will look inside the black box of human behaviour.

The psychosocial issues where it seems that the neoclassical model runs into trouble include:

-   some areas where motivations other than 'maximisation of self-interest' (e.g., altruism, honesty and trust) have important economic effects;
-   inframarginal motivations;[1]
-   the motivations and behaviours that may best be understood in terms of the concepts which Alfred Marshall referred to as 'activities' and 'progress';

- the economic importance of the distinction between needs and wants;
- issues of class, especially in relation to other divisions in human society (along lines of race, age, ethnicity, education, etc.);
- various kinds of power and coercion that arise from or impact upon the economic sphere;
- innovation and entrepreneurial activities;
- and various information and learning-related issues, including the role of advertising, the effects of fashions in thought and belief, and the value of collective behaviour for gathering and sharing information.

This chapter will take up only a few of these issues, as examples of the social economics approach to understanding human behaviours and motivations as determinants, consequences and goals for the field of economics.

VIIA   Altruism   Most people recognise that there are many altruistic motives, including some that have significance for economic behaviour. Although this recognition began with Adam Smith, and continued to be evident in the writings of most of the prominent economists up through the time of Alfred Marshall, it is not really compatible with the core of the modern neoclassical paradigm. There have been many ingenious efforts to integrate it into the core, but none of these have been incorporated into the mainstream.

The issue may be illustrated by reference to one such effort: Amartya Sen's concept of a 'two stage utility function'.[2] Sen's proposal was that we understand utility-driven choices[3] as occurring according to the following two steps: first we decide what kind(s) of utility are involved in a given problem (e.g., are we after the utility we will feel by doing our duty; by that associated with self-improvement; or is it simply hedonistic pleasure?) Having made this choice, we then choose the activity that will maximise the preferred type of utility.

As a description of reality, this is probably inferior to a psychology of choice which is not constrained to employ the vocabulary and concepts ('utility' and 'maximisation') of neoclassical economics. However – again, as a description of reality – it is a distinct improvement upon the restriction of utility to selfish gain which is the most useful definition for the neoclassical core.

Selfish gain is not, of course, the only meaning of utility in the neoclassical paradigm. However, it has been well argued (see, e.g., Chapter 2 in Etzioni, 1988) that attempts to broaden the definition further result in either a tautology or a mystery. This has been particularly true since the historical time of the transition from classical to neoclassical economics. One of the characteristics of that transition was an attempt to excise from the field dependence upon beliefs which, however widely held, could not be proved. In particular, a number of the assumptions of Utilitarianism were formally removed (though their presence often remained felt on an informal or unconscious level). One consequence of this was the following:

> If interpersonal comparisons of utility are impossible, then we are no longer able to maximise the sum of utilities across people. So the neoclassical utilitarian defends a weaker kind of maximisation process in which one maximises his own utility. The classical utilitarian's moral principle, which says to maximise the sum of utilities, is strong in the sense that it sometimes directs people to act against their own selfish interests. The corresponding, weaker neoclassical utilitarian's moral principle says that we should move toward Pareto optimality. This principle is weaker in not requiring individuals to act against their own selfish interests. It is also weaker because in many situations it does not tell us what to do.[4]

The neoclassicist, with his/her beautifully structured system, suffers from a serious problem:

- all normative inputs have (theoretically) been removed from the field;
- 'you cannot derive ought from is';
- yet the economist is constantly in the position of needing to be able to say what *ought* to be done.

The fall-back upon efficiency is often not enough, for the question arises: Efficiency to what end? We shall see throughout this book (and even more in Volume 2) instances of where this untenable situation is uneasily resolved by the injection of normative elements back into the foundations of the field – even into the psychological assumptions, from which they are supposed to be absent. The argument over altruism, and the appeal to sociobiology to settle it (by proclaiming what the nature of Man *must* be, as a result of evolution) is but one symptom of this malaise.

VIIB Trust Karl Marx popularised the concept of a callous 'cash nexus', or web of commercial relationships, which, he claimed, was all that bound people together in a capitalist system. In fact, in a variety of ways, modern industrialised economies are more than ever dependent upon what might be called 'the trust nexus'. There is a web of informal rules, ethical principles, habits and traditions which clearly work for the public good and which often do not (at least in any obvious way) serve the private, selfish interests of those who abide by them. The more complex and interdependent a society becomes, with increasing specialisation and rapidly developing technology, the more critical these are.

Social economics could usefully devote some attention to examining this issue through such questions as these:

–   What different forms does the 'trust nexus' take? How does it vary among different groups of actors (e.g., workers, managers, consumers, entrepreneurs, taxpayers, etc.)?
–   Who plays by these rules, and who does not?
–   Under what sorts of circumstances is it most prevalent, where most absent?
–   What effect, if any, does social science (including economic) theory have upon the trust nexus?
–   How can the trust nexus be encouraged and strengthened? And what side effects might result from efforts to do so?

VIIC Incentives and motivations Inframarginal motivations are an important class of motivations which are hard to discern in the neoclassical system. Examples include the pleasure which is taken in work in the early hours of the day, before fatigue sets in; or a welfare recipient's sense of decreased welfare associated with the boredom, and perhaps a feeling of reduced value to the world, consequent upon not having work to do.

There are, additionally, a large set of incentives which do not get represented in prices. The use of a person's own time may be an example: when I commit my *time* I also commit my *self*. The other 'human values' which are then involved ('What will I learn from this experience? How will it change me? How will I feel during the hours in which I am so engaged?' Etc.) are not easily converted into money values.

Another significant set of motivations which are not normally represented in prices is that associated with non-marketed exchanges and non-marketed work, such as volunteer activities. Home-making and child-care – activities critical to the wealth and welfare of societies – are other outstanding examples. Economists have not neglected these areas; where they have dealt with them successfully, however, they have generally done so by abandoning much of the core of the neoclassical paradigm, stepping, perhaps, into the area to be defined as social economics.

VIID Learning; fads and fashions; familiarity and strangeness There is an educable aspect to humankind. It shows up in such economic places as our ability to adapt to higher petrol prices with energy conservation measures; as well as in the ability of advertisers to manipulate tastes (towards careers in teaching as well as towards the purchase of deodorants); not to mention the advertising industry's manipulation of the values and self-images of large populations. It is, in fact, when tastes, preferences or values change that many interesting economic events are likely to occur. This is precisely when the light of the neoclassical economic system is apt to fail because it takes consumer preferences as 'given' and 'sovereign': in assuming that each person is the best judge of what s/he wants, it fails to consider what people 'should want to want', or the possibility that people might benefit from changing wants through a learning process.

We may refer here to Alfred Marshall's unabashedly normative concept of 'progress'. He assumed that the moral structure which is part of the foundation for individual motivations is, or should be, one of society's most important ends; the ultimate public good lies in a kind of progress wherein human wants are trained so that individuals will increasingly want what is good for them.[5] What is good for people, Marshall felt, is to want the kind of reward which a good person wants; i.e., fame, honour, and the pleasure, for its own sake, of serving others. If the moral structure of the society and of its individual participants can gradually be brought toward this orientation the whole society will be better off, for honour will increasingly replace pay as the most sought-after reward, permitting an evener distribution of income without loss of productivity; and consumer satisfaction will increase as individuals at every level care more about the quality of the work they perform.

Tibor Scitovsky gets at Marshall's closely related concept of 'activities' by dividing the sources of achievable 'satisfactions' into two sets, *comforts* and *stimuli*, where the latter often include activities such as work, sports and cultural pastimes. Scitovsky stresses that an important source of human satisfaction is the mental stimulation that is associated with novelty. This fact, however, creates 'a logical difficulty which seems to rule out consumer rationality in the sense in which we know and accept it as the governing principle of consumer behaviour in other areas of consumer choice.'[6] The logical difficulty comes from the fact that there are stimuli which include novelty (or surprise) among their satisfying elements and which, at the same time, require an 'investment' of time and effort in learning. Why make the investment if you do not know what the reward will be? But if you do know the reward in advance, you are robbed of the element of surprise. An example given by Scitovsky is 'the impossible situation of having to have musical knowledge to be able rationally to decide whether that musical knowledge is worth acquiring. Nor', as he then adds, 'is that problem confined to music; it is common to all forms of stimulus consumption that require a skill for their enjoyment.' (ibid., p. 124). His conclusion is that this paradox is resolved when the previous generation, having experienced the rewards to be had from 'education in consumption skills', provides such 'humanistic education' for the young.

The characteristic which most separates 'comfort' type experiences from 'stimulating' experiences is on the spectrum from familiarity to strangeness, or novelty. A little of the latter is exciting; too much is nerve-wracking.[7] In spite of the varying range of tolerance that different people have for the boredom of familiarity or the alarms of strangeness, one can, nevertheless, make some useful generalisations about the relevance of this point with respect to economic groupings. For example, most people tend strongly to prefer working among people they know to working among strangers. Employers tend to prefer to hire an individual who has some connection, however tenuous, with someone they know, rather than a person who is completely unknown – even though the information gained from the 'introduction' may have no bearing on qualifications for the job in question.

The economics of consumption, as developed in practice by those who produce in order to sell to consumers (and who 'sell' to consumers what it is that they produce) may depend most obviously upon being able to tickle the desire for novelty; but the economics of production, insofar as it relates to relationships among people who are working, brings out the neglected importance of the desire for familiarity.

VIIE   Activities The economics of Alfred Marshall will be a
                      particularly useful source for an area of human
psychology that is notably lacking in the modern neoclassical
paradigm. Marshall saw humans as rounded beings whose human
values are of central importance. He saw those values not as fixed, but
as evolving in response to the environment and, most importantly,
through the activities of their possessors. And he saw the whole society
as the responsible locus both for the value-shaping environment and
for the opportunities for individually value-shaping activities.

Marshall's emphasis upon studying productive activities not only in
terms of their contribution to consumption, but also as forces for
societal, cultural and ultimately economic change, is dramatically
different from what is to be found in neoclassical economics. The latter,
stressing individual wants and their satisfaction, makes no pretence of
attempting to recognise social or cultural change aside from the level at
which existing wants are satisfied. The strongly Utilitarian character
which continues to provide the ethical/philosophical framework for
neoclassical economics casts activities as instrumental. The *process* is
regarded as relatively unimportant (another way of avoiding a dynamic
issue), while the emphasis is upon what one *gets* at the end of the
process. What one *gets* can be fairly easily fitted into a static system.
What one *does* – the activities themselves – the process again, as
distinct from the goal – is a dynamic reality deserving of study within a
theory which would, however, need to be quite different from
neoclassical economics.

A social economics with a practical and sustained emphasis upon the
values of Man as worker – not just after-hours, but the worker on the
job – will have an additional advantage in possessing a special line to
the findings of adjacent fields (sociology, psychology, etc.), and a
special way of using these insights to organise economic concepts and
data. It will also have a point of view sufficiently distinct from the point
of view of neoclassical economics as to help clarify the existence and
the nature of the latter's point of view.

In this connection, the logical structure of the earlier exercise in goal-
definition may be made somewhat clearer. The primary goal, welfare,
analysed in terms of four aspects (survival, happiness, self-actualisation
and moral or spiritual development), is to be understood as referring to
states of being. As such, this is at some remove from the subjects with
which economics can be expected to grapple directly; yet it is critical to
keep the 'being' goals in mind to assist in prioritising and balancing the
secondary goals.

The secondary goals may be roughly categorised under two headings: 'having' and 'doing'.

-   *Consumption* and *sustainability* are mostly about having.
-   Education and work, as examples of *enhancing activities*, may be ends in themselves, and then they are importantly concerned with doing; but under some circumstances they are perceived as more relevantly means to the ends of having.
-   *Hope* has been strongly attached to the materialistic definition of progress with respect to consumption in the last two hundred years; but resource constraints may require that, if this is to remain a goal, it will have to be experienced increasingly with respect to the doing aspects of life.
-   *Economic justice* continues, and probably will continue for a long time, to be most concerned with who gets what ('having'). Normally related to this, of course, is the critical importance of the question of who may participate in what activity. This may, in turn, be closely linked with issues of self-esteem as well as pleasure in life. There are not a few people for whom these last-mentioned 'being' issues are the chief motivation to press for equal access to work and educational opportunities; but for many others the critical issue is a survival level of consumption, for themselves and for their children.

VIII Human groupings and interactions

VIIIA *Issues of aggregation*

Statistical smoothing, as an effect of aggregation, can sometimes cause realistic results to be deduced from unrealistic assumptions. An example is the assumption of maximisation of self-interest. At times this may be unusefully unrealistic, but it should be stressed that there are many other places where it works very well, precisely because, in the aggregate, human behaviour may average out to a pattern which is consistent with the core neoclassical assumptions – even though those assumptions would not be an accurate description of the underlying individual choices.

However, the problems which can arise out of the initial simplifying assumptions may also be compounded by the interdependencies and other types of interrelationships which occur in aggregations, but which tend to be ignored in neoclassical models.

For example, neoclassical economics cannot well accommodate to its areas of real strength explanations or predictions which take into

account the way work groups behave differently from what would be
predicted as a simple sum of the parts (e.g., instances of compensation
for the weakness of a member who does not produce as effectively as
the rest). There is much relevant group economic behaviour wherein an
incentive which would produce a given effect upon most of the
members individually will have a different effect in the context of group
dynamics. Leadership may play a special role here; also concern for
how one is perceived by other people; and a variety of other motives
and interactions, some of which may be subsumed under the term,
group solidarity.

In addition to sorting out the variety of incentives which may go
beyond narrowly construed self-interest, it is also important to note
that incentives may have different impacts, depending upon whether
they are felt by individuals, groups of individuals, firms, groups of
firms (e.g., by sector), by ethnic or interest groups, regions, nations, etc.
'Social systems differ in the relative mix of the different classes (private,
collective, sectoral, spatial) of incentives. Incentives interact and the
system outcome depends upon such outcomes. In some societies the
incentive mix may promote a high incidence of competitive behavior
among the institutions; in others, dominant bureaucratic behavior; in
still others, cooperative behavior, etc.'[8]

VIIIB Institutions,   The term 'institution' is sufficiently broad[9] so
including   that it can be employed to cover most, if not all,
governments of the human groupings wherein additional
               sophistication is needed to explain economic
behaviour. To answer this need social economists might go to the field
of sociology; or they might draw on digests of sociological understandings such as institutionalist economists have sometimes made.
Again, an evolving, standard literature may develop for this area.

Over the years a number of first-rate sociologists have been
individuals who started their educational careers in economics
(Talcott Parsons is just one example), then discovered that economics
was not dealing with the questions that had driven them to the field,
and so moved over to sociology. We need to reverse this drift – to
attract into social economics individuals with a strong background in
sociology, who can bring with them an ability to see *societies as
networks of relationships* – among individuals, creating institutions; and
among institutions as well.

Obviously, not all relationships can be studied at once, and the
defining feature of the field of economics is its focus upon things that

have an economic meaning. The point to be made here is that institutions, governments and networks of relationships must be understood within a more comprehensive context than that traditionally accorded them in the neoclassical system if we are accurately to perceive which of their aspects do, indeed, have the most significant economic meaning. The challenge for social economics is to view whole economic systems – on local, national and transnational levels – *as* wholes; and to see the integral part played by all institutions, including governments, within the systems at each of these levels.

The role of governments is one of the most important of economic topics, and one of the least well addressed. The subject is equally an embarrassment to Marxian economics, where the expectation was stated by Marx that, if everything else was done right, governments would simply wither away; and to neoclassical economics, where, too, the decision to call on government implies a kind of failure ('market failure', in this case).

Among the institutional issues which will require special attention from social economists, two of the most important are power and competition. Economic and non-economic power which can be used to reduce economic competition is one among many anti-competitive forces to be found in human nature and in the nature of institutions.

If, as suggested earlier (in Chapter 1), idealisations of competition and cooperation occur in the neoclassical and the Marxian paradigms as simplifying assumptions which are, however, inadequate to handle some real world complexities – so, too, is another alternative, coercion, inadequately recognised by both systems. In the neoclassical system coercion, as a power relation, is only considered in relation to the activities of government. Relations in society are assumed to be divided up in such a way that free choices about production and allocation always and only occur in the economic (market) realm; while coerced choices, determined by power relations, are seen as exclusively political (governmental). In fact, government is an important actor in the production and allocation of public goods and services; and coercive, power relations are to be found at many points in the economic sphere. Power relations affect, e.g., the purchase and sale of labour power, as well as transactions between large and small firms, etc.

For different reasons, coercion in relation to economic matters is also insufficiently analysed in the Marxian system. The diversity of kinds and sources of power in the economic sphere is hard to see in a system which relegates all power to a class source. Moreover, communist economics are ultimately concerned with the ideal world when political and economic coercion will have ceased to exist. In the meantime, the coercion of the state – one of the outstanding features of life in a communist system – is handled with kid gloves, if at all.

Disaggregation will be important for the social economics approach to institutions. While there are useful things to be learned from finding the similarities between such institutions as families and firms, firms and governments, etc., there are also important differences to be noted. The neoclassical paradigm has tended to use the firm as the typical institution, and has made significant progress in some areas by seeing how far the theory of the firm can then be made to apply to other institutions. There are, however, important areas where maximisation of a single function (by analogy with profit maximisation) is not the most useful assumption to impose upon institutional behaviour.

There is a logical chain to be observed between (a) the purposes for which institutions exist; (b) their actions; (c) policy advice to support those actions; and (d) the theory on which that policy advice is based. Though *goals* (purposes) and *theory* are at opposite ends of this chain, they remain importantly linked; the emphasis of theory needs to be affected by the goals, just as much as the realism of the goals should be affected by the theory.

A concrete example of what is meant here would be the analysis of such public institutions as national governments, or the World Bank. Some recent work in public choice theory has emphasised the positive observation that individuals in these institutions are often motivated by private self-interest, and may be understood from the assumption of selfishness which is sometimes used as the micro basis for the theory of the firm.[10] Such positive observations on the nature of actual human motivations are obviously of great importance, to be discussed and debated without inhibitions stemming from preferences as to the way the world 'should' be. At the same time, social economists who operate near the 'theory and advice' end of the chain would be expected to accept some responsibility for knowing the broad goals of the institutions and for reflecting on the relationship of theory and advice *vis-à-vis* those broad goals, as well as with respect to the narrower tasks for which they might have been called in.

For instance, if a social economist has been called upon to advise a government on which ones, among a variety of available new technologies, should be promoted as most efficient in carrying out some agricultural task, s/he would not only answer the question that was asked, about economic efficiency, but would also comment upon whether the technology which promised the most output for the least investment would also have important impacts upon employment or other elements of the broader welfare to which the government is, presumably, committed.

IX Economic systems   A distinction needs to be made between *a system of economic theory*, as a set of abstractions about the perceived world, and *an economic system*, as the actual structure of some grouping of real world economic activities.

The system of neoclassical economic theory has co-evolved along with capitalist economic systems; it is best adapted to explaining capitalist economies, and to assisting in achievement of the capitalist goal of maximising a society's total consumption opportunities through efficiency in production.

The system of Marxian economic theory evolved on a path that took about seventy years before converging with a real communist economic system, but it is nevertheless designed to aid in understanding communist economies, and to promote their objectives of fair distribution of work and consumption.

With what 'economic system' shall we associate 'the system of social economic theory'? That question can be answered in two ways.

First, we may note that the capitalist system described by neoclassical theory does not, in fact, exist; any more than the communist society described by Marxian theory is to be found anywhere in the real world. Both systems of theory describe ideal economic systems: one of perfect competition, the other of perfect fairness and cooperation. Social economics, rooted in the period when the evolving field of economics was dominated by Alfred Marshall (see Chapter 5, below), is more directly related to neoclassical than to Marxian economics; we could begin to understand its place in the world of actual economic systems by saying that it will attempt to describe some aspects of economic life in so-called capitalist countries with more accuracy and relevance than the neoclassical paradigm can do. If it is successful in this goal, it may then also be of use to historically Marxist or socialist countries, as they, too, seek for an alternative way of organising their understanding of changing economic realities.

The other way of addressing this question is to note that we are living in a time of great transitions, where what have for two centuries been analysed as national economies are now often better comprehended as parts of a global economy – but the latter has yet to be fully analysed or understood. Rules and realities are changing;

issues that had not previously seemed important enough to be included in our accounting are now emerging as critical elements of our economies; and goals, too, may be changing. In many ways humanity is at present more affluent than ever before; that very affluence arouses demands for the subordination of the goal of productive efficiency to the goals of economic and social justice. At the same time the costs, to a rapidly approaching future, of production and consumption are being discovered to be much higher than previously imagined. Something like social economics is needed, not only as an alternative to the neoclassical economic explanation of capitalism, but to promote clear thinking, in an increasingly globalised world, about alternatives to both capitalism and communism – neither of which, in any case, really exists as described by neoclassical or Marxian economics.

IXA Macro   and global   economics   Some elements of macro theory are so loosely or uncomfortably connected to the core of neoclassical theory that they may be regarded as lying outside of the neoclassical pool of light; fair game, in fact, for any other system that can do a better job of incorporating them.

As suggested earlier, the macro elements which do fit into the neoclassical core are, generally, those areas:

– where the aggregation of micro elements can be simply made, because the theory of the atomistic cases is applicable to the aggregation thereof; and
– where social welfare may be achieved by maximisation of individual welfare.

Trade is an example of where neoclassical economics usefully, but in disregard of some aspects of its own theoretical consistency, employs aggregate concepts as though they resulted from a simple addition of atomistic units. Neoclassical economists often present their argument as though they were 'building up' from a one person, one good economy. This procedure is, in fact, a logical impossibility in light of the phase-shift that occurs when people and goods are aggregated so as to permit trade; one of the most important outcomes of the neoclassical system is, indeed, the welfare-raising effect of trade, which could not be predicted from knowledge of all the actors individually, disregarding interactions among them.

With this said, and accepting some theoretical inconsistency, the neoclassical system nevertheless possesses powerful tools for explaining certain aspects of international trade. Other aspects remain relatively less understood.

As an example both of some neoclassical strengths and of some of its weaknesses, we might consider the global grain trade. We can find here many of the ideal conditions listed in the overall description of the neoclassical core areas: there are relatively complete markets which tend to be capitalistic; many of the conditions for perfect competition (e.g., homogeneous products, many final buyers and sellers) are present; and there are such an enormous number of actors (including a majority of the people in the world, one way or another) that at least some local 'irrationalities' get lost in the averaging out of behaviour. Neoclassical analysis has, therefore, a basis on which to build demand-supply diagrams that are quite realistic. However, this approach loses its grip, for example:

–   where attention has to be paid to how the aggregate groups of actors are defined (a nation? a farmers' lobby in the EEC? a multinational trading company? a trading bloc?);
–   where power transcends the neoclassical list of market forces (military or political as well as economic power; or even the power of world opinion or of prevailing fashions in ideas); or
–   where tastes change. For example, the preference for meat is sometimes as relevant as the ability to pay the premium for it. Also cf. the growing taste for wheat (promoted in part by the US policy of PL480 exports of surplus grain at below-market prices) in areas of the world not well equipped to grow it.

In such areas as these, where neoclassical economists have been most effective in understanding the global grain trade it is often because they have, on their own, ventured outside the neoclassical system of theory.

More generally, the issues of aggregation which we have seen both helping and hurting the effectiveness of neoclassical theory are critical of its welfare predictions and prescriptions. It gradually came to be recognised, during the time that Alfred Marshall dominated economic theorising, that the letter of the Utilitarian philosophy could not be followed, for it was impossible to sum up individual utilities for anything like Bentham's 'felicific calculus'. However, nothing has really replaced the concept of maximisation of non-interactive, individual utility sums as a way of linking together neoclassical micro-economics with its macro aspirations to address social welfare. One problem, which social economics must be designed specifically to avoid, has been the over-balancing of the neoclassical system of theory towards a micro grounding. In spite of the rejection of Utilitarian summing just cited, neoclassical theory has continued, in most respects, to proceed as if human aggregations were in no way different from the sum of the parts. Given this bias, it is probably the case that the neoclassical/ Utilitarian approach has the greatest likelihood of contributing to social welfare when it is applied to highly homogeneous societies.

When neoclassical economics is applied to a society with important heterogeneities, it can still *appear* to work if there is a homogeneous group which is sufficiently dominant so that what applies to that group appears to apply to the whole society. Dissenting voices have been raised in Western societies by various groups, including women, who have argued that there has existed an unrecognised division between the most generalised interests of men in these societies, and those of women; and representative of the poor, who have said that their interests, too, differed from those of the dominant group. From such points of view, the most damning criticism which can be made of the neoclassical system of economic theory is that it has often operated like the theory of the status quo; the theory of the group in power; 'privileged' or 'macho' economics.

Macro economics, as it now exists in the neoclassical system, is a theory addressed to the interests of nation states. It is generally accepted that the goal of macroeconomics (its 'definition of success', as this term will be described in Chapter 9, below) is to maximise the welfare (usually interpreted as the GNP) of a given nation, which includes attempting to improve the competitive position of each nation with respect to other nations. For an economist who is an adviser to a particular national government, this is often the appropriate position to assume.

However, 'micro' and 'national' are not the only levels of economic interest. Very different understandings will emerge from a recognition of the place, the goals, and the powers of other relevant actors on all levels. To name just a few of those that should be taken into account:

-   there are cities such as New York, Los Angeles, Bonn or Mexico City, that deal directly with foreign and multinational entities, bypassing their own national governments in important, recognised ways

- there is the United Nations, with its agencies; also the International Labor Organisation
- there are research networks, such as the CGIAR system which has created, supported and disseminated the Green Revolution
- there are multilateral agencies such as the ones formed at Bretton Woods
- NGOs such as OXFAM, Amnesty International, or International Physicians Against Nuclear War
- international professional organisations, such as those to which physicists, psychiatrists, or archaeologists the world over feel allegiance
- multilateral corporations, such as the giant agribusinesses, or firms in microprocessing, telecommunications or automobile production
- international crime syndicates, such as the drug cartels
- internatiuonal accords and agreements such as the Montreal Protocol to limit emissions of chloroflurocarbons
- and there are abstractions demanding allegiance, such as the Sullivan Principles.

All of these examples illustrate the forces which go under, or over, or around, or through, the force-field of the nation states.[11] In addition to their social and political ramifications, they have important economic impacts. Recognition and understanding of these impacts requires a 'global economics' that does not at present exist: neither market analysis nor distinctions of class are sufficient to define the relevant actors on the modern world scene.

Returning to the area that has traditionally been defined as 'macro' economics – the area of the nation and its concerns – there remain important areas for exploration which also require some different approaches. Neoclassical economics has not come to terms with the fact that, even in 'capitalist' countries, the private sector is only one of four: the other three being the government, the not-for-profit, and the non-monetised sectors. Models based upon the assumption of profit-seeking fit poorly when applied to these last three sectors. They go a long way to explaining the allocation of resources within the first sector, but not within the second, third and fourth; and they leave much to be explained regarding the allocation of resources *among* the sectors (one of the most critical issues for a modern economy). Finally, if profit-maximisation is not sufficient, what definitions of success shall be sought for each sector?

IXB   A third   Karl Marx predicted that the defects in capitalist
alternative;   systems would lead to their collapse. With a few
system and   different twists of history he could have been
theory   proved right: the evils of the first century of
capitalism after the Industrial Revolution might
well, had they continued on their path, have led to violent political
revolution. There was increasing consciousness and resentment of such
social ills as great concentrations of power in the hands of property
owners; cruel practices (often virtually necessitated by the system,
regardless of the wishes of individual employers) in the employment of
relatively powerless individuals, especially women and children; the
virtual abandonment of those unable to support themselves in the
market system (orphans, the old or disabled, others who could not find
employment); neglect of such public goods as health care or rural
transportation; and increasingly violent economic swings, the 'boom
and bust' cycles. However, the most critical of these defects were
corrected by what J. K. Galbraith has called the 'Bismarck/Lloyd-
George/Roosevelt revolution',[12] whereby systems of social security, old
age pensions, and unemployment insurance, along with agricultural
price supports and the progressive income tax,[13] irrevocably altered the
nature of capitalism. It ceased to have both the ideal character of
perfect competition and free markets portrayed in neoclassical
economics, and the perfidious character of absolute exploiter
portrayed in Marxian polemics.

As the end of the twentieth century arrives, communist countries are
making decisions which amount to an admission of failure in their
economic systems; the degree to which they have achieved their goals
of equity in allocation of work and consumption seems insufficient
compensation for the loss of efficiency in production. This may make it
easier for capitalist countries, and the economists therein, to examine
the weaknesses, even while they continue to build upon the strengths,
of the socio/political/economic compromises which constitute modern
capitalist systems. Some of the requirements for a new, co-evolving
economic system and system-of-economic-theory relate to the
following points:

–   Change and development will continue to be critical realities and
    needs in all parts of the world – not only the developing countries –
    for the foreseeable future. We need a system of economic theory
    which can perceive, analyse, and, where desirable, give assistance
    to a variety of *sources for change and development*. For instance:

- 'Bottom up' and 'top down' approaches, and ways of combining those two
- NGOs and multilateral organisations of many kinds
- cultural, religious and/or ethical impulses
- centre-periphery relations

• domestic unrest	• foreign inputs
• migration	• markets
• planning	• technology
• education	• basic needs

all of these need to be understood as forces which, for good or ill, may initiate, channel, structure, or block change and development.

- Profit-maximisation rears its head even in communist societies. If it were the ubiquitous force supposed in capitalist societies, neoclassical economics would have smooth sailing in its predictions, descriptions and prescriptions for the socialist as well as the market-oriented parts of the world. In fact, profit-maximising is an important, but not the sole important, motivation; and we need to be able to make use of and encourage, as well as simply to recognise, other impulses and goals that motivate human beings as economic actors.

- The systems of farm supports which are the rule, not the exception, in industrialised countries, make what has been held up as the classic textbook example of the conditions for perfect competition into a state-regulated industry, with effects on national and international markets and prices which threaten increasingly to outweigh the humanitarian claims for protection of the (mostly large) farmers.

  At the same time, from the global perspective, stabilised high prices in one or a few major producing nations may be used (as they were during the late 1970s in the USA) to create global grain stockpiling against times of poor harvest; this is the other side of the coin to the EEC's 'mountains of butter' etc. that have offended the sensibilities of those in favour of free trade and cheap food. It is not clear that completely unfettered agricultural markets are the best mechanism to serve global needs and maximise global welfare in face of the uncertainties of the long as well as the short run.

- Neither the play of market forces nor government interventions have yet shown the way to solve what emerges as the single largest economic problem of modern times: how to make markets and institutions (especially bureaucracies) responsive to broader conceptions of welfare than narrow, short-run self-interest.

Human societies are becoming increasingly global societies in which we find that 'we are all poisoning our neighbour's well, and we are all drinking our neighbour's water'. If the reality were as simple as that metaphor, simple pricing mechanisms would solve our problems. In the astonishingly complex world of ever greater globalisation, a value system (undergirded by appropriately redesigned macro and global accounting systems) which assumes a primary importance for the future of the whole human race is the most efficient way to internalise the intertwined, boundary-ignoring chains of causes and effects.

– In a world where resource constraints will take on a newly compelling force and urgency, we need to think differently about the relationship between consumption and welfare, and between work and welfare. Production needs to be designed, on the one hand, to allow reduced throughput of the '*mm*' factors (see section VIB in Chapter 3, above). On the other hand, if some types of production are thereby limited, the goal must be for other '*ii*' (information intensive) work and leisure, things and activities, to make up for that loss.

– We need a system of economic theory that can deal directly with economic issues that are not all market issues. Problems do not necessarily leave the sphere of economics when they do not have good market solutions. Economists must be able to address the issue of *balance* between markets and other forces: governments, bureaucracies, and the third and fourth sectors – the not-for-profit and the non-monetised (or domestic) spheres of action.

– We need, finally, a system of economic theory which can deal overtly with the multiplicity of irrepressible but not always compatible welfare goals that have been left to the unconscious or unadmitted corners of existing theories. We have to have ways of formally recognising the desirability of dispersion of power and enhanced equality of access to the means and the results of production, for example via democratic institutions and general education, as well as via effective markets.

Notes

1. For the non-economist, marginal analysis is concerned with decisions taken on the knife-point of yes-or-no, when the decision-maker is hard put to it to decide, e.g., Shall I buy this? Shall I employ another worker? Shall I work another hour? Inframarginal motivations are the ones that are made before the worker is ready to decide about his/her last hour of work, or the consumer his/her last item of purchase, etc.
   See also Section VIIC, below.
2. Amartya Sen, 'Rational Fools: A Critique of the Behavioral Foundations of Economic Theory', in *Philosophy and Public Affairs*, vol. 6, 1977; pp. 317–44.
3. Which are probably best understood as instrumental choices – see below. Choice is more readily understood in the context of instrumental than of expressive behaviour.
4. Talbot Page, 'Intergenerational Justice as Opportunity' in Douglas MacLean and Peter Brown (eds) *Energy and the Future* (Rowman and Littlefield, New Jersey, 1982) p. 45.
5. Cf. A. Marshall, 'The Old Generation of Economists and the New' (1987) in *Memorials*, esp. pp. 302–3. Cf. also a comment by Albert Hirschman:

   > men and women have the ability to step back from their 'revealed' wants, volitions, and preferences, to ask themselves whether they really want these wants and prefer these preferences, and consequently to form metapreferences that may differ from their preferences . . . . the concept of metapreference must be of concern to the economist, to the extent that he claims an interest in understanding processes of economic *change* . . . .
   >
   > When a change in preferences has been preceded by the formation of a metapreference . . . it typically represents a *change in values* rather than a change in tastes ('Against Parsimony: Three Easy Ways of Complicating Some Categories of Economic Discourse, *AER*, 74, nos 1–2, 1984; pp. 89–90. Italics in the original.)

   See also Paul Streeten's Appendix ('Recent Controversies') to Gunnar Myrdal's *The Political Element in the Development of Economic Theory* (International Library of Sociology, London, 1953) esp. p. 215.
6. Tibor Scitovsky, 'Can Changing Consumer Tastes Save Resources?', essay written in 1979, repr. in *Human Desires and Economic Satisfaction: Essays on the Frontiers of Economics* (Wheatsheaf, Brighton, 1986) p. 123.
7. See Tibor Scitovsky, *The Joyless Economy* (Oxford University Press, 1976).
8. T. R. Lakshmanan, 'Knowledge Technologies and the Evolution of the Economic Landscape', paper presented at the International Workshop on Technical Change at the Center for Energy and Environmental Studies, Boston University; 11-12 October 1988, p. 13.
9. It is also a word which is rather clumsy to use. For example, 'institution' may refer to the idea of a firm, and to 'this particular firm'; it may refer to the idea of marriage, but not to 'this particular marriage'. It is generally

used, in the social sciences, to mean something quite abstract, e.g., 'recognised patterns of practice around which expectations converge' (O. R. Young, 'International Regimes: Problems of Concept Formation', in *World Politics*, 32, 1980); but in common speech it is probably most often used with reference to something thought of as a building – a jail, or a mental hospital, within which inmates are 'institutionalised'. These semantic difficulties have likely been a factor in the lack of cohesion of the 'institutionalist' school in economics.

10. This matter is, in fact, a little more complicated, as the most elegant firm theories assume profit-maximising as the only motive; and that is not necessarily a selfish one, as it requires the agents' motives to be identical with those of the principals.

11. For more discussion of these 'challenges to sovereignty' see the forthcoming special issue of *World Development, Global Commons: Site of Danger, Source of Hope*, N. Goodwin (ed.), to appear in early 1991.

12. From a lecture by John Kenneth Galbraith at the American Academy of Arts and Sciences, 5 April 1987. The historical sketch presented in this paragraph draws upon his selection of details.

13. As Arthur Okun has commented, 'In their ten-point radical program of the Communist Manifesto, Marx and Engels put [the progressive income tax] in second place – behind only the abolition of private land ownership. Yet, by 1913, that means had become law through a constitutional amendment in this bastion of free enterprise [the USA]' (*Equality and Efficiency: The Big Tradeoff*, The Brookings Institution, 1975, p. 101).

5 Building Anew (Selectively) on the Economics of Alfred Marshall

An economic criticism would make use of the history of economic thought, and be of some use to it in turn. But it would not be the same study. It would be the synchronic match to the diachrony of intellectual history, as literary criticism is to literary history, and economic theory is to economic history. The technique of research used by the macroeconomic theorist Axel Leijonhufvud supplies a case in point. He views the history of economic thought as a decision tree, beginning with, say, Adam Smith, who made such and such a theoretical choice on thus and such a question; continuing through Ricardo and Mill and Marshall, who made others; and so forth down to the present state of economic science. At each branch is a road not taken. When economics reaches a dead end – as it has by common consent, for instance, in thinking about the real side of foreign trade – one can either strike out blindly through the yellow wood or, better, return to the previous branching and take the other road. The technique is 'criticism' of science, in the sophisticated sense of an aid to understanding, for the purpose of helping the science to progress.

Ignorant of the history of economic thought, and misled by an attachment to an unenlightening account of how economic science operates, the modern economist spends a good deal of time wandering in the wood. Returning to the previous branching takes advantage of the useful past of economics.

Donald N. McCloskey, *The Rhetoric of Economics*,
University of Wisconsin Press, 1985, p. 183.

This book has been written as the result of the confluence of three subjects:
1. an early stage in the synthesis and development of social economics as an alternative system of economic theory;

2. an exploration of some issues in the practice and theory of the social sciences generally; and
3. an interpretation and examination of some issues in the economics of Alfred Marshall.

The third subject has several roles to play in relation to the first two. Most of this brief chapter will be devoted to explaining the uses that will be made of Marshall's economics in this book's development of social economics and in its grappling with issues in the theory and practice of the social sciences.

ALFRED MARSHALL AT A FORK IN THE HISTORY OF ECONOMIC THOUGHT
Alfred Marshall is often cited as the first of the great neoclassical economists; at the same time he was the last of the great economists still to draw on the full richness and breadth of the classical discipline, 'political economy'. He thereby managed to encompass in his work a larger view of 'the whole potential field of economics' (as that concept was defined in Chapter 1) than any other economist I know of. In an age with a large vision of the scope of human inquiry, Marshall's combination of depth with range was, I believe, prominent among the reasons why he maintained a position of acknowledged dominance over the field of economics in Britain, Europe, the USA, and in other places looking to the Western world for intellectual leadership, for a third of a century – from at least 1890, when the first edition of his *Principles of Economics* was published, to near his death, in 1924.

The scope of economics has become progressively and significantly narrower since Marshall's time. Neoclassical economics, in particular, has purchased the ability to do a relatively restricted set of things very well at the price of losing its ability to handle well, or at all, many of the issues of human welfare which were of concern to Marshall. For many people whose interest in economics still arises out of questions about human welfare, there is a need for new sources of illumination in the field.

To undertake, in response to this need, the creation of a system of theory from scratch would obviously be absurd. In looking for the point of departure where the greatest number of promising options were still open, Marshall's work is an obvious choice. He provides a starting point for thinking about method, as well as encompassing an exceptionally wide scope in terms of content. Marshall combined, as few or no other economists have done, a commitment to scientific truth with a dedication to human welfare, and a scrupulous methodological carefulness with an unquenchable empirical curiosity. His theory maintained a fragile and sometimes tense balance between dynamic realities and static methods; micro observations and macro outcomes; application and theorising; social and individual welfare; normative and positive elements.

Marshall's neoclassical heirs have tidied up his often messy, even contradictory inclusiveness by, in general, choosing one out of each uncomfortable pair: static, positive methods with a high degree of precision and rigour, ignoring disequilibrium in favour of equilibrium; micro assumptions about individual welfare to which macro outcomes are supposed to be reducible; and a status structure for the field in which theory dominates over application. Neoclassical economics has whittled down the richness of Marshall's legacy, emphasising theoretical simplifications and abstract laws at the expense of empirical specificity and the complications of overtly held goals and applied analysis.

SOME FAMILY TREES FOR MODERN ECONOMIC THOUGHT It will be convenient, in discussing some dynamic issues of the evolution of systems of economic theory, to switch from the metaphor of pools of light, used earlier, into one of 'paths', along which ideas may move, and which may fork. The path metaphor aids in imagining the difficulties sensed by Alfred Marshall as it became increasingly clear that one line of what he was working out was developing in a way that was deeply incompatible with the rest. The path that was to become neoclassical economics had an inexorable logic that led to exclusiveness: it was forced to disassociate itself from much of the humanistic, ethical, qualitative content that had been part of economics since it had evolved, in Adam Smith's time, from a concept of science then only newly beginning to be distinguished from philosophy.

That much-diminished subject, modern Western philosophy, is what has been left over after its line has split repeatedly, with many issues of interest going off on other roads. History parted from philosophy in classical times. The secession of mathematics was aided in the late Middle Ages/early Renaissance by the impact of Arabic thought on the Western world. The medical sciences led the divergence of the natural sciences from philosophy. In the eighteenth century economics split off; in the nineteenth and early twentieth, sociology and psychology.

Looking back, one may see the field of economics as having also endured several branchings.[1] After Smith, the earliest lasting split was the one which took the Marxian path out of the rest of the classical tradition. The remainder of that tradition (still sharing with the Marxians a significant area of overlapping concerns) went on to develop through the 'political economy' of Ricardo and Mill; in 1890 it became the 'economics' of Alfred Marshall.

Out of the still relatively broad system of theory over which Marshall presided, two paths were visible to him. His preference was to proceed simultaneously down both of them, resulting in the ambivalences and the stretching for inclusiveness which give such distinctive flavour to his writing. (His friends as well as his detractors found something a little funny in the figure thus created – one who always saw, and argued, at least two sides on every subject.) Of the two paths Marshall trod, one has been developed as neoclassical economics. The form in which we know this today – fully axiomatised, streamlined for high internal consistency, and heavily dependent upon the ideas of equilibrium and of marginal analysis to define its approach – was nurtured in its early stages by Marshall, even as he expressed his discomfort (throughout *Principles* and in some of his essays, but most of all in his letters) with what he could see it leaving out. Even while he appreciated its strengths he resisted the narrowing made inevitable by those strengths.

Social economics, as the other path on which Marshall can be seen to have walked, has remained relatively latent. In Marshall's work it exists as a potential, something for which many separate elements can be found, their interrelationships not spelled out. Since then it has been taken on unevenly and unsystematically by practitioners under a variety of names. The latter have included some Marxians[2] as well as political economists and proponents of that widely scattered group of ideas, emphases, and observations which are sometimes lumped together as 'institutionalism'.[3] There are others too, who, while sometimes still calling themselves 'neoclassical', have operated on the margins of that paradigm.

It is unlikely that Marshall recognised how real and deep was the division that was forming. The split, as it appeared to him, was a temporary one, between a hope and a stubborn methodological problem. He was, on the one hand, a champion of the hope that economics could become a 'science', modelled, in important ways, on the natural sciences. On the other hand he saw very well, and frequently warned against, the danger that the field would be defined by its methods – that it would concentrate upon what could be treated rigorously, rather than upon what matters. The way in which he hoped to reunite the separating streams of economic thought was by the discovery of techniques which would enable his economics to deal scientifically with what is at the root of the human interest in economics: human values.

While I am (quite evidently) a warm admirer of Marshall in most respects, I believe that here he contributed to a set of logical errors which were almost inextricably incorporated into the foundations of neoclassical economics. While endeavouring to build anew on many parts of what Marshall understood as the field of economics, I will also (especially in Part III) attempt to show where it will be desirable, even at this late date, to disentangle some of the roots of our thinking from his.

MARSHALL   Two purposes have been described for referring to
AS A MODEL   Marshall:

- one is the use of the history of economic thought to help us in understanding economic thinking in the present;
- the other is to give us an historical jumping-off point for the option of an alternative system of economic theory.
- Marshallian economics will also be a natural place to turn for a third use: when seeking certain kinds of examples, or models.

One kind of model for which Marshall can serve is a neutral one: a model of 'what is done'. His work will serve thus, for example, in discussions of particular approaches to be used in the analysis and interpretation of economic texts – using, that is, particular analytical approaches to get at a deeper understanding of 'what is done'. For instance, Marshallian texts will be conveniently available for practising the identification of different layers of meaning (cf. Chapters 8 and 13–16). Such purposes could equally well be served by practising upon the works of a number of other authors, but Marshall's exceptional carefulness and self-consciousness, and the fact that eight published editions of his *Principles* are available for examination, make him a very helpful exemplar.

The other kind of model is the normative one: 'what should (or should not) be done'. Sometimes Marshall's work will be held up as an *positive* example, worthy of emulation (e.g., Chapter 10, the discussion of 'Theory and Empiricism'). The chief example of Marshall as a *negative* normative model is the one just cited, where he built a logically flawed bridge between his humanistic and his scientific ambitions for economics.

THE RELATION   The historical sketch that has been suggested here is
BETWEEN   one in which the field of economics took its second
MARSHALLIAN   major fork since Smith during Marshall's time, with
ECONOMICS   Marshall for a while standing astride the two
AND THE   divergent paths. The proposal of this book is to
MODERN PATHS   return to that fork and to attempt a more thorough
                   development of the latent potential which I have
called social economics. With respect to this proposal the following comments should be made:

1.   While in some areas the task of social economics may be the restatement and renewed employment of elements contained in Marshall's writings that have since been largely ignored, in other areas the goal will be to integrate elements which Marshall himself failed to reconcile.

2.   Social economics will not simply inherit the pieces that are left over after the neoclassical system is subtracted from the broad field of economics claimed by Marshall. Instead it will aim to return to something more like (but not identical to) Marshallian complete-ness – recognising that to do so will entail a trade-off with some of the virtues of the neoclassical development.

3.   Such a return will not be achieved simply by unravelling history back to where Marshall stood. He straddled different paths at a time when their logical conclusions had not yet been worked out. The subsequent development of the neoclassical path makes it clear that certain aspects of its methodology and approach cannot be maintained, as Marshall tried to maintain them, in concert with his broader approach. We cannot for example start from the modern neoclassical structure and add on whatever pieces we would like to include: we would find too many incompatibilities. Neoclassical economics is defined, and confined, by a system of formalisation which determines its application. An alternative such as the proposed social economics will have to be differently formalised.

There will be no attempt to show that all of social economics was foreshadowed in those parts of Marshall's system which have been dropped out of modern neoclassical economics; but in fact one can find historical support for a surprisingly large portion of social economics therein.[4] It should be noted, however, that those ingredients of social economics which were contained in Marshall's work have been available to neoclassicists all along. Indeed, there are neoclassical economists who have availed themselves of some of these, and who would likely claim that in doing so they have not contradicted the core of their branch of economics, but are merely extending it to take in outlying areas.

In any case, as social economics is developed, much borrowing back and forth between social and neoclassical economics is to be expected, and hoped for. Techniques developed in the neoclassical system, when carefully employed in the broader, more methodologically self-conscious context of social economics, may yield different results than they have been able to do while wielded by the science that forged them. However, social economics' greater concern with issues of methodology (its lesser optimism, one might say, that one can arrive at useful conclusions without overmuch regard for the initial assumptions or for how data is fitted into theory), as well as its greater emphasis upon empirical tracking of theoretical progress, should make its practitioners wary of adopting anything, however useful, before they have tested it against their own methodological standards.

BIBLIOGRAPHICAL NOTE It has been necessary to exercise care to prevent this book from being swamped with references to and citations from the enormous body of relevant works by neoclassical economists, Marxian economists, and all the dissidents and critics thereof. The literature by and about Alfred Marshall alone is very extensive. Only in cases where a reference is especially illuminating, and where it accomplishes something that cannot be done more briefly without it, will the literature be brought in. To take the other approach (of appealing to authority, or citing the existing debates on all the topics raised here) would be to overburden this book beyond the reader's – and the publisher's – endurance.

As regards Marshall's own work, my largest emphasis will be upon his *Principles of Economics*. His broadest definition of 'what economics is' is best to be seen in *Principles*; each of his other works deals with some subset thereof. Marshall's other major works, as well as many of his essays, lectures, letters, etc. (especially the group selected by Pigou for the memorial volume) are drawn upon, for the most part in support of what is to be learned from *Principles*. From time to time attention will be paid to the evolution of Marshall's eight editions of *Principles* (a task mercifully aided by the ninth, Variorum, edition).

Most of the time, my use of Marshall's work is something like a comparative statics approach, which emphasises two periods in the history of economic thought (the present, and the era of Marshall's dominance), with only occasional references to points on the path in between. Some early appraisals of Marshall's work, with insights as to its relation to his life, are contained in *Memorials of Alfred Marshall*, edited by Marshall's student, A. C. Pigou. I will note particularly the essay by another famous student of Marshall, J. M. Keynes, since it has been especially influential in shaping modern perceptions of Marshall.

Much of the other work concerned explicitly with Marshall's writings appeared in the decades between Keynes's *General Theory* and Friedman's *Essays on Positive Economics*. Only in Chapter 16, where I will deal with some quite specific, technical issues, will I make much reference to that body of literature.

Existing attempts to find an alternative to neoclassical and Marxian economics are fairly widespread,[5] including both individuals who recognise the essentially truth-seeking nature of all science, as well as others whose motivations (covering the usual human range from individual spite to humanistic benevolence) is largely emotional, without containing a serious appreciation of the intellectual complexities of economic understanding. The (negative) example of Alfred Marshall, who managed to combine an open commitment to moral and spiritual values with a passion for scientific truth, will sometimes serve as a warning of the difficulties and perils of this combination. More often, the positive Marshallian example can encourage the maintenance of high standards of intellectual carefulness, as the essential accompaniment to human caring, in dealing with the aspects of the field of economics that are most important in setting economic policy for the enhancement of human welfare.

Beyond these instances, I owe a debt to more other thoughtful critics of neoclassical economics (more of them actually operating within than outside of the field) than I can name – more, doubtless, than I know, as I have absorbed much along the way without always remarking the source of each thought and inspiration. In the bibliography, and in occasional references through the text, I will attempt to give some indication of this debt.

SUMMARY OF   In the rest of this book we will step down from the
THE REMAINDER   broad overview that has characterised much of Part
OF THE BOOK   I, to look at some specific issues that are central to
                             social economics – although this book will attempt
to cover only a very small part of what was mapped out in Chapters 2
through 4.

Some of the methodological issues that have been raised in Part I will
be dealt with in more depth in Part II.

One of these issues, going beyond methodology, is the tension
between normative and positive economics. I will begin to deal with
this subject in Part III, but will expect to return to it in Volume 2 of
Social Economics.

Part IV will consist of just one short chapter, reviewing what portion
of the social economics project has been covered by this book.

Notes

1. Just as some of the broader lines have at times split and rejoined
    (linguistics, for example, has gone in and out of philosophy more than
    once), so some splits in economics have appeared to be only temporary.
    The line represented by Malthus, for example, at one time appeared more
    divergent from the classical mainstream than it does today.

    Given the strong hegemonic drive of neoclassical economics, it may be
    that some splits which appeared to be healed, in fact were not.
    Samuelson's desire to include the great economists of the past in
    'Modern Mainstream Economics' was responsible, for example, for the
    so-called 'Keynesian synthesis'. (It is interesting to note that his
    inclusionary attitude does not extend to his contemporaries in the
    schools of Rational Expectations, Macroeconomics and Chicago
    Libertarianism; these he places outside of the Modern Mainstream; see
    the 'Family Tree of Economics' on the inside back cover of Paul A.
    Samuelson and William D. Nordhaus, *Economics*, (McGraw-Hill, New
    York, 1985). That 'synthesis' attempted to incorporate the essence of
    Keynesianism into the mainstream, but in fact much that was critical in
    Keynes's work was left on the outside – perhaps to be better assimilated
    by social economics.
2. If a rather jaundiced view of modern neoclassical economics defines it as
    'Adam Smith minus Karl Marx', it is worth noting that many of those
    elements bearing a Marxian tinge which are so successfully avoided in
    today's neoclassical theory had not yet been expurgated from the field as
    it was defined by Alfred Marshall.

3. My debt to this 'school', as I set forth upon an ambitious attempt to pull together existing and new elements into a newly defined theory, is very great. One of its leading modern exponents, Paul Streeten, has spun or inspired many of the strands which I hope to weave together. Harvey Leibenstein's work, also, has provided much insight. Another institutionalist and labour economist, Peter Doeringer, suggested that I use the name, social economics. Many others, at a greater distance, have provided inspiration and ideas.

   Individuals often described as institutionalists include Thorstein Veblen, John R. Commons, Wesley C. Mitchell, J. M. Clarke, Clarence E. Ayres, Gunnar Myrdal, and John Kenneth Galbraith. The following description of the distinguishing characteristics of early twentieth century institutionalists shows particularly well the relatedness of that movement to this book:

   > The institutionalists protested at the overly abstract and deductive character of mainstream economics. They wished to make economics more 'relevant' to social problems and employ it as an instrument of reform. They thought that economics was hopelessly mixed in utilitiarianism and that no real progress could occur until this archaic utilitarian view of man was replaced by a modern interpretation based on the findings of contemporary philosophy, psychology and anthropology. Above all, the institutionalists wished to provide economics with a criterion of value other than the price of commodities. They wanted to distinguish between right and wrong, production and exploitation. They were concerned with economists' preoccupation with the perfectly competitive model and free trade while the world was becoming dominated by big business and imperialism. They emphasized the impact of technology on society and the force of legal and social institutions in determining human choice. Some were even prepared to reject, in their more sanguine moments, the very means of thought of mainstream economists and complimented themselves on their personal use of non-Aristotelian logic. (David Seckler, *Thorstein Veblen and the Institutionalists: A Study in the Social Philosophy of Economics*, Colorado Associated University Press, Boulder, CO, 1975, pp. 1–2.)

   It is hoped that social economics will go beyond institutionalism in developing as a system of theory which is more complete, more coherent, and more systematic. Nevertheless, while not every characteristic instanced in the foregoing passage is appropriately applied to social economics as projected in this book, it is clear that there is a very large overlap which should be acknowledged.

4. See N. Goodwin, *Back to the Fork: What We Have Derived from Marshallian Economics, and What We Might Have Derived*, unpublished doctoral dissertation, Boston University, 1988 (no. 8724711, University Microfilms International Dissertation Information Service, Ann Arbor, Michigan).

5.   There are many individuals as well as groups working on such projects. Those that are active in the United States include:

Amitai Etzioni's Socio-Economics Project in Washington, DC (The George Washington University, 515 22nd St., NW, Suite 401, Washington, DC, 20037);
the Human Economy Center (its newsletter is edited out of Mankato State University, Minnesota, 56001; that university offers a field of 'social economics');
the more populist Co-op America, which publishes *Building Economic Alternatives*;
New Options (PO Box 19324, Washington, DC, 20036);
a group of mostly Catholic economists who have formed the Association for Social Economics, and publish the *Review of Social Economy*;
TOES, North America (a spin-off from the group that originally organised 'The Other Economic Summit' in Great Britain, which is now preparing to publish an annual volume on 'The New Economics'); and the International Society for Ecological Economics, c/o Robert Costanza, Center for Environmental and Estuarine Studies, University of Maryland, Solomons, MD, 20688.

To my knowledge there has not yet been assembled an alternative complete enough to be regarded as a full economic theory, but the effusion of efforts made by those working outside the received theory, as well as by some who see themselves as remaining within its bounds, supplies much material with which to work and many ideas from which to receive inspiration.

Given that my project is different from that of many critics of the neoclassical system of economic theory – I am not setting out to change that system, but to propose an alternative to stand alongside it – I would like to mention three books in particular which share this intention of providing an alternative:

Paul Ekins edited *The Living Economy*, a well-integrated collection of essays on various topics which need to be covered or to receive a different kind of focus in an alternative system of economic theory. I have found this book invaluable as a reference for what other 'alternative economists' have seen as the terrain needing to be covered. With Manfred Max-Neef, Ekins will edit a continuing series of books on 'Living Economics'.

Two other alternatives which I have found particularly helpful are Amitai Etzioni's 'socio-economics', particularly as laid out in *The Moral Dimension*; and the ecologically oriented vision laid out in *For the Common Good*, by Herman E. Daly and John B. Cobb, Jr.

Part II
Textual Analysis and Reality in the Social Sciences

Part II

6 The Stumbling-blocks of Economics: Complexity, Time and Change

This chapter will outline what Marshall saw as the deepest problems in the development of an economic science – problems which, I will claim, have continued to enjoy the same status: as unsolved, if not insoluble. In Chapter 6 these problems will be presented initially through Marshall's eyes: in the rest of Part II they will be dealt with as generalised problems for the field of economics and, in many cases, for all the social sciences. This chapter will be one that will make use of a relatively large number of quotations. These will be numbered throughout the chapter for easy reference.

There were issues of complexity, time and change which Marshall recognised as essential aspects of his subject but which were not readily dealt with by the 'scientific' techniques which he was helping to develop. As he feared, the forces which he helped to put in motion have in fact resulted in a situation wherein these bothersome but crucial issues have been pushed aside by techniques which are powerful in other achievements, but not sufficient for the degree of complexity that interested Marshall.

Much of Part II will be devoted to an exploration of approaches to economics which, it is hoped, will enable social economics to grapple with complexity, time and change in ways which, at best, may ultimately go beyond what neoclassical and Marxian economics have been able to accomplish; at the least it is hoped that the proposed ways of doing social economics will provide a good complement to the existing paradigms.

In anticipation of the discussion of later chapters of Part II we will begin, here, with a small conceptual tool that is so useful that it is worthwhile to make it available now, before going any further: namely, the distinction between two concepts, *accuracy* and *precision*.

ACCURACY AND PRECISION   This is not a distinction that is entirely novel: it is noted from time to time, but it has yet to be taken seriously enough in economics to make the difference in this field that it might. Among those who have pointed it out, one who has put the issue with special force and clarity is Andrew Kamark. His statement on the subject is worth repeating here:

1   'Accuracy' will be used to convey the meaning of 'correctness', or 'true value'. 'Precision' will be used to convey the meaning of 'degree of sharpness' by which a thing or concept is specified. For example: on Cape Cod, where the pace of life is unhurried and casual, you may ask a craftsman in June when he will come to repair your fence. If he answers, 'Sometime in the autumn', he is being accurate but not precise. If he answers, 'Ten a.m., October 2', he is being precise but not accurate – it is almost certain that on October 2, the fish will be running and he will be out in his boat. One of the recurring themes that we will find in our discussion is that too often in economics the choice is between being roughly accurate or precisely wrong.'[1]

Accuracy has to do with what I shall be discussing later under the name 'external consistency': that is, a well-specified and 'realistic' mapping from subjects in the real world to our symbolic representations of these subjects. *Precision*, by contrast, may be judged within the given model, without reference to the fit between the model and its real-world referents (if any). Precision does not necessarily involve *quantification*, but that is one of the most obvious and frequently employed avenues to its attainment. *Qualitative* analysis can be accurate; its precision cannot be measured, but its accuracy can be assessed.

Alfred Marshall sometimes expressed the conviction that, in order to be scientific, it was not enough to be accurate; it was also necessary to be precise: quantitative as well as qualitative description, discussion, and explanation was called for. His argument was a practical one, and perhaps the strongest that can be made on this subject:

2   Mere qualitative analysis, then, will not show the resultant drift of economic forces. It may show gain here and loss there; but it will not show whether the gain is sufficient to overbalance the loss; whether the gain should be pursued in spite of the loss. And yet, for the purposes of practical action, this decision must be made. It is useless to say that various gains and losses are incommensurable, and cannot be weighed against one another. For they must be, and in fact they are, weighed against one another before any deliberate decision is or can be reached in any issue ('The Old Generation of Economists and the New' (1897) in *Memorials*, pp. 301–2).

Marshall's hope was to build a scientific discipline upon the special advantage which he saw economics as possessing, in dealing with subjects which can be at least approximately quantified. Thus,

3   The *raison d'être* of economics as a separate science is that it deals chiefly with that part of man's action which is most under the control of measurable motives; and which therefore lends itself better than any other to systematic reasoning and analysis. We cannot indeed measure motives of any kind, whether high or low, as they are in themselves: we can only measure their moving force. Money is never a perfect measure of that force; and it is not even a tolerably good measure unless careful account is taken of the general conditions under which it works, and especially of the riches or poverty of those whose action is under discussion. But with careful precautions money affords a fairly good measure of the moving force of a great part of the motives by which men's lives are fashioned.'[2]

This passage follows upon a paragraph which refers to 'trained common sense' as 'the ultimate arbiter in every practical problem', and then continues:

4   Economic science is but the working of common sense aided by appliances of organized analysis and general reasoning, which facilitate the task of collecting, arranging, and drawing inferences from particular facts. Though its scope is always limited, though its work without the aid of common sense is vain, yet it enables common sense to go further in difficult problems than would otherwise be possible (ibid.)

The 'appliances of organized analysis and general reasoning' to which Marshall refers are the tools of mathematics, statistics, graphical exposition, etc. One critical question, which he never addressed directly, is: How precise does quantification have to be in order to permit the use of these tools? Will estimates and approximations suffice for these purposes?

From his many comments tangential to this question, it would appear that Marshall often (though not always) assumed that, if mathematical analysis is built upon pretty good approximations, it can yield pretty good answers – though they will never be as precise or as satisfactory as the answers which can be got in the physical sciences.

We will see that he had a lively awareness that such a procedure was filled with dangers. His personal attitude towards mathematics (an attraction/repulsion wherein he felt that mathematics was a seductive game that might lure him away from the serious – i.e., moral – issues in life) sometimes prevented Marshall from carrying his techniques to their logical conclusion. It may be that this inhibition also prevented him from exploring more closely his rather casual assumptions (or hopes) regarding the usefulness of approximate measurements for quantitative techniques.

PROBLEMS WITH COMPLEXITY   Appendix C of Marshall's *Principles*, on 'The Scope and Method of Economics', is a particularly interesting essay which may present an appearance of ambivalence, as though the author was unable to make up his mind on which of two choices to take. In fact I believe the situation was that Marshall saw very well both the values and the pitfalls of a myriad methodological approaches. We have already divided these approaches into the qualitative (including accuracy) and the quantitative (stressing precision): for the purposes of the rest of this chapter we may roughly summarise them as the *intuitive* and the *mathematical* approaches. Marshall's conviction was that economics could only progress to the achievement of its best potential by the use of both; however, he also recognised the difficulty of proceeding thus upon two tracks, along with the attendant danger of trying to avoid that difficulty by concentrating upon one track alone.

Marshall's desire for quantitative analysis, and for sophisticated scientific techniques which could handle a world thus appropriately quantified, stemmed from his appreciation of the fact that the realities of interest to economics were so complex that they could not be handled on an intuitive level: they had to be reduced to 'bits' of information (as we would now say), so that they could be dealt with piecemeal in formal analysis. However, while Marshall was attracted to mathematical – especially statistical – means for handling complexity, he virtually never spoke in favour of these methods without attaching a warning. The following is typical:

5   The longer I live the more convinced am I that – except in purely abstract problems – the statistical side must never be separated even for an instant from the non-statistical: on the ground that, if economics is to be a guide in life – individual and more especially

social – people must be warned off by every possible means from considering the action of any one cause – beyond the most simple generalities – without taking account of the others whose effects are commingled with it. And since many of the chief of these causes have either no statistical side at all or no statistical side that is accessible practically for common use, therefore the statistical element must be kept subordinate to general considerations and included among them.'[3]

The 'general considerations' were, in Marshall's approach, to be the responsibility of 'common sense'. The use of that term has some problems (which will be discussed further in Chapter 9); for now, I would like to ignore the particular term, but think about how people go about dealing with complexity in every day life. My hypothesis will be that, in some respects, under many common kinds of circumstances, we do better at coping with complexity *without* many of the tools and techniques that have been developed for economics than we do with them.

There is a wide variation in the capacity that human beings have for handling complexity on an unconscious, or intuitive level. Even the low end of the normal range is, however, quite impressive. Consider the complex calculation of velocity, angle, acceleration, etc., that have to be made in a split second when a driver considers whether it will be possible to pass a car and to return safely to his/her own lane before an oncoming automobile reaches the place on the road where s/he will be before s/he can pull back into lane. On a conscious, formal level such calculations would either take too long to be practical, or (more often) would be beyond the capability of most of the people who actually drive cars. On that conscious level, comparable calculations can only be done by a translation of the elements involved into mathematical symbols.

Marshall's apparent assumption on this subject is an interesting one, and quite different from what seems to motivate the modern development of economic techniques. He suggested that mathematics and other kinds of analysis can deal with simple situations, but becomes less and less useful as the complexity of the subject increases. Such a conclusion is explicit in his statement that 'The most helpful applications of mathematics to economics are those which are short and simple, which employ few symbols; and which aim at throwing a bright light on some small part of the great economic movement rather than at representing its endless complexities.'[4] Why would an economist of renowned mathematical ability have felt such skepticism? One explanation is in the observation that:

6   numerical instances can as a rule be safely used only as illustrations and not as proofs: for it is generally more difficult to know whether the result has been implicitly assumed in the numbers shown for the special case than it is to determine independently whether the result is true or not (*Principles*, p. 688).

THE USE OF MATHEMATICS TO ADDRESS PROBLEMS WITH TIME AND CHANGE   Marshall's response to the problems of time and change were similar to his response to complexity. On the one hand, he would have liked to have found mathematical solutions to these problems; on the other, he doubted the power of mathematics to deal with these issues fully:

7   while a mathematical illustration of the mode of action of a definite set of causes may be complete in itself, and strictly accurate within its clearly defined limits, it is otherwise with any attempt to grasp the whole of a complex problem of real life, or any considerable part of it, in a series of equations. For many important considerations, especially those connected with the manifold influences of the element of time, do not lend themselves easily to mathematical expression: they must either be omitted altogether, or clipped and pruned till they resemble the conventional birds and animals of decorative art. And *hence arises a tendency towards assigning wrong proportions to economic forces; those elements being most emphasised which lend themselves most easily to analytical methods.* No doubt this danger is inherent in every application not only of mathematical analysis, but of analysis of any kind, to the problems of real life. It is a danger which more than any other the economist must have in mind at every turn. But to avoid it altogether, would be to abandon the chief means of scientific progress.

For reasons similar to those given in this typical case, our mathematical notes will cover less and less ground as the complexity of the subjects discussed in the text increases (*Principles* p. 700; italics added).

It may be that the truly great mathematicians are those whose intuitive ability to calculate is not inhibited by the conscious use of the formal apparatus of mathematics; the conscious and the intuitive operations continue in parallel, each serving as a check on the other, and neither acting to inhibit the other. For most people, however, a switch over into one mode tends to damp down the other. This is particularly evident in the struggles which economics has had in dealing with dynamic issues of time and change. On the intuitive level we live in time, and take change for granted as the fundamental fact of life; but time and change are both destroyed by the analytical processes which depend upon taking reality apart into timeless instants; and when we are engaged with those analytical processes we often fail to see that the dissection has altered that which we wished to study.

The method of marginal analysis has been welcomed for, among other things, its amenability to the calculus. The latter, it has been thought, was a way to deal mathematically with time. In fact, however, the way that the calculus does this comes out the same as though it performed its operations by *stopping* time – which, of course, effectively eliminates it. It appears to permit the calculation of change on the wing, as it were, by quantifying the direction, the rate, etc., of change at a timeless instant; and it can do this for any timeless instant over any period for which the change can be specified in a well-defined function. Not only does this push us back to the empirical problem of defining the function; it also leaves us, when we use these functions for marginal analysis, at a static conclusion. For example, the point of intersection of the rising marginal disutility of work with the declining marginal utility of pay is an infinitesimally thin slice of information. It reduces the dynamic picture of diversely motivated, changing human beings to a single point – in time, in motivation, and in state of being. It permits precision, but it is a precision of dubious accuracy.

The argument I have just made sounds a little like the argument against the idea of infinitesimals, which goes back at least to Zeno of Elea, in the fifth century BC. In 1734 Bishop Berkeley took up the cudgels in *The Analyst*, a book which he wrote in response to Isaac Newton's use of infinitesimals in the development of the calculus. Berkeley referred to Newton's 'fluxions' (infinitesimal 'instants' of time) as 'the velocities of evanescent increments . . . neither finite quantities, nor quantities infinitely small, nor yet nothing . . . the ghosts of departed quantities.'[5]

The introduction, by Weierstrass in 1872, of the use of 'limits' to compute instantaneous velocity is a way around the necessity of using infinitesimals:

8   Instantaneous velocity is taken as the limit of ratios of time and space increments (average velocities) taken over decreasing time

intervals; without velocities referred to as intervals, in contrast to single instants, instantaneous velocity would have no meaning. Although instantaneous velocity [in the limits approach] does characterise motion at an instant, it does so by implicit reference to what goes on at neighboring times.'[6]

The problem here, as we shall see in a moment, is that the concept of 'neighboring times' is translated into mathematics through the concept of the real number line *as a continuum*. The use of decreasing intervals towards a limit of zero is, ultimately, no more effective than the 'infinitesimals' approach to the calculus in creating a genuine identity between the real world and a mathematical concept of instantaneous time (as expressed, e.g., in the question, 'How fast was the car going at 11.15?') Any way that we can think up for tagging or identifying the real-world time, 11.15, must identify a span, or *period*, of time, not an instant.

MATHEMATICS AND THE REAL WORLD I will press this point a little further: as we go on in Part II we will be increasingly concerned with the issue of *what is realistic* – i.e., what approaches to being an accurate representation of the real world. The role of mathematics in creating a language with which to represent reality – or not to represent it – is central to economics. Marshall may have been one of the first to perceive the meaning of the possibility that mathematics could help to grapple with complexity, time and change; he was among the last major economists to express doubt that this hope was, in fact, solidly based. It is of considerable importance, not only to economics, but to all of the social sciences which have followed its lead into mathematisation, that the validity of these doubts be re-examined.

I continue, then, with a few examples of discontinuities between mathematics and the real world. 'Motion at an instant' and 'motion over a period' are two fundamentally different concepts, connected by what may be considered a pun on the pivot-word, *motion*. For a use of this idea which comes to a different conclusion from my own, I refer the reader to 'Zeno and the Mathematicians' by G. E. L. Owen (in Salmon (ed.) 1970). Owen says that Aristotle 'failed to grasp that the two senses of 'moving' are not identical but yet systematically connected' (ibid., p. 161). Such a 'systematic connection' could constitute the basis for the 'mapping' from real world to symbolic representation which, I claim, is not sufficiently present in the mathematical and the common uses of the word, 'motion' to allow consistently accurate and precise use of that word as it shuttles back and forth between its (at least) two different realms of use.

Similar problems beset our notions of *space* and *matter* as those just suggested with respect to *time* and *motion*. All of these problems have in common the notion of 'continuity', or a 'continuum'. These words, too, however, turn out to have different meanings when applied, even on the grossest level, to space and matter on the one hand, and to time on the other. When we analyse these subjects more carefully (as we will do in Chapter 11) we will find that the words 'continuous' or 'continuum' also have different meanings when applied to matter at the sub-atomic level versus at what might be called the 'sensory' level. In part, the problem arises from an insufficiently examined use of analogy:

9   As usually understood, the real numbers (including integers, rationals and irrationals) in their natural order form a mathematical continuum. If we use the real number system to represent time we are assuming that there is an isomorphism between the real numbers and the temporal continuum . . . . One consequence is that instants of time do not have immediately preceding or succeeding instants; between any two instants there are infinitely many others. Another consequence is that there is a super-denumerable infinity of instants, and each instant has zero duration. The same type of situation occurs if the real number system is used to represent points on a line in physical space.' (Wesley Salmon, 'Introduction' to *Zeno's Paradoxes*, 1970, p. 35.)

This problem has to do with the 'denseness' property of the mathematical continuum of the real number line. In ordinary understandings of 'continuity' the term implies that there is no separation between parts: if any part is chosen, it will be found to be 'next' to the adjacent parts in such a way that there is no room for other parts in between. This is precisely *not* the case for the real number line, where, for any two points (numbers) that you can name, it will always be possible to find others between them. Thus,

10 Whitehead and Bergson, for example, have denied the possibility of providing the requisite correlation between the mathematical continuum and physical time. An answer to them must take the form of showing how it is possible to provide a correlation between

the *later than* relation among instants of time having zero duration and the *greater than* relation among real numbers (ibid., p. 36).

Such a correlation may be constructed, and yet the 'systematic connection' we are seeking is still not complete enough for all uses. For the purpose of keeping time with clocks of all kinds, the *later than*/*greater than* correlation has been entirely adequate, for most purposes, for millennia. As we shall see when we examine Zeno's paradoxes of motion (in Chapter 11), it breaks down entirely when we try to carry to its logical limit a conceptual understanding based upon such a correlation.

The point of this detour, using the example of the assumptions and implications of the calculus, has been to pose the question: Where shall we place the use of mathematics in economics, between (on the one hand) the everyday employment of clock time, where the time/number correlation is accurate enough for all practical purposes; and (on the other hand) the purely abstract theorising of Zeno, who 'proved' that all motion is impossible? My argument is that there are places where the subject of economics requires accuracy (in relation to the real world), but where some of the mathematics presently in use in the field can only provide precision, without external accuracy.

Recent developments in the field of pure mathematics may be healthy in this regard, in more consciously stating that some areas of mathematics can legitimately exist at some distance from the real world.

11 Until 100 years ago it was tacitly assumed by all philosophers and mathematicians that the subject matter of mathematics was objectively real in a sense close to the sense in which the subject matter of physics is real. [Query: is that the same sense in which the subject matter of economics is real? or of physical anatomy?] Whether infinitesimals did or did not exist was a question of fact, not too different from the question of whether material atoms do or do not exist. Today many, perhaps most, mathematicians have no such conviction of the objective existence of the objects they study. Model theory entails no commitment one way or the other on such ontological questions. What mathematicians want from infinitesimals is not material existence but rather the right to use them in proofs. For this all one needs is the assurance that a proof using infinitesimals is no worse than one free of infinitesimals. (Davis and Hersh, 1981, p. 252.)

The authors of the book just quoted cite, as an outstanding example of this new freedom, the mathematical conventions that have been adopted to accommodate 'pseudo-real' objects within the 'nonstandard universe' of nonstandard analysis as used, e.g., by A. Robinson. The achievement of this approach, they claim, is *precise definition* of such concepts as an infinitesimal neighborhood. Here (referring back to our earlier definition) we see an example of the word, *precise*, being used to refer to something like internal consistency, quite explicitly eschewing reference to any external reality. Cantorean set-theory is another branch of modern mathematics which has similarly taken advantage of the liberty achieved by not insisting upon a 'systematic connection' between mathematics and reality.

These developments may help to force into consciousness the difference between mathematics and reality; between, for example, a physical understanding or description of the notion of 'distance', and a mathematical one. There are, in mathematical theory, an infinite number of ways of subdividing a physical distance. This is very different from saying that, in physical fact, a distance can undergo an infinite number of subdivisions. Similarly, since Euclid, mathematicians have accepted the notion of a 'point' as something that has position (location), but no dimension. As an *idea*, this is not only imaginable, but exceedingly useful: as a piece of the real world, it does not exist.

In normal life, as well as in mathematics, we have a clear notion of 'boundaries', including the 'edges' of *things* as well as beginning and end points in *time*. These are practical notions for many everyday uses, and they are reflected with precision in many mathematical assumptions and operations; but there are levels of reality wherein it is important to understand that the imaginary line which we conceptualise as constituting an 'edge' or 'boundary' has no real existence. (See Chapter 11 n. 14 for elaboration on this point.)

To give one more example: integers map very well onto sheep in a herd, or passengers in an airplane, or fingers on a hand. They apply *in principle* to grains of sand on a beach, or stars in the sky: even though we doubt that anyone ever *will* count these things, the idea that it would 'in principle' be possible to do so seems acceptable. We begin to get into trouble when we try to apply numbers to 'utils' (that is why units of money are so often used as a proxy for utility; numbers, including decimals, map very nicely onto dollars and cents). We know (roughly, not precisely) what we mean by the word, 'happiness', but there is no reliably accurate way to map this reality onto the real number line.

Some abstract mathematical conceptualisations are well designed to map onto some of the objects of the real world, at some levels of observation. Other such concepts only map onto other abstract conceptualisations. Much of the time, the safest way to treat mathematical applications in the social sciences is to think of them as extended metaphors. A mathematical model does not put something real – the real subject of interest to a social scientist – through a process where the outcome is determined by the inputs, assumptions and techniques: that process only operates upon the abstract descriptions of the subjects of interest. The outcome is, indeed, determined jointly by the inputs, the assumptions and the techniques (as well as the skill of the human being who uses these techniques, and, usually, some additional inputs of intuition, hunches and un-spelled-out assumptions, which are not readily visible in the model) – but it is not necessarily an outcome that has any bearing on the real world.

I have suggested that there are places where the subject of economics requires accuracy (in relation to the real world), but where some of the mathematics presently in use in the field can only provide precision, without external accuracy. In relation to time and change, for example, modern economic techniques offer the use of lagged variables and moving equilibrium growth models, but these techniques requires consistency in change, if they are to be useful. The erratic, unpredictable changefulness of change goes beyond a second, or third, or nth derivative. Often the best we can do, on the conceptual level, is to abstract from the ragged time and change of reality to smooth, continuous functions. The blooming, buzzing confusion of brute facts is the dynamic reality. The formal body of analysis is many steps of abstraction removed from that reality, and its apotheosis is the concept of static equilibrium – a concept that exists in the world of abstractions, not in the world of real time. Here we see the danger that, in compressing our understanding of the world into mathematical forms, we retreat from that which we have wished to study.

A perfectly static set of conditions is relatively accessible to analysis by the tools that were available to Marshall, and which have been progressively refined since his time. To set up that set of conditions as a goal, then to perceive all relevant forces (both economic and noneconomic) as tendencies toward that goal, allows the use of more powerful, consistent techniques than any we know of for dealing with such processes in themselves. Yet the best that we can get out of these techniques is something like Walras' general (but still essentially static) equilibrium analysis, or its modern version in computable general equilibrium models.

MARSHALL'S Marshall was significant in bringing into the centre of
EQUILIBRIUM the discipline an issue whose complexity has since been
ANALYSIS hidden by the simplifications necessary in order to
carry to its present height the theoretical precision of neoclassical economics. Modern economists who have any interest in the origin of their ideas, beyond the publications of the last few years, generally cite Alfred Marshall as a major contributor to the idea of comparative statics, in which is solidly embedded the notion of equilibrium as a description of *where things are*, or *whither things are tending*.[7] In fact, although he never approached Walras' attempt at detailing a general equilibrium analysis, Marshall's achievement in the area of equilibrium analysis is much diminished when it is seen only in the context of comparative statics, as just described. The following statement is characteristic of his position:

12 we look towards a position of balance or equilibrium between the
forces of progress and decay, which would be attained if the
conditions under view were supposed to act uniformly for a long
time. But such notions must be taken broadly. The attempt to
make them precise over-reaches our strength. If we include in our
account nearly all the conditions of real life, the problem is too
heavy to be handled; if we select a few, then long-drawn-out and
subtle reasonings with regard to them become scientific toys rather
than engines for practical work.[8]
. . . though the statical treatment alone can give us definiteness
and precision of thought, and is therefore a necessary introduction
to a more philosophical treatment of society as an organism, it is
yet only an introduction (*Principles*, pp. 381–2).

Marshall most often used the term, *equilibrium*, in a manner which was slightly different from the ideas expressed as 'where things are or whither things are tending'. The short phrase which would generally have been acceptable to him in place of the word, 'equilibrium', (and which he not infrequently used in that way) was 'balancing of forces'.[9] This connotes a dynamic tension, rather than a tendency toward inertia. Marshall was almost always careful to state as exactly as possible what he meant, removing as far as he could any danger of misleading readers into unjustified simplifications. He was at particular pains to bring the reader with him away from a static notion of equilibrium as an end-point or goal, into the ultimately dynamic idea of 'balancing of forces'. He attempted to smooth the way by starting with 'a simpler balancing of forces which corresponds rather to the mechanical equilibrium of a stone hanging by an elastic string, or of a number of balls resting against one another in a basin' (*Principles*, p. 269) before bringing the reader to 'the higher stages' of his work, where he would introduce more complex biological metaphors such as a business firm, which 'grows and attains great strength, and afterwards perhaps stagnates and decays; and at the turning point there is a balancing or equilibrium of the forces of life and decay' (ibid.).

From here he goes on to expand his subject beyond the bounds of what his own methodology will ultimately be able to encompass; indeed, the remainder of this passage (particularly the section which I have italicised) is devastating to his own most ambitious hopes:

13 These considerations point to the great importance of the element of time in relation to demand and supply . . . For, *in an age of rapid change such as this, the equilibrium of normal demand and supply does not thus correspond to any distinct relation of a certain aggregate of pleasures got from the consumption of the commodity and an aggregate of efforts and sacrifices involved in producing it*: the correspondence would not be exact, even if normal earnings and interest were exact measures of the efforts and sacrifices for which they are the money payments. This is the real drift of that much quoted and much-misunderstood doctrine of Adam Smith and other economists that the normal or 'natural' value of a commodity is that which economic forces tend to bring about *in the long run*. It is the average value which economic forces would bring about if the general conditions of life were stationary for a run of time long enough to enable them all to work out to their full effect.

But we cannot foresee the future perfectly. The unexpected may happen; and the existing tendencies may be modified before they have had time to accomplish what appears now to be their full and complete work (*Principles*, pp. 288–9; italics added).[10]

Marshall's painstaking distinctions between the long and the short run were motivated by a number of considerations, of which only the most mundane (the different lengths of time required for adjustments of capital stock versus more fluid factors of production) continue to be well-known. To him the more interesting reason for this distinction was that it seemed to be a way of creeping up on a dynamic science. The need to do so has become especially clear in recent decades, as we have become more aware of the deficiencies in economics which have made it blind to many importance effects of human activity upon the natural environment. A weakness in the existing mainstream economic paradigms has been, precisely, their static character: the assumption of neoclassical economics, that markets adequately represent the future, has proven an insufficient representation of a reality in which present actions have not been guided by sufficient concern for future costs and benefits.[11]

GENERAL
TENDENCIES AND
PARTICULAR
ACTORS;
DEDUCTION AND
INDUCTION;
RIGOUR AND
REALITY

We have seen Marshall write of a state of stable equilibrium to which things tend to return; but that, as he explained elsewhere, is only an illusion of changelessness; it is not a situation where there are no active forces, but rather one in which – as long as those forces remain unchanged – they happen to balance one another out. We have seen him complicate the notion of equilibrium to the idea of a centre *about which* variables tend to oscillate; and then complicate it yet further to an *average*, one which is rarely reached, but which we can imagine *would* be reached, *if* the highly improbable (i.e., long-lasting lack of change) occurred. Above all, the subject of equilibrium was to be thought of in terms of a *process, not of a goal*. Indeed, to slip into the idea that an equilibrium is a goal ('where things are, or whither things are tending') is to commit a logical fallacy, inserting a teleology where there is none.

As Marshall moves from Book V, Chapter i, which is an introductory chapter on 'balancing of forces' (or equilibrium) in markets, to Chapter ii, on 'Temporary Equilibrium of Demand and Supply', he is especially careful to bring in individual, personified actors, so that we can see that any teleology that actually exists is in the minds of human beings. Thus, with a boy picking blackberries, 'Equilibrium is reached when at last his eagerness to play and his disinclination for the work of picking counterbalance the desire for eating' (*Principles*, p. 276).

Later Marshall will comment on the meaning of a stable equilibrium, 'that is, the price, if displaced a little from it, will tend to return, as a pendulum oscillates about its lowest point' (ibid, p. 287); but we are intended to understand, here, that such a 'tendency' is not in any way teleological or normative, except possibly in the minds of individuals who have (more or less perfect) knowledge of the conditions of the market and understand how those conditions will be worked through to an anticipated result.

Mark Blaug has given a trenchant criticism of the situation in which neoclassical economics finds itself, in consequence of its choice of simplifications from the complexities of time and change. Blaug's criticism comes in the form of 'a central question about the entire history of orthodox economics in the last hundred years', namely:

14   that all the substantive finds of modern economics rest on the use of static equilibrium analysis and yet static equilibrium analysis seems to preclude fruitful discussion of such vital problems as the process of competition, the process of capital formation and the role of entrepreneurship'[12]

that is, problems which can only exist in the context of time and change.

It is important to keep in mind, as Marshall did, the reasons why he kept returning hopefully (only to remind himself sternly not to get carried away by his hopes) to quantitative approaches to economics. The subjects which Marshall most wished to be able to measure were in the area of welfare, which he hoped to be able to get at through consumers' surplus; that, in turn, required the ability to have exact measurements of demand – one route to which is a defined aggregate utility function. Marshall pinned many of his hopes upon the law of diminishing marginal utility (in such a murky area, the existence of any law at all seems like a great beam of light; cf. *Principles*, p. 79); but this, it turned out, was not to be sufficient (even if one were to make the enormous leap of taking for granted the measurement of utility) for deriving well-behaved demand curves.[13]

There is, however, an alternative route to the calculation of demand curves, wherein one can, by induction, piece together empirical observations, rather than building up deductively from utility functions. There is a long discussion in Book III, Chapter iii of *Principles*, relating to how, in principle, one might do this. Marshall concludes: 'And therefore if we had the requisite knowledge, we could make a list of prices at which each amount of [a commodity in general use] could find purchasers in a given place during, say, a year.' (*Principles*, p. 83).

The next chapter in *Principles* gives detailed examples of prices and their elasticities with regard to a large variety of things: the price and elasticity 'of wall-fruit, of the better kinds of fish, and other moderately expensive luxuries' (including plovers' eggs in London in April 1894); of wheat in London in 1335 compared to 1336; of bad concerts in small towns and good concerts in large towns; of water, as used by the poorer classes and by the middle classes; *etc. etc.* Marshall concludes these empirical observations with a new section (III, iv, 5) which starts out:

15 So far we have taken no account of the difficulties of getting exact lists of demand prices, and interpreting them correctly. The first which we have to consider arises from the element of *time*, the source of many of the greatest difficulties in economics.

Thus while a list of demand prices represents the changes in the price at which a commodity can be sold consequent on changes in the amount offered for sale, *other things being equal*; yet other things seldom are equal in fact over periods of time sufficiently long for the collection of full and trustworthy statistics (*Principles*, p. 92).

Chapter iv of Book III ends with Marshall's 'Note on the statistics of consumption' in which, again, he stresses the empirical, inductive method, concluding that 'the general demand curve for a commodity cannot be drawn with confidence except in the immediate neighborhood of the current price, until we are able to piece it together out of the fragmentary demand curves of different classes of society' (*Principles*, p. 96).

There are a variety of ways of understanding the constraints which contemporary neoclassical economics has accepted for its investigation of the real world problems which are thought to be of an economic nature. It operates, to begin with, under standards of rigour which have an impact upon the question of what problems a professional economist will be willing to define as falling within his province; hence Blaug's frustration that his own favourite dynamic problems are scanted and even scorned as worthy objects of study.[14]

The meta-constraint which gives rise to the adoption of these perhaps needing-to-be-reexamined standards is the limitations of our abilities (separate limitations on our formal and on our informal, or intuitive, abilities) to deal with complexity. The neoclassical decision on how to deal with complexity has been, in effect, a preference for mathematical types of techniques which can handle simultaneously enormous numbers of variables. The price paid for that choice is that each variable or action entered into such a system must be defined unambiguously and must, usually, be defined so as to be conceptually quantifiable (even if, in many cases, no attempt will ever be made to quantify it).

It has been said that 'the ultimate model of a cat is of course another cat'.[15] The meta-constraint cannot be avoided: however we choose to try to deal with complexity, our systems of thought and analysis can never deal with the fullness of the world as we experience it. In all of our thinking and acting, we have to make do with something less than another complete world as model, as working theory, as construct for understanding. (See Chapter 8, below, for a further discussion of this subject.) The link between this meta-constraint and the kind of constraints under which different economists choose to operate is a process: starting with the limitations upon our abilities to deal with complexity, we may go, via a particular process of simplification, to a particular type of economic theory, the neoclassical. A different sort of process of simplification would lead to a different type of economic theory.

DEVELOPMENTS SINCE MARSHALL   The advent of modern computers has added significant pressure to the drive to find ways to quantify the things and events that are of economic interest in this world. What can now be achieved with quantitative statements has become enormously greater; so the motive to quantify has increased in proportion. But our ability to quantify has not kept pace.

Of all mathematical fields, Marshall had most optimism regarding the assistance that would be provided by statistics, and since his time this field has advanced in ways that seem to have justified his optimism. This has only thrown into sharper relief the distance between the refinement of the techniques and the reliability of the facts on which it has to work. Much of the subject matter of economics – a social science – remains intractable to 'exact measurements'. So we find ourselves in the position of having superb tools poised for use with inadequate material to use them on; we have the knowledge and the patterns to create a suit of armour, but, often, hardly enough material at hand to simulate a fig leaf.

One solution to this dilemma is simply to claim, anyway, that we can make, and have made, a suit fit for an emperor. We may find claims repeated throughout Marshall's writing which almost give the impression that he was prepared to content himself with this solution; but Marshall's personality was not well suited to such a course. Hence the ambivalence which is expressed, on the one hand, in his statements that economics can be made a (relatively) exact science; balanced, on the other hand, by his refusal to accord much respect to any of the techniques which could be used in such a programme. So we return to the practical, if modest, conclusions which we saw in the quotations from Marshall which were numbered 2, 3 and 4 in this chapter. A summary statement of these conclusions is the following:

16 The law of gravitation states how any two things attract one another; how they tend to move towards one another, and will move towards one another if nothing interferes to prevent them. The law of gravitation is therefore a statement of tendencies.

It is a very exact [i.e., precise] statement . . . there are no economic tendencies which act as steadily and can be measured as exactly as gravitation can . . . .

The laws of economics are to be compared with the laws of the tides, rather than with the simple and exact laws of gravitation. For the actions of men are so various and uncertain, that the best statements of tendencies, which we can make in a science of human conduct, must needs be inexact and faulty. This might be urged as a reason against making any statements at all on the subject; but that would be almost to abandon life . . . . since we *must* form to ourselves some notion of the tendencies of human action, our choice is between forming those notions carelessly and forming them carefully (*Principles*, pp. 25–7).

The tension expressed here is, again, between accuracy and precision: if we try too hard for precision in our description of 'the tendencies of human action' we will veer away from accuracy, for, in the real world, these tendencies are not very precise.

These conclusions, if true, are discouraging. We should not let our discouragement make us forget the other side of Marshall's insistence: that this does not mean we should give up the attempt to understand the world, even to understand it 'scientifically'. However, what is 'scientific' in the social sciences may have to be differently defined – may need to draw on a different mix of human mental capabilities – than we find in the physical sciences. The latter have often been used as a model for the social sciences. This approach can only be carried so far; then it becomes necessary to strike off in some new directions.

Since Marshall's time the search for the particular kind of rigour sought in economics has created a situation in which economists can use their tools and techniques most effectively in an analysis of comparative statics, which compares a series of equilibria defined as long run states. There the emphasis is upon equilibrium as a state – a goal – something hypothetically to-be-reached. It is the 'arrived at' version of equilibrium whose characteristics are quantified, defined, and compared with other 'arrived at' versions in other long runs.

An example of the realities which are likely to be hidden by such an approach is the possibility that Keynesian 'underconsumption' may again emerge, at the end of the twentieth century, as a global problem. It may be that the deficit-financed consumption levels of the United States conceal a trend for productive technology to outrun effective demand. One reason why Keynesian economics has never been really well integrated into mainstream neoclassical economic theory (the so-called 'Keynesian synthesis' notwithstanding) is that the hypothesis just suggested flies in the face of the established theory. Underconsumption *should* not be a possibility because productive technology should not be able to outrun consumer purchasing power. Price adjustments *should* always bring supply and demand into balance so that the market will clear.

Standard neoclassical theory shows that this string of statements *must* be true: in the long run the *shoulds* become *wills*. What the theory has never achieved is a precise specification for when the long run, with the anticipated equilibrium conditions, may be expected to arrive. It is possible, even likely, that, in some areas, it never will; for new disequilibrating circumstances will keep occurring before the old ones have been worked out. Underconsumption can be neglected as a 'transition phenomenon' by neoclassicists who (because this is what their techniques allow them to handle) are more interested in the previous, and the next, *state* of equilibrium than in the transition *processes* between them. (One thinks of the Red Queen offering Alice as wages 'jam yesterday and jam tomorrow – but never jam today.') Transition phenomena must, however, be of considerable interest in the real world, where a decade, a lifetime, or (in some cases) the entire imaginable future may be seen as a series of transitions; but they are not in transition to – that is, they will never reach – the theoretically predictable equilibrium.

It may be argued (this is, indeed, one justification for the comparative statics approach) that long-term trajectories have to be plotted at least enough to permit the use of the calculus to derive the direction of change in the instantaneous 'now'. However, the methodology which we have imposed upon ourselves, and which, with its requirement for conceptually quantifiable functions, serves as an additional constraint, may in any case be fancier than necessary; its precision outruns the accuracy of our knowledge. For example, as discussed above, change can only take place over some finite stretch of real time. Nothing can actually happen in instantaneous time: the addition together of any finite number of instantaneities will not take up even a second of real time.[16] Given this reality, it is often sufficient, in the relatively unusual cases where the change in question is amenable to representation in functional form, to use the less sophisticated method of arc estimation of the direction of change.

A companion to the complex of problems relating to the central concept of equilibrium as a goal-state is another complex involving over-emphasis on what happens at the margin; the definition of marginal activities as, generally, 'instantaneous', i.e., not happening through time; and the tendency to push marginal analysis in the direction of this kind of definition in order to make it amenable to the calculus.

Each of the pieces that has been listed here as trapped in the requirements for the mathematisation of economics needs to be shaken loose: more attention needs to be paid to infra- and extra-marginal economic activities and states of being; and some marginal analysis could usefully be reworked within a 'fuzzier' notion of the meaning of a margin, not specified as an infinitesimally thin slice – of time, or money, or whatever. The calculus or more sophisticated techniques are not problems in themselves, but their use both diverts our attention from what we are not managing to achieve, and tempts us to go in the direction of the areas wherein they can be most helpful.

One implication, then, of the problems of complexity, time and change in economics, is that we will come closer to an ability to analyse their effects by the use of *less* rather than *more* sophisticated and difficult mathematical techniques. Emphasis upon:

–   finite, definable time periods, rather than the humanly inexper-
    ienceable instantaneous point of time;
–   the knowable present rather than the never-reached long run; and
–   the process of change rather than the putative (but virtually never-
    reached) equilibrium goal of that change;

all of these bring us away from the abstractions of theory in the economic sense (as mathematical modelling), and towards observable aspects of the real world.

Marshall evidently suspected or even assumed this to be so. Here was one of the places where he made it clearest that, at this fork, he would not continue down the neoclassical path. Given a choice between an elegant and precise model which could not deal accurately with the realities of complexity, time, and change, versus a rougher system, less fully worked out in analytical terms, which would at least recognise the existence of the realities it could not systematise, Marshall's most frequent preference was for accuracy over precision.

This has not been the choice of the neoclassical economists who, coming after Marshall, have preferred precision at almost any cost to accuracy. The reason why the mainstream in the field defines itself as it does today requires some further exploration. That will be the subject of the next chapter.

Notes

1. Andrew M. Kamark, *Economics In the Real World* (University of Philadelphia Press, 1983) p. 2.
   Aspects of this topic have been recognised at least since the time of Aristotle, who said, 'It is the mark of an educated man to look for just as much precision in each enquiry as the nature of the subject allows' *(Nichomachean Ethics*, 1.3).
2. *Principles*, p. 32. This passage was written for the first edition of *Principles*, and retained throughout the seven succeeding editions, essentially unchanged except for the deletion, in the 3rd edition, of a footnote regarding the roles of science versus common sense.
3. Quoted in A. C. Pigou, *Alfred Marshall and Current Thought* (Macmillan, London, 1953) pp. 16–17.
4. A. Marshall, 'Mechanical and Biological Analogies in Economics' (1898) quoted in *Memorials*, p. 313.
5. Quoted in Philip J.Davis and Reuben Hersh, *The Mathematical Experience* (Birkhäuser, Boston, 1981) p. 244.
6. Wesley Salmon, 'Introduction' to *Zeno's Paradoxes*, (ed.) Wesley C. Salmon (Bobbs-Merrill, Indianapolis, 1970) p. 24. I am grateful to Martha Nussbaum for bringing this book to my attention.
7. A fair example of this meaning of equilibrium, taken from a standard microeconomics course at MIT, is the following:

   Realistically, of course, the establishment of the new equilibrium may take an appreciable time; and, in the meantime, other changes of data are all too likely to occur. This means that full equilibrium is never actually reached. But it is still true that our understanding of the laws of motion of a dynamic economy must be based, directly or indirectly, on concepts of static equilibrium. Thus we may visualise the constantly changing economy as always moving in the direction of the static equilibrium, even though that equilibrium may itself be constantly moving. In this manner we can understand why actual prices and quantities are rising or falling, if they are constantly in the process of adjusting toward the moving target of their respective equilibrium magnitudes (Robert Bishop, *Lectures on Microeconomics*; in mimeo).

8. This idea will return frequently, most often tagged by Marshall's phrase, 'long trains of deductive reasoning'.

9. Cf:

Consider, for instance, the balancing of demand and supply. The words 'balance' and 'equilibrium' belong originally to the older science, physics; whence they have been taken over by biology. In the earlier stages of economics, we think of demand and supply as crude forces pressing against one another, and tending towards a mechanical equilibrium; but in the later stages, the balance or equilibrium is conceived not as between crude mechanical forces, but as between the organic forces of life and decay . . . .

The balance, or equilibrium, of demand and supply obtains ever more of this biological tone in the more advanced stages of economics. The Mecca of the economist is economic biology rather than economic dynamics (A. Marshall, 'Mechanical and Biological Analogies in Economics' (1898) in *Memorials*, p. 318).

10. It is interesting to compare this passage with the one from Bishop, in n. 7, above. In many respects, of course, they are pointing out the same things, giving the same warnings. The difference is that Marshall is more reluctant to see 'equilibrium' as anything *but* a process.

11. See the passage from Batie quoted on pp. 266–7 below.

12. Mark Blaug, *Economic History and the History of Economics* (New York University Press, 1985) p. xviii.

13. We will return to this subject in Part III. The literature in this area is immense. For a good summary I would refer the reader to Blaug's chapter on 'Marshallian Economics: Utility and Demand' in *Economic Theory in Retrospect*, 4th edn (Cambridge University Press, 1985; first printed in 1962). See especially pp. 350–1:

The effort to link utility to demand in the Marshallian manner via the 'law of satiable wants' is beset by two difficulties. When we replace additive by generalised utility functions, the law of diminishing marginal utility does not furnish 'one general Law of Demand'. Moreover, a generalised utility function robs us of any operational procedure for the cardinal measurement of utility. With the elimination of cardinal measurement, the very notion of deriving *diminishing* increments of utility from additional units of a good loses all meaning and it is no longer possible to make statements about the welfare effects of a change in price.

No wonder then that Marshall tried to simplify his argument by the device of holding MUe [the marginal utility of money] approximately constant.

14. Cf. the italicised passage in quotation no. 7 above and the quotation from Blaug on p. 394 below.

15. A. Rosenblueth, N. Wiener and J. Bigelow, 'Purpose and Teleology', *Philosophy of Science*, 10, p. 23.

16. See Chapter 11, below, for the concept of a 'pass-through limit': this will be a useful way of understanding both the approach to time described here as adapted to the methods of the calculus, and also the neoclassical use of the ideal concept of equilibrium.

7 Some Sociological Explanations for the Present Condition of Neoclassical Economics

In this chapter we will take a somewhat impressionistic look at the sociology of the field of economics. Given a discipline which, at the beginning of the twentieth century, has problems that it can not resolve, how will it develop, through the end of the twentieth and into the twenty-first century, with the claim that it is a science – indeed, 'the queen of the social sciences'?

MARSHALL'S AMBIVALENCE, AND HOW IT IS PERCEIVED
Since Marshall's time it has become ever more difficult to draw attention to the need for something besides technique to bridge the gap between the world that (presumably) exists outside our heads and the symbols through which we communicate about the world. Those economists who have attempted to lay stress upon this requirement have generally seen this part of their work marginalised under the name of 'institutionalism'. (They include such figures as Myrdal, Hirschman, Streeten, Scitovsky – to name a few.) The neglect of this part of the field may be traced to the neglect or depreciation of a part of Marshall's work; and that began with an essay by John Maynard Keynes.

In Chapter 5 it was noted that Marshall's persistence in bestriding the entire path of economics, even as it divided beneath him, led to a reputation for ambivalence, even inconsistency. Ambivalence, or multi-sidedness, can be understood and evaluated in a number of different ways. The interpretation that is most familiar today goes back to the way Marshall's memory was preserved by Keynes's leading essay in *Memorials to Alfred Marshall*. That essay retains its grip for good reasons: it is readable and astute, both in presenting a psychological portrait, and in outlining Marshall's most specific and solid achievements. It contains, however, some complicated twists.

141

Keynes who (in spite of his disclaimers of any normative tinge) may have been the most effective economist of all time as a giver of advice and meddler in practical affairs, chose, in discussing Marshall, to adopt a heavily positivist tone. Keynes leaves no doubt as to which side *he* regards as the 'higher', when he discusses the 'conflict', in Marshall, 'between an intellect, which was hard, dry, critical, as unsentimental as you could find, with emotions and aspirations, generally unspoken, of quite a different type. When his intellect chased diagrams and Foreign Trade and Money, there was an evangelical moralizer of an imp somewhere inside him, that was so ill-advised as to disapprove' (J. M. Keynes, 'Alfred Marshall, 1842–1924', in *Memorials*, p. 37). Earlier in the same essay, Keynes similarly referred to 'this double nature', saying that 'the piercing eyes and ranging wings of an eagle were often called back to earth to do the bidding of a moralizer' (ibid., p. 11).

The traditional view of Marshall which has grown directly out of Keynes's biographical and critical sketch attempts to downplay the multi-sidedness of the man and his work, as though it is assumed that his memory is best served by overlooking a slightly embarrassing tendency to be inconsistent, even fuzzy-headed. (This tendency was, by Keynes, implicitly interpreted as a result of Marshall's moralising tendency.) In anticipation of the prevailing wisdom of today, when it is assumed that s/he who does something more than economics is regarded as something less than an economist,[1] Keynes regarded some of Marshall's facets as detractions from, not additions to, his contributions as an economist. He was uncomfortable with Marshall's inclusiveness – his 'dual nature' – and tried to carve out of it for memorialisation the part that pointed in the direction that he, Keynes, thought economic science should develop.

It was not by accident, or inadvertently, that Marshall embraced a variety of apparently conflicting ideas. The subject matter of economics is itself full of ambiguities and contradictions: Marshall tried, in his theoretical writing, to be true to the fullness and complexity, even the contradictions, of human experience. That he continually strove to see all sides of a problem, and to avoid expressing himself in such a way that his work could be used in support of any singular or extreme position – this could be regarded as his greatest strength, not his greatest flaw.

Marshall's outstanding methodolgical characteristic was balance: balance between theory and facts, for example; or between tools (i.e., mathematics) and facts. But whereas in the first pair (theory and facts) he saw an essential complementarity, in the second he saw a possible conflict; not one inherent either in the tools or in the facts, but arising out of the frailty of human nature. He foresaw the danger that researchers would lose interest in facts that were not amenable to their tools, or that they would effectively lose interest in facts, as the sophisticated development of some kinds of tools outran the quality of available data.

Marshall remarked in one place that to avoid altogether the danger of distortion of emphasis which accompanies the use of mathematical and other kinds of analysis 'would be to abandon the chief means of scientific progress'. At the same time, he was aware of 'a tendency towards assigning wrong proportions to economic forces; those elements being most emphasized which lend themselves most easily to analytical methods' (*Principles* p. 700). Above all he warned repeatedly against 'long chains of deductive reasoning'; even in the context of his most encouraging statement of the value of 'a training in mathematics' and 'experience in handling physical problems by mathematical methods' – or perhaps all the more so for being in such a context – Marshall is concerned with the danger which he could, it appears, already see in their employment:

> It is obvious that there is no room in economics for long trains of deductive reasoning; no economists, not even Ricardo, attempted them . . . . But a training in mathematics is helpful by giving command over a marvelously terse and exact language for expressing clearly some general relations and some short processes of economic reasoning; which can indeed be expressed in ordinary language, but not with equal sharpness of outline. And, what is of far greater importance, experience in handling physical problems by mathematical methods gives a grasp, that cannot be obtained equally well in any other way, of the mutual interaction of economic changes (*Principles*, p. 644).

A prime reason for Marshall's often-expressed distrust of mathematics was precisely that mathematics permits long chains of deductive reasoning. To modern economists, by contrast, this enabling is one of their most attractive features. Thus Marshall's desire to restrict the use of mathematics to the simpler situations of interest to economics is in radical opposition to much of modern 'scientific' thinking, which calls upon mathematical tools as our only hope of being able to master the growing complexity of human experience.

Looking over the successive editions of *Principles*, one may perceive a tendency in Marshall to suppress his more philosophical, reflective side, especially as it is applied to questions of methodology. A critical reflection was thus deleted from the fifth edition: there he had called for a 'general principle [which would] determine the point in the widening of the scope of economics, at which the growing loss of scientific precision would begin to outweigh the gain of increasing reality and philosophic completeness' (*Principles*, 2nd edn, deleted from the 5th edn; quoted in *Var.* II, p. 763). I do not have much confidence (though I do not entirely rule out the possibility) that it will be possible to enumerate such a 'general principle' in terms that are specific enough to carry much weight. However, the point remains that the field of economics is in need of renewed attention to the balance between 'scientific precision' on the one hand, and 'reality and philosophic completeness' on the other. In the absence of attention to this balance, the modern tendency has been to err in the direction of apparent scientific precision.

A view of what has been achieved since Marshall's time gives rise to the hypothesis that, **given the topics of intrinsic interest to economics, there was, from the beginning, a finite and relatively small subset upon which quantitative methods could effectively be brought to bear**. If Marshall was discontented with the disproportionate attention given in his time to *what could* versus *what couldn't be quantified*, he would be even more so now, as the remaining unexplored quantifiable ground has shrunk to insignificance by contrast to the vast tracts of nearly virgin territory awaiting the development of non-quantitative approaches.

A SOCIOLOGY   In achieving even a summary understanding of how
OF ECONOMICS   economics has developed from where it was at the
                    turn of the century, under the dominance of Alfred
Marshall, to its present condition, there are several trends in recent intellectual history that should be noted. One is the turn towards positivism which started near the beginning of this century and continued as a marked trend for several decades. It is interesting to note that Marshall is only one of a number of broad, turn-of-the-century social science thinkers whose heirs, unable to deal with the full complexity of their vision, whittled it down in a biased manner, retaining the side that lent itself to positivism and ignoring or (as Keynes did with Marshall) belittling the normative, humanistic,

subjective, intuitive, judgment-laden side. Others beside Marshall who have been treated in this way include John Dewey, Talcott Parsons and Henry James. Earlier writers whose works were similarly streamlined to fit the idea of 'science' of the early twentieth century include Charles Darwin and Adam Smith.

Over the course of this century the natural sciences have become progressively less certain of the infallibility or even the unique definability of 'the scientific method'; but there has continued to be a time lag between the methodological development of the natural and the social sciences. Economics, suffering particularly from 'physics envy' in its aspiration to the position of 'the queen of the social sciences', has sought to imitate a positivist mode now considered obsolete in physics itself.

The ambitions of economics, in the optimistic days of the 1950s and 1960s, included a boast of predictive powers. That expectation has been disappointed as the advice and explanations of economists have come into conflict with the events of the 1970s and 1980s (stagflation, fluctuations in the prices of basic commodities, the international debt crisis, etc.) which they had either failed to predict or could not explain, or on which the economics profession had apparently given poor advice. Economists needed, then, to bolster their reputation and image in the eyes of the public and of policy-makers.

The use of ever more sophisticated, difficult and, to the uninitiated, impenetrable, mathematics makes it harder for the public and the policy-makers to judge the conclusions of economics against what is known to make sense in the real world. At the same time, in the USA, the availability of funding through such agencies as the National Science Foundation has increasingly emphasised the desirability for economists of being able to speak the language of science.

I cannot cite a definite causal relationship between this history and the fact that, at this time, it is in academia that the direction of the field is controlled. However the latter fact does appear more firmly established now, at least in the USA, than it was during the 'optimistic times', when a greater number of influential economists could be found with weaker ties to academia than is now the case. Such professionalisation is, in any case, part of a more general trend in the natural and social sciences, as well as in the humanities.

Hence the growing importance of the four academic screening points where all the pressures of the field channel in the same direction. The qualities, skills and understandings

1. that get a prospective student admitted to a graduate department of economics;
2. that help the student to get good grades and achieve an advanced economics degree;
3. that assist in the writing of papers that will be accepted by the major journals; and
4. that lead to academic promotion and tenure of an economist

all encourage abstract or mathematical modelling. As regards factual, historical, psychological, political or other contextual understandings or skills which have a usefulness in practical application of economics, the student develops these at peril of taking time away from studies on 'the cutting edge' of modern 'theory'; and the academic economist employs them with little or no encouragement or reward from within the profession.

Moreover, since the beginning of the twentieth century there has been a drift in the character of students going into economics, as undergraduates in mathematics, physics, and other mathematically oriented fields have increasingly found that they have a comparative advantage when they go on to graduate work in economics. This has continued to be a popular field for graduate studies, so that departments of economics have often been able to select, from among more applicants than they could accommodate, the students who they thought would most contribute to the enhancement of that department's reputation. It is difficult to test for the qualities of common sense, judgment, intuition, imagination, etc. which would make for a thoughtful, broad-minded economist; much easier to devise and to grade tests for mathematical ability. A simultaneous drift has occurred in respected economics journals, towards increased emphasis upon abstract or mathematical modelling.[2]

At the fourth of the academic screening points listed above we encounter the two modern academic imperatives: 'publish or perish' and 'up or out'. The tenure system as it now exists sets a competition which must be winnable by the young; the whole system tends to get skewed to allow older faculty to give high praise to the younger colleagues whom they would like to attract, and to allow young professionals to acquire the requisite publishing credentials. The virtues of elder members of the profession must stand aside in favour of what can be offered by recent graduates. The things that require many years to learn (roughly summarised as wisdom, and including judgment) have to be devalued relative to The Latest Techniques, for it is in those that recent graduates are likely to be ahead of their mentors.

The people who are most competent in the skills of youth are, then, the ones who gain the best jobs and set the continuing standards as to what shall be taught, what published, and how the academic screening points will continue to be managed. The likelihood that the skills of youth will occur in people who also possess, or will later develop, the qualities of common sense and judgment is, fortunately, not zero; there are some outstanding examples of individuals who have both. But there is little or no direct cultivation of judgment and wisdom in the field.

THE CHOICE OF LANGUAGE: WHERE WE ARE AND WHAT MIGHT BE DONE The preceding section gave reasons why the lead in defining the major modern systems of economic theory (Marxian as well as neoclassical) has increasingly been taken by *those individuals capable of doing the most difficult mathematics*. The effect of this situation is thrown into relief by considering what would be the result of a different situation. If, for example, the leading edge of the field were defined as contained in the work of economists with another sort of skill – such as the sorts of analytical skill (clear, logical thinking, and imagination) required in the work of Harvey Leibenstein or Albert Hirschman – there would be less pressure for all the rest of the practitioners in the field to strive to show that they can operate on a mathematical frontier which may, in fact, be beyond their knowledge or understanding.

The common desire of the 'rank and file' in any field to emulate the leaders has both advantages and disadvantages. If the leaders are outstanding for their conscious reliance upon common sense and intuitive perception, inferior imitations may take the form of mushy thinking, even while the frequency of outright absurdities may be reduced. In the current situation in economics, occurrences of mushy thinking take a different form, being disguised by the apparent crispness of mathematics, and rendered invisible to their perpetrators by their own frequent inability to interpret their results in real-world terms. The requirement that *economic modelling should have a meaning in real-world terms* is, at the moment, given scant attention in the dominant academic arm of the field.

Whichever approach is dominant, the prevailing methodology and techniques of a field will not be used only by those who can do so with full competence. The reality of economic practice is not confined to the very best practitioners; an analysis of the value of techniques must include the ways in which they are, in fact, used. It is often said that nothing is gained by criticising a field through a criticism of its worst practices. However if bad practices are widespread, and are repeated in journals and taught in classrooms, this tells us something not only about those practitioners, but also about the structure and sociology of the field which tolerates, encourages or even rewards them.

Users of mathematical language are too often tempted into wading in above their heads. It is hard enough for a first rate mathematician to make him/herself understood by the general public; that becomes downright impossible when a second-rate mathematician – or even, in fact, a first-rate one – has fallen into the trap of the Peterkin Principle[3] and has given in to the temptation of going one step beyond his/her own capacity to translate the final mathematical steps back into a verbal language. Not only does this remove the analysis from the reach and judgment of any but a few specialists, who do not have time to check the meaningfulness and realisticness of all their colleagues' work; it also deprives the individual thus stretching to his/her outer limits of the chance to check the results intuitively.

There are a variety of values to be weighed in the choice of language, in addition to the just-cited question of accessibility to a broad range of critics and to intuitive assessment. Another question is whether it is more desirable to permit, or to exclude, ambiguity. That is,

– Is ambiguity a proper and useful reflection of a complex reality; and is a language loaded with ambiguity the only possible way of making a bridge of translation between the complex world and our complex minds?
– Or, alternatively, is the gain in rigour more significant than the loss in reality when we force our experience into a set of singular, mutually consistent 'truths'?

One great strength of mathematics (when used correctly, which they often are not; in situations of extreme complexity mathematics are only used correctly when they are used brilliantly) is that they exclude ambiguity. One definition of a properly phrased mathematical statement holds that it can only have one meaning; a properly phrased mathematical question can only have one answer. By contrast, a great strength of most verbal languages is that they *permit* ambiguity.

Depending upon which value is stressed, the preference between abstract/quantitative and intuitive/verbal languages may shift. This chapter should not lead to the conclusion that, because of the dangers stressed so far in relation to non-verbal languages, they should never be used. What it should lead to is:

- a recognition that there are trade-offs in the choice of language; and
- a motive to further investigation as to what is the full set of trade-offs relevant to any particular situation.

Some additional institutional innovations may also be necessary in order to make it possible to develop a new way of developing and teaching an alternative system of economic theory. For example, in order to emphasise different qualities and skills than the 'skills of youth' now brought to the fore by the culture of 'publish or perish – up or out', there may need to be changes that would permit more individual development and intellectual (and other) maturation between the time a student finishes graduate school and the time that s/he must be considered for tenure. One way to accomplish this would be to say that, where social economics is taught, it would have different tenure rules than other areas: e.g., no social economist would be put up for tenure until s/he had completed something like three four-year stints at different locations; and some non-academic experience in that time would be regarded as desirable (rather than being a liability).

Given the conservative nature of bureaucracies, any change is difficult to achieve, and the particular suggestion just put forth may not, in any case, be the best one. It was suggested here mainly to emphasise two central points:

- A new kind of economics will require new approaches to the education both of those who go on to practice it in the real world and those who go on to develop and teach it.
- Changes, of some kind, within universities will be required to support such novel educational approaches.

WHY THE FIELD OF ECONOMICS NEEDS MORE THAN THE EXISTING SYSTEMS OF THEORY The sociology of contemporary economic study and practice shows a strong tension between the two poles of *academic* versus *empirical/applied* economics. The definition which was proposed in Chapter 1 for the broad field of economics – starting from 'the questions asked of economists', and then modifying these with a recognition of economics' relation to adjacent fields of study, and of the cluster of goals which are especially attached to this particular field – contained a definite bias towards application; social economics, in particular, is in large part designed to fill an important area, which might be labelled *policy economics*, and which is inadequately illuminated by both the neoclassical and the Marxian systems of theory.

Ultimately, the content of the field of applied, or empirical, or policy economics is determined exogenously, by the questions that people outside the field (in government, business, policy-making in general) not only ask of economists, but are willing to pay them to answer. By contrast, the methodology of academic economics has developed quite separately from this exogenously-determined content, and is often poorly suited to it; and the content emphasised in academic economics is, I contend, to a large degree determined by its methodology.

One reason that this situation is of concern is that the education of all economists, wherever they will end up upon the spectrum between the applied/theoretical poles, is in the hands of the academic group. It is questionable whether those who will ultimately operate somewhere at the applied end are well prepared by a training programme designed near the opposite pole.

Attempting to respond to the challenges of the real world, individual economists find themselves using informal, seat-of-the-pants methods when they step outside the area illuminated by the formal theory. A major goal for social economics is to create a framework within which the best of such applied work can find a home – a framework for generalisation about the useful real-world activities of economists – so that it will be possible to teach that kind of economics to those who wish to learn it. Such a framework will have to be found in another part of the field of economics than that now claimed by the currently dominant systems of theory.

A premise of this book is that it is unlikely that the dominant economic paradigms can or will expand to fill the conceptual space of the whole potential field of economics. I will suggest here only briefly my reasons for coming to this conclusion, and will, moreover, confine this reasoning mainly to a consideration of neoclassical theory.

The first reason to assume that neoclassical economics cannot expand to fill the rest of the space defined as the entire field of economics is that many excellent efforts to do just this have been expended without avail. Economists such as Leibenstein; Simon; Sen; Scitovsky; various game theorists; and many individuals working in the areas of labour and, above all, development economics – all have made valiant efforts to insert into neoclassical economics a more realistic understanding of human nature and more realistic models of economic behaviour, as it has seemed that these things were necessary to an expanded application of 'economics'. Each such endeavour has ended up like a grain of sand inserted into an oyster: the irritation has produced accretions directly around the grain of sand, sometimes resulting in a little globe of interesting ideas; but the oyster – the system of neoclassical theory – has remained unchanged.

Possible reasons why this system of theory is so resistant to change include the following:

1. Neoclassical economics has achieved a very tight (though not perfect) degree of internal consistency. It thus effectively excludes a large class of novel elements which, in changing some parts of the whole, elaborately interrelated system, would throw out of kilter their relationship to the rest.

2. Neoclassical economics has developed its methodology in relation to its content in such a way that the two aspects are virtually inseparable; but the methodology has become the tail that wags the dog. This system of theory is inhospitable to any content which cannot well be handled by the elaborately developed methodologies now in use, because it would be unthinkable to reverse the direction in which the methodology is developing. Also,

3. The explanation behind reason 2 is as much sociological as intellectual. The reward systems and status orderings which have become attached to neoclassical economics (as, over time, some sort of reward and status systems inevitably become attached to any developed system of theory) are now closely related to a unidirectional type of progress which contains little possibility of doing anything other than extending the accepted methodologies.

Reference was made, earlier, to the Peterkin Principle. The name comes from a fictional family who always chose the most complicated available solution (as, for example, when they sought to reconstitute a cup of coffee chemically, after mistakenly putting salt into it instead of sugar). The Peterkin Principle states that:

a social scientist is tempted by the reward systems of modern academia to use the most abstract level of mathematics of which s/he is capable; at which point of mental stretching the individual has gone beyond his/her ability to translate the mathematical analysis back into a verbal language – to check the results intuitively.

Contemplation of this principle and the story behind it may suggest two conclusions for the subject at hand.

The first is that economists (and all other social scientists) need to exercise discipline to resist showing off the most difficult techniques of which they are capable. Instead,

- in order *to press forward the frontiers of knowledge*, it is advisable, most of the time, *to operate well inside of the frontier of available techniques.*

The second conclusion is that,

- if the existing systems of economic theory do not suit all our needs, we may be wasting our time trying to reconstitute the paradigms from their present condition

in other words it is time to pour out a new cup.

The next three chapters of Part II will attempt to provide some tools that will be useful in the development of a new system of economic theory. In part, these are offered as tools which would be helpful in the early stages of the development of any new system of theory in the social sciences. More particularly, they are some elements of what I will suggest will be needed to fill the tool kit of the social economist.

Notes

1. We may contrast John Stuart Mill's comment, that 'a person is not likely to be a good economist, who is nothing else' (quoted by Marshall in *Principles*, p. 636).
2. As early as 1953 Pigou had commented upon this trend, saying that 'To anyone who has taken in the *Economic Journal* over a long period a notable change will have been apparent. At the end of the last century . . . in general the articles and memoranda were written in ordinary language – *ordinary* language, not even the specialist jargon language which some people so much enjoy. Now they are predominantly mathematical in tone' (Pigou, 1953, p. 5).
   The continuation of this drift has been widely noted. See, for example, 'On the Efficient Use of Mathematics in Economics; Some Theory, Facts, and Results of an Opinion Survey' by Herbert C. Grubel and Lawrence A. Boland, at Simon Fraser University, Vancouver, in manuscript. I am indebted to Vassily Leontief for bringing this paper to my attention.
3. See the end of this chapter for elaboration of this principle.

8 The Peculiar Place of Meaning in the Social Sciences

Here we return to some issues that were raised in Chapter 6. In some important respects the difficulties experienced by the social sciences, including economics, in coming to grips with the problems of complexity, time and change, are similar to those experienced by natural (or physical) scientists as well. In other respects they pose different kinds of challenges to these two areas of human understanding.

One theme that will unfold as we continue in Part II will be the importance of being aware of both the differences and the similarities between the natural and the social sciences as they are pressed to the limits of what they can achieve.

Another continuing theme is the distance between the world that exists and the words, symbols, models, etc. that we use to represent it and communicate about it. We go outside of the areas which neatly submit themselves to rules and formulae whenever we think about how we are to use theories, definitions, assumptions and simplifications, as ways of bridging the distance between 'the real world' and 'communication'.

(*Note: The term 'communication' will be used as a short-hand reference to all the activities we undertake in which we rely upon some translation from the reality presumed to exist outside of our heads and the symbolic version of that reality which we, in some sense possess: these activities include writing and talking; reading and listening; and just plain cogitating.*)

This second theme will be taken up at some length in Chapter 10. For now, suffice it to say that the qualities (skills, characteristics, or whatever) that a human being, as scientist, must bring to bear in bridging the distance between world and idea are subjects which have received insufficient attention within many fields. Social scientists, often led by economists, have pursued techniques as though that pursuit alone would build the needed bridges.

153

Alfred Marshall stands out among the great economists who have repeatedly called for something else – something which Marshall called 'common sense' but which I will generally refer to as 'judgment' – to play a companion role to technique. Focusing upon the activities of the social scientist, we will see (this will be the focus of Chapter 9) that judgment has a role to play in selecting the important assumptions remaining to be spelled out; the meanings most relevant or important to dissect; the words and symbols that should be looked at most carefully; the methodological points to stress; the areas where one should begin the search for logical contradiction or incompleteness; etc. A third theme of Part II will be the conscious definition of some of these critical areas where judgment is called for.

SOME PRELIMINARY COMPARISONS BETWEEN THE PHYSICAL AND THE SOCIAL SCIENCES   The social and the natural sciences had a common ancestor in philosophy – an area of speculation which (from what we know of the pre-Socratics in Greece), at least as soon as it grappled with issues of meaning and morals ('what matters'), was also trying simply to identify and begin to comprehend what's out there – 'what is'. In reading modern physics it sometimes seems as though the wheel has come full circle: simply the attempt to identify the essential components (if they may so be called) of the universe – energy, matter, space, time, 'space-time', etc. – and to comprehend their nature, often seems to engage our philosophical as much as our scientific selves.

In this respect, when we consider the difficulties which economics has in dealing with time and change, we find in the physical sciences something similar, but more conscious, and likely to be carried to a deeper, more philosophical level. Some delightful examples of the perplexities arising in this area may be found in a collection of essays, called *The Nature of Time*,[1] which was written by members of the Oxford University faculty in the physical sciences and philosophy. In Chapter 11 I shall attempt to show, in a discussion of some of the kinds of paradoxes that have been with us since the time of the Greeks, that our concepts of measurement, when applied to both time and space, break down when carried too far in the direction of certain limits. The economic problems with time that were mentioned in Chapter 6 – e.g. the impossibility of capturing the instantaneous 'now' in a freeze-frame that does not erase its context, time; or the difficulty of writing algorithms that do not, at some nth derivative, finally deny further changes in the process itself of change (a parallel statement in commonplace language is: 'the interesting events are the ones that could not be predicted') – these reappear, in more elemental and abstract form, in the musings on time of philosophically sophisticated physicists, or philosophers with knowledge of physics.

The problems posed by *complexity* in the physical sciences are somewhat different from the problems posed by *time and change*. At the outset they resemble the struggles we have seen in economics. It was from the natural sciences (including mathematics) that the statement came, which was quoted in Chapter 6: 'the ultimate model of a cat is of course another cat'. To dramatise the meaning of this, let me describe how it came home to me.

In the 1970s I was working on a modelling exercise with the architect, philosopher and mathematician, R. Buckminster Fuller (most often remembered as the inventor of the geodesic dome, and originator of the term, 'Spaceship Earth'). His conception of the accuracy and detail of the model to be created was extremely ambitious, and his colleagues experienced much frustration in their inability to produce anything even close to what he had in mind. My own frustration expressed itself in a dream in which, to show the resources, human trends and needs of the whole Earth, Fuller's team created a three dimensional globe that became larger and larger as the necessary detail was entered. Finally in the dream it became so large that it could no longer sit on the Earth; we had to push it off into space, where it hung side by side with the original; it was at last complete when it was the same size as the original, and an exact replica in every respect. The only true model of the Earth is, ultimately, another Earth.

The usefulness, of course, (as well as the practicability) of modelling exercises rests precisely in the fact that they never come anywhere near the 'ideal' or limit case of that dream. The *ultimate* (ideal) model of a cat or an economic system may be another cat or economic system, but we conceptualise it through words, mental images, etc., that depend upon much simplification.

Here, however, the physical and the social sciences begin to diverge, for in experimental science the 'ultimate' model *is* available. Mice are more often used than cats, but both are common enough in laboratories. The physicist who wants to communicate about electrons will employ many kinds of abstractions (diagrams, words, etc.) to do so; but ultimately s/he also has the option (at least the ideal, well-financed physicist has the option) of dealing (not 'directly', to be sure, but via complicated machinery, both for finding and for perceiving the particles) with the real things-in-themselves.

The relative infrequency with which the social scientist, *as scientist*, can deal directly with the *ding-an-sich* is one point of difference which we may note. At the same time, in his/her daily life the social scientist not only deals with, but *is* an 'ultimate model' for some part of his/her subject: because the subject of the social sciences is human beings. This brings into this area of human understanding an element of subjectivity, which, I would argue, cannot be wholly excluded, however much we may try. Indeed, since what the social scientist often wants to know about is a direct result of (if, indeed, it is not in fact) something subjective like motivation, belief, thought, or emotion, and since our only direct knowledge of these things arises through introspection, it is the case that *the more successfully subjectivity is excluded, the more the knowledge base for the social sciences is constricted.*

It is, most of all, the subject matter that makes for the most dramatic differences between the physical and the social sciences: human beings (in terms of their mental and behavioural, rather than their physical existence) are the subject of the social sciences. The aspect of this difference which may be most salient – and which will be the topic for much of this chapter – is the fact that, given that the subject is the mental and behavioural aspects of human beings, then a new dimension for study comes to the fore: the dimension of *meaning*. Not all of this large subject can be explored here. The aspect from which we will start will be that of the meaning – and meanings – which have to be dealt with in creating and communicating about the subject matter of the social sciences.

CREATORS AND RECIPIENTS OF SOCIAL SCIENCE TEXTS   What you, or I, know of the work of other social scientists is not what is in those other minds, but is rather what we receive at the end of the form of communication which they extend. As we start to move into this topic it will be useful to examine the possibility that there is a significant area for what could be called creativity at the receiving as well as at the originating point of communication; and that, if this is so, then we have to regard the way that we read and listen as important parts of the reality of our field. This section and the next three will position this activity within certain social sciences traditions. Starting with the section entitled 'a conscious Approach to Conscious and Unconscious Levels of Meaning', a particular critical tool, which has the potential for broad application and usefulness, will be described.

Economists communicate with each other and with the rest of the world in several ways; most notably through what they write, through formal verbal presentations (e.g., lectures), and through informal verbal presentations (e.g., conversations). Any of these communications may be regarded as texts, and subjected to textual analysis. Textual analysis is not only done in one known and stated way; at the extreme, one could claim that there are as many kinds of 'readings' as there are 'readers'. Retreating from such fine distinctions, I would nevertheless say that there is a technique, called 'discourse analysis', which has some important differences – some of them quantitative, and some qualitative – from the kind of reading that is most commonly afforded to economic texts. This technique, arising historically from the concept of 'close reading' of texts in literature studies, has increasingly been applied to 'texts' outside of the usual realm of literature-seen-as-art (e.g., to advertisements, speeches, newscasts, etc.), and then to other areas of human activity (television performances; structures – e.g., prison designs; laws; unwritten rules; institutional guidelines; etc.) which are 'read' as 'texts'.

To date, these methods have been employed largely from the critic's side of the fence. However, methods growing out of discourse analysis can also be taken to the other side, and employed by those who create social science texts; not only the writers of books and articles, but also, for example, economic practitioners.

Unfortunately, much of what has been written about, and many examples of, discourse analysis is arcane and jargon-ridden. However, the essential features of possible use to social scientists need not require a lifetime of language study to master. An additional goal of Part II will be to set out a simple and preliminary codification, or set of guidelines, starting on the critic's side of the fence, which can be employed on the other side as well, to assist social scientists in general, social economists in particular, to gain the self-consciousness which is the key to reaching some new relationships between goal and analysis; between theory and fact; between academic and empirical science.

Social science texts attempt to lead to, convey, or examine, purportedly true statements about human beings in society. In the spirit of Donald McCloskey[2] I claim that the quality most sought for in such texts is credibility; the effectiveness of an author is shown in the degree of credence, or belief, which s/he can claim from the recipients of the text. (Note: 'most sought for' here does not mean 'best' – it means no more than it says.)

The credibility/credence nexus in a social science text connects its creator with its recipients in a somewhat different manner than either the aesthetic element of a novel or a poem, or the invitation to repeated experimental proof in a natural science text. The types of communication involved in the three broad areas of scholastic discourse – arts and humanities, social sciences and natural sciences – is sufficiently different so that we should expect to find that the most useful types of discourse analysis will also fall into three general types, along the same lines of division. What will be offered here is a preliminary outline of some of the sorts of activities (including but not limited to activities which might go under the heading of 'discourse analysis') which will be used in this book (especially in Part III), as an approach which is particularly useful for the social sciences.

Specifically, I will name, distinguish between, and, to a limited extent, describe, a number of the different types of critical activities which I have employed in reading texts by Marshall and other economists, in my endeavour to learn some of the important, less obvious things about economics in particular, social science in general. This discussion will be written in a more personal tone than most of the rest of the book, as it will draw, for examples of procedure and methods, on my own experience with the material to be analysed later in the book.

THE FIRST TOOL OF ECONOMICS: THE MIND OF THE ECONOMIST   A fundamental question will be concerned with the very basis upon which economics over the past half century has been structured. When one stops to think about it, there is something more than a little odd about the way this discipline has chosen to build itself, as though starting from a vacuum of knowledge about its subject. The very idea of axiomatisation in a social science is so counter-intuitive (for all that we have become accustomed to it) as to deserve a reappraisal.

The normal way for the human mind to work is to take each new piece of information or new speculation and evaluate it for truth, or usefulness, or other merit, *against the background of a life's experience.* The whole life's experience is not consciously present, but a tremendous amount (there are no really solid guesses as to how much) is 'stored' in some way, so that correspondences between the new input and the stored material call forth judgments on the new information.

By contrast, the economic view of the human being, since Marshall's time, has operated as though starting from nearly complete ignorance on the part of the economist him/herself. During the early period of modern formalisation a pitifully small amount of ideas about human motivation and behaviour were permitted to be 'known' in the consciousness of the field of economics. Then, as though these things were being discovered for the first time, an odd lot of singular observations about human nature was grafted on, in a rather haphazard way. The basic assumption of rational maximisation of self interest was padded out, here and there, with the 'rotten kid theorem'; the idea that people might choose to exercise 'exit, voice or loyalty'; 'bandwagon' and 'snob' effects; situations that could be named a 'prisoner's dilemma', or characterised as 'moral hazard'; etc.. What a curious, and incomplete collection! It does not seem likely that simply extending this collection is the way to achieve any kind of sufficient completeness.

The economic approach to human nature, in fact, has been to behave as though engaged in an effort to programme a computer to predict behaviour. A computer only knows what it is told. Nothing can go directly from the human unconscious into the computer's works: all that it receives must be delivered via programming (which is a conscious, intellectual activity) out of conscious human knowledge. In their areas of strength, computers can outperform any human mind. What they do not have access to is the stored experience of a human unconscious.

Even if a computer were programmed with far more than the above-cited collection of memorable names for bits of behaviour which have been economists' recent additions to the basic behavioural assumptions – even if, for example, it were fed all the factual descriptions of human motivation and behaviour contained in all the psychology, sociology, anthropology and history textbooks in existence (and were given some way to sort and prioritise the conflicting information contained therein) – it would not possess the ability to understand and respond which exists in human beings. The human ability to understand and respond which is different from, and more powerful than, the computer's ability, derives from that unconscious part of our mind which we cannot translate into a computer programme.

The point of this comparison is to suggest that the way we have gone about developing our 'human sciences' may not be the way that can best take advantage of our starting point – ourselves. It is not to say that we should not use computers – of course we should – but rather that we should also use ourselves, and we should not use ourselves as though we were computers.[3]

In formal neoclassical economic work we are using only a scant fraction of what we, as individuals, understand about the common subjects of the social sciences: human motivation and behaviour. In recent years the analogy with computer sciences has lent weight to the idea that all assumptions and all knowledge about human motivations and behaviour can, and should, be made explicit in any scientific work: that which is not made explicit is presumed not to exist (i.e., our models are assumed not to tap into anything like 'unconscious belief'). The attempt to impose this particular kind of 'rigour' throws away so much information that it is worth questioning whether the gain has been worth the loss.

MATHEMATICAL   When confronted with an economic problem, the
MODELLING   approach of neoclassical economics is to 'apply a
                     model'. By contrast, the approach of social
economics will be, first, to apply a trained intelligence.

What is the ideal of a model, as currently employed in economics? It is a set of assumptions which, in the most stringent modelling exercises, are supposed (a) to be exhaustively spelled out, and (b) to comprise the totality of knowledge/understanding about the world which is to be included in the particular modelling exercise. Normally, in fact, both (a) and (b) are impossible. (See n. 3.)

The models which are generally considered the most sophisticated examples of modern neoclassical economic reasoning may be accurately described, in Marshall's words, as 'long chains of deductive reasoning'.[4] They normally start with a set of simplifications which would be considered merely absurd if it were not so apparent that, for this type of reasoning, such simplification is essential. The inputs from reality, thus stripped down, are then manipulated through long, often impressively difficult, mathematical exercises. What emerges at the end cannot be expected to bear *more* relation to reality than what went in at the beginning; frequently, some of what relevance there was to start with has been lost, as when, for example, highly stylised behavioural assumptions are employed recursively to demonstrate the effects of the passage of time. If the results of each iteration (to take a typical example) are taken as the starting point for the next period, while important influences have been left out through the necessary simplification process, and the behavioural assumptions were only a fair representation of reality under very limited and special circumstances to begin with, the multiplication of errors can take the conclusions a great distance away from reality.

There are, of course, some good uses for modelling techniques.[5] Short and simple models (eschewing *long* chains of deductive reasoning) can be a helpful expression of understanding, to clarify an individual's own thinking, or to assist in communicating an idea.

The other, more difficult road is to use mathematical models creatively, to uncover previously unknown facts. The acknowledged master of the technique in our time is Kenneth Arrow: his most striking results, while highly creative and illuminating, are essentially descriptions of the very narrow limits to what we can hope to prove when using these techniques with maximum rigour and honesty.

The question, as always, is: What are the alternatives? I will summarise here what will be spelled out further as we go on, in this section and throughout the book. Possible answers – or directions as to where to look for answers – include suggestions that the inputs to social economics should include:

- human values, those of both the subjects of the analysis and the analyst (these are now, as they must be, an input to existing systems of economic theory, but their role is not overt);
- material from the other social sciences; and particularly
- a recognition in social science analysis of what may be called unconscious processes, including intuition, judgment, and the full store of personal knowledge, only a small part of which is consciously present at any given time.

Can these matters be scientifically incorporated into a science of economics? Probably not, in the way that economics has defined science. Is there some other way? Probably so, and this will be a major task for social economics: it must find *a way to incorporate intuition, judgment and personal knowledge, along with human values, into a theoretic framework that is, to a sufficient extent, judgeable, teachable and applicable.*

THE STANDARDS REQUIRED FOR 'SCIENTIFIC BELIEF'   There will unquestionably continue to be uses to justify putting some (not, perhaps, as great a proportion as at present) of the human resources available to the whole field of economics into the continued development of sophisticated techniques. However, we also need a system of economic theory that can develop scientifically in a different direction. What this may require is an altered definition of what it means to be 'scientific'. In this respect, economics may be trailing behind the pack which it thought it was leading: the demise of positivism is older news in some other areas of the social sciences than it appears to be in our field.

It is increasingly clear, as we digest the Heisenberg uncertainty principle,[6] along with Gödel's demonstration of the nonreflexiveness of mathematical proofs, that the positivist position, insofar as it depends upon claims to knowledge with certainty, is untenable. It is not the case, nevertheless, that the only alternative is then to turn to complete relativism. The 'facts' we hold in our minds may be best understood as *beliefs* rather than as *certain truths*; however, this is no reason to rush to the extreme of saying that all beliefs are equally good. We can work to define rules and procedures which both indicate (a) how to arrive at 'better' or 'worse' beliefs, and also (b) how to recognise which statements held out for our credence are 'better' or 'worse'. (Of course, our statements in these two areas, (a) and (b), will only be offered and held as 'beliefs', not as 'certain knowledge'.) Deeply, this is what methodology is about, and what makes it interesting.

Let us explore these issues a little further. It has become almost automatic to inquire, of any standards that are not taken as absolute, whether we should in that case interpret them as strictly relativistic. Relativism, in this context, can be of two kinds: moral relativism, which holds that any one person's or society's *values* are as good as any other's; and epistemological relativism, which says that, since knowledge with certainty is impossible, any belief is as good as any other. It must be stressed that neither of these, in the extreme form just described, is a logically necessary result of the debunking of the extreme positivism which flowered for a while earlier in this century. There is a good deal of reasonable ground between the two poles. An alternative to relativism, for example, is the philosophical position of realism. In the context of economics, it is described by the philosopher of economic methodology, Uskali Mäki, thus:

> realism says that, independently of what economists think about the referential and representational capacities of economic theories, there is an objectively existing real world, and that the terms, statements and theories of economics can be used to refer to aspects of this reality (world realism) and can represent them truly or falsely (truth realism).[7]

Mäki goes on to consider 'the idea that truth and certainty somehow go together: to commit oneself to truth realism is to commit oneself to the possibility of certitude', and says,

> This view is mistaken. Take the law of demand as an example. It is a statement about the relation between the price of a good and the demand for it. As such, it may be either true or false (perhaps with some qualifications of scope), in virtue of certain facts about social reality. Up to this point, I have made claims (on a semantico-ontological level) about truth but I have said nothing (on an epistemological level) about certainty. Certainty will enter the picture upon the formulation of an epistemological statement about the law, to the effect that, e.g., 'the law of demand is (or can be) known to be true (or false) on infallible evidential grounds.' I think this epistemological statement is false; but it does not follow from this that the law of demand is false. Truth and certainty belong to different realms, and should not be confused with each other. (Ibid, p. 97)

On the epistemological side it is important to look at what happens when the shift is made from 'certainty' to 'belief'. Both of those are mental states, which may be defined thus:

– *Certainty* is the conviction that a direct, perfect, reproducible mapping can take place between the 'facts' of the real world and the mental constructs in an individual's mind. A person in a state of certainty believes that his/her mental constructs are, in some relevant sense, a perfect image of reality.
– *Belief* is the state of mind which obtains when a person holds that, even though a perfect mapping between real facts and mental constructs is not possible, nevertheless his/her mental constructs are a pretty good approximation to a picture of reality.[8]

The state of mind described as 'certainty' holds that it (that state of mind) is directly created in response to facts of the real world; fact, and only fact, can produce certainty (according to those in that state of mind). 'Belief', however, recognises that it can, and usually does, come about in a number of ways: in part 'you believe what you see'; in part 'you believe what you are told'; in part 'you believe what you want to believe'. In other words, we may hope that, as in the construction of certainty, 'facts' have played the dominant role in constructing belief;

but we know that even perception ('what you see') is affected by prior beliefs and expectations; by our methods of sorting and categorising information as it reaches us; as well as by our wishes and values.[9]

We cannot, ultimately, prove that there *is* a reality 'out there'; nor can we define, without reference to our sensory experience, the correspondence between what our senses tell us and the presumed reality which we take to be the source of that sensory information. These are the discouraging conclusions which have pushed thinkers to such extreme positions as mysticism or complete relativism (moral or epistemological or both). Another, more moderate reaction is equally reasonable. It may be described as follows:[10]

- Although the scientific attitude prevents us from certainty about 'reality' or about 'truth', yet the alternative of rational, non-absolute belief need not be despised. *The recognition that one is operating in a science dependent upon belief rather than certainty is not inconsistent with standards that have long been associated with the ideal of scientific truth.*

- Absence of proof should not be regarded as absolute disproof. When we step away from the world of 'certain-yes or certain-no', a whole array of shades between belief and disbelief – with 'wait and see' attitudes in the middle – may come into play.

- Making inferences from the words and actions of others, and comparing these to our own sensory experiences, we may assemble images of 'the real world' which, while they remain subject to revision, are employed as beliefs about reality.

- An important goal is to establish rules for discovering and selecting (subject to further evidence) which particular beliefs are the ones we should choose to hold. (The art of rhetoric may be – though it is not always – understood as adhering to this goal.)

- While we accept (more or less reluctantly) that we can never be *certain* that our statements are perfectly true (or even that they are true at all), we strive nevertheless, with all the ingenuity and thoughtfulness we possess, to avoid practices which will obscure presumed-(though-not-known)-to-exist truth, and to adopt practices which will bring our beliefs into conformity with external reality. (This last statement summarises, I believe, the nature of all science.)

A great scientific apparatus was developed to ensure the recognition of truth as something certain; much of that apparatus can be used for the more modest goal of making our beliefs as good as we possibly can, i.e., to give them what we (the people we respect, and we ourselves) deem to be the highest probability of having the closest correspondence with the guessed at (though never perfectly 'known') reality.

The conclusions, here, are similar to McCloskey's:

- It is important to understand how our beliefs, as economists, are formed; in order to achieve that understanding, we have to look farther than the 'simple facts' to which these beliefs are supposed, by some, to relate in a simple and straightforward way.

- The person who labels his/her epistemological constructs as 'beliefs' recognises that these constructs are subject to persuasion. Moreover, s/he will be sceptical that beliefs can be safely viewed as 'purely positive' or 'value-neutral' in any areas in which the people involved have feelings or values.

- Some of the ways of looking for the antecedents of economic (or other social science) beliefs include the study of intellectual history; the methods of discourse analysis; and an examination of levels of meaning.

The last item on this list will be the central subject for the remainder of this chapter.

A CONSCIOUS APPROACH TO CONSCIOUS AND UNCONSCIOUS LEVELS OF MEANING   It is only fairly recently that the social sciences have claimed a place in the Western scientific tradition. By so doing, they have put themselves in the shadow of the natural sciences – trying to live up to a concept of what it meant to be 'scientific' which came from that so much older, so much better developed tradition. Quite recently the juxtaposition of psychoanalysis with other social sciences has begun to bring a new light onto the comparison, pointing up an important way in which separate terms are required for an understanding of the social versus the natural sciences.

A partial explanation for the impact which psychoanalytic psychology has had upon individuals in the Western world, upon Western societies, and upon the sciences which deal with humans as individuals and in society, arises from what it says about meaning. It insists that we must add to our appreciation of *conscious, intended* meaning an anticipation of at least one additional, deeper, *unconscious* level. What we say, what we do, what we perceive, even what we think and believe, all may be examined for meanings on at least two levels, roughly called conscious and unconscious. There are many views on the validity, or lack thereof, of psychoanalysis; in spite of debate on that issue, the social sciences reflect the effects of a fairly wide absorbtion of this critical perception about individuals and groups.

Discourse analysis is the formalisation of one way to try to apprehend meaning at more than one level. Building upon what good literary critics have always done (at least unconsciously), discourse analysis may be consciously used to free ourselves from the constraint to look only at the meanings that are claimed on the level where an actor or spokesperson consciously, intentionally conveys a conscious, intended meaning to the conscious level of perception of the recipient(s).

As long as only one kind, or level, or dimension, of meaning is recognised, a dramatic difference between the social and the natural sciences remains unexplored. This critical difference stems from the fact that the social sciences, in dealing with human beings, must deal with meaning. This difference remained in the background so long as the social sciences were assumed to be concerned, like the natural sciences, with a single-level kind of meaning, identified with a singular 'reality'.

The natural sciences try to discover and elucidate facts and principles that belong to the single plane of the natural world – that is the reality with which they have to deal. It has often been assumed that the social sciences were doing pretty much the same thing, even though the components of their reality happened to be human beings. However, the reality with which the social sciences try to deal has multiple (e.g., conscious and unconscious) meaning-planes. Thus we cannot expect the operations of the social sciences to be easily mapped onto the single-meaning dimensions of the natural sciences.

A foreshadowing of this recognition might be seen in discussions of 'unintended' consequences, in Adam Smith, for example. But those unintended consequences were understood either in a purely naturalistic mode (a pendulum will describe its natural arc, whether or not the releaser knew, understood, or intended that trajectory), or else in a religious mode (Man proposes, God disposes). The workings of the invisible hand might be understood in both these ways; the unintended consequences of Men obeying their natural (hence God-ordained), self-serving impulses could also be seen as the intended consequences of a benificent deity. But God's meanings were never self-contradictory or divided. The thickness of multiple meanings, hence multiple understandings, only comes to the forefront in the sciences of Man when the layered, inherently self-contradictory nature of Man, the subject, is accepted through something like psychoanalytical awareness.

This is not to suggest that that layered, contradictory nature was utterly ignored before psychoanalysis. Great psychologists have recorded their observations for millennia; their understandings have been generally best preserved in literature, either oral or else written down in poetry, fiction or drama. The absence of the vital psychoanalytical concept for conscious understanding of this layered complexity gave rise to a specific type of adjustment; the psychologists of the past recognised the presence of contradictions, but, lacking the concept of distinct levels of meaning, often explained this recognition to themselves and to their audiences by the concept of hypocrisy. There are, of course, people who are consciously hypocritical – who purposely mislead others as to their real purposes. However, hypocrisy may be a less probable explanation for behaviour resembling that of the notable hypocrites of literature (Iago, Molière's Hypocrite, etc.) than the psychoanalytic explanation which suggests that people don't always know, on one level, what they mean on another; they may talk and act at some times on one level, at other times on another – or on several levels at once.[11] The multiplicity of not necessarily dishonest, even when contradictory, meanings which authors put into texts and which their readers take out of them is now – through discourse analysis following upon psychoanalysis – available for non-judgmental critical examination in the social sciences.[12]

IDENTIFYING AND SORTING OUT DIFFERENT LEVELS OF MEANING The dualism of 'conscious' versus 'unconscious' is only one way of slicing layers of meaning in the human sciences. I would like to propose, and will use through the remainder of this book, another approach which I have found particularly useful in social science textual analysis. My emphasis, here, will be upon the real-life form of economics – what is practised – more than what is preached. This emphasis will reveal differences among social science meanings on three levels:

1. What the social scientist formally and openly claims to be doing; the 'stated' or 'conscious' level.
2. The 'effective' or 'unconscious' level; the implied or taken-as-if-implied meanings that are adopted and built upon, both by the author of those meanings and by others.
3. The operations that are performed on the 'logical' or 'technical' level.

Before going on to develop these 'levels' in greater depth, I will give a few examples of the ways in which they are already familiar to us.

When someone is sceptical about the relationship between theory and practice, or when a reader or critic protests that the logic of a piece of social science does not support the claims made for it, s/he may be referring to a divergence between the first and third of these levels.

It is also possible to find situations where there is mutual congruence on the first and third levels, while these both diverge from the middle level. For example, an economist might make a (level 1) disclaimer as to why, in a particular situation, scientific rigour cannot be maintained; and yet at the same time the results may be presented and received (on level 2) as if they were on scientifically firm grounds. The deepest level of meaning (level 3) may include the reality that what is *in fact* being offered is a mix of common sense, opinion, analysis, and fact. Sometimes this deep level is accurately reflected on level 1, in an overt statement or disclaimer; however the world demands simple statements to lead to action, and then the result may be that neither the overt statement nor the deepest level of meaning are the ones which have the most impact.

An example of a level 1 statement which will be of interest to us in Part III of this book is the following, from Chapter II of Marshall's *Principles*:

> An opening is made for the methods and the tests of science as soon as the force of a person's motives – *not* the motives themselves – can be approximately measured by a sum of money, which he will just give up in order to secure a desired satisfaction; or again by the sum which is just required to induce him to undergo a certain fatigue.
>
> It is essential to note that the economist does not claim to measure any affection of the mind in itself, or directly; but only indirectly through its effect (*Principles*, pp. 12–13).

I will claim, in Part III, that while most of Marshall's actual practice (on level 3) accepted the limitations stated in the foregoing, the message that went out on level 2 through much of Marshall's writing was far too easily understood as a claim that economists, in fact, can and do measure such 'affections of the mind itself' as desires and satisfactions. We will see, in Chapter 15, that such commentators as A. C. Pigou and Marc Blaug responded, and objected, to this level 2 implication.

John Maloney, a contemporary economist who, like myself, has found Marshall a useful starting point from which to address many of the same issues as those confronted in this book, made a generalisation which is similar to the one I have been making:

> Indeed this writer doubts if economists' qualifications of their own theories does anything to dislodge them from their readers' minds. Faced with, say, a standard account of the neoclassical theory of the firm, with a few half-hearted 'real-life' exceptions tacked on to it, the reader may merely congratulate the writer on his realism, openmindedness and intellectual honesty, and take the paradigm as being all the more authoritative. Listing exceptions and qualifications may also make the reader feel that the more that is wrong with a paradigm, the more must be right with it, to have justified so much trouble in exposition (Maloney,1985, p. 215).

The economists' qualifications and exceptions cited here are offered on level 1; the readers' response, as Maloney describes it, fits on level 2.

It is the effect of the meshing of the readers' needs and wishes (e.g., for simple truths) with something offered on an inexplicit or unconscious level of the text which carries through into the way the text is then used. It is level 2 which has the most impact upon any audience of readers or listeners, and which is most likely to lead to further action. The effective level of meaning is the one in which the *as if* behaviour has its effect. Disclaimers, such as those instanced by Maloney, may state that a given procedure cannot be truly scientific for lack of adequate data, or of methods for putting the available data into quantifiable, commensurable, aggregatable form, etc. But on the effective level of meaning, the social scientist may nevertheless proceed *as if* all the necessary ingredients for scientific analysis were at hand; 'scientific' analysis is performed upon not-quite scientific data. When this is convincing, as it often is (often simply for lack of anything else that is *more* convincing) it is *used* as though the effective level were the 'real' (or logical) one.

Although the terminology I have chosen may be unfamiliar, this way of breaking down levels of meaning is a common-sense approach which has been employed by others. Such a consciousness, for example, is implied in the question, 'What does so-and-so *really mean* here?' Although that is a common kind of question, it is open to a good deal of complexity in the answer. First of all, it suggests that there is an 'apparent' meaning, but that the questioner is looking for something distinct from that: the 'real' meaning. Then the question arises: is there only *one* 'real' (or, for that matter, only one 'apparent') meaning?

Common references to 'real' meanings usually attempt to get at what I have called the third, or logical, level of meaning. When people suggest that we should dig deeper, past the apparent level to the real one, they may, by the 'apparent' level mean *either* level 1 or 2: thus there is a basis for disagreement on what people more-or-less casually think someone has said, before they even get down to disagreeing about what was 'really' said.

None of this is news in the realm of public discourse; it is not even news for discourse in the physical sciences.[13] If it has been late in coming to the social sciences, this is perhaps because they are the most threatened by it; the contextual and individual (subjective) character of meaning in the social sciences is particularly obvious and significant, therefore particularly threatening to their claim to being scientific – when the concept of science, taken from a now outmoded concept in the physical sciences, means 'objective' and 'provable'.

Considerable attention will be paid in Part III to highlighting the differences in these kinds, or levels, of meaning as I have found them in Marshall's texts. Additionally, almost all of the remaining types of analytical activity which I will describe in this section depend to some degree upon an everpresent consciousness *that meaning does occur on a variety of levels; that most authors do not clearly signpost what is going on at which level; and that a more complete understanding of a text is possible when these levels are sorted out.*

Let us return to a more detailed description of the three levels:

- *Level 1*: What the social scientist claims to be doing. The 'conscious' or 'stated' level of meaning is most typically to be found in self-consciously worked-out formal statements.
- *Level 2*: What the world acts as if it thinks the social scientist is doing.[14] The 'unconscious' or 'effective' level of meaning may be thought of as something that does not exist in the text standing alone; it is created interactively, being revealed as the receivers of the text interpret (by the light of their own experience) something as vague as its 'general tone', to form a basis for both general and specific expectations, and for their own further thought and action.

  Some people, of course, bring exceptionally idiosyncratic experience to all that they do, including their reception of texts. In speaking of a generalised 'level 2 meaning' of a text, I, as textual analyst, am referring to the cluster of interpretations that I assume are most commonly made, or that I guess to be most likely. (I will comment further, below, on the 'assumptions' or 'guesses' of this nature that the critic must make, and the basis on which they may be made.)

The impact of level 2 meanings may be carried through to logical, intellectual activities, but the 'effective' level of communication passes, most commonly, from the pre-cognitive processes of one mind to the pre-cognitive processes of others.[15] Interpretation and analysis of such communication necessarily contains a highly subjective element.

Note that level 2 is often used as the basis for work on level 3 – both by the person whose work generated the particular level 2 meaning, and by other people.

- *Level 3*: Those parts of what the social scientist is actually doing that can be defined or schematised in logical terms.

  Unlike level 1, which takes the form of a *statement*; or level 2, which takes the form of a *belief*, the 'technical' or 'logical' level of meaning is a set of *operations*; it is the level on which inputs (statements, axioms, beliefs, etc.) are operated on by the methods of logic (or whatever other methods are used) to produce an output different from whatever the author took as the inputs to his/her work.[16]

DISCUSSION OF LEVEL 2, 'THE EFFECTIVE LEVEL OF DISCOURSE'   If there is any subtlety in the foregoing model which might make it hard for the reader to translate the proposed levels of meaning into terms which s/he is accustomed to using, it is in level 2. Another way of describing this level of meaning is to point out that it is *what is taken as the basis for action or for further understanding* (hence the name 'effective level'). I will elaborate a little further.

It is in unfriendly criticism that one is most likely to encounter attention to the 'effective level' of discourse. In Chapter 13 I will use Marshall's contemporary, Joseph Nicholson, as an example of such an unfriendly critic. He brought attention to level 2 of Marshall's work for reasons which may be explained as follows.

A reading of almost any part of Marshall's work would lead most readers (Nicholson included) to believe that Marshall had a broad concern with all classes of people, and especially with the poorer members of society; that Marshall took needs (especially in the context of poverty) to be at least as important as wants; and that he believed that an understanding of motivations (including needs, wants, values and satisfactions) are at the heart of economic inquiry. Nicholson stressed that, by contrast to this expectation, Marshall's most rigorous logic does *not* deal with needs, motivations, values, or even with satisfactions; it only deals with wants, and with them only as they are 'effectively' expressed in market power. Blaug, similarly, expressed his astonishment that Marshall's logic would retreat to the narrow range of events which can be assumed to 'affect in about equal proportions all the different classes of society'.

The reason to be surprised or disappointed in this aspect of Marshall's logic is that one had expected something different: the 'real' (level 3) meaning disappoints us as compared to what we had taken to be the 'apparent' meaning. But here, I claim, our disappointment derives from an expectation stemming from the apparent meaning *as it is found on level 2* – an expectation which we infer from the general tone of Marshall's writing, rather than from formal, explicit statements. By contrast, if we had derived our expectations exclusively from level 1 – Marshall's overt claims or formal statements – we would find that most of the time (especially if we ignore the early writings) his statements are quite consistent with the narrow working out of his logic. This was the consistency which Edgeworth emphasised (also discussed in Chapter 13, below), referring to statements of Marshall's which had, after all, promised no more than the use of prices as indicators of relative well-being within a very narrow range of circumstances.

My own interpretation of the general tone (level 2) of Marshall's writing is that it suggests that his hopes for the use of prices in economic studies were broader than this. But how have I identified the effective level of Marshall's discourse? It is worth taking a look here, using myself as an example, at an individual's interaction with the text, out of which level 2 is created.

I have said that, in speaking of a generalised level 2 meaning of a text, I am referring to the cluster of interpretations which I assume are most commonly made. Sometimes I make such an assumption on the basis of a good deal of evidence; at other times it represents a guess about how people in general are likely to react. That guess is conditioned in part from my own lifetime experience which has generated a set of expectations about typical human reactions to each given situation; these expectations are, of course, modified by my own reaction to the particular experience, with an attempt to correct for whatever of my own responses experience has told me are not 'typical'.

In identifying the effective level of Marshall's discourse, then, first of all I took into account my own reactions. Specifically, by the end of my first reading of *Principles of Economics* I found myself in a state of cognitive dissonance; on the one hand I had been convinced (mostly by the general tone – level 2 – but also by some overt statements on level 1) that prices could be used as the windows onto a tremendous amount of knowledge about human motivations and satisfactions. On the other hand, I seemed to be missing some critical pieces of the logical operation which could thus connect prices with the said human motivations and satisfactions. I reread the book, and found that I had missed that operation because it did not exist.

The general sense of the whole book (level 2) seemed to support the belief that the prime subject of Marshall's economics is *values*, in the sense of 'what matters to human beings', and that he had succeeded in dealing with this subject objectively, quantitatively and 'scientifically'. At the same time, there were a number of clear statements (on level 1) disclaiming such a wide ambition. And the ambition was not fulfilled on the operational level (level 3).

My own sense of having been led to expect something which, upon closer analysis, proved to be elusive on level 3 and was frequently disclaimed (though sometimes, contradictorily, claimed) on level 1, made me look for a similar disappointment in other readers. I have commented on my findings with respect to Nicholson, Pigou and Blaug. I would be willing to argue (but it would require a long discussion) that a similar sense of disappointment was among the motivations for Maloney's book, *Marshall, Orthodoxy and the Professionalisation of Economics*. More important, but virtually impossible to prove, is my hypothesis that the economics profession at large has adopted Marshall's level 2 hopes into its institutional belief structure.

THE IMPLICATIONS OF LEVEL 2 IN MARSHALL'S WORK FOR THE SUBSEQUENT DEVELOPMENT OF ECONOMICS The hypothesis just cited grows out of the following observations and reasoning (which will be expanded in Part III): Marshall's programme was to establish a consistent relation between the intangible subject of human welfare and the tangible measure of money, or price. He himself may have been seduced into this attempt by the fact that, in common parlance there is one word – *value* – which can be used to refer to both sides of the desired relation. Marshall was careful to restrict his own *formal* use of the word to its 'exchange value' side, saying more than once that he would not employ it in the sense of 'use value'. However, in talking of the 'real worth' or the 'real cost' of things he was, in effect, using 'value' as the pivot on which he could turn to either of the desired directions.

The result of using a word which had different meanings on levels 1 and 2 was confusion on the logical level, where Marshall, often without announcing (or, probably, recognising) that he was doing so, would operate on one meaning, and then switch midstream to use of the other. Thus, as I will attempt to show, Marshall built some of his economic operations upon a much broader level 2 meaning of 'value', *in spite of* its conflicts with his more restricted level 1 statements.

Moreover (this is the largest logical leap, to be critically examined by others), I contend that his level 2 meanings were sufficiently widely taken into the field generally (first by economists who read Marshall's work, then by others who were taught or influenced by those who had read his work), so that the beliefs and expectations generated therein continue to be perpetuated even today. Economic writings and discussions continue to be based upon scientific-sounding references to a variety of 'values' broader than those simply communicated through prices.

I will claim, further, that neoclassical economics is designed to deal with – and is received, on level 2, as though it can and does deal with – questions about how humans actually act on the basis of what they perceive as their wants. However, the theory is formally limited to consideration of effective demand – a much more limited concept than 'what humans perceive as their wants'.

As I go on, later, to discuss economic writings which seem to me to build upon level 2 in Marshall's writing, I will assume that there is, at any given time, a general sense of what economics is about, what it can and should attempt, and what it has already achieved; I do not pretend that all of that general sense of the field derives from readings of Marshall, but I will try to trace threads in that general sense for which Marshall's writing forms a credible source. Note that it would be possible to compile a set of statements from published economic texts which would support the above cited level 2 perception of what economics can and does provide; and another list of statements in the literature which would show full awareness of the logical limitations of the field. We would then be in the situation of having two sets of level 1 statements, the first set proposing to do something more ambitious than what turns out to be possible on level 3; the second set recognising the limitations of the logical level. What are we to make of that?

We might simply say that those economists who maintain level 1 statements more ambitious than what can be supported by the most sophisticated and subtle level 3 logic are bad economists, and should not be considered in our discussions. Such a conclusion would not necessarily be in accordance with the status ordering of the field at any given time; it sounds like a good idea, but under the current sociological structure of the field it cannot be enforced so as to protect the unwary from such 'bad economics'.

More useful may be the adoption of practices which would legitimise the perceptions of even those who are not the most economically sophisticated, when they find that the pictures drawn by economics are not just simplifications from, but are distortions of, the real world. Recognition of the author's responsibility for the level 2 meanings contained in his/her text may prove to be an effective way to provide such legitimation. This may be an alarming or even a distasteful idea: who wants to be held responsible for flawed interpretations or misuse of his/her work? I quail at the thought, myself, as I imagine the fuzzy thinkers who might latch onto my abjuration of the kinds of 'rigour' called for in mainstream economics, using this as justification for a sentimentalist approach with which I would not be in sympathy.

All the same, given the quantity of material now being written in all the social sciences, it is not only possible but necessary to impose higher standards than ever before for what shall be culled out as the 'best' work. Those standards can and should include a requirement for writing to be as clear and direct as possible, so as to reduce the possibilities for misunderstanding and misuse. The *natural* ability to express oneself lucidly has always been valued. To this can be added a *learned* ability to recognise different levels of meaning in what one is writing, as well as in what one reads and hears, so as to avoid sending out unintended messages.[17] Here again, what is being proposed has to do with how the discipline is taught as well as with its content.

DISCUSSION OF LEVEL 3 Contemporary analysis of economic texts is most likely to be carried out with regard to their level 3 meanings. This is often done as if it is, in fact, the only level of meaning.

To see the use made of logical implications in ordinary analysis of economic texts, we might look at any of the commentaries on Marshall that will be described in Chapter 16, below (e.g., by M. Friedman, L. E. Fouraker, D. A. Walker, E. B. Wilson, J. M. Bailey, etc.), where there are many attempts to disclose 'what Marshall is actually doing' (on level 3). The process of 'following through logical implications' has led me along a path closely parallel to that marked out by the commentators whom I will examine in Chapters 16 and 17. There I will discuss this process in sufficient detail so that I will not describe it further here, but will merely summarise two of its principal elements.

One is the procedure of *pointing up areas of incompleteness, with their implications*. Again, Chapter 16 will exemplify this technique of textual analysis; here I will simply suggest as examples some criticisms of Marshall's statements about demand, which were incomplete in specificity of definition and in mathematical analysis. For instance, he failed to specify what, exactly, he meant by 'constant marginal utility of money'; what, exactly, he intended to hold constant at any given time; when he did and did not intend to restrict his analysis to commodities relatively unimportant within total expenditure; etc.

The other most striking element of level 3 analysis is the technique of *revealing contradictions: internal, external, and methodological*. Modern neoclassical economists are most apt to stress internal inconsistencies; this kind of analysis is what is most thoroughly exemplified in Chapter 16. There I will also look at the charge that some of Marshall's procedures and assumptions are inconsistent with the realities which he claimed to be studying. These might be described as *external inconsistencies*, since they refer to a contradiction between, on the one hand, some element within the Marshallian system and, on the other, that reality onto which the system was intended to be mapped.

We will also see (it will be Pigou who points it out) that there is a *methodological inconsistency* in Marshall's apparent fall-back upon assuming a direct measure of utility as a foundation of the system by which he hoped to be able to deduce measurements of utility.

INTERNAL AND   In Chapter 16 I will take up a question which has
EXTERNAL   puzzled Marshall's commentators: namely, how could
CONSISTENCY   he have continued employing a particular group of
assumptions which were mututally contradictory? I will suggest there that Marshall may have been less concerned with the model's internal consistency than he was that each of its elements be brought, as well as possible, into consistency with the known world. The following is my summary of the trade-off we confront between internal and external consistency:

Our knowledge is imperfect. Imagine that element A' of our model is a simplified reflection of our best understanding of some aspect, *A*, of the real world, and similarly for B', C', and so on in relation to elements *B*, *C*, etc., in the real world. Imagine, also, that we have particular difficulty in perceiving, say, the reality, *C*; then the result may be inconsistency between A', B' and C" (so designated to indicate that its difference from C is greater than permissible).

What is the right solution to such a situation as this? Obviously, the *best* solution would be to identify the source of error, and correct it. But the problem is that our knowledge is imperfect, and we probably do not know which modelled element – A', B', or C" – is the one containing the most serious divergence from the real A, B, and C. In such a situation of ignorance, if we begin to fiddle with these elements so as to bring them into consistency *with one another*, we are more likely to end up with some form of A", B", C" than with our desired A', B', C': there are more ways of guessing wrong than of guessing correctly.[18]

Marshall rejected what many commentators would have liked to impose as a requirement, namely that he carry his models through to their logical conclusions (which would have alerted him to their *internal* inconsistencies). His method was, instead, to pay more attention to the relationships between what I have schematised as A' and A, B' and B, C' and C, etc. than to what he saw as secondary relationships, between A', B', C', etc. In other words, as compared to the more 'rigorous' economists of today, he often gave greater emphasis to 'external' versus 'internal' consistency.

To summarise what is implicit in these distinctions: if a model contains some elements which are, in some way, 'wrong' (e.g. they simplify from experience in ways that produce undesirable distortions in understanding and/or prediction), then internal consistency is not necessarily a virtue, and may be a disadvantage. Economics may have taken on the ambition of being internally consistent when it was yet too young to make a virtue of this quality; as the standard theory exists today, it contains a great number of effectively 'wrong' elements which are simply compounded in the rigorous consistency of its logic. This suggestion will not be employed as a blanket approval for all of Marshall's inconsistencies, but rather as a reminder of the too-rarely mentioned possibility that internal inconsistency may sometimes emerge as an alternative to something worse.

Anyone who employs this argument to justify an internal inconsistency in his/her own logic must, of course, be making an open admission along the lines of: 'Evidently some piece of what I am putting forth is a particularly poor description of the world; at this stage I don't know how to find or correct that external inconsistency, so the internal inconsistency remains as a reminder of the flaw in my mapping from reality.' There are many places in the economic literature that already exists where such an admission would be appropriate, and healthy. Some changes in the social structure of the field will be necessary, however, before they could be made with confidence that they would be evaluated appropriately.

I am not proposing that Marshall himself consciously thought through a defence of internal inconsistency such as I have suggested here; I put it forward to explain the emphasis I will choose later, in Part III, when I examine Marshall's demand theory and what it has led to. Given Marshall's strong desire to be 'scientific', instances of sustained internal inconsistency in his work raise very interesting questions, e.g.: Why did he accept this – instead of what alternative? What may his successors have lost, in the process of resolving what appeared as internal contradictions in Marshall's work?

The attention which I will give to the analytical problems in this area of Marshall's work will not emphasise the internal inconsistencies in themselves, but will regard them, rather, as important among several kinds of indicators which point to the deeper problem which can be summarised by saying that Marshall was trying to do something which was impossible – and which, I will later suggest, he intuitively suspected to be impossible.

Marshall in fact attempted to continue to walk upon two paths, one increasingly dependent upon quantitative methods, the other including the richness of the political economy tradition of Adam Smith. However, it is not clear that this is still possible, at least not in the way that Marshall did it. The neoclassical path has proceeded a very long way from the fork where the two paths diverged. Were it to try to reintroduce the ambiguity of Marshallian language it might lose too much of the very real progress which it has made.

It is for this reason that I have thought in terms of developing an alternative path, of social economics. We have an option, in charting out a course which Marshall only began, but did not carry as far as I would like to go: now is the time to explore whether social economics must continue in a straight line away from the other path, or whether it may bend close enough to the neoclassical path to be able to borrow some of its tools.

For the neoclassical path to borrow much from social economics may be impossible; neoclassical economics starts from a context which is committed to the exclusion of ambiguity. But if the social economics path includes some recognition and acceptance of ambiguity in its very foundations, it will have the freedom to borrow tools developed in the exclusive context of neoclassical economics. Some of these tools will be considered in the next two chapters, as we continue to consider the uses of 'judgment' as a companion/alternative to the neoclassical (and, increasingly, the Marxian) emphasis on technique.

Notes

1. (Basil Blackwell, Oxford, 1986) ed. by R. Flood and M. Lockwood. I am indebted to Dan Dennet for bringing this book to my attention.
2. Donald N. McCloskey, *The Rhetoric of Economics* (University of Wisconsin Press, Madison, 1985).
3. In all of this it may be that the field of economics resembles that of mathematics more closely than economists realise, in different ways than they would wish. A delightfully funny, and all-too-true, portrait of 'The Ideal Mathematician' is drawn in the book, *The Mathematical Experience*:

    > His writing follows an unbreakable convention: to conceal any sign that the author or the intended reader is a human being. It gives the impression that, from the stated definitions, the desired results follow infallibly by a purely mechanical procedure. In fact, no computing machine has ever been built that could accept his definitions as inputs. To read his proofs, one must be privy to a whole subculture of motivations, standard arguments and examples, habits of thought and agreed-upon modes of reasoning (Davis and Hersh, 1981, pp. 36–7).

    The authors of the book then imagine a conversation between The Ideal Mathematician and a student, who asks, 'Sir, what is a mathematical proof?' The Mathematician answers:

    > what you do is, you write down the axioms of your theory in a formal language with a given list of symbols or alphabet. Then you write down the hypothesis of your theorem in the same symbolism. Then you show that you can transform the hypothesis step by step, using the rules of logic, till you get the conclusions. That's a proof.
    > Student: Really? That's amazing! I've taken elementary and advanced calculus, basic algebra, and topology, and I've never seen that done.
    > I.M.: Oh, of course no one ever really *does* it. It would take forever. You just show you could do it, that's sufficient . . . .
    > Student: Then really what *is* a proof?
    > I.M.: Well, it's an argument that convinces someone who knows the subject. (ibid., pp. 39–40.)

4. See, e.g., *Principles*, pp. 637–8 and 644: quoted in Chapter 10, below, and 7, above.

5. There are, obviously, many discussions on this subject. One I particularly like is in Chapter 2, 'Theory, Formal Model and Reality' of Jànos Kornai, *Anti-Equilibrium* (North-Holland Publishing Company, Amsterdam, 1971) see esp. p. 16.

6. This asserts that there is an incompatibility between measurement of position (e.g., of electrons) and measurement of momentum: you can know either separately, but both together are immeasurable. Indeed, it seems that an electron is not simultaneously characterised by both momentum and position; when one characteristic is observed, not only is the other then unobservable – the other characteristic then does not exist. Hence the ordinary understanding of the Heisenberg uncertainty principle, that it refers to the way that observation affects the fundamental characteristics of the thing observed.

7. Uskali Mäki, 'How to Combine Rhetoric and Realism'; *Economics and Philosophy*, 4, 1988, p. 96.

   While Mäki has used McCloskey's work (and, to a lesser extent, that of Arjo Klamer) as a most useful foundation for further development of these subjects, he also makes an important criticism:

   > There seems to be an interesting incongruence or tension between how Klamer and McCloskey see the nature and tasks of economics on the one hand and the metatheory of economics on the other. They seem to be (implicitly) committed to the following normative statement: Whereas it is not and should not be the goal of economists to strive for truth about the economy, it should be the goal of metatheorists to pursue truth about economics (ibid., p. 97).

   What he points out is that, in emphasising the role of rhetoric (the art of persuasion) in economics, McCloskey and Klamer have adopted an anti-realism, excessively relativistic stance – even while, as metatheorists (individuals who theorise about theory) they implicitly hold themselves to a standard of 'truth realism'. Like Mäki, I believe that it is the 'metatheoretical' stance of the proponents of recognising rhetoric in economics which, in accepting 'truth realism' even without certainty, represents the best side of the 'rhetorical' strand in modern economic thought.

8. A third possibility is *faith*, which holds that there is some underlying truth 'more true than reality' such that real facts are not required to prove that which is held by faith; the most absolute faith may not even be shaken by contradictory 'evidence' from the real world.

   A fourth possibility, *delusion*, is defined similarly to faith, except that a delusion is a belief-held-in-the-face-of-evidence, which belief (unlike the belief of 'faith') is *not* supported by the surrounding society.

9. See Chapter 10, below.

   A famous (though quite inconclusive) discussion of these issues is to be found in the notes by Ludwig Wittgenstein which were printed as a book called *On Certainty*, ed. by G. E. M. Anscombe and G. H. von Wright (Harper & Row, New York, 1972). Especially interesting for our consideration is Wittgenstein's connection of a state of mind (whether it be called *belief* or *knowledge*), which results from confrontation with 'facts' or 'evidence', with something like trust, regarding *which* evidence, *which* facts to accept: knowledge, Wittgenstein says, 'is related to a decision (p. 47e).

A way of preserving the term, *knowledge*, but toning it down to accord with what I have called *belief*, is presented by J. R. Lucas (in Flood and Lockwood (eds) 1986, p. 126), who says: 'Knowledge is . . . subject to a retrospective withdrawal proviso. So long as the prediction works out, you really did know all along: but if the prediction proves false in the event, then the knowledge claim has to be withdrawn, and you never really knew what you thought you did.' Cf. again Wittgenstein (in Anscombe and Wright (eds) 1972, p. 3e): '"I know" seems to describe a state of affairs which guarantees what is known, guarantees it as a fact. One always forgets the expression "I thought I knew".'

10. What is described below is logically just as relevant – and appears to be at least as acceptable – to the physical as it is to the social sciences.

11. For those who still seek to see all behavior explained by a single, rational motive, a modern approach is described by Etzioni:

> A thesis shared by several members of the Public Choice school and several other neoclassical economists is that individuals will lie, cheat, and violate other moral precepts and laws whenever they expect they can get away with it or when the penalty will be smaller than the gain. Williamson argues that rational actors who pursue self-interest are expected to act opportunistically, which often entails acting immorally. For example, those who are skilled at dissembling realize transactional advantages. Economic man, assessed with respect to his transactional characteristics, is thus a more subtle and devious creature than the usual self-interest seeking assumption reveals (1975, p. 255). (Etzioni, 1988, p. 58.)

12. For a similar approach, see the Introduction to the paperback edition of *James and John Stuart Mill; Father and Son in the Nineteenth Century*, by Bruce Mazlish (Transaction Press, New Jersey, 1988). This work is an excellent example of an historian's broad application of the insights of psychoanalysis to a range of other social sciences.

13. Cf. the 'externalist' tradition, associated with the names of J. D. Bernal (e.g., *The Social Function of Science* (Routledge, London, 1939) and of Boris Hessen, whose 1931 paper, 'The Social and Economic Roots of Newton's Principia' (printed in *Science at the Crossroads* (Frank Cass, London, 2nd edn, 1971)) presented at the Second International Congress of the History of Science in 1931, attempted to 'recontextualise' science: to recognise, that is, that even in the 'hardest' sciences there is room for interpretation, which is affected by the social and economic context of the human scientist. (Hessen may be read as distinguishing between a core of 'hard fact' which is not affected by the social context; and all the deductions, applications, etc., therefrom, which are.) A recent paper by Loren R. Graham, 'The Socio-political Roots of Boris Hessen' (in *Social Studies of Science* (Sage, London, Beverly Hills and New Delhi) vol. 15,

1985), has done for Hessen – treating the latter in his role as social scientist – what Hessen did for Newton, as a physical scientist.

14. By 'the world', as referred to in the description of level 2, I mean either the world of policy-makers and citizens who regard economists as experts; or the rest of the economics profession, which is often only too eager to proceed as if some knotty problem had been resolved. A good example of the latter, to which my attention was drawn by Pankaj Tanden, was the response to the publication of Robert Willig's 'Consumer's Surplus Without Apology' (*AER*, September 1976). Errors in emphasis, definition and analysis have been pointed out which throw significant doubt upon Willig's claim that 'observed consumer's surplus can be rigorously utilized to estimate the . . . correct theoretical measures of the welfare impact of changes in prices and income on an individual' (p. 589). However, in numerous subsequent references to this article, which implied or stated that the measurement of consumer's surplus was no longer a problem, the profession exhibited a credulity which is best explained as prompted by the desire to believe that there are rigorously adequate quantifiable proxies for the important unquantifiable variables in welfare economics. (Willig's article will be discussed in some detail in Chapter 17 of this book.)

15. I do not attempt to deal, here, with the area of manipulative or propagandistic communication wherein the communicator *knowingly* puts out covert messages that may be at variance with his/her level 1 statements or level 3 logic, but which are intended to sway the audience through emotional or other non-cognitive means.

16. A fourth level could be added to the above: (level 4) the effect the social scientist ultimately wishes to have, i.e. what s/he would most like to achieve through the work being examined, as the ramifications and consequences of that work unroll in the world. What Alfred Marshall, for example, wanted as the ultimate effect of his work was a world of greater economic prosperity of a type which would contribute to the 'progressive' development of the human spirit. However, this goal may perhaps be better kept separate from the categorisation of *meanings*; it does spill over into meaning, but is most directly understood as *goals*. It has already been discussed under that heading, in Chapter 2; for a further development, it will have to await *Social Economics*, volume 2.

17. An alternative possibility is that a social scientist may choose to bring the intended operations on level 3, and the formal statements of level 1, into accord with the messages sent out on level 2, once s/he has recognised what those messages are.

18. This point is not unique to the social sciences; an example of recognition of the same problem in the natural sciences is ascribed to Francis Crick, who said that 'a good model is one that does *not* account for all the data, . . . for some of the data are bound to be wrong.' (George Johnson, 'Two Sides to Every Science Story', a review of *What Mad Pursuit* by Francis Crick, in *The New York Times Book Review*, 9 April 1989, p. 41.)

9 Assumptions, Success and Responsibility: Examples of the Uses of Judgment

Reference has been made to the use of judgment as a companion and, I would suggest, as a guide, for technique. Here I will begin to lay out in some detail a few of the most critical tasks to which judgment must be directed.

Neoclassical economics, in basing itself upon a particular set of psychological assumptions, derived from a reading of Adam Smith narrowed by the Utilitarian emphasis and supposedly justified by Darwin, has accepted simplifications and abstractions which are constantly at risk of being invalidated when some of the particulars which have been lost assume a new or unexpected importance. Questions were raised in Part I regarding the long-term impacts that such assumptions may have upon a maturing system of theory. These issues will reappear in this chapter as it begins, from the critic's (or reader's) side, with the textual analysis necessary for recognising the assumptions which a writer has made, and upon which a piece of social science may be based.

LOOKING AT ASSUMPTIONS FROM THE CRITIC'S SIDE The search for the underlying assumptions in virtually any text may be endlessly interesting – and it may also be just plain endless. Certain kinds of modern theory, especially those which are designed to permit computer interaction, often claim that the beauty of their methodology is that it forces them to spell out all relevant assumptions. Such a statement depends for its truth upon how relevancy is defined. There is no algorithm for making such a definition; it must come back to common sense, or judgment.

The belief that it is *possible*, let alone a matter of practice, for people to know consciously all of the assumptions behind a particular piece of writing, is naive. It is surprising that such a belief has been so often stated in writings about economics, and has received so little challenge to its realisticness; yet one can find instances of this belief stretching back throughout the history of the field.[1]

The web of assumptions in any one person's mind is so deep, subtle, and many-layered that a complete confession of all those that bear in any way upon the subject at hand would likely be both impossible and excruciating. Given this, it is not necessarily the case (though it might be so, in some instances) that it is a criticism to state that an assumption has not been spelled out by the author. The good critic does not automatically leap upon such an omission saying, 'Aha! now I've got you!' Rather, the interesting question is: *among the set of assumptions not made plain by the author, which are the important ones to consider?* That is to say: which are the unstated assumptions whose statements would materially alter our understanding (on any level) of the text?

That is largely a matter of the critic's judgment. The deepest questions in almost any pursuit: the question, 'What matters?' and also (on the next level away from the general toward the specific) 'What is important in the given context?' – these cannot be answered by any scientific method; their answers usually come from a pre-cognitive area of our mental processes.

Several procedures may assist in getting one's attention caught by important unstated assumptions. One way is to have other assumptions in mind which serve as contrasts. The normal assumptions of everyday life are not a bad place to begin. Everyone possesses, of course, a large stock of these. Unfortunately, the training given to many economists tends to have the effect of making them deaf to the voice of common sense, so that they learn, when operating as economists, not to attend to dissonances between the everyday assumptions upon which they otherwise operate and the assumptions which they encounter in the field. One can, with a little effort, unlearn this deafness. One useful, small activity in this regard may be the cultivation of a habit, while reading economic texts, of actively seeking for places where one can pencil 'PQA' (for 'Particularly Questionable Assumption') in the margins. (Another is the marginal note, 'RM', for 'rigor mortis' – used to mark where the techniques have killed off the meaning of the questions which they were designed to answer.)

A more significant aid is to keep adding to one's familiarity with work in other social sciences, so as to have in mind, for comparison with the implicit assumptions of economics, some of the assumptions of psychology, sociology, anthropology, etc. Without becoming a professional in these other fields, one may still benefit from a different point of view which, if it does nothing else, enhances one's alertness to the restrictiveness of the assumptions in one's own system of theory.

ASSUMPTIONS
ON THE
CREATIVE SIDE
OF SOCIAL
SCIENCE
By now, more than a half century after Marshall's death, modern neoclassical economics is believed by many to have been fully axiomatised, constructed in such a manner that every chain of proof unravels back, if followed all the way, to a few axioms about human nature. The essential assumptions on this subject which have been accepted as the basic axioms of the field have not come out of the field of psychology; rather they are deductions from (not to be found explicitly in) the work of Darwin.

Modern neoclassical economics attempts to deal with human beings only through well-known and carefully stated assumptions – a procedure which has the merits of rigour, but which was carried out, perhaps, too quickly, with too little thought given to whether the assumptions employed were those that would best serve as a foundation for an entire discipline. The field has been left with only a scant handful of statements about human beings, as such: all contained in the statement that *rational individuals attempt to maximise their (perceived) utility.*[2] Explanations of the meaning of this statement come down to three jointly tautological definitions:

- maximisation of (perceived) utility is what rational people do;
- (perceived) utility is what rational people maximise; and
- rationality is the characteristic of those who maximise their (perceived) utility.

Others have attacked this system as inadequate.[3] Rather than repeat those arguments here, I will continue to chip away at the more general issues which surround the question of how we choose our assumptions, how we employ them, and how we know when it is time to move on to new ones.

RECOGNISING
THE
DEFINITION
OF SUCCESS
Of all the assumptions, and of all the normative or ideological elements, in any piece of social science, perhaps the most important to recognise is the existence of a *definition of success*. I will first explain what such a definition involves, and then go on to cite an example of the importance of its recognition.

It is helpful to begin by looking in an area where the definition of success is particularly salient. The influence on economics (as well as on other fields) of the evolutionary and, more recently, the sociobiological, models may in part be ascribed to the clarity, power and wide applicability of those models' definitions of success. They assess the relative success of individual humans and other living things according to *their ability to maintain or increase the representation of their genetic material in the gene pool of future generations.* The route to this type of success is defined as 'maximisation of inclusive fitness'; in other words, anything that maximises the future replication of the DNA of an individual *ipso facto* maximises its 'inclusive fitness'.[4]

It is important to recognise what, in the current enchantment with the power of these models, tends to get forgotten: that such a definition of success is essentially arbitrary. A large reason for its appeal, however, is that its arbitrariness *appears* so objective: this is not a definition that comes from the inner searchings or moral position of any individual, but one which sees 'the individual as a survival machine built by a short-lived confederation of long-lived genes'.[5] Yet it must be remembered that this seemingly objective statement is also the projection of Man's search for order upon the events of the world. Genes do not actually form purposive confederations, nor do they act with the intent to maximise anything. If something is, in fact, maximised, this can only be inferred, after the fact, by a mentality possessing a particular ability to generalise about causes and effects, and to enunciate laws therefrom.

However useful may be the metaphorical construction of the laws of evolution, they nevertheless have no constraining power upon actual human preferences (which are, let us recall, among the essential subjects of economics), unless some individuals choose so to be constrained. The philosopher Mary Midgley has stated this point well: 'Motives have their importance in evolution and their own evolutionary history – but they have also each their own internal point, and it is virtually never a wish to bring about some evolutionary event, such as the maximization of one's own progeny. Confusion between the aims of individuals and the "aims" of evolution – if there can be said to be such things – is ruinous.'[6]

Upon reflection, it indeed appears that many individuals have made decisions which did not maximise their inclusive fitness. One thinks, for example, of the band of Greek women who walked, singing, off a cliff to their deaths rather than be taken by Turkish soldiers – who would doubtless have given them opportunities for genetic representation in future generations. Or of the Shakers, who upheld their religious beliefs in not reproducing, so that they are now extinct, leaving behind a strange, brief trace in human history, and a few infants' skeletons under their floor-boards. These are examples of 'maladaptive' moral codes such as the sociobiologist, William Irons, referred to when stating that the idea of cultural relativism can and should be borrowed from anthropology and used as a meta-context for the conclusions of sociobiology: 'The statement that a particular form of behavior is adaptive to a particular environment is a statement about its effect on survival and reproduction and nothing more. Whether that behavior is also good – morally, esthetically, or otherwise – is a separate issue.'[7]

It must be stressed that it is a matter of choice whether the definition of 'success' that we choose in any particular context is to be more nearly allied with the achievement of something which is good ('morally, aesthetically, or otherwise'), or with adaptiveness, or with something else. In addition to the examples already given we might recognise a variety of other definitions of success, e.g.:

- that of a yuppie family which, in order to maximise a 'success' that is largely defined by personal consumption, is likely to limit its offspring, perhaps to zero;
- that of the Catholic church, which defines success in terms of the total number of souls 'saved'; hence individuals who embrace this religion line up with the sociobiological goal of maximising the number of their descendents;
- or that of a Utilitarian who is concerned with the quality as well as the quantity of human life.[8]

The possible definitions, then, can include individual goals, such as living according to a code of honour or of religious doctrine; the amassing of material goods; or the 'otherworldly' success of being accepted in Heaven. They can also include goals for society or the species, e.g., maximisation of numbers of people going to Heaven, or of the pan-human sum of 'utility' or 'satisfaction'. And we can easily imagine extensions of the list: e.g., people who will risk death or the annihilation of their offspring for the sake of ambition (Lady Macbeth), or for revenge, or in the hope of being remembered; or people who are concerned not only for the human species but for gorillas, whales and obscure fishes; for the Amazon forests; for the whole Earth's ecosystem. The emphasis upon accounting which appeared in Chapter 2 (above) was, in effect, directed towards defining and then evaluating an acceptable measure of success. The 'sustainability' ethic which was adopted there is well represented by Kenneth Boulding, who has said that

The essential measure of the success of the economy is not production and consumption at all, but the nature, extent, quality, and complexity of the total capital stock, including in this the state of the human bodies and minds included in the system . . . . Any technical change which results in the maintenance of a given total stock with a lessened throughput [that is, less production and consumption] is clearly a gain.[9]

It was because I had in mind a question about how neoclassical economics defines success that I became sensitised to the issue (to be developed in *Social Economics*, volume 2), of the 'point of view' of the field of economics. There are, as I have been stressing, very many ways in which a person could define success: why did neoclassical economics adopt the definition I have here ascribed to the yuppies (before the latter were even invented as a category)? Marshall's definition was very different, with 'consumption' being subservient to his ultimate goals of improvement of Man's spiritual and mental life, and the exercise and development of Man's 'highest faculties'. Why the divergence since his time?

One answer to that question appeared as I recognised that, as compared to the neoclassical development, Marshallian economics was based upon a *social* – rather than neoclassical economics' *individualistic* – point of view. Moreover, in contrast to both Marxian and neoclassical economics, it adopted neither a *workers'* nor a *consumers'* point of view, but attempted to embrace *both*. Here I had stumbled upon one of the rewards of keeping in mind a question about the definition of success – a definition that almost assuredly exists in the form of some assumption behind any text. Such a question will lead the recipient of the text toward a recognition of the point of view taken by its author, as well as some insight into the point of view of the field which s/he represents. More generally, the search for the definition of success is helpful in revealing the essential values – the sense of *what matters* – embedded in a social science text.

Such an understanding of a text is more readily achieved by a reader who possesses some knowledge of the context in which it was written, as well as some understanding of the viewpoint of the author. The increasingly ahistorical character of education in neoclassical economics requires us to emphasise, under the heading of methodology, contextual issues which, half a century ago, were routinely considered as part of the intellectual history which it was taken for granted would be learned by all entering the field.

NORMATIVE AND/
OR IDEOLOGICAL
ELEMENTS;
STARTING WITH
THE ASSUMPTION
THAT THEY PLAY
SOME ROLE

As was remarked with respect to assumptions in general, it is probably also impossible to lay out every normative or ideological element that has played a part in the writing of virtually anything. Nevertheless, such elements do play a critical role. A more detailed discussion of this subject will have to await the next volume of this work; here I will simply give an example of the way in which one may read between the lines to find normative assumptions or evaluations which affect the apparently positive conclusions to a piece of analysis.

An economist involved in development policy might be expected to address such a question as the following: 'Will the urban cost of living rise or fall if farmers are prevented from importing capital equipment?' This question should elicit a tracing-through of the immediate, secondary and more distant impacts of the suggested policy upon farm machinery importers, food importers and/or exporters, domestic farm machinery producers, farm owners and workers, those who sell other goods and services to the foregoing, etc. The answer, to be truly useful to a policy maker, should not only state the probable net increase or decrease in urban prices, but should decompose these into effects on food prices; on goods and services sales to rural landowners and to rural workers; on domestic farm machine manufactures; etc.

If the facts thus elicited are then used to state a bottom-line figure on whether the urban cost of living has gone up or down, *implicit evaluations have been made which assume that an aggregate cost-of-living index which subtracts one person's loss from another's gain does represent some sort of social welfare function* (one strongly tinged with classical Utilitarianism). Built into this assumption is likely to be the further assumption, allowed in by default, that *every unit of exchange is of equal value*, regardless of who pays or receives it. Thus the 'cost-of-living' concept in the initial question had, to start with, smuggled in value judgments in the making and acceptance of an aggregate price index. (Indeed, the everyday concept of a 'bottom line' does the same.)

Suppose the analyst's summary answer to the question posed above is as follows:

In the short run, as labour is substituted for imported capital equipment, there will be more rural employment, reducing the migration pressure on the cities; at the same time, domestic food production will decrease, creating political pressure for increased food imports and/or higher food prices. In the urban areas in the short run there will be less pressure on the employment capacity of the industrial sector, while in the long run, as production of domestic farm machinery is stepped up, there will be increased urban job opportunities; and thus, on average, urban incomes will rise. All of this will contribute to urban price inflation.

There is no purely logical transition between this string of facts (which are simply predictions of the consequences of an isolated act or set of acts) and any welfare conclusions which may arise from it: '*ought* cannot be deduced from *is*'. However, even putting aside the evaluation of relative importance which is concealed in the method of aggregation of the summary concept of overall price inflation (will every urban dweller be similarly affected by the 'urban price inflation'?), we need to give a little thought to the economist's decision to accept the implication of the initial question: that implication was that *a priority in assessing the proposed policy is to consider its effects upon the urban price level.*

THE SOCIAL RESPONSIBILITY OF THE SOCIAL SCIENTIST: GETTING THE QUESTIONS RIGHT   The economist is a human being whose choice of response to a question, on the basis of his/her special knowledge as an economist, always includes the alternative of asking, 'Does the question you pose actually ask what you intend to ask? Will the answer to the question which I *hear* respond to the question which you *intend*?' There exists, too, the even more 'humanistic' alternative of pointing out (if this is what the economist happens to observe): 'There is a question of higher priority (more relevant or more important from some point of view) that should be asked about this subject, before the one being posed.' Accepting this alternative, however, means accepting that the role of 'expert professional' includes a responsibility for helping those who pose questions to understand the consequences of formulating them in one way, rather than in another.[10]

One consequence of such an approach is to open seriously the issue of the social responsibility of anyone in the position of 'expert professional'. Such a role should include a responsibility for helping those who pose questions to understand the consequences of formulating them in one way, rather than in another. This is contrary to current economic thinking, which tends to ignore the process that goes on in the posing of questions; even when the theorist poses his/her own questions, s/he generally acts as if the questions had been 'given'. Such a pose, like the pretence that a social welfare function will have been 'given' before an economist gets to work on welfare problems, virtually precludes attention to important issues regarding the normative or ideological content of economic theory. The first requirement for understanding these issues is to drop the pretence that either questions or welfare functions are 'given' in some way that is completely outside the activity and the concerns of the economist.

The question which a policy-maker wants to ask of a specialist is not usually, 'if I do such and such (e.g., if I finance the Panama Canal in the following manner), and if nothing else changes, then what will the consequences be?' Instead, the policy maker will most probably want to ask something more like, 'given the following objectives and constraints, what is the total set of reasonable alternative ways of financing the Panama canal; and which of them will do the best job of meeting the weighted bundle of objectives?' If the question is one which has a significant economic component, an economist, employing his/her total package of personal resources (comprising individual 'judgment' attributes plus specialised expertise) may be able to give the most useful response to the policy maker's needs.

Some of the situations where the economist's answer may *not* be the most useful one include: (a) a situation where other expertise is more crucial than that of the economist; e.g., if the impact of the decision will depend more upon political, cultural, etc. variables than upon economic ones. (In this case, the economist should be employed as an adviser to the politician, anthropologist, sociologist, etc.; or some sort of team should be made up, of members of the relevant sciences, to come to a joint decision); or (b) a case where an economist has a deficiency in judgment which overbalances his/her expertise in economic knowledge and skills. (It is worth asking whether the kind of academic economic training currently available does not tend to produce a disproportionate number of economists with such a deficiency.)

The examples given in this section stress the difficulty of making clean distinctions between normative and positive economics. This difficulty should be kept in mind before we take for granted one of the basic tenets of scientific thinking: that there is no logical connection between a purely positive statement (or question) and a normative statement (or answer). The operative word here is *purely*; when questions or statements appear positive, but implicitly contain normative assumptions or evaluations, then answers may be logically derived therefrom which also have normative implications. In such cases the simple statement, 'you cannot derive *ought* from *is*', may just not apply. Most often 'ought' is already mixed in with 'is', in the original formulation; and it *is* possible to derive 'ought' from a mixed 'is/ought' statement.

THE ECONOMIST'S RELATION TO THOSE WHO ASK THE QUESTIONS: THE EXAMPLE OF ECONOMETRICS The for-a-while accepted primacy of prediction, within an image of 'positive' science, has driven many economists to the only honest position that seems compatible with such an ethos: the promise of delivering accurate 'if . . . then' statements. Such statements are often not, in fact, what is wanted by the people who ask the questions to which economists respond. Most clients of economics are motivated by a need to make decisions. Often the most useful economic output, from their point of view, would indeed be prediction, but of the boldest sort. When economists do venture to make predictions they normally assume that all existing policies and forces in the society will stay as they are. The really useful prediction, however, would be one that could state, 'this is what is going to happen given all of the other changes which will also take place'. That is getting into the realm of science fiction; under no significant circumstances does any actor know what all the other actors are going to do over an extended time.

The question to be looked at here is: given that economists cannot provide the kind of prediction that would be most useful, what are the next best alternatives?

Some economists have turned from *prediction* to *description*. The version of the latter currently considered most scientific is econometrics, which, in some forms, offers descriptions of 'what is', with hints that may be employed in analysing 'how it got that way'. Nevertheless, a straight dose of econometrics is, in actuality, sheer *description*, without *understanding*: the understanding has to be supplied to some extent by the users (depending upon their knowledge of how to read statistics) and to some extent by the economists, in whatever interpretation they offer. Understanding, in effect, always requires interpretation: a shipload of radios and a table of statistics may be differentiated as 'a tangible fact' versus 'a form of descriptive statement', but both require an additional infusion of meaning in order to be of any use either to a planner or to a theoretician.

'Meaning' is very different from 'fact', and 'description' is somewhere in between the two. Understanding is impossible without all three. It is possible to do social science with a much greater level of awareness and understanding than is now common, with regard to meaning, and to different levels of meanings. The process of making such awareness and understanding widespread may look reductionist, because it will call into question many claims that are now considered necessary for upholding the rigorous scientific standards to which we think we adhere. Those standards in fact not infrequently disguise a confusion between fact and meaning, knowledge and belief, proof and persuasion.

THE OUTPUTS OF ECONOMICS: A WAY OF COMPARING SOCIAL AND NEOCLASSICAL ECONOMICS Givers of advice generally steer the seekers toward the type of advice which they, the givers, have to offer. The response from economists has typically come in one of three forms:

1. a *ceteris paribus* 'if . . . then' type of prediction, based upon a model abstracting more or less appropriately from the relevant situation;
2. an econometric description of reality, in which the lessons to be drawn from that description in fact (but not avowedly) depend largely upon the *judgment* exercised in data selection and preparation, and the *meaning* attributed to the results by its interpreter; or
3. a seat-of-the pants, common-sense type of response, in which the economist draws upon his/her life experience and accumulated understanding to point out the most salient features of the situation (description and understanding) in light of the interests which s/he thinks are most importantly at stake (evaluation and goal-definition), and then offers suggestions along the lines of: 'These are the events you can influence, and the means you have to influence them; the best place for your intervention is probably the following . . .' (prediction and prescription).

The first two of the above types of advice are readily claimed and proclaimed by neoclassical economics. The third, though it is often what is actually given by people who happen to be neoclassical economists, does not really fit within the neoclassical methodological framework. (The neoclassical economist who actually gives this type of response may feel it necessary to go back and dress up his/her output in econometric or modelling terms.)

Social economics will need a legitimate way to formalise, to the appropriate extent (and not only in economic applications, but also in the teaching of the field), what was just described as the third common form of response, so as to make the best use of the life experience, judgment, intuition, etc., of the economist. This will most likely look very different from the kind of formalisation now accepted as appropriate in neoclassical economics.

One way to begin may be to reconsider our conceptualisation of the outputs of economics. The most obvious candidates for consideration are those that have just been mentioned: *understanding, description, prediction, evaluation, goal-definition* and *prescription.*

The first thing to be said is that economists always have done, and probably always will do, some of each of these. A corollary is that, given such diverse activities, diverse types of standards are probably required. Take, for example, standards with respect to 'precision': certain types of *description* can be expected to be precise; the best *predictions* may give a general, not a precise, idea of the general nature of expected change; while a *prescription* should be precise enough to be implementable, but if it is a prescription for actions that are to take place over time it generally needs to be recognised that, after the first stage, generalised guidance will increasingly become more helpful than precise directives. Similarly, it is necessary to adjust standards of, for example, 'certainty', 'responsibility', 'responsiveness to the client's needs', 'breadth of application', etc., depending upon the types of output which each piece of economic analysis is designed to produce.

If neoclassical economics continues to stress a more simplified, stylised understanding and description (e.g., emphasising the 'classical' conditions of competition, etc., that lead to a competitive equilibrium) than is chosen by social economics, this will be an important methodological distinction between the two. At the same time, social economics will have to pay a price for increasing the complexity of its descriptions; this will probably be most evident in the area of prediction, where it will have less to say about the 'theoretical' (in the sense of mathematically modelled) consequences of *ceteris paribus* changes within idealised situations. The choice may be between a system of theory which describes, and can accurately predict, events in a different world from the one in which we live; versus a system which describes, but is modest in predicting, events of our own world. At the same time, social economics could be expected to be more methodologically self-conscious about (because more accepting of) the outputs of *evaluation, goal-definition* and *prescription.*

Social economics should be able to achieve a self-conscious methodological flexibility which will be built upon the recognition that the use for which the economic output is sought – the questions which it seeks to answer – will influence how much emphasis is put upon each type of output. Thus

- *evaluation* may respond to such questions as: 'Who is hurt, who helped, to what extent, for what period of time?'
- *understanding* to: 'What are the existing conditions which are most significant in influencing the events of interest? Why and how do they produce these effects?'
- *prediction* to: 'What changes in the current flow of events may be expected? What will be the outcome in a given time if the current flow continues unaltered?'
- *goal-definition* to: 'What are the most important questions to ask here? From what point of view should they be formulated?'
- *description* to: 'What is the range of choice for action?'
- and *prescription* to: 'Out of the possible actions, which should be taken?'

THE DIVISION OF LABOUR BETWEEN SCIENCE AND COMMON SENSE   Marshall had a vision of the social sciences as a collection of disciplines which have grown up around different particular ways of viewing different particular aspects of Man's social existence, with common sense, or judgment, operating as both a unifying principle (to allow comprehension of problems which cross disciplinary lines), and also as the only basis for real-world decision making. In this picture, common sense is seen as external to the sciences, even while it is, in Marshall's view, essential to their right application and even to their ability to make accurate perceptions.

The following passage makes explicit Marshall's division of labour between science and common sense:

In some parts of the science [of economics] the province of exact reasoning extends so far, that it can go near to indicating the right solution of practical problems. But in every practical problem it is common sense that is the ultimate arbiter. It is the function of common sense alone to propose a particular aim; to collect from each department of knowledge material adapted, so far as that department can do it, to the special purpose; to combine the various materials; to assign to each its proper place and importance; and finally to decide what course is to be adopted.[11]

The scientific process, which (in the thinking behind this passage) is evidently a purely positive one, stops short before the decision or policy making process begins. Then another individual than the economist, or another part of the same individual, but speaking from Common Sense, not from Economic Authority, takes over. Science, in general, can analyse; it is left to common sense to draw, from the analysis, the conclusions which are to apply to the real world.

This is a curious procedure; a little untidy, and perhaps hard to implement; but, if it were practically possible to divide people up in this manner, it might be one of the better approaches to policy- and decision-making. The trick is to get people first to recognise for themselves, and then to admit outwardly, when they are speaking as economists, and when as possessors of common sense. The difficulty of achieving this is possibly a driving force behind the attempt to purge science of all normative elements. In the social sciences generally today there are very few who give to common sense the esteem that Marshall had afforded it; among the majority it is an idea which has fallen into disrepute.[12]

There are, indeed, many valid objections to what passes, in everyday speech, under the name of common sense. For one thing, it is not at all 'common', in that it can bring different people to different conclusions. For another, our common sense tells (most of) us that common sense is a far more serviceable faculty in some people than in others; but it is hard to imagine ways of defining this faculty so that we could agree on who has what brand of it, let alone how to develop it in those in whom it seems wanting. And yet common sense continues to play, by default, many of the roles which Marshall ascribes to it, simply because it is needed, and because nothing has been found to take its place.

This unacceptable reality creates a problem for actual economic practice. The rhetoric of economics, insofar as it maintains a claim to being strictly positive, effectively eschews a policy or decision making role. Modern positivists would say that there is something or someone external to the social scientist – the politician, the citizen as voter, or the moral philosopher (the reference in the classical writings, e.g., Smith and Mill, was to 'the statesman') – who plays the role that Marshall claimed for the common sense aspect of the social scientist. It is difficult, however, to delineate exactly the moment when analysis stops and conclusion-drawing and decision-making begin. Insofar as the economist allows his/her imagination or perception to go on beyond the exact endpoint of analysis, and gets involved in its consequences (let alone the assumption-making and goal-setting which preceded it), s/he is acting on something which goes beyond what Marshall called the economic organon, and which might be called common sense – or what I have tended to refer to as judgment.

It is a fact that, in the real world, economists are called upon to be active in every stage of policy- and decision-making processes, from that least dangerous step that Marshall countenanced, of saying 'what probably won't work'; through the ranking of various alternatives (often according to some kind of cost-benefit analysis); all the way up to stating what should be done, and even to helping the statesman to determine the ends that s/he should pursue. Given all this, it would seem desirable that economic theory itself should at least recognise these realities.

The most conservative way of doing so would to build into the teaching and the theory of economics the statement: 'This body of theory is often used to bring practitioners to the point where another capability of the human mind – common sense or judgment – takes over from economics.' A more radical approach would be to include within the theory and the teaching of economics some ideas about how an economist can make that transition, along with some guidance on using judgment/common sense to interpret and apply economic theory.

The internal division which Marshall made, within the individual economist, between the use of theory and the use of common sense, may not be altogether satisfactory; but the alternative seems to leave an even more severe gap between theory and practice.

An economics which defines itself strictly according to the narrower interpretation of the field afforded by Marshall[13] is no more than a tool, and economists who believe in this definition, and are true to it, are also only tools to be used by whoever possesses the qualities which would permit him/her to draw conclusions from economic analysis. But if common sense ceases to be highly regarded, and if nothing else takes its place, then there is no basis upon which anyone can claim authority for using economics in the real world. There is then no link between theory and application.

Many of the most humane economists of this century (those whom I would want to claim as 'social economists') have stressed the necessity for observing the distinction between the endpoint of analysis and the moral judgments we might make on its practical application. What I would now like to add to several decades of concern over this distinction is the recognition that it is unrealistic to assume that social science analysts generally can or will stop short of knowing or caring about the consequences of their analysis. The social sciences, more than any other area of human endeavor, require a set of guidelines *both* for guarding against the worst pitfalls of, *and* for making the best use of, *the reality that intentions or hopes as to consequences precede, and to some extent determine, most social science analysis.*

When this fact is accepted it becomes evident that we cannot cordon off of the operations of common sense/judgment from those of mathematical modelling, econometrics and other techniques; these two contributions to analysis have to be employed together and conjoined within any individual who wishes usefully to apply economics to issues in the real world. With this recognition we return – but we will not pursue this further here – to a subject of Chapter 2 (Section IIIB): how to design educational curricula so that they contribute to the development of judgment as well as of techniques.

Notes

1. Marshall's position, for example, may be exemplified by two passages in *Principles*. The wording employed in the Mathematical Appendix – 'each particular difficulty, each source of possible error, is pushed into prominence by the definiteness of our phrases' (*Principles*, p. 700) is somewhat more conservative, and therefore more accurate, than another, more absolute claim that 'people . . . insist on knowing what is, and what is not intended to be assumed' (*Principles*, p. 71).

2. The rational expectations school would not think it relevant to include the word 'perceived', since they find it convenient to proceed as if it were the case that there is no difference between perception and reality. Others might cite a relativist philosophy which states that we have nothing to go on *but* perception, hence 'perceived' might as well be omitted here; it is to be taken for granted everywhere.

    It is critical for others (those who believe that there is a conceptual difference between perception and what we call 'reality' – even if we can only infer reality *via* perception – and who believe that this difference is an important one, with real-world consequences of which the economist must take account) to include the word 'perceived' in this definition.

3. For an especially good critique of the tautological nature of this utility definition, and of the neoclassical efforts to escape pure tautology, see Etzioni, 1988.

    The 'selfishness' implications of the 'rationality assumption' will receive a little more attention in Chapter 11, below.

4. There is less agreement in evolutionary biology upon how the success of a *species* should be defined. Recent suggestions have included definitions of a species's success in terms of absolute growth of biomass: of relative share of Earth's biomass; of relative activity in the absorbtion and/or processing of Earth's resources; or in terms of numbers of individuals. Older suggestions, more obviously designed to make Homo sapiens, by definition, the most successful of all, have stressed such qualitative measures as 'complexity' or 'differentiation of functions'.

   This question in any case no longer receives much attention, as the emphasis in most branches of evolutionary biology falls increasingly upon individual, rather than species, survival and 'success'.

5. Richard Dawkins, *The Selfish Gene* (Oxford University Press, 1976) p. 46.

6. Mary Midgley, *Beast and Man: The Roots of Human Nature* (Cornell University Press, New York, 1979) p. 142.

7. William Irons, 'Behavioral Biology and Anthropology', in *Evolutionary Biology and Human Social Behavior*, ed. by Napoleon A. Chagnon and William Irons (Duxbury Press, North Scituate, Mass., 1979) p. 38.

8. Some interesting issues in this area are raised by an essay of Wilfred Beckerman, in which he poses the questions: Should individuals choose to continue their own lives? Or to make sacrifices which will promote the continued existence of the human species? Beckerman explicitly contrasts economic rationality – emphasising, he says, the *welfare* of human populations – with evolutionary rationality, where each individual's success is contingent upon maximising the numbers of its own descendents. (Wilfred Beckerman, 'Human Resources: Are they Worth Preserving?' in Paul Streeten and Harry Maier (eds) *Human Resources, Employment and Development*, (Macmillan, 1983).)

9. Kenneth Boulding, 'Economics as a Moral Science', *American Economic Review*, 59(1), 1969, pp. 9–10.

10. I witnessed a concrete example of this alternative when Buckminster Fuller was asked by a New York City planner, 'How can we accommodate the projected growth in number of automobiles in New York City?' Fuller's answer was, 'You should be asking, instead, how to reduce the number of automobiles that are in the city', and he gave several good environmental, economic and psychological reasons why, even if they could be accommodated, more automobiles were not the best solution to the city's needs. This response, it should be noted, fell on deaf ears: the questioner was a traffic designer whose understanding of his job was that he was to take the probable consumer choices on transportation as given and to adjust accordingly.

11. *Principles*, 1st edn, pps 88-9; abbreviated in the 2nd edn and deleted in the 3rd edn; quoted in *Var*. II, pp. 157–8; italics added. For a passage on this subject which was retained through the final edition of *Principles*, see quotation 4 in Chapter 6. Compare also: 'The only resources we have for dealing with social problems as a whole lie in the judgement of common sense' (A. Marshall, 'The Present Position of Economics' (1885), in *Memorials*).

12. Among philosophers of science when the idea of common sense is used formally it seems to be limited to knowledge of that which is most superficially evident to the senses.

13. Cf.:

> Sometimes indeed the economist may give a practical decision as it were
> with the authority of his science, but such a decision is almost always
> merely negative or critical. It is to the effect that a proposed plan will
> not produce its desired result; just as an engineer might say with
> authority that a certain kind of canal lock is unsuitable for its purpose.
> But an economist as such cannot say which is the best course to pursue,
> any more than an engineer as such can decide which is the best route for
> the Panama canal.
>
> It is true that an economist, like any other citizen, may give his own
> judgement as to the best solution of various practical problems, just as
> an engineer may give his opinion as to the right method of financing the
> Panama canal. But in such cases the counsel bears only the authority of
> the individual who gives it: he does not speak with the voice of his
> science. And the economist has to be specially careful to make this
> clear; because there is much misunderstanding as to the scope of his
> science, and undue claims to authority on practical matters have often
> been put forward on its behalf (A. Marshall, 'The Present Position of
> Economics' (1885) in *Memorials*, pp. 163–5).

10 The Micro Foundations for Textual Analysis

I have spoken of the sciences as attempts to map onto some 'communication' a scientist's perceptions, observations, or beliefs regarding the nature of the real world. (As mentioned previously, the 'communication' considered here may also include what goes on inside the mind of a scientist, even in solitude, as s/he tries to order observation into understanding.) In the case of the natural, or physical, sciences, it is the physical nature of the world that is of concern; in the case of the social sciences, the subject is the behaviour of human beings, usually in the context of human societies.

Behind all of the issues to be considered here is a concern with the way the sciences reflect reality. This concern emerged in Chapter 8 as we looked at the way that the meaning intended by the 'creator' of a text is transferred to its 'recipient'; and in the question of what kind of belief, or knowledge, the social scientist (or, indeed, anyone) accords to the claims of science. In this chapter the concern with the way the sciences reflect reality will be reflected in some discussions of the process of abstraction whereby human minds (and sensory functions feeding into the mind) process information about the world, and of the tension between empirical and theoretical attitudes. The chapter which follows will then continue with a discussion of some dangers that beset a theory when certain kinds of unreality are imported into it. The last-mentioned subject has special significance for the study of economics, because it goes against several decades of theoretical work that has been carried out on the claim that only the output of economics was important; the realisticness of the input did not have to be examined.

Returning to the carriers for the mapping from 'real world' to 'communication': words, models, and theories are what most obviously serve as such carriers. This chapter will begin with a consideration of these carriers as the essential building blocks for the communication which occurs between the creator and the recipient of a text. It is worth taking a little time to look at how words and symbols get attached to the things and ideas which they are intended to represent. They are not, in some simple way, directly engendered out of these things and ideas, but are associated with them by a connecting chain composed of several links.

THE CHAIN OF CONNECTIONS FROM THING OR IDEA TO WORD OR SYMBOL Figure 10.1 attempts to schematise, if crudely, some of the links in the chain that was just described. This figure depicts only a small piece of the full process on which we depend for virtually every interaction with the world. Note that steps (c) and (d) represent a part of the process of translating from world to thought (or 'fact') which is largely biological, but which is as necessary as any intellectual part of the process. Much is required on the biological level alone to interpret the distinct impulses of the relevant neural receptors so that they present to the mind a concrete, integrated image such as 'a tree'; this complex process is symbolised, in (d), by the action involved in turning the 'upside-down' picture created by the lens in the human eye, at one point in the process, into a 'right-side-up' image whose 'top' and 'bottom' will correspond with where we feel those parts to be when we put out our hands to confirm with our sense of touch the messages from our visual receptors.

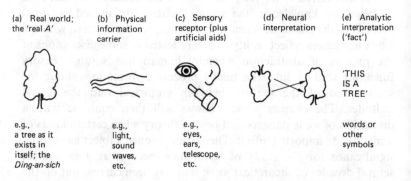

Figure 10.1 Part of the process of abstraction from world to word; the initial perceptual process

The raw data of the world is translated into 'facts' only with the assistance of experience, generalisations from experience, and something akin to theory. A certain level of sophistication is required (one which is, evidently, found in many other living species besides Man) to recognise that oaks and pines and dogwoods all belong to the same category, 'tree'. As our categories become more complex and meaning-oriented – 'hardwood tree', 'commercially useful hardwood', 'unhealthy specimen of a commercially useful hardwood' ('meaning' includes, but is not limited to, use) – it becomes clearer yet that, even just to put our observations of the world into words, theory is essential.

The purpose of indicating the extent of what is involved is to drive home the fact that words are often not just the *building-blocks* of theories, but are also the *results* of theories. The process shown in Figure 10.1 already takes a huge jump into abstraction – depending upon what could be thought of as 'previously held theories' – between steps (d) and (e). Yet the analytic interpretation – step (e) of Figure 10.1 – occurs, most of the time, on the unconscious or reflex level.

One definition of a theory is **a system of generalisations and abstractions employed to make sense of and connect together in the mind the raw details of the world as they are received by our senses and presented to the intellect by (largely unconscious) analytic interpretation**. I will return, later in this chapter, to consider a little more fully what 'theory' must mean as contrasted with 'empiricism'. First, however, it will be useful to look more closely at some of the things we do as we create and employ the words and symbols which are both the building blocks of theory and, very often, the frame for our empirical observations.

LOOKING CAREFULLY AT DEFINITIONS In the parts of this book where there is textual analysis of the work of Alfred Marshall or of other economists, considerable attention is paid to definitions of certain words which have been used as though their meaning was straightforward when it turns out, upon close examination, that they are being used differently by different writers, or in different contexts. Such close attention makes any science a more effective tool; it is especially needed in the social sciences whose vocabulary is more dependent upon everyday speech, with all its richness and ambiguity. The upshot of such close attention need not be a departure from common speech (that way jargon lies), but it may lead to using ordinary language with heightened care and consciousness.

'Value' is an important example, in economics, of such a dangerously multi-meaning word. Another situation where words have a special economic meaning, different from the common one, is exemplified by 'desire' or 'demand'. When employed by economists these words often (though not always) imply *effective* desire or demand, i.e., that which can be backed up by purchasing power. As with 'value', these words can be pivots upon which the level 3 operations can swing to employ *either* the formal economic meaning (likely to be claimed on level 1), *or* the everyday meaning (which may help create the 'general tone' of level 2).

Similarly, in Part III, I will comment on the importance of the placing of the apostrophe in 'consumer's (versus consumers') surplus'. Depending upon where it is placed, we have two terms which sound identical and look very similar, and yet pose very different problems. Failure to be clear about which term is the one under consideration glosses over the enormous difficulties of the aggregation issue, with all the problems of interpersonal/intertemporal comparisons that it raises.

A related, but not identical, issue is the way in which, within a scientific discipline, word usage may be distorted from common speech in order to maintain a particular status ranking in a field. A salient example of this is the way in which 'theory' in economics has been wrested away from its common usage. In general speech, as suggested earlier, 'theory' connotes a system of generalisations and abstractions employed to make sense of and connect together in our minds the raw details of the world as brought to us by our senses. As employed by most economists, however, the term now refers to a very specific subset of that general concept: a particular kind of mathematical modelling technique. Most people, if asked, would agree that 'theory' is a good and necessary thing; by a semantic imposition, the mathematical modelers in the field of economics have managed to gain a virtual monopoly over claims to 'theoretical' strength.

With respect to each of these issues, the first and best defence for both the critic and the creator of social science texts is a sensitivity to the meanings of individual words and phrases, and a habit of scepticism over whether it is really such a short step as it appears, to go from the meaning of one word or phrase to another which appears similar: e.g., from 'demand' to 'effective demand', or from 'consumer's surplus' to 'consumers' surplus'. Similarly, it is helpful to note when a word, especially an abstract noun, may have importantly different uses, and to watch for unannounced 'pivoting' about such a word from one use to another.

CONSIDERATION OF A SPECIAL CLASS OF ABSTRACT WORDS: 'UNICORN WORDS'   This chapter began with a symbolic representation of how symbols relate to reality. The underlying assumption evidently is that there *is* something which is 'real': that we can talk about reality, and define 'truth' as a good match to reality, and that we can seek truth – though not assuming that we will know 'for certain' when we have found it. All of this presupposes the philosophical position which, in Chapter 8, was described as 'truth realism' (see the section on 'The Standards Required for Scientific Belief').

The discussion of reality could be refined to a debate about different kinds of reality – about what it would mean to say that *goodness* is a word that refers to something real; or *happiness*, or *death*, or *life*. I myself would contend that there is some kind of meaning (here I am slipping in an implied relationship between 'reality' and 'meaning') to a statement such as: 'I have a happy life'. I would have more trouble with a statement about the habits of unicorns; to be meaningful, that would have to be understood in a different context, not intended to represent reality.

This subject is taken up in *The Mathematical Experience*, where reality is discussed in terms of *what exists* (or, the old pre-Socratic concern, 'what is'). 'The unicorn', it is said, 'as a literary legend exists. As a zoological blueprint it exists. But as a live creature, which might potentially be caught and exhibited in a zoo, it does not exist.'[1] Some words or phrases are of a type which may be called 'unicorn words': we all know what they refer to, but that to which they refer is something invented by human beings – it is not to be found in the real world, outside of the human mind. As we shall see in the examples that follow, 'utility' is a good example of a unicorn word; so, for another example, is 'general equilibrium'. Consider:

> There exists the word, 'utility'; and there exists an ordinary conceptual understanding of what the word is supposed to mean, so that two people can hold a conversation in which that word is used, with some hope that they will emerge from the conversation with a similar understanding of what had been communicated. Yet neither the existence of the word, nor the ordinary, shared understanding of what the word is supposed to mean, guarantees that anything in the real world has an existence corresponding to it.[2] (If there is any doubt about what this passage is intended to convey, try rereading it, substituting the word, 'unicorn' for the word 'utility'.)

It is possible that the term, 'total value', which will be employed quite freely in this book, should nevertheless also be regarded as a unicorn word (or phrase). The word 'total' implies measurability; if value (in the sense which I have indicated by saying 'human value') is immeasurable, then their joined use in a phrase is at least an oxymoron. This may be another way of understanding Marshall's difficulties with consumer's(') surplus, which caused him to conclude that it was 'a theoretical but not a practical tool in the economist's workbox'.[3] Consumer's(') surplus is, in effect, the difference resulting from subtracting the practical datum of exchange value from a theoretical construct ('total value') which is either an oxymoron or a unicorn phrase; subtracting the concrete from the undefinable leaves another undefinable.

All of this is not to say that unicorn words should never be employed. A good example is i, defined as $\sqrt{-1}$. The usefulness of this concept is undeniable, and, indeed, it turns up frequently in formulas which express truths about e.g., the geometrical relations of shapes which we have observed in the real world (cf. Euler's formula, $e^{ix} = \cos x + i \sin x$). I am not about to suggest that the unicorn nature of i means that we should ban it, but it is important, under some circumstances, to remember that $\sqrt{-1}$ does not exist in nature. For example, suppose an economist performed a calculation intended to predict inflation as a function of twenty variables, and $\sqrt{-1}$ got into the computations somewhere along the way, and then stayed in. If the economist then went to a policy-maker and said, 'We've plugged your data and your objective functions into our model, and can state that, with the given parameters, in twelve months the rate of inflation will be $15.6i$' – it would be obvious that something had gone very wrong.

Startling as it may seem, if you think carefully about this you will probably agree that 'infinity', like $\sqrt{-1}$, is also a unicorn word. Davis and Hersh take up this issue:

Mathematics, then, asks us to believe in an infinite set. What does it mean that an infinite set exists? Why should one believe it? In formal presentation this request is institutionalised by axiomatisation. Thus, in *Introduction to Set Theory*, by Hrbacek and Jech, we read on page 54: '*Axiom of Infinity. An inductive (i.e. infinite) set exists.*' Compare this against the axiom of God as presented by Maimonides (Mishneh Torah, Book 1, Chapter 1): '*The basic principle of all basic principles and the pillar of all the sciences is to realise that there is a First Being who brought every existing thing into being.*'

Mathematical axioms have the reputation of being self-evident, but it might seem that the axioms of infinity and that of God have the same character as far as self-evidence is concerned.[4]

Even more than 'the square root of minus one', infinity is a critically useful idea, but it is not something that is found in nature. There are a lot of blades of grass, and a lot of stars, but not an infinite number of them. The same may be said for molecules, atoms and subatomic particles – even if the latter are to be understood as probabilities, rather than as entities. A distance is, in theory, infinitely divisible, but theory is not identical with reality until proven to be so, and no distance ever has been divided into an infinite number of infinitesimal segments. The most infinite thing I know of is the gap between the real, finite world and the theoretical infinite. And that one is also a theoretical, not a 'real-world', infinity.

While it is an essential mathematical concept, infinity is also a dangerous one, because its 'unicorn' character is so seldom recognised. This is especially so in the field of economics, where mathematics is widely employed as though a mathematical proof were a proof about the real world, and where economists often fall into the danger of talking, and advising, as though the difference between 'almost infinity' and 'infinity' were not, itself, infinite. (For further discussion on this issue, see the next chapter.)

PREEMPTIVE, PERSUASIVE AND PACKED DEFINITIONS Amitai Etzioni gives some poignant examples of the way that a dominant paradigm, by definitions and by choice of words, can preempt the ground on which discussion is to occur (this is, indeed, an aspect of the art of rhetoric):

Intellectual circles in Europe were preoccupied for more than a century shadow-boxing with the ghost of Karl Marx, trying again and again to show that history is not dominated by economic or materialistic factors, that ideas matter. Similarly, social scientists and attending intellectuals, on both side of the Atlantic Ocean, have been preoccupied – and still are – with extolling, questioning, and attempting to shore up the notion of Rational Man (or *homoeconomicus*). Indeed, even those who challenge this notion often define their position in terms of various deviations from the rational model. This is evident in the frequent references to their concepts as dealing with a residual realm, the 'non-rational', rather than a category that can, by itself, be positively defined. Moreover, non-rationality is often confused with irrationality and tends to carry a negative connotation. '*The trouble is that once one starts to talk*

208 *Textual Analysis and Reality in the Social Sciences*

about rationality, it preempts the way we organise our views of human thought and behavior. We tend to think always in terms of default from a standard . . .'[5]

Neoclassical economics is full of examples of such preemptive definitions, from 'rigour' and 'theory', to 'free trade' and 'perfect competition'.

The latter two are also good examples of what the philosopher, Charles Stevenson, has called 'persuasive definitions'.[6] 'Perfect' and 'free' are not neutral words; they are morally loaded to be persuasive on the point that, e.g., this kind of competition (as opposed to 'impure' or 'imperfect' competition) is something desirable, something the achievement of which would make us feel, 'There! We've finally arrived at the place we were trying to get to!'

It is interesting that it is hard to find a description for the kind of competition economists want to talk about which is not morally loaded, if not in the 'good' direction, then in a way which makes it sound 'bad'. 'Untrammelled' and 'unfettered' competition make us think of 'Nature red in tooth and claw'; they imply that competition *should* be trammelled or fettered. If we use these terms we risk aligning ourselves with those who feel that competition isn't nice, and who have a nostalgia for some state of society (feudalism?) where everyone knew his/her place, and relations were so regulated as to leave little scope for competition. The most neutral term I have been able to find is 'unrestricted competition'.[7]

Closely linked to persuasive definitions, social science abounds with (indeed, one could say it is largely made up of) definitions which carry a large freight of assumptions. In accepting such definitions we are, unwittingly, accepting the assumptions packed into them; and as questions are formulated, using these definitions, they smuggle in as assumptions a part of what we might have expected would emerge, after analysis, in the answers. To take one example, a seemingly straightforward question about how a given policy would affect inflation may hide, in the terminology used, the myriad ultimately normative assumptions that were necessary in order to *define* inflation. The definition is normative because prices rarely move with perfect uniformity; to extract a general change in price level from various prices moving at different rates, sometimes in different directions, it is necessary to accept conventions regarding the assignment of weights.

'Conventions regarding the assignment of weights' sounds neutral enough, but underneath such conventions must be some way of determining which things are *more or less important* (either for the society at large or for the particular use to which the convention is to be put); this is the subject of value-definition. (It is also the subject of accounting, which was discussed in Chapter 2.) The *use* of a rule always looks relatively impersonal, therefore impartial; but the *formulation* of any rule for defining price levels implies decisions about how to weight the marginal evaluations of different groups of people – where the marginal utility of money, let it be remembered, varies across individuals with different levels of income (it is likely that it varies within income levels, as well). For instance, a rule specifying that 'the weight is to be the commodity's share in GNP' makes the implicit decision that the preferences of the rich are to be taken more into account (because their expenditures are larger, per person) than the preferences of the poor; and it determines how industrial and governmental expenditures are to be weighted in relation to personal expenditures. 'One dollar, one vote' is a rule which, once established, may be impartially applied; but its establishment is not impartial. (We will see more of this subject in Chapter 16, as 'Fallout from the Aggregation Problem'.)

Aggregation is one of the most intransigent problems in welfare economics. Some aggregation-related problems can be understood as arising initially out of a failure to specify the concrete issues which have been dealt with too exclusively on an abstract level. Given an individual case, and enough facts, there are many situations in which economists can specify how a particular policy will impact upon a particular family or firm, or upon a carefully defined, relatively homogeneous group or class of individuals. What they cannot do – and perhaps should not be expected to do (but they are) – is to define the 'net' or 'bottom line' effect as a *summation of impacts that affect different individuals in different ways and to different extents*. It is, unfortunately, most frequently the case that some people are helped and some hurt by each proposed economic policy or action. Here the contemporary economist is tempted to throw up his/her hands and say to the politician, '*You* decide how to weight the different effects'. Unfortunately, the politician is often strongly motivated to shunt that responsibility right back to the 'experts' (what a science fiction writer has called 'passing the buck on a Möbius strip'). It is questionable whether there is any training that would make a person an 'expert' in the subject of how to weight different people's gains and losses; but, as this is a problem which so often confronts economists, it is one to which the profession should at least give some serious, formal attention.

CHOICE OF LANGUAGE: TRANSLATING THROUGH MULTIPLE LAYERS OF ABSTRACTION Marshall remarked that 'an inference from one set of facts to another, whether it be performed by instinctive or by formal reasoning, involves not one process but two. It involves a passage upwards from particulars to general propositions and ideas; and a passage downwards from them to other particulars ('The Old Generation of Economists and the New' (1897) in Memorials, p. 298). Most of the methodology of which social scientists are aware concentrates upon the middle process – the 'inference from one set of facts to another'. Economists today pay relatively little attention to the distance between the thing-in-itself (element (a) of Figure 10.1) and the abstractions out of which theory is created. While this whole process is so complex that no single piece of social science work, attempting to convey, examine or lead to, purportedly true statements about Mankind in society, could, at the same time, lay out the origins of each of the understandings on which that work is built – nevertheless it is worthwhile to develop sensitivity to this subject. In particular, it is helpful to note the words or symbols that serve to bridge the gap between the concrete and the abstract.

As there is a need to be clear about the precise meaning (or, if it is imprecise, the imprecise meaning – this is an important point) of each word, there is no less need to be clear about the meanings which are to be attached to abstract symbols. When abstract symbols are employed it is often forgotten that they usually are replacements for words (which are, themselves, of course, abstract symbols.) No matter how theoretic, analytical, or symbolic a piece of work in economics may be, economists must deal with the fact that symbols used alone are normally incomprehensible; in the end the meaning of each symbol or collection of symbols must usually be reducible to words. This statement is, in fact, true for mathematics and for the natural as well as for the social sciences:

> Interpreting a symbol is to associate it with some concept or mental image, and to assimilate it to human consciousness. The rules for calculating should be as precise as the operation of a computing machine; the rules for interpretation cannot be any more precise that the communication of ideas among humans.
>
> The process of representing mathematical ideas in symbolic form always entails an alteration in the ideas; a gain in precision and a loss in fidelity or applicability to its problem of origin (Davis and Hersh, 1981, p. 125.)

In the necessary going-back-and-forth between symbols and words there is additional opportunity for lack of clarity to be ignored or disguised. When a word (e.g., 'utility') has been replaced by a symbol (e.g., 'U') the dangers of unaware unicorn thinking are hidden in yet another layer of abstraction.

It is generally simpler to check a verbal statement against reality than a mathematical one; the latter must first be translated into words. For example, if one is in the middle of a set of calculations which employ the imaginary number, i, it is impossible to check this reasoning against reality until the calculations are followed out to where the i has been got rid of. This does not mean, of course, that imaginary numbers should not be used; just that this should be a recognised disadvantage, to be weighed against their other conveniences. Deductive logic does not require that the symbols it uses, including words, be paired with anything in the real world; however it is more obvious in the case of a discussion of the mating habits of unicorns that this cannot be checked against reality than in the case of, e.g., a statement that $\log L = \log w - U(l)$.

The verbal language with which any human being is familiar – whether it be Mandarin, English, Spanish, or Swahili – is a complex system of symbols representing concrete and abstract things, ideas, actions, states of being, etc. A mathematical language is another system of symbols. Many of the common things that are daily talked about through the use of words are relatively easily translated from one verbal language to another. 'What a nice day this is!' or 'Is political freedom essential for the full development of human potential?' can be translated from Urdu to Rumanian, and back, in such a way as to communicate approximately the same thing – although cultural as well as personal differences place (probably undefinable) limits on the extent to which any phrase does in practice mean the same thing to two different people. By contrast, these two phrases would be difficult to translate fully into a set of mathematical symbols. Some other kinds of statements, dealing with other subjects, are easier.

The fact that some things are relatively easily – i.e., concisely and accurately, and requiring relatively simple definitions – represented in mathematical symbols is one of the reasons that economists like Marshall have been attracted to that method of writing down and/or communicating thoughts.

Much the same can be said for another kind of symbolic communication, graphical representation, which may be employed to regularise the thinking in back of a verbal or other symbolic representation. At the same time, part of the power of a graph is its ability to express the summary of a large number of ideas, assumptions, simplifications and other abstractions, all in one image. Such a summary does not usually specify all the clues to its expansion into that-which-it-summarised; many conventions go into the reading of a graph, and the conventions may change without warning from one sub-area of economics to another, even from one article in a journal to another. With a little patience one can usually discover the conventions governing the reading of a particular graphical representation, but even then one is left with unnamed and undiscussed simplifications and assumptions which may require special cautions.

The standard economics of today operates on the basis of what (if it is thought through) must be enormous optimism about the ability of economists (and not only the few very best economists) to carry in their heads, and to maintain in proper relation to one another and to reality, thick layers of nested abstractions. The discussion of this chapter is motivated by some scepticism as to whether this optimism has been warranted with regard to much of what is written and taught in the field. The function of such scepticism in a critical analysis is to prompt the critic to translate into more concrete form the meanings embedded in all the layers of abstraction of the text under discussion.

A procedure which can be useful here is to rephrase, in quotation marks, what one thinks is being said by someone else. Although as a conversational gambit this sometimes requires more explanation than it is worth (most of my friends still have not got used to my doing it), as a tool for textual analysis it can be valuable in clarifying to oneself as well as to prospective readers just what is one's interpretation of some text.[8]

Where the text under consideration depends heavily upon symbols other than words, the device of restatement is first of all helpful simply in translating into words critical points in the logic and the conclusions. Economists ought routinely to do this for their own work; when they fail to do so, this becomes one of the first functions of textual analysis. Even when non-verbal symbols do not carry the main burden, if jargon or some kind of 'shorthand' has been employed, it may be useful to expand the text.

It often turns out that a confident statement (in which X puts 'in other words' what s/he thinks Y has said) is not seen, by Y, as the same thing at all: or X and Z might each put Y's statement in such different 'other words' that they will discover a strong disagreement whose existence they would not have guessed if they had not attempted the rephrasing. Discussions of a text which do not begin by stating what each of the discussants think it says are often, in effect, parallel discussions of different texts.

THEORY AND   Let us, at this point, refer back to the complex of
EMPIRICISM   biological and cognitive processes, a part of which was
sketched out in Figure 10.1. We saw there a little of the process of generalisation and abstraction which could result in such a simple recognition as 'this is a tree'. I would like now to stretch our understanding to see the kinship between a concept such as 'tree', and another such as 'general equilibrium'.

Both of these concepts are generalisations which are built, fundamentally, upon the biological/cognitive processes of abstraction from messages conveyed to the brain by the senses. However, one represents more steps away from the starting point in the world, towards abstract understanding.

– The generalisation, 'tree', though more immediately related to the input of our sense, is still much more than 'this particular leafy thing that shades my window', or than 'that particular structure that I climbed, and fell out of, as a child'. By creating, in our minds, the category, 'tree', we bring the individual case into association with a wide range of experiences and bits of knowledge.

– 'General equilibrium' is the result of yet more steps into abstraction, because it is built upon so many intermediate generalisations and abstractions. It includes, for example, the idea that some human beings, in some of their acts, may be recognised as 'suppliers'; also the idea of a 'supply curve', which summarises what many suppliers would do under a variety of circumstances; etc.

It should be evident that 'pure theory' and 'pure empiricism' are each equally impossible, for reasons which begin with the way in which we, as physical beings, relate to the world. Anything that could be conceptualised as 'a purely empirical fact' can exist only outside what we think of as mind; by the time it has entered our minds so that we can think about it, it has already been massaged by something like theory. The 'fact' – 'this is a tree' – is a construct, just as 'general equilibrium' is a construct; both constructs may be held more or less in common by many beholders, but neither exists outside of the minds of the beholders.[9]

What, in Chapter 6, we viewed as a tension between mathematical versus intuitive methods, may now be reconceived, as a tension between deductive and inductive approaches; and these, again, can be paired with theoretical versus empirical ways of understanding. Economics has a particular relation to the idea of human welfare. An essential question to raise here is: how tight are the restrictions which the scientific method must impose upon the humanitarian aims of economics? Much of modern neoclassical economics works within very tight (or 'rigorous') restrictions indeed. The areas where these restrictions seem most irksome (and where they continue to be most often broken through by the abandonment of one or another of the requirements that go with being 'scientific') are in the economics of labor and of development, and in welfare economics. Each of these fields contains, at one extreme, theorists who for the sake of scientific rigour are willing to jettison whatever elements of reality or of humanitarian aims seem to stand in the way of such rigour; and, at the other extreme, practitioners who will let rigour go by the boards when it cannot deal with the fulness of what they see as the relevant reality of the requirements of their aims. Most theorists and practitioners, of course, lie somewhere in between these extremes. In Marshall's words, 'all are bound more or less to collect and arrange facts and statistics . . . and all are bound to occupy themselves more or less with analysis and reasoning on the basis of those facts which are ready at hand'; however, there are some people who 'find the former task the more attractive and absorbing, and others the latter' (*Principles*, p. 11).

Referring back to the 'certainty versus belief' discussion of Chapter 8, I propose a tentative hypothesis: that those social scientists who are temperamentally most desirous of *certainty* are also the ones to whom theory is the ultimate attraction; while those who are content with *belief* are the ones who are more likely to claim an empirical approach. Such preferences can only lead people to a relative, not an absolute emphasis. However, the status structure of the field of economics today lends its support to a relative emphasis which is very far on the side of theory. Marshall anticipated this danger in a letter to Edgeworth, written in 1902:

In my view 'Theory' is essential. No one gets any real grip of economic problems unless he will work at it. But I conceive of no more calamitous notion than that abstract, or general, or 'theoretical' economics was economics 'proper'. It seems to me an essential but a very small part of economics proper: and by itself sometimes even – well, not a very good occupation of time.

The key-note of my *Plea* is that *the* work of the economists is 'to disentangle the interwoven effects of complex causes'; and that for this, general reasoning is essential, but a wise and thorough study of facts is equally essential, and that a combination of the two sides of the work is *alone* economics *proper*. Economic theory is, in my opinion, as mischievous an impostor when it claims to be economics proper as is mere crude unanalyzed history. Six of ye one, 1/2 dozen of ye other! (Quoted in *Memorials*, p. 437).

MARSHALL AS A MODEL IN THE ISSUE OF THEORY AND EMPIRICISM Given that there can be neither pure empiricism nor pure theory in the social sciences, is there some 'best' way of realising the interplay between these two unicorn constructs? Probably not; as Marshall said, there is room and need both for scholars with an emphasis upon collection of facts, and for those with an emphasis upon reasoning about the facts at hand. The question comes down to one of emphasis. That is worth thinking about, even though we may not expect to find the 'ideal' emphasis. It is especially important to think about it now, in the late twentieth century, when the emphasis especially in economics, but also in some other social sciences, has swung rather far in the theoretical direction.

Chapter 7 gave a sketch of where the field is now in this regard, and how it got here. At this point I would like to take a look at where Marshall stood on the issue. Throughout this book Marshall is used as an exemplar of many different things, not all of them things which will be set forth for emulation. In this particular connection however, he is a model in the normative sense: his interweaving of theory and empiricism has not been improved upon by any other economist.

One reason for Marshall's excellence in this respect is his methodological self-consciousness. He considered with conscious care what is involved in turning sensory perceptions into intelligent observations; observations into useful theories; and theories back into the bases for practical action.

When it came to the third of these tasks (using theory as a basis for practical action), Marshall felt, in fact, a good deal of ambivalence, which was illustrated in the sections on 'The Social Responsibility of the Social Scientist' and 'The Division of Labour Between Science and Common Sense', in the previous chapter. His concern regarding the application of economics to practical matters stemmed from two particular worries: one was his distrust of Man's ability to predict the future, based on any social or other science; the other was his conviction that the analytical tools of science must only be servants to other aspects of Man's mental capacity.

Marshall's best hopes for prediction[10] related to the statistical smoothing of heterogeneity:

> For our present purpose the pliability of the race is more important than the pliability of the individual. It is true that individual character changes, partly in an apparently arbitrary way, and partly according to well-known rules. It is true for instance that the average age of the workmen engaged in a labour dispute is an important element in any forecast of the lines on which it will run. But as, generally speaking, young and old, people of a sanguine and a despondent temperament are found in about like proportions at one place as at another, and at one time as at another, individual peculiarities of character and changes of character are a less hindrance to the general application of the deductive method, than at first sight appears. Thus by patient interrogation of nature and the progress of analysis, the reign of law is being made to invade new fields in both therapeutics and economics: and some sort of prediction, independent of specific experience, is becoming possible as to the separate and combined action of an ever-increasing variety of agencies.
>
> The function then of analysis and deduction in economics is not to forge a few long chains of reasoning, but to forge rightly many short chains and single connecting links (*Principles*, p. 638).

This is about as encouraging a statement as one can find anywhere in Marshall's writings on the possibility of useful theorising of the type which represents variables from experience as symbols or numbers, and then manipulates them through a process of mathematical (essentially deductive) reasoning, to produce, at the end, a statement or prediction regarding real human behaviour in the real world. His emphasis upon 'short chains' and 'single connecting links' has, however, a meaning which is worth spelling out in greater detail.

What Marshall himself did, and what he recommended, was to intersperse the thinking which he performed at a distance from the subjects of his thoughts with a 'return' to the world. He put little faith in any 'long chain of reasoning', but felt that the conclusion at the end of each link should be tested against observation of the world. (He himself spent much time in first-hand observation, walking about the industrial cities of England, talking with manufacturers and union workers in England and America, etc.)

This seems like a very simple piece of advice. It is, however, one whose importance for the usefulness of the social sciences can hardly be stressed enough; and it is advice which is far too seldom heeded today. Marshall himself is partly to be blamed for his. His stated goal was to 'deal with facts that can be observed and quantities which can be measured and recorded; so that when differences of opinion arise with regard to them, the differences can be brought to the test of public and well-established records; and thus science obtains a solid basis on which to work' (*Principles*, p. 22). The problem, here, was Marshall's reluctance to recognise that many of the facts of importance to a *social* science are *not* in the nature of 'quantities which can be measured and recorded' – in spite of his own recognition of the danger that economists would emphasise 'those elements . . . which lend themselves most easily to analytical methods.' (*Principles*, p. 700).

The base of a social science *cannot* be as 'solid', in the quantifiable, measurable ways Marshall wished for, as the base of a physical science. Yet this is no reason for social sciences to cut loose from experience and observation. Given the fuzziness of the initial observations on which subsequent deductions are to be built (e.g., the observations of human behaviour which have been stylised into the image of 'rational economic man', upon which so many deductions have then been erected), there is all the more reason to follow Marshall's prescription: keep going back to check whether the real world is proceeding according to the theory.

How frequent should this be? That is a matter of judgment. Marshall saw that an approach emphasising empiricism could also be carried too far, and he cautioned (especially when thinking of the German Historical School) that 'facts without theory are mute'. However he sensed, accurately, that the errors of the coming generation were less likely to be in the overly empirical direction than in that which was in fact taken by the neoclassical school – the masters of 'long trains of deductive reasoning'. To correct today's excesses he would doubtless counsel shortening the sections of models which are strung between observations. Social economics, following this guidance, would encourage only relatively short excursions into the mole-tunnels of perfectly abstract modelling, requiring its practitioners relatively frequently to come up for air and test their progress against what they know of the real world.

Related to the foregoing is the issue of the tension between *induction* from 'observed' or otherwise 'known' facts, versus *deduction* which uses theory (most generally understood) to go from the 'facts of the real world' to a set of proposed 'facts' which have not yet been observed in the real world. Here, again, Marshall took the correct, if uncomfortable stance, of championing both sides at once. He pointed out that each, in pure form, is impossible.[11] The discussion, at least for the social sciences, must be about where one chooses to be on the spectrum shown in Figure 10.2. Social economics, as it is proposed in this book, would distinguish itself from neoclassical economics by existing somewhat farther to the left on this spectrum.

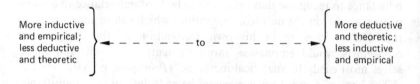

More inductive
and empirical;
less deductive
and theoretic

to

More deductive
and theoretic;
less inductive
and empirical

Figure 10.2 The spectrum from empirical to theoretic

What, in practice, does this mean? For one thing, a more empirical, less deductive science will have to foster different ideas and expectations about simplicity versus complexity. An area where this is particularly evident is in the matter of *brevity*, which, in turn depends upon *choice of language*.

It is often impossible to abbreviate the content of a statement of understanding in the social sciences in the same way as may be done in the natural sciences; there is no social science formula whose 'power' is comparable to $E = MC^2$. However, neoclassical economists, in their desire to create a discipline which would be 'scientific' like the natural sciences, respond to a very strong internal motivation (and external pressure, from their colleagues, journals, etc.) first to axiomatise, and then to summarise. Of even the most complex and subtle argument, regarding even the most difficult matters, it is widely believed that, if 'what this economist is really saying' can't be compressed into a few pages, then it must not be very significant.

A prime counter example to such a belief is Alfred Marshall's *Principles of Economics*; there is no way to boil down his 700 page book into something short which would convey 'what Marshall is really saying'. Incidentally, the same is true of Samuelson's fat volumes of introductory economics. The style of the latter is far less ambling, in an idiom that is more familiar to modern audiences; but it remains true for Samuelson, as it was stated by Marshall, that 'every plain and simple doctrine as to the relations between cost of production, demand and value is necessarily false: and the greater the appearance of lucidity which is given to it by skillful exposition, the more mischievous it is' (*Principles*, p. 306).

'SIMPLIFICATIONS' AND OTHER TYPES OF 'UNREALISTICNESS' As another way to describe the relationship between theory and reality, it is sometimes appropriate to say that the former is composed of elements which are simplifications of the latter. The need for simplifying the experience of our senses in order to construct abstract models for the better understanding of the world is generally accepted – and it is accepted by economists with particular enthusiasm. One of the deficiencies in the field of economics is the lack of a well-thought-through and well-known methodology on the subject of simplification. There are at present virtually no generally accepted rules, or even guidelines or suggestions, regarding how far a social scientist should take the necessary simplifications of the experience of the real world. Economists simplify to whatever extent serves their purpose of the moment. Their work, once in print, is subject to critical scrutiny, but the criticism they receive is rarely on such methodological grounds.

In his 1953 'Essay on the Methodology of Positive Economics', Milton Friedman contended that the realisticness of assumptions does not matter. In response to this, Uskali Mäki has written extensively on the general subject of 'unrealisticness'. His categories make a useful starting point for our discussion:

> Let us say that a statement is an *idealisation* if it is formulated or can be formulated in terms of a variable that is assigned the value 0 or ∞. An idealisation, in other words, involves so-called limit concepts. Notions like frictionless surface in physics and perfectly elastic demand in economics are dependent on idealisations. A statement is a *simplification* if it modifies some of the characteristics of its object so as to make it look simpler than it in fact is. Examples are spherical planetary motions in astronomy and linear production functions in economics. A statement is an *exaggeration* if the value of a quantity it attributes to its object is larger than its real value. Some idealisations are extreme exaggerations.

Idealizations, simplifications, and exaggerations are strictly false statements. An *isolation*, on the other hand, may be true of its object which it isolates from the influence of other objects for closer inspection. Physical experiments in laboratory conditions are based on material isolation, while isolations in economics are conceptual in character.[12]

It is commonly understood that a given theory does not aim to cover all of reality; one way of describing a theory would be to say that those parts of reality which it does intend to include are represented in the form of symbolic simplifications (e.g., words or mathematical symbols, sentences or mathematical phrases) of a small, carefully selected, *subset* of elements of reality. As Mäki points out, however, there are different ways of reducing reality to symbols, and some of them are strictly false, while others are not.

The type of 'realisticness' which I shall favour, in this section and in the next chapter, is a type which assumes that 'the whole truth' is not symbolically representable, but which makes clear distinctions between 'nothing but the truth' and something which is clearly *un*truth. As a start, such a 'safe realism' will:

- make it clear when its categories are, and when they are not, referring to real things that exist in the real world;
- though not describing all elements of the area of interest, strive for accuracy in describing the chosen elements;
- not so isolate the chosen elements from the context as to give a strictly false definition; and
- in general avoid making counter-factual statements; when these cannot be avoided, guard against them by making clear their nature, as statements contrary to fact.

Even in such 'safe realism', there will be distortions which will increase toward the margins of the areas, elements or characteristics receiving most theoretical attention. This is why there will always be competing versions, even within safe realism, none of which will be wholly true, but some of them more useful for some purposes, some for others.

The term 'simplification' is, itself, normally understood to refer to a construct which represents some, but not all, of the aspects or characteristics of the reality which it partially reflects; it may not reflect even those aspects in their entirety, but what portions of them it does convey are conveyed faithfully. A Picasso sketch of bullfighters (using lines as representational elements, instead of using words or mathematical notations as symbols) may convey faithfully the essential elements that strike the eye, in such a way that, although each line segment alone is virtually meaningless, the result appears as a faithful, although greatly simplified, representation of the portion of reality chosen by the artist.

By comparison, many aspects of economic theory are not in the same sense simplifications from reality; they are not reduced statements of fact (or statements of reduced fact), but are statements contrary to fact. For example, the world described in the first and second theorems of the formal theory of welfare economics is not recognisably the world we inhabit.[13] Here, a series of statements, mostly of the 'if . . . then' form (i.e., 'if the world did conform to these conditions, then the following further conditions would hold . . .'), have been combined to produce, at the end of a long chain of deductive reasoning, the conclusion that 'every Pareto optimum is potentially achievable through the operation of market mechanisms under conditions of perfect competition'. This is not a false statement, in the sense of containing contradictions to its own internal premises. Neither, however, is it a recognisable sketch (like the simplified Picasso drawing) of the real world.

The central problem is that the concept of a world of perfect competition is not a *simplification* from our real world; it is *a picture of a different world.* Many of the 'classical conditions' under which neoclassical theory operates are not simplifications in the sense of representing a stripped-down, but still faithful, representation of the world; often they are simplifications only in the sense that they simplify the work of the theorist.[14]

The same may be said of the 'single-cause/single-result' fallacy; i.e., the (perhaps in part aesthetically motivated) tendency of scientists to assign to each result a single cause, and to each cause a single result. The problem with such a procedure may be dramatised by a thought-experiment in which we imagine an important happening (a war, let us say, or a major inflation), and we imagine, also, that we are in the God-like position of knowing the 'true' causes of the happening. Let us imagine that what we know is that there were, in fact, 100 true causes, each bearing about equal responsibility. It is probable that an economist using modern techniques for testing correlations would not come out with anything approaching the true answer; and if we were to offer the true answer to the profession, it probably could not get published in an economics journal. The true answer would simply appear too unsatisfactory; it would leave people saying, 'Yes, but what was the *real* reason?' We would be told, 'You will have to simplify your conclusions if you want to publish them.' To do so, however, would, again, be not a simplification but a distortion.

Mäki's term, *isolation*, is particularly applicable to the convenient notion of *ceteris paribus*. That Latin term asks us to consider 'all other things remaining the same' while we concentrate our attention upon a particular action or effect. Certainly there are useful understandings to be achieved by imagining a 'simplified' world wherein only one or a few changes are permitted at a time. The critical question to keep in mind is: what useful understandings are kept beyond our reach as long as we thus restrict our imaginations or our perceptions?

Additions could be made to Mäki's list of types of 'unrealisticness'. One that I would propose is *incorporated metaphors*. We can hardly speak without using metaphors; for example, when we speak of time 'flowing', we are unconsciously adopting a metaphor which regards time as a river; when we say a politician 'clawed his or her way to the top' we have metaphorically viewed the politician as a member of the cat family; etc. For rigorous philosophical speculation on the nature of time we will find we have prejudged the issue if we employ the river-metaphor, with its unidirectional flow; and for a rational debate on politics the cat-metaphor, too, states a pre-judgment. Nevertheless, ordinarily we do not feel that our perceptions have been distorted by commonplace use of such common metaphors. However, there are metaphors which sometimes get incorporated into a discipline and then treated as reality, and there the danger of distortion may be acute.

I will argue later (in Chapter 17) that an important example of this problem in neoclassical economics is the concept of the welfare function, which depends upon the implicit metaphor that the society is an individual being, and its welfare can be understood like the welfare of an individual. The graphic or other mathematical representation of, e.g., indifference maps can also be viewed as a metaphorical activity which sometimes gets out of control and is incorporated into our way of thinking as if it were a direct, not a metaphorical, representation; 'Here is the individual's (or the society's) indifference function' says the teacher, pointing to the blackboard.

The activity which I associate with all of the foregoing observations of types of unrealisticness in economics is an examination of theories to see what are the basic building blocks of which they are constructed; in this examination I recommend questioning so-called simplifications, with a distinction in mind between actual simplifications versus distortions. A theory built on the latter, I hypothesise, is particularly prone to run into trouble of the 'external inconsistency' type that was described in the previous chapter, and that will be the subject of the next one. There we will be especially concerned with the type of 'unrealisticness' which is commonly known as an *idealisation*.

Notes

1. Davis and Hersh, 1981, p. 146.
2. Machlup has pointed to the same issue, using the phrase 'the fallacy of misplaced concreteness' for the situation where a 'thought-object' is mistaken for 'an object of sense-perception, that is, for anything in the real, empirical world' (Fritz Machlup, 'Theories of the Firm: Marginalist, Behavioral, Managerial' *American Economic Review*, 57, p. 26).

   Plato suffered from, and purveyed, a 'unicorn word' confusion when he first encountered a class of words which had only just been introduced to the Greek then spoken: namely, abstract nouns. His, and his audience's unfamiliarity with such words is evident in the way that (particularly in the early Dialogues) Plato kept inserting explanations, e.g., 'Beauty – by which I mean "the beautiful"'; 'Justice – I mean, "the just"'; etc. Out of this unfamiliarity came the idea of what have been called 'Platonic Ideals' which expressed the notion that: if there exists a word such as *beauty* or *truth*, and we can comprehend and communicate what that word is intended to mean (the commonality of such comprehension is, of course, another whole subject for debate), this must be so because there exists, somewhere in the universe, an actual form or pattern to which the word refers.

   In modern usage I would only think of an abstract noun as a unicorn word if it is employed in a manner similar to Plato's: to imply that there is some *thing* to which the abstraction refers.
3. C. W. Guillebaud, 'Some Personal Reminiscences of Alfred Marshall', in John C. Wood (ed.) *Alfred Marshall, Critical Assessments* (Croom Helm, London, 1982).
4. Davis and Hersh, 1981, pp. 154–5. If you are not yet persuaded that the concept of *infinity* requires a special place in our mental organisation of concepts – closer to *unicorns* than to *chickadees* or even, I would claim, than to *happiness* or *hunger* – consider the following conversation between a sceptic and a person who had never questioned the realism of the concept, 'infinity':

   Sceptic: Nothing exists in reality which has the characteristic, 'infinity' – there is no actual thing to which one can apply the adjective 'infinite'.
   Believer: That's nonsense! What about the number of times you can halve the distance, say, between, zero and one?

S.: Zero and one what?

B.: Well, inches.

S.: Here's a line an inch long on this piece of paper; let's start halving the distance from the beginning to the end point . . . after a while the area we're trying to mark off is all black, we can no longer distinguish further 'halvings'.

B.: The problem is that that pencil isn't infinitely sharp.

S.: What pencil is? *Conceptually* we could go on halving the distance forever, but in reality we cannot.

B.: Alright then, what about the series of real numbers; surely you'll concede that that is infinite?

S.: In theory, yes; in reality, there does not exist anywhere a thing to which can be put the name 'the infinite series of real numbers'. That is, while we cannot name the number that is the last one in the series, we also cannot point to anything in reality that corresponds to the infinite length of such a theoretically infinite series.

B.: But you know perfectly well the meaning of an infinite series: it would be expressed by our starting to count, and never stopping –

S.: But we *would* stop.

B.: Why?

S.: We would die.

B.: Then suppose we set up an institute for counting, and every generation would assign someone fulltime –

S.: (*helpfully*) The counter could go by millions, or billions.

B.: That wouldn't actually make any difference –

S.: You mean no one would ever actually reach infinity?

B.: No, but the *concept* is there –

S.: I'll believe it when you can show me a real example of it.

5. Etzioni, 1988, p. 93; italics added. The passage which Etzioni quotes is from Robert P. Abelson, 'Social Psychology's Rational Man', in S. I. Benn and G. W. Mortimore (eds) *Rationality and the Social Sciences* (Routledge and Kegan Paul, London, 1976) p. 61.

6. See Charles L. Stevenson, *Ethics and Language* (Yale University Press, paperback edn, 1960).

7. Although I am inclined to favour this term as one which does not prejudge the issue, it may be that the social sciences are *not* best served by simply recommending the avoidance of 'persuasive definitions'. While the intent behind their use may be to persuade, to the sophisticated reader/listener their function is also to *signal the position* (or point of view) of the author/speaker. We might ideally require of social scientists that they first know, and then state, their prejudgments or ideologies; but until that ideal is put into practice there is at least some gain in the use of words which warn us of those positions.

Marshall struggled with the semantic problem just discussed, but from a different point of view worth noting; to him the word 'competition' itself carried with it such *negative* connotations that he protested 'we ought . . . not to brand the forces, which have made modern civilisation, by a name which suggests evil' (*Principles*, p. 6); and then went on to say,

> We need a term that does not imply any moral qualities, whether good or evil, but which indicates the undisputed fact that modern business and industry are characterised by more self-reliant habits, more forethought, more deliberate and free choice. There is not any one term adequate for this purpose: but *Freedom of Industry and Enterprise*, or more shortly, *Economic Freedom*, point in the right direction; and it may be used in the absence of a better (*Principles*, p. 8).

One could hardly find a clearer example of a persuasive definition! Marshall evidently recognised their existence, but (like most people who are aware of persuasive definitions) objected to their use only if they were persuasive in the wrong direction.

8. A good example of this procedure is found in the discussion of a paper by Muth, in pp. 92–96 of Donald McCloskey, 1985. Another illustration may also be found at the end of the discussion of Harberger, in Chapter 17, below.

9. It is, of course, the *construct* (the set of associations and generalisations which come together in a category to which human beings can give a common name – and to which other animals also have a demonstrated capacity to attach a common concept abstraction) that exists only in the minds that hold it. While we cannot prove that the *ding-an-sich* does exist outside of our minds, it seems reasonable to believe that it does. (This, again, is the philosophical position of world realism.)

10. A wish poignantly revived, in the 1960s, by the excitement surrounding the Club of Rome models, and their implicit promise that computers would be able to do what mankind had so long sought from magic. With the brief flowering of 'projection as prediction', it seemed that such magical powers really were attainable by human beings, upon attainment of a PhD in economics or in systems analysis. Some disillusionment has set in since then. On the idea that the science of economics might someday be able to fulfill the ages-old human wish to be able to predict the future, Marshall commented, in one of the last pieces of economic writing of his life, thus:

> Prediction in economics must be hypothetical. Show an interrupted game at chess to an expert and he will be bold indeed if he prophesies its future stages. If either side makes one move ever so little different from what he has expected, all the following moves will be altered; and after two or three moves more the whole fact of the game will have become different (*Memorials*, p. 360; 'Fragments by Marshall'; dated 1922.)

11. Unless, as may be the case, some or all of pure mathematics may be described as purely deductive, without any necessary base in the real world. If this is an exception to the statement just made in the text, it is not one which weakens my claim, as far as the social sciences are concerned.

12. Uskali Mäki, 'Types of Unrealisticness in Economics: The Case of J. H. von Thünen's Isolated State', paper prepared for presentation at the Annual Meeting of the History of Economics Society in Richmond, Va., 10–13 June 1989; preliminary draft, p. 10.
13. These theorems are discussed in Chapter 13, below.
14. Note that this statement implies a belief about the nature of the relevant part of reality – namely, that virtually no economy that actually exists is perfectly competitive. We will press further, in the next chapter, on the question of the usefulness of describing reality as though it is approaching such an idealisation as perfect competition; there, too, we will return to the 'external consistency' issue raised here and in the preceding chapter, regarding the mapping of communication carriers (words, models, theories) upon 'the real world'.

11 Stories That Blow up: How to Anticipate When the Realisticness of Assumptions Will Matter[1]

As was suggested in the previous chapter, the approach that is here proposed for social economics will finally bring the issue of making bridges between the concrete and the abstract down to questions about the nature of reality. It is not, after all, just any 'concreteness' that is being made abstract: it is something real, something 'out there', beyond our minds. In most attempts to apprehend this reality it is reasonable to assume that there are many descriptions which are approximately equally accurate (arguably, none of them is perfectly accurate), but there are also some which are less accurate, and there are some descriptions which do not relate to reality well enough to serve usefully as inputs to a science.

As we return to subjects which were raised in Chapter 6, the thesis of this chapter will be developed with special care, because it will dispute a contention that has remained dominant in neoclassical economics for more than thirty years: namely, that

> **the realisticness** (or lack thereof) *of the assumptions employed in* **economics** (by extension in the other social sciences too; as also, **some economists have supposed, in the physical sciences**) *does not* **matter.**

This idea, somewhat carelessly stated by Milton Friedman and even more carelessly used by myriad economists after him, has been extensively written upon and effectively disputed.[2] It nevertheless continues to prevail in economics and in other social sciences which are influenced by the methodology of economics.[3]

This chapter will attempt to provide a new framework for understanding when, and in what ways, the realisticness of certain

227

assumptions does matter. It will begin by building upon the discussion of the three preceding chapters, where the relation between theory and reality was considered in terms of bridges between the concrete things of the real world on the one hand, and, on the other, the various methods of abstraction (neuronal, linguistic, theoretic) which symbolise these things in the process of 'communication' – still stretching the term 'communication', as we have done throughout Part II, to include writing or speaking; reading or listening; or using one's logical and intuitive faculties to work over an idea.

VARIOUS APPROACHES TO THE SELECTION AND USE OF ASSUMPTIONS

A news item in the summer of 1989 was a decision by voters in conservative Orange County, California, to legislate for expensive restrictions and requirements on businesses and consumers. The goal was to reduce the contributions made by Orange County to ozone depletion and global warming.

Economists might view these voters as acting irrationally. Orange County alone cannot save, and probably cannot destroy, the Earth's ozone layer. A more 'rational' kind of behaviour would be to let everyone else bear the costs of trying to do something about the problem; if Orange County could manage to be a free rider in this situation, it could reap handsome economic rewards. A prediction of how the vote on this issue would go, based only on neoclassical economic assumptions about the way rational individuals behave, would have been wrong. The distance between such a prediction and what actually happened in Orange County is a very mild case of what I will call 'stories that blow up'. The more extreme cases strike us more forcefully, as paradoxes or bizarre absurdities.

Economics, like most other social sciences, is almost entirely concerned with the way human beings behave. Understandings, descriptions and predictions of human behaviour are based upon beliefs about human nature. In economics, particularly, these beliefs have been axiomatised to a set of core assumptions which may be summed up by saying that '**Rational individuals maximise their perceived utility**'. Many other, secondary assumptions follow from this; particularly assumptions about markets, as collections of rational individuals. Another assumption may be discovered to be necessary to the development of this basic assumption into a system of theory which is supposed to apply to what happens in real economies: namely, that most people behave rationally most of the time. Given that most people behave rationally, and that the meaning of rationality is utility maximisation, the rest of neoclassical economics follows.

Some neoclassical economists define the words in the critical sentence '**Rational individuals maximise their perceived utility**' so that, tautologically, it must be true. (For example, defining rationality as the maximisation of perceived utility.) Others go to sociobiology to 'prove', by evolutionary history, that rational individuals are programmed to do nothing but maximise their perceived utility. That argument can be stated convincingly, to meet all the requirements of internal consistency; all the same, there are times, as in the case of the Orange County voters, when it creates a situation of external inconsistency, where the conclusions drawn from the assumption of rational maximising (non-tautologically defined) are contrary to the facts of the real world.

Other neoclassical economists take the position that the assumption of rational maximising is not *strictly* true, but that it's a 'good enough' approximation. And others, like Milton Friedman, have said we simply shouldn't be worrying about the realisticness of our assumptions: his position has most often been interpreted as saying that: **the goodness of the results we get shouldn't be judged by, and won't depend upon, the realisticness of the assumptions upon which we have built our theories**.

Beyond the core set of assumptions which a social science may hold, there are also provisional assumptions, taken on for the sake of a particular exercise. We might say, for example,

1. 'Let us assume perfect competition'; or
2. 'Let us assume that the interest of every actor in every long and short run is represented in a perfect market'; or
3. 'Let us assume that utility will be maximised when preferences are satisfied.'[4]

Even more commonly, we build into our models an assumption that

4. 'Equilibrium is where things are, or whither things are tending.'

The first of these assumptions is quite often made explicit: the other three are more often assumed than stated. What relation does 'assumption' bear to 'belief'? When closely questioned, most of the time we don't really believe that perfect competition *really* is a fact of life (1), or that perfect markets do exist which perfectly represent all interests (2). Many economists probably believe by default the third assumption, of the identity between utility-maximisation and preference-satisfaction simply because it has not occurred to them to question this, but when brought to think about it, many or most economists would be a little uneasy about committing their personal belief to this as a fact of the real world. They might be even more uneasy with a positive or teleological definition (4) of equilibrium as 'where things are or whither things are tending'. It is, however, much easier for us deal with certain economic problems, especially within the neoclassical framework of analysis, when we act as if all of these were our beliefs.

Such *as if* behaviour is not without implications. In the case of perfect competition, for example, as for any assumption which has to do with perfect markets, it requires us to go further: to assume a world where buyers and sellers are too small and powerless to dominate the market; where there is no collusion; there is perfect information; and all the other familiar conditions. Assumptions 3 and 4 have different kinds of implications, of a slightly less 'cognitive' nature. Assumption 3 has to do with an additional belief about human nature, which might or might not be considered a part of the rationality assumption: namely, the assumption that people know what is good for them – or at least, that every individual is the best judge of what is good for him or herself. This belief, like any alternative which may be offered, has strong political overtones. A gravitation toward assumption 4 may, indeed, have as much to do with temperament as with intellect.

As was the case with the *core* assumptions, individual social scientists respond to their, and their colleagues', *provisional* assumptions on a spectrum which goes from Friedman's position – that the realisticness of the assumptions doesn't matter – to the alternative, which holds that unrealistic assumptions will always produce inaccurate and unuseful theories. The latter extreme is, practically, an even more difficult position to maintain than is Friedman's, because any process of thinking is an abstraction – a *remove* from reality. It becomes extremely difficult to theorise at all if we try to ban all unrealistic assumptions.

What I hope to contribute to this debate is some common sense, and then some systematic thinking. The common sense is the observation that sometimes unrealistic assumptions do seem to lead inevitably to bad theory and sometimes they don't; sometimes the realisticness of the assumptions matters more and sometimes less.

The systematic thinking is where I hope something new and interesting may turn up.

- What if it were possible somehow to characterise the situations in which unrealistic assumptions have the greatest potential to lead us into trouble?

- I would like to work towards a system that could predict, for example: 'if you proceed with such and such an assumption, you are going to end up with results that won't be useful.'

In order to dramatise this, I will use as examples of what I mean by 'running into trouble' some stories that stray so far from reality that they blow up into paradoxes. Some of the classic paradoxes in philosophy, economics and other areas may turn out to be examples of what goes wrong when unrealistic assumptions are pushed to their limit. Before I take on some paradoxes, however, I would like to introduce a few more conceptual tools.

REALITY, UNICORNS AND A METAPHOR   In the last chapter I proposed the terms 'unicorn word' or 'unicorn phrase' to indicate a word or phrase which refers to something people can talk about in common – something we have all heard of, so that we each have a reasonable idea of what others mean by it – but where the thing itself does not exist. I suggested that some of the very common and useful concepts of mathematics (infinity, i, lines, points, instants, continuity) may be best categorised as unicorn terms. I stressed – and will want to stress this again, and yet again – that this does not mean we should not use these concepts, in economics or anywhere else: only that we should use them with rather more care and caution than has been common.

At this point I would like to introduce a deliberate use of a little piece of mathematics, emphasising that its use, throughout this chapter, will be *as a metaphor*. It will be developed as an aid in understanding what I will put forth as a resolution to the paradoxes that will be discussed in this chapter. It will be particularly important to recall the metaphorical character of this discussion when we come to Zeno's paradoxes, for some commentators have slipped into error by thinking that the mathematical example below was a literal, not a metaphorical solution to the problems of motion that Zeno posed.

The mathematical metaphor I wish to use may be illustrated by the unbounded integral where, as X approaches infinity, Y asymptotically approaches zero. Since Y never reaches zero, one would think that the area under such a curve would be infinite: this is, in fact, the case for 'the integral from one to infinity of one-over-X, dx' (see Figure 11.1).

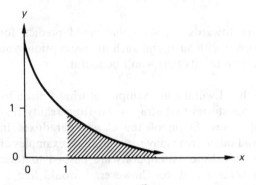

Figure 11.1 The graph of $\int_1^\infty \frac{1}{x}\, dx$

However, $\int_1^\infty \frac{1}{x^2}\, dx$ ('the integral from one to infinity of one-over-X-squared, dx' – the graph of which looks almost identical to Figure 11.1) *has a finite area* (equal, in fact, to 1). This gives us an illustration of an extra-natural limit $[X \to \infty]$ which, in one case, pulls its consequences outside the real world with it; in the other, it returns a result which has a place within our experience. Note that either result – convergence or nonconvergence – can occur in a situation where the limit is infinity, even though 'infinity' is a unicorn word.

The first use I want to make of this metaphor of mathematical limits, and what happens to functions when we take them to their limits, is to establish a comparison with the set of *assumptions that could be characterised as idealisations*. 'Perfectly competitive markets', 'maximising behavior', and 'perfect precision' are all examples of this kind of assumption. They are also concepts which can be described on a spectrum, such as the spectrum from less to more competitive markets, or the spectrum from lesser to greater precision.

We may feel intuitively that, at least in their middle ranges, 'precision' and 'competition' lie on continuous spectra. What happens, however, when we approach the limit case, or idealisation, of perfect precision, perfect markets? Is there a discontinuity, such as we find in some mathematical functions, between the limit and the limit minus epsilon? **I would suggest that such a discontinuity, if it exists, is not to be looked for where we depart from the *actual*, but where we depart from the *possible*.**

Thought-experiments often ask us to explore conditions which do not actually exist in the real world. The thought-experiments which have the potential to end up as paradoxes, I am going to suggest, are those which contain some premise that is not only counter-factual, but is also counter-possible.[5]

The metaphor being developed here depends upon a comparison between, on the one hand, a mathematical function that goes toward some limit; and, on the other hand, an explanation that depends upon the idea of real events tending toward some 'ideal case'. When the mathematical limit is outside reality (e.g., infinity), or the ideal case is something not encountered in the real world (e.g., perfect markets), it will sometimes, but not always, happen that the integral will blow up, or the model will break down into paradox or absurdity. Without trying to define, on the mathematical side of the analogy, what are the contexts within which functions approaching certain limits do or do not converge, I will ask the question: what is the relationship between context and idealisation (or 'limit case assumption') which will result in 'nonconvergence' in a description of the real world?

My hypothesis is that nonconvergence – meaninglessness – is the fate of any argument, model, theory or system of theories where two conditions obtain:

1. first, when there is a discontinuity between the limit case idealisation and the real world;
2. and second, when the action in the argument, model, etc., is required to go continuously along the idealisation all the way to its limit.

Light is shed upon both of these conditions by a comparison between an idealisation commonly used in economics – perfect competition – and one from the physical sciences upon which economists have often drawn for analogy – the perfect vacuum. In such analogies it is often stressed, from the social science side, that the spectrum from less, to more, to a perfect vacuum, is continuous, with no phase-shift involved in the achievement of the limit. The analogy implies that the same may be said of all the social science idealisations which are employed as assumptions.

When, historically, this analogy first began to be employed, the perfect vacuum of the natural sciences was something of which no human being had had direct experience (indeed, Aristotle denied that such a thing *could* exist). During the formative period of the early 1900s, when the young science of economics was looking to physics for methodological guidance,[6] physicists were optimistic that a perfect vacuum could be achieved. The methaphor has remained influential, even though the prevailing beliefs in physics have changed.

If a perfect vacuum is not to be found in nature, is a perfect market? Not, I would suggest, strictly defined: there are anti-competitive characteristics in human nature, such that, as long as humans and their institutions continue to be the chief actors in markets, the counter-balance to perfect competition will always be effectively in play.[7] In particular, there may be a discontinuity (something like a 'phase shift') between the kinds of information actually found in the real world and the perfect information required for perfect markets. (More will be said on this in relation to Newcomb's paradox.)

If, indeed, perfect markets as strictly defined in economics not only do not but *cannot* occur in nature, this still does not mean that it will never be useful to think about them, or to assume them for certain modeling exercises. Their explosive potential for such use depends as well upon the second condition given above.

The second condition – **that the action in the argument, model, etc., is required to go continuously along the idealisation all the way to its limit** – applies to the context in which the idealisation is treated in a particular model or theory. If the context is carefully defined so that the action only depends upon the middle ranges (e.g., where behaviour is quite competitive, but never required to be completely so), then the potential for serious trouble need not be realised.

PASS-THROUGH   I have suggested that the determination of whether
LIMITS   an idealisation is to be understood as a 'continuous' or a 'discontinuous' limit is a first step toward discovering what circumstances will create paradoxes or absurdities (the analogy to which, in mathematics, is nonconvergence). Besides 'continuous' or a 'discontinuous' idealisations, there is another category of assumptions which I would call a 'pass-through limit'. A pass-through limit is an idealisation which you keep aiming at, until you find yourself on the other side of it, but there is no duration of real time when you can say, 'Here I am at the limit'. Put differently, it is a case where the coincidence of the conceptual limit and the real-world experience never exists in real time, but where, in the real world, we seem to go *through* the conceptual space which may be identified as a limit-case to reality. I am reminded of a grafitto in the women's lavatory at Boston University (the university where I took my economics doctorate): 'The long run will never come, and equilibrium is where you're never at.' In many instances equilibrium is set up in

such a way as to be a pass-through limit. The concept of instantaneous time may also be usefully described in this way. Zeno's paradox will provide a more concrete example of this concept.

Mathematicians, when talking about a non-convergent integral, sometimes say that it 'blows up'. That is what happens, I will claim, to logic that tries to integrate real-world reasoning with an ideal case that stands outside of the possibility in the given context. A number of examples of logic 'blowing up' in this way have been preserved in the special form of paradoxes. The approach which is being suggested here, with the three categories of 'continuous', 'discontinuous' and 'pass-through' limits, may be able to slice through the Gordian knot of a number of logical paradoxes.

APPLICATION As a start, let us consider Newcomb's paradox,[8]
OF THE LIMIT where a 'predictor' (possessing an extraordinary
METAPHOR ability to predict, from knowledge of a person's character, what that person will do) has set up
A Newcomb's rewards based upon foreknowledge (or an extra-
paradox ordinarily good guess) of which of two boxes a subject will choose to open. Specifically,

There are two boxes, (B1) and (B2). (B1) contains $1000. (B2) contains either $1000000 ($M), or nothing . . . .
You have a choice between two actions:
(1) taking what is in both boxes
(2) taking only what is in the second box.[9]

The catch is that the 'predictor' (initially described as, possibly, an extra-terrestrial being, to account for its exceptional predictive powers) will decide what to put in box (B2) *depending upon* its assessment of what the subject will choose, in the future, to do. Thus,

if it predicts that the subject will take only what is in the second box, then it will put $M in the second box:

but if it predicts that the subject will open both boxes, then it leaves the second box empty.

Importantly, the subject knows these rules; the subject also knows that *the predictor has almost never been wrong.*

The sequence of events appears in our familiar linear time to be as follows:

(t_1) predictor deposits rewards

(t_2) according to some decision rule, the subject chooses to open box (B2) only, or else both boxes

(t_3) the subject gets the reward that was already in the box(es) when s/he opens it (them).

Normal, rational rules of decision-making would assume that the result, at time (t_3) depends only upon what happened in prior times (t_1) and (t_2), *and not vice versa*. Given that the rewards are already in the boxes at time t_2, the dominance principle would say that, whatever decision the predictor has already made, at time t_2 it is the case that the subject has a better chance of getting a higher reward if s/he chooses to open both boxes. However, this story contains the appearance of backwards causality, linking the choice at (t_2) to the event of (t_1) through the predictor's extraordinary abilities. This is how Nozick argued it:

If one believes, for this case, that there *is* backwards causality, that your choice causes the money to be there or not, that it causes [the predictor] to have made the prediction that he made, then there is no problem. One takes only what is in the second box. Or if one believes that the way the predictor works is *by looking into the future*; he, in some sense, sees what you are doing, and hence is no more likely to be wrong about what you do than someone else who is standing there at the time and watching you, and would normally see you, say, open only one box, then there is no problem. You only take what is in the second box. *But suppose we establish or take as given that there is no backwards causality*, that what you actually decide to do does *not* affect what he did in the past, that what you actually decide to do is not part of the explanation of why he made the prediction he made . . .' (ibid., p. 134; italics added).

The paradox, as the story is presented here, is that there are two plausible, mutually exclusive, courses of action; on the face of it, there exist reasons both necessary and sufficient to support each one, but only one course of action can be taken. It is, in (Nozick's) actual experience of discussing this paradox with a variety of people, very difficult to persuade the proponents of either course of action that the other is right; worse yet is the situation of the person who can feel the force of both sets of arguments – and yet who knows that only one decision can be made.

My answer is that the problem was set up in an 'impossible' way – a way that was *bound* to 'blow up', rather than converging upon a single solution that would accord with all parts of the story. The problem is that

(a) we are asked to believe that there is no backwards causality (conditions which seem to abide by the laws of our known world); and, simultaneously,

(b) we are asked to believe in a very, very high degree of predictive ability on the part of the predictor (conditions which go beyond the limits of what is possible in this world).

The individuals who come down strongly in favour of one decision *or* the other are those who choose to place their credence according to (a) *or* (b) – effectively managing to ignore the other request for belief. The individuals who suffer from simultaneously feeling the force of both arguments are those who somehow did succeed in accepting, with approximately equal weight, both (a) *and* (b).

Belief (a) is consonant with what we know of this world. On the face of it, belief (b) is described so as to make it, also, plausibly part of the world we live in (especially because we are *told* that there is no backwards causality); but this is where something illegitimate is slipped in. Under the mask of the insistence that backwards causality is not involved, we are asked to believe in a degree and kind of predictive power that simply does not exist in this world.

We (human beings) can make very good predictions about the way certain chemicals will react together under a set of stated conditions. We have learned to make pretty good predictions about how pigeons will respond to a variety of stimuli, and we are learning, all the time, additional quite reliable predictions about more pigeon responses to more diverse stimuli. We can make some predictions about large patterns of human behaviour (e.g., marriage, or voting) that seem to hold for a while after they are first made, but that disintegrate slowly over time. As individuals, we may be quite good at predicting some of the choices that will be made by other individuals to whom we are close (which of two recipes my husband will prefer; what my son or daughter will do on the first night at the end of the school year; etc.) But the skill we are asked to believe in, of the extra-terrestrial predictor, does not fall into any of these real-world categories. Essentially, we are asked to believe in a predictor so accurate that it can know things about the subject's character which the subject him/herself does not know until the moment of irrevocable choice – *general truths about character which will absolutely (or almost absolutely) determine a particular choice.* In effect, we are asked to accept actions or states being codetermined by 'personality' or 'genes' in a way that does not fit our known world.[10] If the predictor does not have supernatural powers of prediction, it can only make its extraordinarily good guesses about the future by deduction from what it knows about the subject's state at t_1 – knowledge, one can only presume, which must be about either personality or genetic make-up.

Such deduction, I claim, is outside of possibility. Many actual people, actually thinking about this story, have found themselves so divided between the two choices that they might well come down one way on one day, the other on the next, depending upon random outside events that might have affected their moods, etc. Experience suggests that few if any individuals are entirely consistent: the best possible knowledge of an individual is likely to yield, not an absolute prediction of behaviour, but a probabilistic one, such as: 'Faced with such and such a situation, the subject will take choice (A) 75 per cent of the time'.

The first discontinuity in Newcomb's paradox is its assumption of a consistency in human behaviour, arising from 'genes' and/or 'personality', which permits (nearly) perfect prediction. The next discontinuity is the assumption of the combination of knowledge and understanding (of 'genes' and/or 'personality') which must be present in order to make the (nearly) perfect prediction of the story.

The story is told as not necessarily reaching the limiting cases (of *perfect* predictive ability, or *perfect* consistency in behaviour), but it ignores what I perceive as a discontinuity between the limit and the limit-minus-epsilon (the best possible prediction, the highest possible degree of consistency). It is doubtful that we would ever be able to describe conclusively what constitutes 'the best possible prediction'; but I suggest that the supposed (perhaps extra-terrestrial) predictor and its predictable subject have been described in a way that depends upon assumptions that go beyond the limits of any possible reality of this world. The attempt to apply rational decision rules to the problem is paradoxical because of an absurdity in trying to apply this-world behaviour to what is, in effect, another world.

B The paradox of the 'selfishness gene' It will be useful to compare this conclusion, briefly, with a plausible resolution of what some have seen as a paradox in the theory of evolution.

By some interpretations, a particular strand of sociobiology[11] shows that reality cannot be as we, in fact, know it to be. The puzzle is posed thus:

> Suppose a species to be genetically programmed for altruism, so that individual members will risk their lives for the good of other members or of the whole (e.g., in rescuing an endangered individual).
>
> Now suppose that a mutation arises such that individuals carrying the mutated gene are 'selfish': they will be 'free riders' on the altruism of the rest of the group, but will not put themselves at risk to enhance the welfare of others.
>
> Such selfish individuals will therefore, on average, live longer than the altruistic members, have more children, and pass on their selfishness to a disproportionate fraction of the next generation. This will be repeated until most of the population carries the 'selfishness' genes instead of the altruistic ones. By similar reasoning, we see that, in a generally selfish population, it would be impossible for a self-sacrificing gene to arise.
>
> Yet (here is the paradox) we know that there actually are a number of species in which individuals will perform acts that reduce their own 'inclusive fitness' (at the extreme, sacrificing their lives) for their children, for the children of other individuals, or in defense of a larger group. How can this be?

The answers proposed by the philosopher, Mary Midgley, depend upon finding the limit case assumptions implicit in the statement of 'the selfishness gene paradox', and showing these assumptions to be discontinuous with reality in the given context. She starts with the 'atomising approach to impulses' which, projecting from what is known about genetic determinism of physical characteristics (certain chunks of DNA can be isolated as critically affecting e.g., eye colour in humans, maturation speed in fruit flies, etc.) assumes that there are also isolable DNA groupings which can be – and someday will be – recognised as determining any psychological characteristic one cares to mention. Midgley says:

> If you believe that the tendency to each specific sort of action is inherited separately, then all tendencies carrying personal danger are

surprising, because it should have been possible to eliminate them
while keeping all the rest. But in fact there seems no reason to suppose
that these tendencies are inherited in such small units, however
convenient that arrangement might be to games theorists . . . .
It seems unrealistic to talk as though the tendency to rescue people
were something that could be carried by a single gene. Something
like a tendency to give warning cries might conceivably be so. But
rescuing is plainly far too complex a phenomenon to be governed in
this way. This is true partly because the kinds of danger, and
therefore the kinds of rescue possible, do not follow a single pattern
– but also because, in any fairly complex creature, the undertaking of
dangerous actions *must* involve other traits in the character besides
the impulse in question; the whole character has to be such as to
permit them. Such behavior cannot stand alone.[12]

In particular, Midgley emphasises

the absolute necessity of treating altruism as an aspect of motivation,
and therefore as something that makes sense only in the context of a
given emotional constitution. It cannot be dealt with if it is defined
merely by results. The higher animals – unlike, perhaps, the social
insects – have characters, general forms of life typical to their species.
Their particular behaviour patterns have to fit into these. When a
particular species puts something high on its priority system – for
instance, dominance, territory, or the care of the young – then it will
face danger for that . . . . It does not seem likely that the power to
rescue others from severe danger makes much difference directly to a
species's survival, though it can certainly do so to that of a small
group. What does make an enormous difference, however, is the
power to form the strong social bonds that make rescue possible.
When we consider what is involved in the relation of parent and
child in a slow-developing species, and remember that this bond
shapes the early experience of every member of that species, further
gradual progress to mutual help among adults does not seem too
hard to imagine. And in that context, rescue is intelligible enough. It
has to be explained not as an isolated gamble, but as part of a whole
pattern of motives, which as a whole is advantageous (ibid.,
pp. 137–8).

The world depicted by Midgley is strikingly more complex than that
assumed in simplistic uses of sociobiology. The limit-case idealisation,
'one gene controls one characteristic', is a way of thinking that works

fairly well at the level of Gregor Mendel's experiments with peas. However, it contains a hidden bomb that will explode '**when the action in the argument, model, etc., is required to go continuously along the idealisation all the way to its limit**': e.g., when, as we just saw, it is carried into a context where complexity is more critical. To generalise Midgeley's point, when we have to include 'patterns of behavior' in our analysis of survival schemes (as is the case with virtually all animals, as well as at least some plants), then we are dealing with contexts where the discontinuous idealisation, 'one gene for each characteristic', will disable the story.

C Zeno's 'dichotomy' paradox   Newcomb's paradox and the paradox of the selfishness gene are particularly interesting for the social sciences because they deal with human choices.

At the same time, it is instructive to see the same approach applied to something that may appear, on the face of it, to be a paradox about the physical world, but where the problem in fact hinges on generalised assumptions of precision, divisibility and continuity which are commonly made in social sciences (such as economics) where mathematics are much employed. Zeno's paradoxes of motion may also be seen to have a 'solution' (if it is a solution to point out that the problem, as posed, simply does not belong to our known world) through application of what I have been calling the limits metaphor.

We will look particularly at the one of Zeno's paradoxes which is known as 'the Dichotomy'. We will find that it is like the paradox of the selfishness gene (and unlike Newcomb's paradox), in that it imagines a situation which is inconsistent with our experience of reality (rather than creating an internal inconsistency). The paradoxical conclusion of the Dichotomy is that **motion is impossible** – a conclusion which, of course, everyone knows, by experience, to be false. And yet, the argument is very compelling.

The argument, most simply stated, proceeds thus:

If you set out to run a mile, you first have to run a half mile; but before you can get to the half-mile mark, you have to get to the quarter-mile mark; and so on. The image is one of paralysis in the face of infinite regress: since infinite divisibility (e.g., of a distance) is assumed, you can never reach point B, because you are always required, *first*, to get to the point halfway between A and B. That halfway point is redefined as the new point B, and the problem is repeated, *ad infinititum*.

A more rigorous statement of the problem, connecting it with modern mathematics and physics, is the following:

> Among the four paradoxes with which Zeno sought to discredit the possibility of physical motion, two are of primary relevance to contemporary mathematical physics, because of that discipline's affirmation that the time variable ranges over the real numbers just as the space variable does. More particularly, it is the denseness of the ordering of the points of space and of the instants of time that provides the point of application for Zeno's polemic. The claim that for any point on the path of a moving object, there is *no* next point, anymore than there is an immediately following or preceding instant for any instant during the motion, enables Zeno to ask incisively: In what sense can the events composing the motion be significantly said to succeed one another temporally, if they succeed one another densely rather than in the consecutive manner of a discrete sequence? This question takes the form of asking . . . how can a temporal process even begin, if, in order to survive the lapse of a positive time interval T, a body must first have endured through the passage of an infinite regression of overlapping subsidiary time intervals $\frac{T}{2^n}$ ($n = \ldots, 3, 2, 1$) *which has no first term* because the denseness postulate entails infinite divisibility . . .?[13]

A logical trick which allows us to deal with one aspect of the Dichotomy is to perform (theoretically) the exact same operation upon *time* as that which is being performed (theoretically) upon *space*: one hour, infinitely divided, would surely suffice to walk one leisurely mile, infinitely divided. Here an infinity (whose size is 'alph naught' in Cantor's terms) of infinitesimal increments of time is paired up with the same type of infinity of infinitesimal increments of space. However, a logical problem still remains after this operation: there is no reason to think that an infinite addition of infinitesimals (if they are true infinitesimals, with zero dimension) would add up to a finite distance or time.

Alfred Marshall has not been the only person to find that time and change are stumbling blocks on which the scientific method must repeatedly bark its shins. In the introductory essay to the book just quoted, the editor, Wesley Salmon, comments that Henry Bergson

> takes the paradoxes of Zeno to prove that the intellect is incapable of understanding motion and change. In his celebrated 'cinemato-

graphic' characterisation of ordinary knowledge he maintains that the usual approach to a physical process consists in accumulating a series of static descriptions of its successive states, much as a motion picture consists of a large number of still pictures. By stringing these static representations together, Bergson argues, we can never come to grips with movement and change themselves . . . . It is only by entering into the process and perceiving it directly that we can genuinely understand physical becoming. Such insight cannot be achieved by mathematical analysis or by logical reasoning; metaphysical intuition is the only way (Wesley Salmon, 'Introduction' to *Zeno's Paradoxes*, p. 19).[14]

Continuing the discussion in Chapter 6, a first cut at the Dichotomy paradox might be to say that the problem is that space and time are continuous, while matter is discrete (it is discrete *as matter*: it's less clear what one can say about it on the level at which it resolves to energy). Moreover, 'discrete' and 'continuous' have different meanings when discussed in the context of (1) 'matter', (2) 'space', (3) 'time', and (4) 'energy'. If we suppose that the very first use of the words *discrete* and *continuous* was presumably with respect to material objects, then we should treat the later application of these words to space, time, and energy as *metaphorical extensions*, not as identical usages. Bergson (who is imprecise but, I think, accurate, as far as he goes) says that Zeno's paradoxes 'all consist in applying the *movement* to the *line* traversed, and supposing that what is true of the line is true of the movement.'[14] What one needs to add is that what is assumed in Zeno's story of the immobilised runner is true only of a theoretical line, in theory, not of any real line, in reality. This point has been made in a variety of commentaries, such as the following: (this is from a discussion of another paradox of Zeno, 'Achilles and the Tortoise', but it is equally applicable to the Dichotomy):

In a physical race, what can we do in the way of marking points on Achilles' distance corresponding to the terms of the infinite geometric series? We may mark many such points. But they are physical points and are therefore unlike mathematical points that have no size. Physical points always have some size. Hence arises the difficulty of packing an infinite number of them into a finite distance. Even if we make the points extremely small, this cannot be done. Even though we make them as small as we please, they still, so long as they are physical and thus greater than zero, cannot be

244 Textual Analysis and Reality in the Social Sciences

packed into a finite distance. And, if they are reduced to zero, they are no longer physical, but mathematical and no longer relevant. Nor can any device of 'infinitesimals' enable us to pack in an infinite number of them: 'vanishing quantities', 'ghosts of departing quantities' of whatever minuteness greater than zero can always by amassed in too great numbers to be packed into a finite distance.

This, I think, is the easiest way of seeing that Zeno's premise cannot characterise a physical race: the 'and so on' is inapplicable because somewhere two neighboring physical points will touch each other and it will be impossible to subdivide the distance between them without altering the assigned size of the points (J. O. Wisdom, 'Achilles on a Physical Racecourse', in Salmon, 1970, pp. 86–7).

As with Newcomb's paradox and the paradox of the selfishness gene, there is something in the way Zeno's problems are set up that brings an other-world assumption into a real world situation. A salient problem is the assumption of infinite divisibility of matter, space, time and motion: the same word, *continuity*, is used with all four, and the *theoretical possibility of infinite divisibility* which accompanies 'continuity' is assumed to follow.

It is difficult to accept that an idea like infinite divisibility, which has become so familiar to us, has no real world meaning.[15] Another way to think about problems of measurement is to focus upon the fact that *perfectly precise* physical measurement requires the identification of *points*; e.g., if you wish to measure the distance between A and B, you have to define precisely the points where A and B are located.

Suppose we try to get around this by deciding that, rather than dealing with pre-existing, real world points, we will create points which, *a priori*, are twelve inches apart. In conception, this seems reasonable; what happens when we try to put it into practice? As we take out stronger and stronger microscopes with which to focus on the two ends of our real-world, twelve-inch-ruler, we will find the ruler to be more and more bumpy. We will have to make judgments on whether to measure from the end of *this* molecule or *that* (for a while we are back in the terrain of fractals); then, as we get down to the atomic, and finally the subatomic, levels (moving into the field of physics), we will find that there is much more 'space' than there is 'matter'; that the matter, such as it is, refuses to stay still; and that there is no way of locating '*the* point indicated by the end of the ruler'.[16]

A similar argument will show that 'the point halfway between' the two ends of the ruler – or between points A and B – *has no real world existence.* Zeno supposed that before we go *to* the end point we must go *to* the halfway point. The Gordian-knot-cutting fact is that, in this real world, where location is as uncertain as fractals shows it to be (see n. 15, above), *we never go 'to' any points.* The best we can do, in trying to use language to bridge the gaps between metaphors and molecules, is to say that the only relation *real objects* can have with the *ideal concept* of 'points' (in time or in space) is that they go *through* them; hence the notion of the pass-through limit.

In the world of mathematics, we may have dimensionless points; in the real world, dimensionless entities (such as photons?) play no role in dividing up space; dimensioned space is only partitioned (and never precisely so, even at the molecular level) by other dimensioned entities. Nor do the possible interactions of real entities include the idea of precise juxtaposition which Zeno evidently had in mind when he spoke of going *to* a point.

My foot may go *through* a point (when the latter is defined as a dimensioned area), or else it may come to rest *on* it (if the 'point' is imagined on the ground). There is no way that my foot can come to rest 'right next to' a dimensioned point B, because both objects, being material, are composed of a combination of matter and space, where, at the subatomic level, (we are told by physicists), the relations between matter/energy and space are such that the space around each subatomic particle is proportionally like the space around a few dust-motes in a great cathedral. There is only probability to tell us about the relative positions of a particle in my foot and a particle in the graphite pencil mark signifying point B; the probability of their actually colliding (being right 'next to' one another – does that phrase still have a meaning at this level?) is vanishingly small.

Summarising this discussion we might say: 'You can't get there (to the world of mathematics) from here (the physical world)'. A very simple example of this fact emerges from Zeno's Dichotomy: you cannot subdivide a real distance so as to arrive at a point. In the real-world game, points are out. Similarly, 'However many moments you can mention you are still only specifying the limits of the periods that separate them, and at any stage of the division you like it is these periods that make up the overall period.'[17]

A note is in order here on the metaphor which introduced the approach of this chapter to certain paradoxes. I am far from the first to have noticed a similarity between the idea of a convergent limit and Zeno's paradoxes of motion. However, I have been careful to keep my use of the limit idea a metaphorical one, while others (e.g., Alfred

North Whitehead and Charles Sanders Pierce[18]) have claimed that Zeno's story really *is about* an infinite series which, in the limit, is convergent. That is what the *mathematical* version of the story is about, but this is precisely why it creates a paradox, for there is another, *real* version of the story, which is about real motion through real space in real time; and this version has nothing to do with infinity.

EMPIRICISM What may be found particularly alarming about the
(AGAIN)   preceding discussion is that it is so empirical. I have
             depended upon what I believe about the real world –
including beliefs that stem from a lay reading of modern physics, similarly from experimental psychology, as well as from personal experience with decision-making and prediction in myself and other people – to suggest that what have seemed to be paradoxes are, in fact, situations where unreal assumptions (a degree of predictability in human behaviour; a one-to-one relation between definable genes and predictable outcomes; the possibility of accurate measurement to an infinite degree of precision; the idea that material things in the real world may be positioned 'right next to' one another; or the translation, from mathematics, of the concept of a 'point' as something that has meaningful existence in the real world) have been introduced into an otherwise plausible story. Each story blows up – it produces conclusions that are mutually contradictory, or else that contradict our experience of the world – *when such an unrealistic assumption is pushed too close to its limit.*

Past attempts to 'solve' such paradoxes have depended, for the most part, upon logic operating *within* each story. The assumptions of the story were accepted as written, and the game was to try to use the rules of logic to operate on the given elements so powerfully as to escape from their paradoxical traps.[19] I have proposed an empirical approach which, in addition to logical analysis of internal consistency, inspects the story to see how it relates to our beliefs about this world.

If an integral is calculated, and found not to converge to any real number, we do not try to use logic to find ways around the answer: we accept that a given function, integrated up to a given limit, is one that simply does not converge.

When encountering a story that contains a paradox we may, similarly, choose to examine, for plausibility, the way the 'plot' of the story (Achilles tries to overtake the Tortoise; a human subject tries to decide which box to open) combines with the built-in assumptions (space is infinitely divisible; genes or personality 'determine' choices).

Some, at least, of the persistent paradoxes kicking around in the literature of philosophy, mathematics, etc., represent cases where the flaws are not to be found in the internal logic. What then remains for examination is the possibility that it is 'external inconsistency' which has made the story fail to converge. I have suggested that what we should be on the look-out for is an element which has been allowed to go unchallenged because it appears reasonable in the 'middle ranges' (some degrees of probability in some kinds of prediction fit within the real world, as do measurements and locational activities down to some degree of precision; there is a middle range of influence – rarely, absolute determinism – from genes upon behaviour; etc.), but which has slipped too far along toward its limit, or ideal case (e.g., perfect prediction, or perfect precision).

There may be something alarming in such a suggestion. For many of the people who are good at what it takes to be successful in academia it is easier, more pleasant, cleaner, somehow, to work on the logic of internal consistency than to get mixed up with the 'external consistency' issue of how theories, models, etc. relate to empirical facts. Then, too, there is so much known today; as soon as one steps outside of a very narrowly defined area of expertise one will encounter others who know much more than one does oneself. One risks being wrong. If one is *shown* to be wrong, this is embarrassing and uncomfortable, and may be professionally damaging. As academics, we have gotten where we are because we have demonstrated a fairly good ability to protect ourselves against being logically wrong. If, however, we are to lay ourselves on the line in terms of facts about the real world, and, worse yet, if we cannot always choose the factual area to be discussed – if we are expected to address any old kind of reality whose nature happens to be at issue – then there is absolutely no surety. There is no one of us who could not make mistakes in some – many – areas.

All that being said, it is hard to believe that there is much future in an academic attitude that does not try, ultimately, to test theories, hypotheses, models, and other constructs against all that is known about reality. We don't have to be experts on everything to be able to make a first cut at what is reasonable.

The greatest difficulty we are likely to encounter in such an endeavour is with fields that are currently in the process of shaking up old, 'common sense' notions – replacing them with what will probably be the common sense of the future. There, what seems 'reasonable' may now be under attack by the experts, and may cease to seem reasonable a few years hence. For example, at the time of the classical Greek philosophers, many of the discoveries which were most surprising and upsetting to existing beliefs were coming from mathematics; indeed, perhaps it was his effort to accommodate some of the new concepts in mathematics that led Zeno to postulate the impossible situations that have come down the centuries to us. In the nineteenth century such unsettlement came dramatically from evolutionary biology. At our own time in history – indeed, throughout much of the twentieth century – physics has been the area of understanding which most often seems to shake us on matters which we might have thought empirically obvious.

Recall the 'unicorn word' idea which encourages us to draw distinctions between what we believe to be real and what we believe does not belong to this world. We may find it useful to refer to a gnomic formulation:

That we haven't experienced it doesn't mean it isn't.
That we can imagine it doesn't mean it is.

It becomes more difficult to keep these distinctions between reality and conception in mind when we wander into abstruse subjects such as theoretical physics. Modern physics obliges us, for example, to consider it an open question whether such familiar concepts as 'space' and 'time' may be unicorn words. Some of the contentions of modern physics appear to us as paradoxes, in creating conclusions which we intuitively feel to be inconsistent with reality. A prime example is the story of Schrödinger's cat, which extends (to what appears, in commonsense terms, to be an absurdity) the contention that the context of the experiment of the observation will determine, in a deeper way than is familiar to us in ordinary life, the nature of reality at a given moment.

Context, again, is critical. It seems likely that Heisenberg's or Shrödinger's conclusions on the interaction between reality and observation are more relevant to the wave versus particle nature of electrons than to our more commonly experienced reality. What causes an idealisation (such as 'pure observation') to create a 'nonconvergence' is not whether it is, alone, a discontinuity from reality; but whether it is discontinuous from reality in the particular context wherein we are considering it. For example, Schrödinger proposed very special conditions where the state of a cat would depend upon the probabilistic behaviour of subatomic particles. The cat may be simultaneously both dead and alive (just as the particle is, in some probabilistic sense, in more than one position) *as long as it is not observed*; its state will resolve to one or the other only as a result of observation.[20] However, in most situations it is reasonable to assume that the state of a cat in a box is in more determinate than this, even while the cat is not being observed.

THE USEFULNESS AND THE DANGERS OF THE IDEA OF IMPOSSIBILITY Consider the modern physicist's beliefs (e.g., Heisenberg's or Schrödinger's conclusions on the interaction between reality and observation) as tools. Consider human nature, with its nearly irresistible urge to use, on every object at hand, any new tool that it has in hand. A great deal that is of value – much, indeed, of what we regard as human civilisation – has resulted from this tendency. *Ex ante* we would usually not wish to restrain such exuberance (at least, in the case of *abstract* tools; when the tool is something physical, like a hammer, we may wish to exercise some restraint over the child who has just discovered it!). Nevertheless, *ex post* we can say that some uses of such and such a tool are better than others; and some are positively misleading. Zeno had applied a set of tools – the abstract idea of infinity, and its corollary idea, infinite divisibility – to a piece of reality where it had no place. This inappropriate application is hard to spot, because the ideas are entirely appropriate with respect to some things (e.g., the real-number line, or set theory) whose dissimilarities from the stuff (real time, real space) to which Zeno had applied them are not immediately obvious.

The concept of 'inapplicability' to which I have just appealed depends upon the idea, brought out earlier, of 'impossibility'. It is important to post some warnings on this subject. History is littered with impossibilities disproven, and of successes which could only be achieved by ignoring the very idea I have been promulgating, of skirting impossibilities.

A good example is a story which is told of Albert Einstein: when praised for his mathematical prowess, he replied that there were many better mathematicians than he; his successes stemmed from the fact that, when his mathematics led him to what seemed an impossible conclusion, he went ahead with the mathematics instead of being blocked by the common sense notion of what is possible. It appears that this was an appropriate and useful frame of mind for a physicist in Einstein's time; it is likely that there will be other times in other disciplines where it is also the essential precondition for progress.[21]

In this, as in so many things, there is a pendulum of fashion. In the Victorian era, imaginative writers railed against the prevailing fashion of thinking, which required that people only believe in 'hard facts' – in what they could see in front of their noses. The influence of Einstein and his followers in physics has doubtless played a part in turning this fashion around; the field of physics has had such an impact in this century that what works there is bound to be tried out almost everywhere else. In any case, intellectuals now seem eager to follow the advice given to Alice by the Red Queen – to practice believing a few impossible things every day, before breakfast.

I can propose no algorithm for testing when the 'Einsteinian' frame of mind is, and when it is not, appropriate. The ability to believe the seemingly impossible is obviously of great importance in some cases: in other cases, dogged insistence on remaining within the bounds of what seems to 'make sense', though less romantic, may be the strategy that will stay closest to the truth. The 'Einsteinian' frame of mind may have been, and may continue to be, the doorway to knowledge in physics (though perhaps it has somewhat overused by now). In the field of economics, which is, after all, largely about subjects that are on the human scale of magnitude (because the subjects are human beings), I would suggest that, in the majority of cases, we should only as a last resort abandon (though we should always be willing to reexamine) our common-sense beliefs about what is possible in this world. Ploughing the fields of the counter-intuitive has been practised so much in recent economic work that what was to be harvested therefrom may almost all have been gathered in.

At the same time we must be warned that, while the set of 'the possible' may (or may not) be finite, it seems most likely that it is, in any case, unbounded. If we rule certain topics, approaches, packages of ideas, etc., 'out of bounds' because they seem to us to make an 'impossible' use of some idealisation, we could be running the risk of letting common sense blind us to some important counter-intuitive reality. We are in a situation like that of statistics, where every action that decreases the alpha risk increases the beta risk.

There is, and always will be, a tug-of-war between common-sense empiricism and theoretical speculation. These two aspects of human nature often pull in opposite directions. At the same time, each is essential as a complement to the other. Perhaps the chief effect of this chapter's extended use of a metaphor from the mathematical concept of limits, with their properties of convergence, divergence, etc., is to give aid and comfort to the common sense side of this 'dichotomy' in human nature. We all knew, all along, that altruism exists, even though some users (or misusers) of sociobiology claim that it cannot; and we all know that we are capable of moving, whatever Zeno may have 'proved'. What I have tried to show is that the common-sense response to these paradoxes of external inconsistency – 'I don't care what you say you've proved; that's not the way the world is!' – is soundly based: the paradoxes arose because the stories incorporated assumptions which are, in fact, contrary to the way the world is.

The particular counter-factual assumptions which we encountered in the paradoxes of this chapter fell into two groups:

A   Some had to do with **human nature**: how and to what degree it is determined by personality; and how and to what degree personality is determined, in turn, by genetic composition. From this there arise questions about how accurate and precise predictions about human behaviour can be made to be; and on what such predictions would be based.

B   The other group had to do with **the nature of the physical universe**. Some aspects of this physical reality are unlikely to be the basis for a paradox because they are sufficiently obvious that we could not easily be fooled into accepting their denial as part of a realistic story. (For instance, if Zeno's stories began with the statement, 'In order to travel any distance it is necessary to be able to move at infinite speed', we would reject it outright. By contrast, the statement 'Before you can go the whole distance, you must first traverse half the distance' raises no problems; only later is the corollary slipped in that, to traverse half the distance you must *come to the half-way point*; that is a subtle enough issue that it, too, fails to raise our intuitive hackles.)

Those aspects which were teased out in the discussion as containing hidden problems had to do with the realisticness of applying the ideas of e.g., 'points' and 'lines' and 'infinity' to the natural world; if these things are called into question, we then have to consider that an idea such as 'precise measurement' may also be without real-world meaning (although it has plenty of abstract meaning.)

To extend our knowledge of the physical world as far as possible, it was necessary to appeal to some of what is becoming the subject of common belief in the field of modern physics. Some of the conflicts which arose here could be seen as between, on the one hand, pure mathematics (with its zoological garden of unicorn concepts such as infinity, the square root of minus one, and other far fancier impossibilities), and, on the other hand, applied physics (which reveals more than is evident to the unaided senses about the nature of matter, space and time – although all of these concepts tend to suffer identity-shifts when examined at great removes from ordinary sensory experience). Economics, which has for so long suffered from physics-envy, can take comfort at least in this: that, to the extent that physics is 'about' real things in the real world, and mathematics is not, economics is more similar to the former than to the latter.

Notes

1. This chapter was first presented as a seminar at the World Institute for Development Economic Research in Helsinki. I am extremely grateful to WIDER for the opportunity there afforded me to receive much helpful commentary.
    The title originally referred to 'realism', but a participant in the seminar, Uskali Mäki, suggested the change on the grounds that 'While realism is a philosophical doctrine (or divides into many such doctrines), realisticness is a property (or many such properties) of representations, including economic theories and their assumptions.' (Uskali Mäki, 'On the Problem of Realism in Economics', in *Ricerche Economiche*, special issue on 'Epistemology and Economic Theory', March 1989 Abstract). See further Mäki's definition of the philosophical meaning of realism in economics in Chapter 8, above, under 'the Standards Required for "Scientific Belief"'.

2. Some of the debate is summarised in the 1979 essay by Lawrence Boland, 'A Critique of Friedman's Critics', *Journal of Economic Literature*, 17, pp. 503–22.). Some later commentaries include:
    Bruce Caldwell, 'A Critique of Friedman's Methodological Instrumentalism', *Southern Economic Journal*, 47 (1980), pp. 366–74;
    William Frazer Jr and Lawrence Boland, 'An Essay on the Foundations of Friedman's Methodology', *American Economic Review*, 73 (1983) pp. 129–44;
    Abraham Hirsch and Neil de Marchi, 'Making a Case when Theory is Unfalsifiable; Friedman's Monetary History', *Economics and Philosophy*, 2 (1986) pp. 1–22;
    Uskali Mäki, 'Rhetoric at the Expense of Coherence: A Reinterpretation of Milton Friedman's Methodology', *Research in the History of Economic Thought and Methodology*, vol. 4 (1986) pp. 127–43.
    Uskali Mäki, 'Friedman and Realism', forthcoming in *Research in the History of Economic Thought and Methodology*, vol. 8 (1990) (preliminary draft, March 1989).

I have found Mäki's work especially helpful, and have further benefited by discussion with him. His formulation of Friedman's view is the statement that

> economic theories should be accepted as good predictors (but not believed to be true) and rejected as bad predictors (but not believed to be false). According to this conception, nothing follows from acceptance of a theory about its truth and about the existence of its objects. Beliefs about these questions (i.e., the truth value of a theory and the existence of its objects) are formed on grounds independent of accepting or rejecting a scientific theory (Mäki, 'On the Problem of Realism in Economics', p. 25).

3. The sociology-of-knowledge kind of reasons why Friedman's approach has continued to have such force are well laid out in Mäki, 'Friedman and Realism'.
4. I am grateful to Thomas Schelling for mentioning this to me as a particularly questionable frequently made assumption.
5. This line of reasoning, if it proves fruitful, may ultimately require definition of the implications of different kinds of impossibility; but it will not be possible to pursue that here.
6. See Philip Mirowski, 'The Probabilistic Counter-revolution, or How Stochastic Concepts Came to Neoclassical Economic Theory', *Oxford Economic Papers*, 41 (1989) pp. 217–35). Also, Mirowski's history of the influence of physics upon economics, *More Heat Than Light* (Cambridge University Press, 1989).
7. This subject will be discussed in *Social Economics,* volume 2, where the counter-balance to competition just cited will be given the name of 'the pan-human conspiracy'.
8. This paradox was first constructed by the physicist, William Newcomb, of the Livermore Radiation Laboratories. It was first published by the philosopher, Robert Nozick, in 'Newcomb's Problem and Two Principles of Choice', in *Essays in Honor of Carl G. Hempel*, ed. by N. Rescher *et al.* (Reidel, Dordrecht, 1969). Among the many articles that have been written about it since, two that are particularly relevant to the discussion that will follow are J.L.Mackie, 'Newcomb's Paradox and the Direction of Causation', *Canadian Journal of Philosophy*, 7 (1977); and M.Dummett, 'Causal Loops', in *The Nature of Time* (R. Flood and M. Lockwood, (eds) (Basil Blackwell, 1986).
9. R. Nozick, 'Newcomb's Problem and Two Principles of Choice', p. 114.
10. Cf. Nozick's footnote:

> But it also seems relevant that in Newcomb's example not only is the action referred to in the explanation of which state obtains . . . but there is also another explanatory tie between the action and the state; namely, that both the state's obtaining and your actually performing the action are both partly explained in terms of some third thing (your being in a certain initial state earlier) (ibid., p. 146).

11. The strand of sociobiology here referred to is often taken to derive from Richard Dawkin's book, *The Selfish Gene*. He was not, however, talking about a *gene for selfishness*, which is what is at issue here. Martha Nussbaum kindly suggested to me the term, 'the selfishness gene'.

12. Mary Midgley, *Beast and Man: The Roots of Human Nature* (Cornell University Press, New York, 1979) pp. 128 and 134–5. It is regrettable that this excellent book is now out of print.

13. Adolf Grünbaum, 'Modern Science and Refutation of the Paradoxes of Zeno', in Wesley C. Salmon (ed) 1970. (With respect to the references to 'modern physics', note that this essay was written in 1955.)

    For further discussion of continuity and the denseness postulate, refer to Chapter 6, under 'the Use of Mathematics to Address Problems with Time and Change'.

14. Henry Bergson, 'The Cinematographic View of Becoming', in Salmon, 1970, p.64; italics added).

15. If we require persuasion that we have been much too optimistic in combining the notions of *precision, measurement* and *divisibility*, we may appeal to the field of fractals, which has brought into mathematical consciousness the imprecision of measurement and of location. The fractal emphasis upon level of focus shows that a different level will produce different measurements, e.g., the famous example of attempting to measure a shoreline, which runs as follows:

    If you take a thread and lay it carefully on a map's depiction of a piece of shoreline – let us say, the shoreline of Cape Cod – you may then stretch out the thread and, by translating back into the measurement of reality from the key of the map (e.g., 'one inch equals five miles'), you will have a statement of the length of that shoreline. However, if you do the same with a map made to a much finer level of detail (e.g., one inch equals 1/2 mile), wherein the gross outline of promentories and bays is resolved to more detailed ins and outs, you will come up with a measurement considerably longer than the first.

    Now if you drive to Cape Cod and start laying a tape measure along the shore, curling it around each rock that meets the water, the measurement will become much longer again. It will increase once more when you begin using a thinner, more malleable tape, so as to account for all the roughnesses and barnacles on the rocks, and for the individuals granules of sand. When you get out your magnifying glass, and then your microscope, using appropriately more refined measuring instruments, the 'shoreline' will continue to have a greater measured length, as smaller and smaller bumps and indents are accounted for.

    I will not propose imagining that you continue measuring down to an infinitely fine level of detail (!); the picture is quite complicated enough without that. Which measurement, of those within the realm of conceivable, this-world possibility, represents the 'true' length of the shoreline of Cape Cod?

    For a trenchant illustration of how too glib a transition from the mathematical idea of a continuum (with infinite divisibility) to the spacial reality of a continuum can suggest that a finite space can contain an infinite amount (of copper, in the example given), see Daly and Cobb, p. 40.

16. Another way of understanding this was suggested to me in a comment by a physician, Richard Rockefeller: at the atomic level of reality it is meaningless to discuss matter in terms of *location*; matter resolves to energy, which never stands still, so that it can be said to 'come to' or to 'be at' any place.

 If we try to locate our 'points' by means of triangulation – e.g., 'Point A is three metres south of the exterior corner of this building, and five metres west of that path' – we will be right back to where we began: how do we find the 'edge' of the path from which to measure five metres? Moreover, any way we devise of bringing out the measurements from the corner and from the path will have a thickness: the two real world representations of abstract 'lines' (even if they are laser beams) will intersect in an area, not a point – unless we do it only in our heads. The point, once again, is the difference between the idea and the reality.

17. G. E. L. Owen, 'Zeno and the Mathematicians', in Salmon, 1970, p. 158.

 Putting this idea into more mathematical terms, 'the division of an interval effects *no* reduction in the cardinality of the resulting subintervals as compared to that of the original interval.' (Adolf Grünbaum, 'Zeno's Metrical Paradox of Extension', in Salmon, 1970, p. 191). Grünbaum discusses the idea of 'a line' within Cantorean set theory, where it represents the kind of infinity called 'non-denumerable'; any subdivision of such a set is also a non-denumerable infinity. Since points do not exist in the world of material things, and the distance between any two objects is a real distance (even if it cannot be represented, in the real world, by a line, because lines, like points, do not exist in this sphere; and even if its length and end points cannot, in actual fact, be measured and located with absolute precision) – this should make us wonder about the meaning of Grünbaum's introduction of a word to arithmetic from set theory, when he explains a finite interval as 'the union of a continuum of degenerate intervals' (ibid., p. 193). These 'degenerate intervals' (i.e., points) do not actually exist; they cannot be arrayed 'in a continuum' because you never move away from the original dimensionless point when you put other dimensionless points 'next' to it: 'next to' a point is right there, in the same place.

 'Union' has a perfectly good meaning in set theory. The attempt to apply it to a spatial description must be recognised as, again, a metaphor, and not a very successful one, for it does not suggest any new or real answers to the original paradox. Grünbaum indeed concludes that 'We are here confronted with an instance in which set-theoretic addition (i.e., forming the union of degenerate subintervals) is meaningful while arithmetic addition (of their lengths) is not (*ibid.*).

18. 'Writing early in the twentieth century, Pierce remarked of "The Achilles" that " . . . this ridiculous little catch presents no difficulty at all to a mind adequately trained in mathematics and in logic". I presume his low opinion reflected a belief that the entire source of the paradox was Zeno's inability to realise that an infinite series could have a finite sum' (Salmon, 'Introduction' to *Zeno's Paradoxes*, pp. 25–6).

19. E.g., for an analysis for Newcomb's paradox which attacks the story from many angles, but in each case focussing only upon the *internal* logic, see Isaac Levi, 'Newcomb's Many Problems'; *Theory and Decision*, 6 (1975).

20. I would hazard the guess that this story may, indeed, be a true paradox, not merely a situation that appears paradoxical because of our naiveté about physical reality. The limit case that creates the problem could be any one of a number of things. One candidate may be the simplistic pairing of the on/off states of life/death with two possible sets of behaviours of the particle, so that either it *will* trip the hammer that breaks the flask that empties the poison that kills the cat – or it *won't*; the probabilistic behaviour of particles may not resolve so neatly. Examples of other places to look for a discontinuity between the limits assumed in the story and what is possible in reality are: the assumption that what is true for particles is true for the things they affect; or the assumption that all of the things which we think of within the category, 'observation', are continuous in their nature and their effects.

21. There are physicists who would say that Einstein could have made contributions to the emerging field of quantum mechanics, but that he drew back because he ran up against the limits of his credulity: a flexible space/time concept was acceptable, but a world stochastically determined was not – in his famous comment, 'God does not play at dice'. The 'Einsteinian position' cited in this chapter refers to his earlier willingness to give credence to the apparently incredible.

12 Implications and Conclusions From Part II

The emergence, in Classical times in the Western hemisphere, of the combined art-and-discipline, philosophy-and-science, sprang from a concern with the question:

1 'What is?'

The ethical counterpart, which will be especially relevant to Part III of this book (and will be examined further in Volume 2 of *Social Economics*), is:

2 'What matters?'

The questions addressed in the preceding chapter have revolved around:

3 'What is possible?'

Comparing questions 1 and 3, the last is a more speculative deduction from 1. Not only do we deduce that everything that *is* is *possible*; we also make certain postulates about what is *not* possible, even while reserving the expectation that there are possible things beyond what we believe actually exists.

All of this brings us back to the issues of belief/knowledge/ certainty which were addressed in Chapter 6. It is important to repeat here – even at the risk of becoming monotonous – that this author is not trying to claim that the 'reality' cited as the reference-point throughout Chapter 11 is something for which she, or anyone else, can claim certain knowledge. Modern philosophical discussion seems (at least for the nonce) to be converging upon an inability to disprove that there may be a plurality of mutually contradictory theories which are consistent with observed data. It is not dreadful (once one has accustomed oneself to it) to contemplate the possibility that there is more than one 'best' way to understand the world (or that slice of it to which any one of us is privy). There would, however, be something dreadful about being obliged to accept the position of 'anything goes'.

Even for a person who takes the position that truth is, in some basic sense, unitary, the argument of Chapter 11 may be useful in pointing the way towards a first cut at recognising, and setting aside, an impossibility set. 'Stories that blow up', with paradoxes as prime examples, are useful warnings. They force us to reexamine our knowledge of the world from three angles. The reexaminations which will most often be fruitful are:

(a)   If the story blows up into an external inconsistency – i.e., if it comes to what we regard as an impossible conclusion – we must inquire whether we have to alter our idea of what is possible.

(b)   Whether the paradox, or 'blow-up', of the story takes the form of external or of internal inconsistency, we must examine the internal logic to see if that is the source of the problem.

(c)   What was emphasised in Chapter 11 was a third requirement, to reexamine the assumptions behind the story. The possibility was suggested that the problem may have existed, in latent form, in some assumption that was discontinuous with reality; the context of the story then caused that latent potential for trouble to be realised.

IMPLICATIONS   With the tools that have been assembled in Part II let
FOR ECONOMIC   us now return to some questions that were posed
THEORY   much earlier in this book, in Chapter 2, namely:

–   Using a limited approximation to human psychology as a basis for understanding economic activity, how far can we spin out our theories before the limitations of the original assumptions will interrupt the usefulness of conclusions derived within this system?

–   Can we predict, from the limitations of the original assumptions, the character and scope of the pool of light that will be cast by the theories based upon those assumptions? And

–   Are there a variety of possible ways of employing the assumptions we make?

In Chapter 11 a systematic approach was proposed for beginning to answer such questions. It was suggested that we should consider whether, in the context of a particular model, theory, or system of theory, the assumptions employed have the character of idealisations (or limit cases). Where they do (for example, most of the psychosocial assumptions of the neoclassical system of economic theory do have such a character), then we should be able to make some predictions about where these assumptions can remain useful, in the sense of permitting the creation of theories that remain consonant with the observations which they are intended to explain. The set of contexts wherein the initial assumptions are employed out to the point of discontinuity are the contexts which will lie outside of the pool of useful illumination shed by such a system of theory.

To be more specific, we may cite two problems which are widely recognised as major pieces of unfinished business in the field of economics:

A   finding a better fit in the correspondence between *micro* and *macro* economics
B   making the phase shift from *static* to *dynamic* understandings and presentations of economic realities.

To these issues we may add the relations, sometimes also seen as problematical, between

C   *disequilibrium* and *equilibrium*; and
D   *short* and *long run*.

Beneath all of these is the tension – in part methodological, in part content-related – between *empirical* versus *theoretical* approaches to the *inputs* to economics; and the *applied* versus *theoretical* character of its *output*.

Building upon the conclusions of the preceding chapter, I now suggest that a major reason why these issues have remained unresolved is that the existing systems of economic theory have paid inadequate attention to the fact that *under some circumstances the realisticness of assumptions does matter*. In fact, in parallel to this deficiency there has also been a lack of attention to the fact that *the realisticness of conclusions also matters*. Neoclassical economists, in particular, have not infrequently found themselves in the position of having proved what, to the uninitiated, would seem to be impossible. They have then sometimes taken the heroic stance (like Einstein, as described at the end of the last chapter) which holds to the assumptions, the mathematics, and what emerges therefrom, even in the face of an apparent 'blow-up'.[1]

In contrast to this heroic stance, I suggest that blow-ups should be taken more seriously, and subjected to examination from all three of the angles described in the introduction to this chapter. The third question posed there – whether the story contained any assumptions which might be problematical according to the two conditions set out at the beginning of Chapter 11 – is the one that was most emphasised in the last chapter. There it was suggested that assumptions about the fundamental issues of a field should not be made, once for all, absorbed into the field, and then forgotten. In the social sciences, at least, an inevitable characteristic of assumptions is that they, in some way, simplify from or otherwise distort reality. Though this has to be accepted as inevitable, it also must be regarded as a source of potential trouble. As they are introduced into each new context, assumptions should be reexamined to see whether the particular distortions, in conjunction with the particular context, will create the type of problem whose extreme, most obvious form is the paradox.

One additional implication for economic theorising may be drawn out of Chapter 11. This has to do with the long-running debate over whether a theory deserves to be called a theory if it cannot be tested, and what would constitute a proper test for a theory in the social sciences. Without going into all the details here, I will simply suggest the following:

> Without being so ambitious as to require our theories to make testable predictions, we can at least require them not to fall below the threshold of making testable sense. An alertness to 'stories that blow up' is a way of testing whether theories lead to conclusions that are both internally and externally consistent. If the conclusions contain impossible internal contradictions (like Newcomb's paradox), or if they contradict what we believe about the world (like Zeno's paradox, or the paradox of the selfishness gene), then they must be subjected to the three types of reexamination listed at the end of the introductory section to this chapter: (a) reexamine our idea of the possible; (b) reexamine the internal logic; and (c) reexamine the assumptions according to the procedure suggested in Chapter 11.

Although the emphasis throughout the last chapter was on the realisticness of assumptions, it should be noted that what we have come out with is a strong focus upon the realisticness of *conclusions* as the first best test for the totality of a theory. Some absurd theories could, of course, slip through this test: the double negative of highly unrealistic assumptions with poor logical development *could* combine to result in a series of plausible conclusions. One can only assume that flaws in logic and assumptions will show up sooner or later in conclusions which, if they are required to make 'testable sense' as suggested above, will start people asking penetrating questions about the elements of the theory.

IMPLICATIONS   Social economics may have a chance of being able to
FOR SOCIAL   deal with what I cited in the preceding section as the
ECONOMICS   four outstanding pieces of unfinished business in
                 economic theory by beginning with an emphasis upon
a process of communication (including, again, writing or speaking; reading or listening; or using one's logical or intuitive faculties to work over an idea) wherein the approach of *axiomatisation* is put in its proper place – *as a tidy and appealing procedure which is rarely actually employed in social science, and should not be appealed to as the norm.* Social economics would emphasise a use of judgment and of personal experience wherein axiomatisation would be understood to be only one of many ways of employing human powers of reasoning to advance a social science.

This proposal may be felt to point to a severe loss in rigour. To assuage such a feeling it is only necessary to remember, again, that the ideal of developing models, theories, and systems of theory as if they contained no beliefs other than the formally stated assumptions, or as if (as was said in Chapter 6) the theorist was programming a computer – this is *only* an ideal. It is not the way social scientists proceed. (We have also seen it suggested – cf. Chapter 8, n. 3 – that this is not the way natural scientists proceed, either.) To abandon this ideal is to drop a pretence, not to reduce the rigour of actual procedure.

As an alternative to this pretence we may, again, use Marshall as a model. Like all other economists he took a good deal for granted, as common human knowledge, or as the subject of 'common' sense. He did not, however, attempt to make any single, succinct statement which would lay out his assumptions on human nature in the form of axioms upon which to erect a tidy, consistent system of thought. What he did provide was, on the one hand, recurrent reminders that the reality in which a science of Man must be grounded is immensely complex – full of contradictory forces, varying capabilities and, on an individual level, unpredictable responses. On the other hand, Marshall sought for laws and regularities in all this so that, where individual actions are unpredictable, yet a statistical smoothing might emerge in the aggregate. His most ambitious hope (but this, I will suggest in Part III, was falsely based) was to establish a sufficiently reliable relationship between expenditures and their psychological under-pinnings to permit the erection of a science.

If we are left with most of Marshall's procedure to use as a model, *minus* the 'most ambitious hope' just referred to, are we not rather discouragingly moving backwards? Indeed, it is discouraging to think we may have to take a quite different approach to all that has been so carefully erected in this century in the name of economic rigour. Only those who have perceived the conclusions of economics 'blowing up' with increasing frequency, and who have been troubled by the inability of the existing systems of economic theory to come to grips with the questions which it seems most obvious to bring to this field, are likely to be willing to undertake the hard work implied in the conclusions emerging here.

The major prescription that arises from Part II of this book is that the makers and, to a lesser extent, the users, of theories need to know how to take a theory apart, down to its constituent parts, and examine each part for its appropriateness within the whole. The generalisation by which Alfred Marshall indicated this necessity was in his interdiction of 'long chains of deductive reasoning'. I will reword what I believe this means – starting, again, with an analogy.

I once sat in an orchard and watched a mole tunneling its way along, lifting the short grass in a moving ridge. I don't know whether the mole had any particular destination in mind, but I was struck by how often it would stop, poke its long snout up into the air, sniff about as though getting its bearings and then dive back down. The scene reminded me, by contrast, of much of the economic theorising to which I had been exposed, where the tunneller never seems to come up to check his or her bearings between the start of the exercise, and the end. It seemed to me that too many economists reason thus:

> You can find a symbol for anything you can think of: for example, 'H' is as good a symbol for the idea, 'history', as is the word, 'history'. Once you've got a symbol for an idea, you can then put the idea through any process of formal, logical or mathematical reasoning you like. Until you get your symbol out again at the end, you don't have to worry about what it stood for when you put it in at the beginning.

What I tried to show in Chapter 11 was that the inputs to a theory may – indeed, in economics they most likely will – include some abstractions which have the particularly dangerous quality of being idealisations. It is unsafe simply to find a symbol for such an abstraction, plug it into a process, and let the whole thing run without pausing frequently to take one's bearings.

Such an unwary-mole procedure is, I have suggested, made even more dangerous when the procedure in question is dependent upon mathematics. I have made some efforts to drive a wedge between mathematics and economics, stressing that the former operates in a world quite different from the latter: what is 'true' in mathematics is *not* necessarily (though it also may be) 'true' in the human world, in whose comprehension economics is intended to assist. Economics is about people, what they want and how they get what they want. When economists speak of people, wants and efforts, it is assumed, at the foundation of the field, that these words refer to real things in the real world. It is very hard to imagine where the interest of economics would lie if this were not so. But none of this is true of modern mathematics, which has finally accepted (or at least most of its practitioners have accepted) that many of its most interesting and fundamental concepts do not correspond to something in the real world.[2] Mathematical procedures can be enormously useful to economics, but, as a generalisation, it is safest to understand these procedures as something like metaphors.

Much neoclassical economic theorising tends to use 'dangerous' idealisations as inputs, and then tends to run them through procedures that come from a quite different world of discourse (mathematics). If we find these procedures, and their results, less useful than we wish, how are we to develop more useful procedures, to generate more useful results? Most of Part II, one way or another, was an attempt to suggest answers to this question, stressing, in particular, the kinds of mental processes which need to be exercised for intelligent social science communication. These activities may now be reconsidered in the light of Chapter 11, as contributing to our ability to avoid having our assumptions 'blow up' our theories. More positively, these activities should help us to break through the barriers which have kept economists from proceeding satisfactorily with what were referred to, above, as the four 'major pieces of unfinished business'. In conclusion to this chapter, and to Part II, I will briefly outline the ways in which this approach may help us to go beyond these barriers – rather as it was suggested that, in real life, the injection of a sharper understanding of reality can overcome Zeno's theoretical barriers.

A The   More realistic assumptions, along with the
correspondence recognition that assumptions which are accept-
between micro   able in one context may cause 'nonconvergence'
and macro   in another, should allow the recognition that, for
                    different issues, or for issues at different levels of
aggregation, it is allowable and necessary to use variants on our
assumptions.[3]

Some assumptions appropriate to, e.g., firms acting in isolation, will
break down (due to such problems as the fallacy of composition, the
law of large numbers, or some other interaction phenomena) when we
move to consideration of a national or a global industry. Conversely,
an assumption about human behaviour may usefully represent the
averaged out behaviour of a large sample in a given time period, while
the *reasons* for the behaviour are normally left out of the assumption.
That is appropriate: the power of the large sample lies in the fact that it
may simplify from such individual things as reasons. Nevertheless, over
time, many individual reasons (related to tastes, fears, aspirations,
beliefs, etc.) may change in a way that will shift the whole average.

It is legitimate to build up from micro observation to macro
conclusions, or to go from macro observations towards finer levels of
theory, only when we accompany this process with a reexamination of
our basic assumptions as they are used on varying levels of
aggregation.

B The phase The light cast upon the static/dynamic problem by the
shift from   empirical approach suggested here is slightly different
static to   from the use of that approach for the first (micro/
dynamic   macro) issue. In this case, the starting point is the fact
                  that *reality is dynamic: there is no such thing as a static
reality*. (You can freeze a frame in a movie, but you are still living and
breathing in time as you look at the 'frozen' frame.)

For simplicity, and in order to be able to use mathematical
techniques, much economic work starts from an assumption of a
static state. Such an assumption, I would claim, is discontinuous with
reality, and has a high potential to produce nonconvergence in a
dynamic world. One of the deepest traditions in economics is the habit
of beginning with the simplest case and working up, 'relaxing' some of
the simplifying assumptions as we try to progress towards reality. The
'simplifying assumption' of a world at rest is, I suggest, in a very wide
range of contexts, a classic example of a discontinuity: ordinarily
nothing can be found to bridge the distance between the limit case of

perfect timelessness and 'the limit minus epsilon' – would that be 'a very slightly dynamic world'? That may be a meaningless concept in the context of ordinary experience.

To escape the impossible situations engendered by 'the simplifying assumption of a static world', it will be necessary to start much economic theorising almost from scratch, eschewing, to begin with, any technique that seems to require static assumptions, and asking how we may apprehend a world of time and change. Words, I propose, do this reasonably well – not perfectly, but they at least do not *deny* time and change. The careful uses of words described in the first five chapters of Part II constitute the core of the techniques which I would propose for social economics.

C   Disequilibrium   and   equilibrium   As with the preceding issue, the critical thing here is not to *start* with an assumption of equilibrium. When we do not blind ourselves with that assumption, we may then see the world as a place in which equilibrium is a fairly rare exception, rather than a rule.

It is a modern fiction that the fast-paced change we experience in modern life is an abrupt discontinuity from the way things were in some past time, when the norm was a state so changeless that it could be called an equilibrium state. When we talk, for example, about the way colonial rule disrupted indigenous social, cultural and economic institutions in Africa, and we look at the interconnected deterioration of resource use and resource base which may be perceived over the last two decades in many parts of that continent, we assume that this was a change imposed upon some previous situation that had existed for a long time, made possible by an equilibrium relation between the demands of Man and the bounty of Nature.

It is almost certainly true that the patterns imposed by colonial rule in Africa created dramatic changes; what is not so clear is that *change itself* was something new. What is difficult to conceive (more for emotional than for cognitive reasons) is an alternative possibility wherein social, cultural, economic and demographic patterns may have changed over time, occasionally reverting to a pattern similar to one that had appeared before, then perhaps going off in some new direction, or trying out a new variant of something else that had arisen previously. Sequences of change could have gone on like this since the emergence of the human species, without ever converging towards any pattern that had special features, elevating it above the others, in a way that would merit the term, 'equilibrium'.

I deliberately place this speculation in Africa, so long thought of (by outsiders) as 'the Dark Continent', precisely because we possess few long records of precolonial African history; where we are without such a record, we are free to conceive of what reality might be without the categories we are almost forced into by historical 'knowledge' of other regions. In Chapter 6 there was some discussion of the difficulty, because of its emotional appeal, of freeing our thinking of the assumption of equilibrium. Historians too often focus upon a single period of time, which may then be described as an end point, with all that came before understood as 'leading up to' the time that receives the focus.[4] Sociologists and anthropologists (particularly those in structural-functionalist, or 'neoclassical' traditions) similarly simplify their work with the implication that *the way things are now is an inevitable result of an inevitable series of changes.*

Sociobiology is used or misused to support the notion of 'evolutionary' (often taken to mean 'deterministic' and/or 'progressive') change in human culture (most broadly defined, to include economic as well as social, sexual and other behaviour). Social scientists are joined by natural scientists in looking for ways to see the world in terms of tendencies toward predictable or stable outcomes. Economists, in their desire to be 'scientific', may have gone the farthest in creating a dependence upon the idea of equilibrium. The reason that there has come to be a problematical relation between ideas of equilibrium and ideas of disequilibrium in economics is that the first is a relatively rare state, commonly assumed; while the second is the more general situation, widely ignored.

The attitudes of human ecology – the field which studies the interactions between Man and Nature – have coloured the perceptions of those economists who have become interested in the idea of sustainable development. The profound effect of this new input to a field's thinking is reflected in the work of a leading agricultural economist (also quoted earlier, in Part I):

> The concept of economic equilibrium also does not fit well in the new sustainable development ethic. Mechanistic systems, so predominant in neoclassical economics, are suitable for stable, predictable systems. While equilibrating systems are not required in neoclassical economics (Kaldor), the neoclassical perspective, in general, maintains the assumption of a stable and reversible process (Norgaard, 1985). Most of econometrics assumes the world is inherently predictable (Williams and Findlay). Yet, ecological

science and environmentalism increasingly incorporate the concepts inherent in 'the science of surprise' that began from theoretical developments in mathematical catastrophe-theory and nonequilibrium thermodynamics (and which can also be found in post-Keynesian economic literature – see Earl and Kay; Ford; Hicks; Shackle). The principles surrounding the 'science of surprise' stress the impossibility of prediction and the irrelevancy of probabilistic approaches to uncertainty management. These principles mean that the world is one of continuous disequilibrium (Williams and Findlay); uncertainty is replaced by unknowability (Ford); exogenous shocks, catastrophes or surprises replace homostasis. Because the limits to growth for sustainable development advocates are perceived as conceivably resulting in catastrophe and irreversible outcomes, the assumptions of stable equilibrating systems are frequently rejected. These perceptions mean that much of the conventional neoclassical economics paradigm in which the discipline of agricultural economics is rooted is rejected by proponents of sustainable development (Batie, 1989, p. 22).

As in the case of dynamic (versus static) realities, we need some powerful means to wrest ourselves out of existing thinking, so deeply rooted in assumptions of equilibrium. The empiricist conclusions of Chapter 11, buttressed by the tools of discourse analysis of the rest of Part II, may be used to give ourselves a fresh start. They should assist us in moving towards the ability to see the world neither as equilibrium nor as disequilibrium states – not as *states* at all, but as *processes*. The idea of an equilibrium state (or, for that matter, of a disequilibrium 'state') would then appear only as a limit case (a pass-through limit), to be employed with great caution in our thinking, as being, in many contexts, discontinuous from reality.

The conclusions here converge with the earlier conclusions on statics and dynamics: all of our tools will need to be reexamined, to see which of them can accommodate to this way of thinking, and which ones pull us back towards the assumption of equilibrium.

D The short versus Several different kinds of issues come into the
the long run problematic relations between the short and the
long run.

First is the simplistic assumption that we are talking about *one* short and *one* long run. That is often not the case, and many problems in this area can be quite easily resolved simply by realising that it is not the case. For instance, some 'difficulties' would resolve into mere 'differences' if we were to specify, empirically, that:

- while in case A we might be talking about the distinction between the choices made when thinking about a single production run, versus those made with respect to any longer time frame;
- in case B, the issue is the profit picture within the time before it becomes necessary to replace any capital equipment, versus profits as they are affected by capital investments not yet in the pipeline;
- and in other cases the 'short' and the 'long' runs are defined in still other ways.

When we have sorted out which long and short runs we are talking about, we can then turn to the next empiricist point: that a long run which will never arrive (such as the imaginary time wherein most significant equilibria may be expected) is of little interest. There is a world of difference between those who are interested in the future as a reality that will some day arrive, versus those who are interested in the concept of long-run equilibrium.

A very different kind of issue in this area is the ethical one. Individuals involved with any kind of public policy are constantly required to weigh the interests of different groups. The same groups, as well as different ones, often also have quite varying interests as we vary the time-frame within which we consider them. What are the moral obligations to take these added complexities into account? And which different time-frames should we emphasise – tomorrow, next year, next generation?

DEFINITIONS OF RIGOUR FOR SOCIAL ECONOMICS   The burden of the discourse analysis approach of Part II was, first of all: Know what you are talking/reading about! As an example of the importance of such self-consciousness, we may note that all four of the problems just discussed begin to be more tractable when you question yourself, your texts, your colleagues or your teachers to find out what time period is under discussion.

Most critically, the four issues just discussed need to be understood *in relation to one another*. For example, while equilibrium is a dubious concept for the long run (the two ideas together creating, often, the chimera of a 'long run equilibrium' that never arrives in real time), yet we may usefully talk about some specific, time-limited concepts of equilibrium on both the macro and the micro levels. Again, the meaning will be significantly different depending upon whether we are talking about the one (e.g., an equilibrium price on global or national markets) or the other (e.g., Marshall's boy picking blackberries). Further, a *static* equilibrium has a different meaning and usefulness – and the consequences of its use may be very different (leading to a 'blow-up', if pushed too hard) – from the harder-to-pin-down meaning of 'equilibrium' within a dynamic understanding of reality. The latter, however, tends to become so abstract a notion that it may be better not to use it at all.

Similarly, if we are going to use the concepts of 'micro' and 'macro' intelligently, so that they add to our understanding of the world, rather than limiting our vision, we must understand the ways in which these terms are affected by the other lines of our focus: static versus dynamic; different time periods; etc.

Such awareness will help us to see how it is necessary to make adjustments in our ways of constructing theory as we deal with different aspects and phases of reality. These are adjustments which we make all the time, usually quite well, in our intuitive response to perceived reality; but the types of rigour increasingly sought in economics over the last hundred years have rigidified economic theory until it has lost the ability to respond to the meaning, for human beings as economic actors, of differences between small and large, now and then, still and moving, near and far. I have proposed social economics as a system of theory that would be constructed with different standards and types of rigour, emphasising verbal logic, 'deep intellectual honesty' (see Chapter 2), and a sophisticated under-standing of 'communication'.

None of the activities that were described in the middle three chapters of Part II is foreign to a good literary critic, but the term 'literary criticism' does imply that its techniques are specified for use on creative (i.e., fictional or poetic, not scientific) literature. Their collective application to another sort of discourse, such as economic texts, could therefore be described as belonging to the modern, at present too faddish and esoteric, school of discourse analysis. If a relatively straightforward, non-mysterious application and description of these techniques, such as I hope to have provided in Part II, helps to make discourse analysis a little less mysterious to those who do not happen to have much grounding in literary criticism, this will have been a useful exercise.

This chapter and the last have expanded the discourse analysis approach of Part II with an emphasis upon empiricism. This emphasis suggests that an assumption which, *in a particular context*, is outside the bounds of possibility, will play havoc with the model, theory or system of theory which depends upon such an assumption (or simplification, or limit case) in such a context. The point of this approach has been to try to drive a wedge, if not between the true and the untrue, at least between the possible and the impossible.

We will now turn, in Part III, to an analysis of the role(s) and meaning(s) of 'value' in economics – an especially slippery and hard-to-pin-down topic. The aspect which this topic wears in contemporary economics is, I believe, best understood by tracing its historical roots, importantly found in the writings of Alfred Marshall. We will need all of the techniques that have been laid out in Part II to do this historical detective work, and then to apply our findings to the dominant form of economics now practised in the West.

Notes

1. An example is the contention of what Elliott Morss has called the New School in economics: that consumers are identically affected by a government's decision to raise a given sum of revenue, regardless of whether the sum is raised through a tax increase, by issuing bonds, or by printing money. (See e.g., Robert J. Barro, 'Are Government Bonds Net Wealth?', *Journal of Political Economy*, vol. 82(6) 1974; and Laurence J. Kotlikoff, 'Taxation and Savings: A Neoclassical Perspective', *Journal of Economic Literature*, vol. 22(4) 1984.)

    This 'New School' conclusion is based upon a chain of logic which pushes two related assumptions to their limits, past, I would claim, a severe discontinuity with reality. One is the rationality assumption; the other is an assumption that rational individuals behave, on average, as if they possessed both perfect information and perfect understanding. The information and understanding required in the particular case includes knowledge of what the government will choose to do throughout the future, understanding of how any legislation will affect actual tax incidence, etc. (See Elliott Morss, 'Do Deficits Matter? A Review of the Evidence', draft, December 1988.)

2. Cf.:

    The concept 'true' does not tally with the assertions of pure geometry, because by the word 'true' we are eventually in the habit of designating always the correspondence with a 'real' object; geometry, however, is not concerned with the relation of the ideas involved in it to objects of experience, but only with the logical connection of these ideas among themselves (Albert Einstein, *Relativity, The Special and the General Theory* (Crown, New York, 1961) p. 2).

3. This, of course, is what may be done when a theorist, moving from a simpler to a more complex model, says, 'now we will relax the assumption of . . .'. The point is to recognise why it is critical to abandon ('relax' is too gentle a word) certain assumptions at certain times, so that we don't leave it until too late.
4. For an historian who recognises, and objects to, this bias in history, see, e.g., Norbert Elias, *The Civilizing Process*: vol. 1, *The History of Manners* (American edn, Urizen Books, New York, 1978).

Part III:

Marshall's Search for a Scientific Way of Inserting Values into a Social Science; His Legacy to Welfare Economics

13 An Historical and Philosophical Context for the Concept of 'Value' in Economics

The methodological issues that were discussed in Part II will receive a more particular application in Part III, as I set out to show why it is important to understand the use of the word 'value' in economics: a word which historically entered in the garb of normative discourse, and has been reformulated as a (supposedly) positive term.

A NOTE TO
THE READER   Some of Part III is more slanted towards the economist reader than the rest of the book has been. Chapters 13 through 16 will include some sections which I hope will continue to be of interest to the non-economist who wishes to deepen his/her understanding or practice of the critical approaches discussed in Part II; such a reader may wish to read selectively here, but s/he should be prepared simply to skip long passages which are unlikely to be of interest to anyone but an economist, and where the attempt to keep the language generally intelligible has been abandoned.

Although I am normally an admirer of Marshall, the project of his which will be examined in Part III is one which I believe was misconceived from the start. Marshall's goal was to devise a true 'science' of welfare economics, using such natural sciences as physics or biology as his models. The method on which he pinned most of his hopes for reaching this goal was to look for a scientific way of dealing with values based on 'a system of measurement of efforts, sacrifices, desires, etc.'[1] Specifically, he proposed to take as objective data the values of all members of society, not as subjectively reported by others or as sensed by the economist, but as revealed through prices. The belief – or hope – that prices can be used to reveal something deeper than that tautologically limited set which is now called 'revealed preferences' is so seductive to an economist who would like to regard

275

him/herself as a scientist that Marshall, for the sake of that belief, kept reworking fuzzy thinking which he would not have tolerated elsewhere.

Chapters 16 and 17 are submitted as evidence for my contention that some of the inconsistencies of Marshall's work which may appear to have been banished have only been driven underground. Chapter 16 will describe subsequent criticism, which has been addressed almost solely to level 3 of Marshall's writings; and Chapter 17 intends to show how the 'effective level' of Marshall's discourse has continued to provide the substructure for some aspects of modern welfare economics.

Much of the analysis in Chapters 13 through 15 will consist of a close reading of Marshall's works, especially his eight editions of *Principles*, where I will try to read between the lines of what he wrote and how he edited. The emphasis upon *Principles*, in this context, is suggested by a wish to be as fair as possible to Marshall: it seems right to look at how he most cautiously, carefully and intentionally represented his programme, in order to summarise:

1.   what he said he was doing – i.e., what he purportedly wanted the reader to carry away as a set of beliefs regarding economic matters;
2.   what he acted as if he was doing – i.e., where Marshall himself appeared to be taken in by the unconscious assumptions and hopes (of whose strength, if not their existence, he appeared to be unaware) that exist on the 'effective level' of his own discourse; and
3.   the actual logic of his work.

Since the approach of analysing 'levels of meaning' which was laid out in Chapter 8 will be employed here, I will refresh the reader's memory by running through the levels once again – in reverse order, for a change:

'Level 3', 'the logical level of discourse', is the level at which the logic is (or is not) actually worked out. Critics subsequent to Marshall (whose writings will be sampled in Chapter 16) have pointed out many places in which the intentions on the 'stated' level (level 1) cannot be fulfilled, because of logical or technical level 3 difficulties unmentioned (or inadequately taken into account) by Marshall.

'Level 2' is 'the effective level of discourse'; it constitutes the meanings that have in fact been adopted and built upon, whether by the author of those meanings, or by others. The meanings that have been adopted and built upon may be different from the overt statements of intent, and may also be different from what has actually, on the logical level, been achieved.

'Level 1', 'the stated level of discourse', includes the formal statements in which the author directly proclaims his/her intentions and states what are the logical or technical constraints which will limit his/her ability to achieve the stated objectives.

Successive editions of Marshall's *Principles of Economics* showed changes to which I will give some attention as I deal with a subject in which Marshall was more than usually self-contradictory, as he repeatedly attempted to re-work an argument without ever being able finally and fully to correct the logical and reality-contradicting flaws of which he was uneasily aware, but which he was unwilling or unable to confront. Admiring intellectual heirs such as J. M. Keynes may have wished to see only Marshall's more sophisticated side, wherein 'succeeding editions of Marshall's *Principles* were marked by increasing caution and reticence as the work of Edgeworth, Fisher and Pareto began to undermine the earlier notions of measurability, additivity and comparability' (Blaug, *Economic Theory in Retrospect*, pp. 326–9). However, a large part of Marshall's work – and a not inconsiderable part of what we have inherited in the field of economics today – can only be understood in the context of his earlier, less cautious and reticent, use of marginal utility theory.

GENERAL INTRODUCTION   The purposes of Part III will be:
TO PART III

– to set forth Marshall's thinking on **the idea that economics could be made scientific by finding a way to make quantifiable subjects (money or price, as economic values) stand for the human values that enter into motivations and satisfactions;**
– to summarise the principal problems in this idea; and
– to give evidence that Marshall was aware of these problems, and that he chose to go on struggling, unsuccessfully, against them, rather than simply excising from his economics the area in which they appear. I will attempt throughout, also,
– to suggest why this ambition, its non-achievement, and Marshall's ambivalence about that non-achievement, are all relevant for the field of economics today.

What I will hope to contribute of some originality is a persuasive argument that – although many of Marshall's premises about the possibility of dealing scientifically with human values are, according to almost any modern understanding of science (my own included), indefensible unless worded in a very restrictive manner – yet much of what he built upon these foundations, in their less restrictive form, remained embedded in the effective meanings of his *Principles of Economics*, and is, indeed still widely accepted and used.

The dilemma of welfare economics, in Marshall's time and in our own, has been the fact that human values are at the heart of the subject: in a discipline which is determined to be a science, how are such values to be incorporated? Their *de facto* incorporation, on the effective level, is at odds with what can actually be achieved on the logical level, as also with the claims and disclaimers made on the stated level.

The deductive links which are essential to hold together facts, or even assumptions, within a theory, have to be fabricated out of something. We will see in Chapters 14 and 15 that Marshall hoped to fabricate these links out of regularities of behaviour which would allow him to use money as a measure of motivations and/or satisfactions: thus he would be able to go back and forth, across scientifically constructed bridges, between observable expenditures and unobservable real welfare; between observable prices and the unobservable feelings of both workers and consumers.

This was a broad goal containing a narrowing technique. Marshall, somewhat inconsistently, clung throughout his life to both the goal and the technique. Neoclassical economics, in its self-conscious statements, has opted for consistency defined by the technique. Yet even the consistency of neoclassical economics has not prevailed totally. Certain inconsistencies had already been built into the very foundations upon which it erected its rigorous edifice. Neoclassical economics' claim to being scientific still resonates with the echoes of Marshall's hopes.

To be sure, when backed into a corner, few modern economists will dare to claim that they can deal scientifically with any kind of values other than exchange values; and yet economic writings and discussions are filled with scientific-sounding references to broader values than those contained in prices. On the theoretical side, the references may be rescued by the fact that no actual attempt is being made to measure actual human values; the pictures of indifference curves and the symbolic representations of utility functions are all perfectly abstract. On the applied side, the defence is that we cannot accurately calculate shadow prices, or consumers' surpluses; nevertheless, decisions must and will be made; questions come to economists from the real world, and they respond to requests for assistance by making the best guesses they can. That is reasonable; but it is not scientific – not, at least, as Marshall and his descendents have hoped to make economics scientific.

There are two aspects of Marshall's approach to economics which will be especially important here.

(a)   One is the set of motivations which caused him to enter the field, and to devote his life to it. These motivations were clearly and without any embarrassment expressed by Marshall as the desire to improve the human condition.

(b)   The other was the conviction that, in order for economics to be as useful as possible (along the lines of (a)), it had to be scientific.

Aspect (a) emphasises that there was a normative element in Marshall's science from the start; the point of the whole exercise is based upon value-judgments about what constitutes improvement in the human condition. Aspect (b) builds (with the idea of 'usefulness') upon this normative element; and yet the idea of being 'scientific' is generally thought to imply a sharp and clear distinction between normative and positive questions and answers. We have, here, a dilemma which has remained, ever since Marshall's time, at the heart of welfare economics.

In combining these two aspects Marshall was, in effect, searching for *a scientific basis for a prescriptive social science*. Throughout his writing there is evidence of Marshall's ambivalence about economists, as such, giving advice (cf. Chapter 9, n. 13); and yet it is clear that he wanted his science to reach beyond simple description.

At one level, what I will offer here is a critique of Marshall's use of prices to illuminate underlying human values. Beneath that is a critique of the logical gaps in welfare economics. This may be further generalised, to the extent that the goals and hopes of welfare economics are integrally bound up with a larger part of neoclassical economics. Each reader will have to judge for him/herself how strongly Marshall's personal normative bias – **that the reason to do economics is because one hopes to be able to contribute to human welfare** – is present in his/her own work, and in the profession at large, in order to come to a conclusion as to how much of modern economics should be viewed in terms of the criticisms which will be laid out here.

The remainder of this chapter will note some of the salient points in the development of welfare economics from Marshall's time to our own.[2] The empirical/theoretical division in the field today will be highlighted through a discussion of the first and second theorems of the modern formal theory of welfare economics.

A BRIEF   Adam Smith had distinguished between two sorts of
HISTORICAL   evaluations: use values and exchange values. It was
CONTEXT   evident that there was a relation between the two, but
              the nature of that relation was not given precise
definition. A century later Alfred Marshall brought to economics the
hope that such a definition could and would be found; and that this
would permit economics to develop as the most scientific of the social
sciences.

Over the course of his career, as Marshall faced serious difficulties
with most of the specific forms in which he attempted to formalise this
hope, he turned increasingly to the idea that *marginal utility* might be
the term that could mediate with precision between use value and
exchange value. He was not much more successful in achieving this
ambition; nevertheless, he bequeathed to the field not only his vision of
what it would take for economics to be scientific, but also a largely
unspoken belief that *this vision had, in fact, become a reality*. Marshall
was not, of course, the only shaper of the wishes and beliefs of
neoclassical economics, but his repetitions of hopes or intentions in this
area, delivered as though they were already facts, may usefully be
examined as a part of the foundations/assumptions on which
economics continues to be constructed.

If Jevons, Menger and Walras are generally credited with the
invention of marginal utility theory in its modern form, Marshall is
seen as the English economist who (after marginal utility had been
discovered several times without making any real impact upon
economic theorising) had finally grasped, developed and publicised
its great potential for the field. J. M. Keynes compared Jevons' 'bright
idea of reducing Economics to a mathematical application of the
hedonistic calculus of Bentham' to 'the great working machine evolved
by the patient, persistent toil and scientific genius of Marshall' (in
Memorials, p. 23). The implication here is that Marshall went beyond
Bentham's utility theory; and so he did, but he never managed to
reduce the dependence of economic theory upon Utilitarianism as
completely as he or his descendents might have liked. Marshall did not
want his work to be associated too closely with the Utilitarian
approach, with its emphasis upon a 'felicific calculus' normally
understood as entirely subjective. However, he did not go all the way
to Pareto's concept of 'ophelimity'.[3]

The abandonment of cardinal representations of utility was overtly
(if reluctantly) accepted by Marshall, but he did not relinquish the
central concerns which he had inherited from classical economics –

namely for 'material welfare, income redistribution, and alleviating poverty. This orientation contrasts sharply with the new framework provided by the ordinalists [or Hicksians]. Using positivist methodology, ordinal utility, and the scarcity definition, the ordinalists' agenda centered on the production and exchange of commodities' (Batie, 1989, p. 14).

The development of economic theory from Marshall to Pareto, to Hicks, to Samuelson, has included the progressive abandonment of assumptions which were seen as not necessary to the logically minimum foundations for positivistic *explanations of prices*. By contrast, Marshall wanted a system which, using prices, would be able to produce scientific answers to normative questions about how to improve the human condition. The logically minimum assumptions of Marshall's system are more extensive than what Samuelson and his followers required for their stated objectives; Marshall's normative ambition and the subjects of interest to him went beyond the interesting, but limited, goal of explanation of prices.

Subsequent use of Occam's razor has made the discipline more streamlined than what Marshall required in the central part of his system. For many modern purposes, for example, it is no longer necessary to assume constant marginal utility of income (an heroic assumption to which Marshall was repeatedly driven by his determination to derive welfare consequences from marginal utilities as revealed by prices), because modern economics, by and large, has a narrower ambition than Marshall's. However, where a modern economist does seek to answer welfare questions, s/he quickly finds that, in pruning away some of the complexities, or even obscurities and contradictions, of Marshall's economics, the field has accepted stringent logical *restrictions upon its objectives*; and when individual practitioners refuse to accept these logical restrictions, then the type of rigour which they support must be sacrificed.

In his essay, 'Was there a Marginal Revolution?', Blaug rather impishly reminds us that, while all today agree upon the central importance to economics of marginal theory, it is not so clear what it actually changed:

Unfortunately, there appears to be no agreement as to just what the new paradigm was that Jevons, Menger and Walras put forward. Was it a new emphasis on demand rather than supply, on consumer utility rather than on production costs? Was it something as ambitious as a subjective theory of value, which was to supplant the objective labour-cost theories of the past? Was it rather the extension of the principle of maximisation from business firms to households, making the consumer and not the entrepreneur the epitome of rational action? Was it perhaps the equimarginal principle, enshrined in the proportionality of marginal utilities to prices as the condition of consumer equilibrium? Was it instead, as Schumpeter like [sic.] to say, the explicit or implicit discovery of general equilibrium analysis? Or lastly, was it simply the first conscious recognition of constrained maximisation as the archetype of all economic reasoning? (Blaug, *Economic History and the History of Economics*, p. 213).

I hope to provide some evidence regarding what, from Marshall's point of view, the answers to Blaug's questions would have been. No, the emphasis was not to be shifted disproportionately onto the consumer or onto demand.[4] Yes, it did extend the notion of rationality to all actors, and it permitted constrained maximisation, though this was not something that would be featured very openly in Marshall's writing. Marginal utility analysis marked out a road towards general equilibrium analysis which Marshall would have liked to traverse, but was not able to take very far. It certainly included the proportionality of marginal utilities to prices, even as early as Marshall's 1876 essay, 'Mr. Mill's Theory of Value' (see quotation 2 in the next chapter); but Marshall recognised even then that it is impossible to establish a proportion among raw utilities, or between utilities as such and other things. A sacrifice, an effort, a guinea – all must be submitted to 'an artificial mode of measuring them in terms of some common unit'. And yes, implied in the foregoing was something which was extremely ambitious and which in many ways came close to being – though it never claimed outright to be – a *subjective theory of value*. The assymptotic approach to a subjective theory of value in Marshall's work will comprise much of the subject matter of the next two chapters.[5]

During Marshall's own lifetime there appears to have been more awareness in the profession than there is today of the extent of his ambitions. Perhaps this awareness stemmed from the fact that there was then more sympathy with Marshall's humanitarian goals, as an integral part of economics, than would generally be admitted today. One of the most interesting contemporary debates occurred when F. Y. Edgeworth came to the defence of Marshallian economics in an exchange with Joseph Nicholson over the latter's *Principles of Political Economy.*

Edgeworth's defence emphasised the congruity between meaning-levels 1 and 3 in Marshall's economics. His argument may be understood to say that Marshall's logic (on level 3) was sufficient to support the scope of his science as he had hedged it in with his most cautious disclaimers (on level 1).

Edgeworth stressed the cautious (level 1) version of Marshallian economics, emphasising

(a)   that price, or exchange value, could be used, not as a measure of absolute well being, but as an *indicator* of *relative* well being – i.e., the more a person could buy, at prevailing prices, the better off he could be assumed to be;

(b)   that Marshall only proposed the application of consumer surplus analysis to changes small enough so that there would be no alteration in the marginal utility of income; and

(c)   that in measuring such small, relative changes, the measurement of total utility is unnecessary.

With the existing situation taken as the starting point, the function of consumer surplus analysis (Edgeworth said) was simply to compare the way in which, under different proposals, consumer surplus would vary from its original quantity.

These were all points which Marshall himself made, and they went a long way towards responding to some criticisms of internal inconsistency; unfortunately, however, Marshall was not consistent in maintaining these positions, with their ramifications and supporting propositions.

As unfriendly critics are more likely to do, Nicholson chose to look at the 'effective level' of discourse. This (level 2) emerges from a reading of Marshall which is oriented to Marshall's – or the reader's – humanitarian goals. Nicholson emphasised the distance between what Marshall's effective level of discourse would lead a reader to expect, and what was actually provided in Marshall's logic, by emphasising that:

–   for changes to have so little impact on the marginal utility of money as that suggested by Edgeworth or Marshall, they could not be changes in the provision of necessities;

— and that even in other than necessities, changes would always
    threaten to affect the marginal utility of income unless the theory
    were restricted in its application to 'a few careless millionaires'.[6]

Describing what has happened to marginal utility economics
progressively from 1871 up to the present, Blaug remarks that

> In the end, as Hutchinson has said, what was important in marginal
> utility was the adjective rather than the noun. Utility theory was
> gradually deprived of all its bite and reduced from cardinal to
> ordinal utility and from ordinal utility to 'revealed preferences' . . . .
> Could anyone have foreseen in 1871 the tortuous path by which
> marginal utility economics led via Paretian welfare economics to
> cost-benefit analysis and dynamic programming? (*Economic Theory
> in Retrospect*, p. 306.)

Hicks, building upon Pareto's work, claimed that with information
on the marginal rate of substitution we could construct indifference
curves, as a step towards an empirical science of human wants and
needs. Samuelson established that the logically minimum requirements
for price theory did not need to go deeper into the human psyche than
one could go via 'revealed preferences' – his update on ophelimity. For
welfare economics Samuelson required only the one additional
assumption that is summarised in the doctrine of consumer
sovereignty: that *individual preferences matter* – marginal preferences,
that is, as revealed by marginal decisions, and congealed in prices. It is
worth noting, here, that this essential building block of neoclassical
economics is an entirely value-determined response to the question,
'What matters?' Nor does such a value-judgment come out of a
vacuum; its roots may be seen in the tradition of individualism which
are conventionally traced back, in the West, to the seventeenth century,
and perhaps even earlier.

The practical and ethical results of the adoption of this basic value
will be considered in the final chapter of this book. Here it will only be
contrasted with Marshall's early position, very close to classical
Utilitarianism, where the goal was to address and deal with utility
itself, as a measurable variable that could guide us to a simple
calculation of the optimal position for society – the maximisation of
total human utility. Marshall himself, over the course of his life, moved
a part of the distance from his own original position towards the one I

have identified with Samuelson. I will look at the evolution of Marshall's thinking as an early segment of the 'tortuous path' referred to by Blaug.

THE DILEMMA OF WELFARE ECONOMICS: THE NEED FOR VALUES   Price theory is a good way of explaining why (most) prices are (approximately) what they are; it is an even better way of explaining what prices *would* be in a particular, well-defined, ideal world. But Marshall (and this applies to other economists, to the extent that they share some of his motivations) was after something else. *He was less interested in explaining price formation than in using prices to reveal the 'values' which were essential data in his system.* Via marginal utility theory, prices were to shed light on *what matters to human beings.* Without such illumination, there can be no basis for welfare economics.

The justification for the last sentence is that economic work which is to any extent tinged with welfare concerns must be able to produce conclusions concerning 'values' of some kind; and if there are to be values in the output of an analysis, there have to be values in the input to it.[7] It is generally accepted that scientific means may be defined for the achievement of any ends, including cases where the ends do not have a scientific character; but in order to perform positive, descriptive science as a means for achieving some normative, prescriptive ends, there must be a way of keeping the means clearly separated from the ends. If scientific procedure requires an effort to keep the personal values of the economist or policy maker discreet from the analysis, what other kind of value is there which can be inserted scientifically as an input to economic welfare analysis?

The answer is fairly obvious; it is, indeed, contained in the value-assumption, cited earlier, that *individual preferences matter.* Marshall, and all economists since him, have employed *the values of other people* – the subjects of the study (whether as individuals or in some aggregate form) – as the objective data of the social scientist.[8]

The use of other people's values as the data which will define the goals of welfare analysis is not impossible, but it imposes some strains on the scientific separation of normative from positive. However, Marshall never overtly questioned the assumption that these inputs could be combined with other facts from the real world and subjected to formal analysis in such a way as to produce an output which would be both descriptively sound and prescriptively useful.

WELFARE In the decades since Marshall's time the area of welfare
ECONOMICS economics appears, at least at first sight, to have evolved
IN MODERN to something much narrower than what was conceptua-
TIMES lised by Marshall. Is my earlier statement, that welfare
economics requires insights into 'what matters to human
beings', still relevant to the modern, narrower form? I will argue that
although this statement, along with many of the concerns and
endeavours of Marshall to be described in this chapter, has taken a
much reduced place in the most rigorous formulations of modern
neoclassical welfare economics, nevertheless such basic principles
continue to be critical to welfare economics *as it is applied.*
Marshall's inconsistencies, as he tried to serve his two masters (of
real-world human needs, and formal descriptive completeness with
logical rigour) are not overtly (on level 1) represented in the
foundations of modern economics as they appear on paper.
However, the post-Pareto tidying-up of welfare economics has
required the adoption of some absurd assumptions (such as the
existence of classical competitive conditions in the world, distortion-
free transfers, etc.), which gravely diminish the relevance of the formal
theory to sustained practice. Hence we have a relatively unscientific
applied welfare economics, and a scientific *theoretical* welfare
economics, with no better bridges between the two today than was to
be found at the beginning of the century in Marshall's system of
inconsistent, or ambiguous, inclusiveness.

The meaning of these criticisms is perhaps best illustrated by a brief
discussion of the first and second theorems of the formal theory of
welfare economics, which state:

1 that every perfectly competitive equilibrium (i.e., one which
   includes Arrow's 'universality of markets' condition[9]) is a Pareto
   optimum; and
2 that each and every Pareto optimum is potentially achievable
   through the equimarginal principle whereby the market mechanism
   in a perfectly competitive world causes all expenditures, at the
   margin, to be of equal value when evaluated according to each
   individual's marginal value of money.[10]

The well-known implication of these welfare theorems is that the best
of all possible worlds is obtainable through the mechanisms of a
perfectly competitive market. (They contain no explicit evidence that

this optimum cannot also be reached in some other way; but they are generally discussed with a fairly strong presumptions that that is so.)

There are four distinct types of problems in going, in practice, from the welfare theorems to the optimum that they predict in theory.

1   One type of problem deals with the question of whether a Pareto optimum is necessarily, from all points of view, the best of all possible worlds. This may be questioned on several grounds:

(a)   We may prefer a point, inside of the production possibility frontier (PPF), which will not be stably attained by the untrammeled workings of a free market. For example, the PPF refers to production using all available resources; there might be reasons to prefer leaving some resources idle. Only under the full set of restrictions implied by Arrow's conditions (M) and (C) (see n. 10) can we be certain that the PPF coincides with *preferences*. Biased bargaining costs, information imperfections that are biased (i.e., not randomly distributed), externalities, public goods and other market imperfections can make an interior point preferable even by Arrow's social-preference-ordering-as-function-of-individual-preferences criteria.

(b)   We may be sceptical of how the choice of the best Pareto optimum is to be made – and by whom. Can those with the social power to make it be trusted to give fair (and does that mean equal?) weight to all interests? If (as is more than likely the case) there is not a single solution which is optimum from all points of view, how is society, or the decision maker, to decide which point of view to take?

(c)   The general equilibrium results which generated these theorems are essentially static: they ignore, for example, the possibility of technological change, as well as Marshall's notion of progressive wants. Thus it is conceivable – indeed, highly probable – that, by the time market forces have worked through to the desired competitive equilibrium from the initial redistribution (and who knows how long that will take?), such a competitive equilibrium will no longer represent the Pareto optimum.

2   Even given a decision as to which is the 'best' Pareto optimum, and given the 'optimum' initial endowment – i.e., one that will lead to it – we may not be convinced that all the classical conditions (of perfect information, including accurate knowledge by each individual of what actions will actually maximise his/her utility; convexity in preferences and in production; no market power; etc.) actually exist or can be made to exist. If not, we fall back on the theory of the second best, which says that the outcome of an attempt to achieve the 'best' result under circumstances which do not conduce to its achievement may be normatively inferior to the result of some different strategy, which takes account of the actual conditions.

3   Although we can show in theory that there is an inevitable relationship between each Pareto optimal point and some initial endowment, we may not believe that human beings have, or could ever have, sufficient knowledge and understanding to select the correct initial endowment, i.e., the 'optimum' endowment that corresponds to (will bring about) the desired Pareto optimum outcome.

4   Even supposing that we have the power to identify the 'optimal' initial endowment which will generate the 'best' Pareto optimum outcome; and supposing, further, that we believe the world is so organised that the optimal initial endowment *will* automatically lead to the desired outcome – we may still have reason to doubt that it is in our power actually to achieve the optimal initial endowment by distribution or redistribution. The formal welfare economics solution as to how to achieve that endowment is to employ the concept of lump-sum transfers. While that concept may be freely employed to achieve – in concept – the desired results, it is rarely put into practice, for at least five strong reasons:

(a)   One is political: possession is nine-tenths of the law; the likely losers in such a transfer are often in a position to resist it more effectively than the likely winners can or will support it. (Asymmetrical distribution of knowledge is part of the issue here; news of an impending loss is likely to be more effectively disseminated and believed than news of a possible gain.)

(b)   There is also the practical problem of finding the pure rents or surpluses or other areas upon which a tax must fall if it is not to have allocational effects. In reality these things are rare in their pure form, and are unlikely to occur in large enough quantities, in the right places, to allow the desired lump-sum tax levies.

(c) Another problem is the transaction costs which are associated with any tax; lump-sum transfers are conceived as occurring instantaneously, on a one-time basis, without warning or repetition, so that there will be no behavioural adjustments to changed expectations; but in the real world, events have to take place in real time – even in bureaucratic time – so that expectations will be altered, and incentives will be distorted accordingly. Hence, the perfectly competitive world in which the perfect market mechanisms were to have worked through to the desired result is already disturbed.

(d) The concept of 'endowment' is closely associated with that of 'wealth'. Real-world experience with attempts to distribute wealth (including productive assets) more evenly in order to generate a more even income distribution shows that it is often difficult to make an endowment allocation 'stick'. Especially under the free-market conditions which are supposed to be in force once the endowment is settled, it is unlikely that it can remain settled once and for all – or even for any reasonable length of time.

(e) The final reason brings us to a problem of Marshall's which is central to this section; namely, the problem of measurement of utilities. The use of lump-sum transfers to compensate for changes made in order to reach a Pareto optimum implies an ability to establish the value of such changes to the individuals affected, in terms of a lump sum.

The overall conclusion is that we don't have, and aren't likely to achieve, the initial distribution which will produce, via a perfect market, the optimal solution perceivable from our present state of of the world. We also don't have, and aren't likely to achieve, a perfect market. Therefore there is no reason to believe that the first best solution of general equilibrium analysis, to be reached via unrestricted competition, is a solution of sufficient relevance for the real world to be the basis for a useful welfare economics.

I have taken this rather long detour through some implications of modern welfare economics because much of Part III will be about the problem of distinguishing between reality and theory, along several parameters. The theory is often so aesthetically and intellectually, if not ideologically, pleasing that there is an enormous temptation to keep forgetting that it diverges rather widely from the real world. We have to be prodded to remember, again and again, that the theory really is not the reality.

OUTLINE OF THE   Questions about whether there is a significant part
REST OF PART III   of *economic practice* (arising out of level 2) which is
                       ignored, or even denied, in *formal economic statements* (level 1) bring up issues of considerable subtlety. A close examination of the work of Alfred Marshall can shed light on these questions, not because he was representative (no single economist could meaningfully be said to be that; and he was, in many ways, *un*representative, in being more self-consciously honest than most), but because he was a first-rate economist, and an important figure in the field. The point of my examination, in regard to the question of whether there are significant differences between various levels of statement and meaning in economic practice and theory, will be to try to reveal both (2) *the effective* and (3) *the logical levels* of Marshall's use especially of demand theory, in order to compare those with (1) *what he said he was doing*. My conclusion will be that Marshall was engaged in an attempt to achieve something which he could not and did not achieve. His overt statements (level 1) sometimes accepted this impossibility and sometimes boldly denied it. His effective practice (level 2) – and sometimes, also, his logical procedures (on level 3) – at times continued *as if* the achievement were possible, or had even been accomplished.

The problems I will discuss regarding this part of Marshall's work are not novelties in the history of economic thought. In particular, criticism of the specifics of Marshall's definition and use of consumer's surplus, as well as his persistence in using additive utility functions, and even an early hope for employing cardinal utility functions, has been very extensive and often acute. I will not undertake anything like a comprehensive survey of these critiques. For the interested reader, Chapter 16 will examine a few of the issues raised, primarily to indicate the extent of the overt recognition now given to the technical problems which Marshall overlooked in order to proceed towards his goals. In Chapter 17 this overt recognition will be compared with the continuing acceptance of the Marshallian programme on the effective level of economic belief.

In the direct presentation of that programme, which is to be the subject of Chapter 15, I will stress two particularly interesting critiques: Pigou's, because its incisiveness is informed by an especially sympathetic understanding of what Marshall was trying to do; and Mark Blaug's, because his work effectively summarises a great deal of what has been said up to the present. However, my purpose is not directly to assess or add to these specific critiques; rather I will employ them principally to sharpen this exposition of the three levels upon which one can understand Marshall's programme, as it emerged in his own writing and as it has been carried forward by his intellectual descendents.

Although in general I believe that J. M. Keynes missed the point in his disparaging remark that 'The piercing eyes and ranging wings of an eagle [i.e., Marshall's far-ranging intellect] were often called back to earth to do the bidding of a moralizer',[11] here the comment takes on some validity. It was not, strictly speaking, the *moraliser* in Marshall who wanted to believe something so badly that he failed to tally up the pieces of the truth that he had in his hands, and to see that the sum contradicted many of his assertions; it was the *aspiring scientist* who made belief subservient to wish. It was the wish *to make economics scientific* which was so strong as to be able to dim the eyes of the eagle. However that wish can, after all, be fitted within what Keynes called the 'moralizer' in Marshall; for it was a wish to be able to improve the human lot, and to believe that economics could be made a powerful tool to this end. For economics to be such a tool, it had to fit within Marshall's notion of what was 'scientific'.

Notes

1. A. Marshall, 'Mr. Mill's Theory of Value' (1876) in *Memorials*, p. 126.
2. An excellent, and more complete, treatment of this subject may be found in Hicks's 'The Scope and Status of Welfare Economics', first published in *Oxford Economics Papers*, vol. 27 (1975) no. 3; reprinted in Hicks, 1981.
3. Pareto used that Greek word to refer only to *the utility which arises from economic actions*, and only *to the extent that that utility may be measured by those actions*. It explicitly does not include all utility, but denotes a specific subset two cuts down from that larger concept. The difference

between Pareto's ophelimity and Marshall's price measure of 'desires or satisfactions' is one of scope of ambition; Marshall had a larger idea of what he hoped to sweep in with his measure, while Pareto's word was pre-defined to refer only to that which was, in a particular context, observable and measurable.

4. Although, as Marshall pointed out in his famous scissors analogy, there was some redressing to be done of a former imbalance, where production costs had been overstressed as the determinants of price:

> We might as well reasonably dispute whether it is the upper or the under blade of a pair of scissors that cuts a piece of paper, as whether value is governed by utility or cost of production (*Principles*, p. 290).

5. Sir John Hicks places the marginal revolution, historically, as part of a longer stream in economic thinking which he calls 'catallactics'. He describes this as 'The construction of a powerful economic theory, *based on exchange instead of on production or distribution*' ('The Scope and Status of Welfare Economics', p. 236; italics added). In Hicks's view, the chief opposition to catallactics comes from welfare economics, of which Marshall was one of the major exponents; thus, while Marshall's name is associated both with welfare economics and with marginalist methods, the weight of Marshall's work comes down most heavily in support of the former. Hicks remarks that the reason that Schumpeter treated Marshall and Pigou 'somewhat grudgingly' in his *History of Economic Analysis* was that Schumpeter 'always judges economists by their contribution to economics in the catallactic sense', while Marshall and Pigou, Hicks states, 'belong to the other party'. (Hicks, n. to p. 238).

6. Nicholson, quoted in Maloney, 1985, pp. 78–80. John Maloney, to whom I am indebted for a very helpful description of this debate, sides with Nicholson in asserting that 'Marshall sanctioned interpersonal comparisons of utility between different income groups' (ibid.). Pigou, as we will see, also supports Nicholson's position on this point; and, while in some places Marshall denied such interpersonal comparisons of utility, we will see that in other places he did engage in them.

7. The next chapter will begin with a careful consideration of different meanings to the words 'value', values', and 'value judgment'.

It might be noted that the abstract output of a social science (i.e., in terms of ideas, whether in the heads of students and other receptive persons, or as written statements) may include any part or parts of a spectrum which, in principle, goes from purely normative (e.g., policy prescriptions, suggestions for changes in beliefs or behaviours, statements of *what should be*) to purely positive (statements of *what is* in the form of description aided by analysis: Marshall's 'reasoned catalogue of the world as it is').

It seems reasonable to expect that the quality of the output, as well as its place on the normative-positive spectrum, will be affected by the qualities and types of 'values' used as inputs. This consideration has sometimes led to a call for 'value-free' social science; but this subject deserves a more profound, as well as a more realistic response than that.

8. One use of this assumption is formalised in Arrow's 'An Extension of the Basic Theorems of Classical Welfare Economics' (in J.Neyman, (ed.) *Proceedings of the Second Berkeley Symposium on Mathematical Statistics and Probability*, University of California Press, Berkeley, 1951), where the preference ordering of the society is assumed to be exclusively a function of individual preference orderings. Unless this conception can be stretched to include the preference orderings of the future, under every possible state of the world – including that in which tastes and motivations have been altered so that individuals 'want what is good for them' – then it is not sufficient for Marshall's 'progressive' notions of the contributions of economics to society. (See *Social Economics*, Volume 2 for an exposition of Marshall's position in this regard.) The Utilitarian summation of individual (*existing*) utilities tends to lack progressiveness, although it could in principle be construed to include, or even to emphasise, utilities resulting from the possession and satisfaction of 'improved' future wants.

9. Arrow's short definition of this term is 'that the consumption bundle which determines the utility of an individual is the same as that which he purchases at given prices subject to his budget constraint, and that the set of production bundles among which a firm chooses is a given range independent of decisions made by other agents in the economy' ('The Organization of Economic Activity: Issues Pertinent to the Choice of Market Versus Nonmarket Allocation' in the *91st Congress, 1st Session, Joint Committee Report*, 'The Analysis and Evaluation of Public Expenditures: the PPB System', A Compendium of Papers Submitted to the Subcommittee on Economy in Government, US Government Printing Office, Washington, DC, 1969, p. 49).

10. Again, to use Arrow's terminology: given (M) the universality of markets, and (C) the convexity of household indifference maps and firm production possibility sets, 'then any Pareto-efficient allocation can be achieved as a competitive equilibrium by a suitable reallocation of initial resources' (ibid.).

11. Keynes, 'Alfred Marshall: 1842–1924' in *Memorials*, p. 11.

14 Marshall's Programme

Marshall hoped to use demand theory, marginal analysis, and consumers' surplus as the tools and techniques which could reduce an intangible subject – human welfare, or what I will be calling 'human values' – to a tangible measure: money, or price. The idea of such a mapping will be discussed first generally, and then in terms of the words Marshall used to refer to it. A difficulty arises in the fact that an important one of these words, 'value', is employed to refer to both the tangible and the intangible sides of the mapping: 'value' may mean human value, with reference to an underlying idea of welfare; but it may also mean exchange value, or, simply, price. We will see how value (but by which definition?) was the link between consumer's surplus on the one hand, and the economics of human welfare (seen by Marshall in the context of 'the high theme of economic progress') on the other; and why Marshall was so enthusiastic about the idea of consumer's surplus as to allow himself some uncharacteristic lapses into imprecise wording and incomplete logic.

Two of the great achievements of modern economics are the development of marginal analysis to explain price formation, and of the equimarginal principle to give a definition to a particular kind of optimum. Marshall would have been content with neither the explanation nor the definition unless they could be shown to be tied to some idea of 'human values'; i.e.,

1   What is the relation between prices and *the real worth of things*? That is to say, recognising that not only 'willingness to pay', but also the underlying 'sense of real value', are, in most cases, purely or largely relative terms; is there, nevertheless, some regular or meaningful relation to be found between these two terms? and,

2   How does the optimum produced by the equimarginal principle working out under conditions of perfect competition compare to the way we would really like the world to be? What values, that is to say, would be optimised if the 'classical conditions' existed and were given free rein?

Should such questions be left to the field of philosophy, or is there any place for them in economic theory? Marshall's writings indicate

294

his interest in speculations such as these. The difficulties into which they led him may well stand as justification for their relative neglect, on a philosophical level, by contemporary economists. However, this neglect may in fact have taken us even farther into treacherous territories than did Marshall's concern.

In this chapter and the next, as these will employ a method of textual analysis that is best supported by relatively numerous quotations, I will again number quotations for easy reference.

SOME In ordinary speech there are two groups of meanings
MEANINGS attached to the word, 'value'.
OF 'VALUE' The first group clusters about material things: it
includes the dictionary definitions of (1) 'a fair return or equivalent in goods, services or money for something exchanged', or (2) 'the monetary worth of something: marketable price' (definition 2 here most clearly refers to 'exchange value').

The second group of meanings is more abstract, e.g.: (3) 'relative worth, utility or importance: degree of excellence', or (4) (what I will call *basis values*) 'a principle or quality [which is] intrinsically valuable or desirable'.[1] This last is the use which is assumed, for example, in the work of the contemporary philosopher, Nicholas Maxwell, when he says: 'In the end there is just one basic problem for philosophy and for inquiry as a whole: *How can we realise what is of value in this strange world in which we find ourselves?*'[2]

In the foregoing definitions the dictionary wisely avoids the question of whether these meanings (especially the second group, but also definition (1)) may be understood on objective ('positive') as well as on subjective ('relative') grounds. The subjective interpretation would understand, e.g., 'relative worth' or 'intrinsic value' to be in reference to an individual's system of evaluations: it would assume that basis values only exist in the heads of individuals. The objective interpretation, by contrast, would assume that there exist some principles, apart from human beings, which, for example, make truth or beauty or goodness available as foundations for human values; an appreciation of these objective principles can be used to help us recognise or define these qualities as they appear in particular cases.

This interesting Platonic issue is not completely outside of our subject; indeed, as soon as we include in economics such a concept as progress, it becomes central. Those who, like Marshall, assume that there are objective criteria for defining progress, still have to face the fact that they are making a subjective interpretation of these objective 'realities'.

A modern example of the Platonic position that 'basis values' exist objectively, whether or not they are apprehended by human beings, is that of the more extreme advocates of the sustainability value, the so-called 'deep ecologists':

1   In the view of many of these advocates, 'something is intrinsically valuable if it is valuable in and for itself – if its value is not derived from its utility, but is independent of any use or function it may have in relation to something or someone else'. While an argument can be made that existence value (that is, human satisfaction derived from the knowledge that the ecosystem services continue to exist and prosper) represents the 'intrinsic value' to which environmentalists refer, this is a utilitarian view. Intrinsic value to many sustainable development advocates is a biocentric concept recognising ethical obligations to ecosystems in their own right.[3]

I include this description of a rather extreme view to illustrate how totally such a view must exist without logical foundation (there is no fact upon which all can agree from which this set of values can logically be deduced) – and then to admit that my own thinking on this subject also employs the concept of basis values in general (and my own basis values as particular facts) as *prima mobilia*, unsupported by deduction from anything else that stands on firmer scientific ground.

My understanding is this: for each individual there is some, usually amorphous, non-logical and and non-deductive 'sense' of what is valuable. (The best analogy is perhaps to such intrinsic quasi-values as a sense of proportion, a sense of symmetry, or an aesthetic sense.) Such a sense of 'basis value' doubtless has biological components; a new mother's sense that her infant is, above all, what matters – what is valuable in the world – may be cited as something so well adapted to the species' survival that it seems reasonable to surmise that this sense of value is somehow encouraged by genetic programming.

For some individuals, as for the 'deep ecologists' just cited, the 'sense of value' persuades them that there can be intrinsic value in things that are unused by, even unknown to, human beings. Other people believe that basis values are only related to human use; to their nation's use; to their family's use; or to their own use. The beliefs that people will state if asked about these things are not, by the way, necessarily the same as what may be revealed in their actions. The citizens who say that there are environmental values worth protecting 'regardless of the cost' (cf. a *New York Times* survey in August 1989) have probably not thought about possible trade-offs. At the same time, it is probably the case that a more careful survey which asked people to decide what they would do when facing various terrible situations ('supposing you had to choose between the preservation of a rain-forest and your sister's life? Your own life? The survival of your city?') would also not produce 'real' answers: part of what is non-logical about basis values is that individuals may and often do hold more than one as absolutes: there is then *no* solution, no answer to certain projected trade-offs.

Having said all this, and having referred to these basis values as non-logical and usually amorphous, I would like to remind the reader of the value judgment, discussed in the last chapter, that 'individual preferences matter'. This basis value, adopted in neoclassical economics (most overtly in the conception of consumer sovereignty), is neither more nor less logical, though it is more precise, than the kind of basis value I have described as characterising the average citizen. It, too, is a first cause, an 'unmoved mover' which cannot be deduced from anything outside of some individual's value system.

The issue of whether values ultimately *are* subjective or objective is unprovable. I personally find that I act as if my beliefs leaned toward the objective, Platonic side of this debate (even while I am not actually sure what I believe on this matter; it does not fit within the class of cognitive elements wherein I am more accustomed to defining belief). The important thing to get out of this discussion, fortunately, does not depend upon proof; it is merely the logical distinction between (A) basis values, as just defined and discussed, and (B) 'exchange value', or 'the monetary worth of something: marketable price'. (B) clearly exists in the real world: it is observable and measurable. About (A) we should ask, 'Is this a unicorn concept?' I am inclined to say it is not; my observation (of myself and of other human beings) leads me to believe that, with the term, 'basis value', I have described something which exists in most, if not all people, and which is an important moving force. It is not, however, measurable, and it tends to be amorphous, often shifting under examination or under the pressure of circumstances. In these respects it differs from the concept 'utility', which, I have claimed, has been defined and employed in neoclassical economics in such a way as not to resemble anything that actually exists in the mental (spiritual?) functioning of actual human beings.

Exchange value is, ultimately, dependent upon individual preferences, which in turn are dependent (at least in part) upon basis values.

If one were to say that 'economic behaviour is value-driven', this would mean – and most people would understand it to mean – that at the root of all economic activity is some assessment that comes out of the basis values; some sense, to put it another way, that some things intrinsically matter more than others – even though it may not be possible to provide a perfect ranking for all things of value. Indeed, if we ask ourselves *why* we value *X* more than *Y*, and find that we can give a satisfactory answer, then *X* and *Y* probably should not be regarded as basis values, but as preferences. The characteristic of basis values is that there is no other value which can be offered as justification for them; they are the justifications for all other values.

Basis values, as I am defining the term, are absolute; they do not submit to hierarchical arrangement. Human beings are often uneasy with a situation where it is impossible to find causes of causes; they wish at least to find *one single* cause of all other causes.[4] Feeling uneasy in the face of a possible multiplicity of absolutes, people often try to propose thought-experiments which will 'reveal' a hierarchy. Such an attempt to find an answer where there is none is one way of generating absurdity, i.e., meaninglessness. For example, if I hold *beauty* and *human welfare* as two basis values, and if I am asked to make the hypothetical choice between protecting a trainload of soldiers and a trainload of irreplaceable art works, I contend that any answer I give is essentially without meaning. Absurd situations sometimes exist; and a response, of choice or action, is sometimes required; but the result is an absurd choice or action which does not either confer or convey meaning.

I have been using, and will continue to use, the term 'human values' (or sometimes 'real value' or 'real cost') to refer to a complex of basis values-*cum*-preferences. Basis values are, I have suggested, neither cardinal nor ordinal; they are absolute, and are deeply hidden in most human psyches. I propose to spend no more time here on the attempt to identify and define them. Preferences are strictly ordinal, and relatively superficial. 'Human values' are the combination of basis values and preferences which we employ for the everyday actions which we do not have time to base upon deep philosophical reflection but for which, nevertheless, we regularly draw on a reservoir that goes deeper than a mere ordinal arrangement of preferences. 'Human values' are routinely used in answering questions from: 'is this pair of shoes worth (to me) what the merchant is asking for it?' to: 'should my daughter apply to law school?' to: 'what shall I say to my son about the girl he wants to marry?'

MONEY AS A
SYMBOLIC
SYSTEM
Underlying any social science there must be a system for recognising, referring to, defining and, in some way, assessing such human values. Such a system must be, at least in part, a symbolic system; 'human value' (assuming it is real and not a unicorn) nevertheless is an abstraction which cannot be apprehended as a thing in itself. It must at least sometimes be dealt with through a symbolic medium.

Marshall claimed, essentially, that the single abstraction, *money*, with its practical manifestation, *price*, could serve as the basis for such a symbolic system. A characteristic early statement of this claim may be found in a passage from 'Mr. Mill's Theory of Value', written in 1876:

2 When we speak of a ratio between an effort and an abstinence, or even between two diverse efforts, we assume, *ipso facto*, an artificial mode of measuring them in terms of some common unit, and refer to the ratio between their measures. The pure science of Ethics halts for lack of a system of measurement of efforts, sacrifices, desires, etc., fit for her wide purposes. But the pure science of Political Economy has found a system that will subserve her narrower aim. This discovery, rather than any particular proposition, is the great fact of the pure science (*Memorials*, pp. 125–6).

Various later versions of the claim are to be found throughout *Principles*. Marshall's most careful formulation, worth reproducing at length, was the following:

3 the steadiest motive to ordinary business work is the desire for the pay which is the material reward of work . . . . it is this definite and exact money measurement of the steadiest motives in business life, which has enabled economics far to outrun every other branch of the study of man . . . .
    The advantage which economics has over other branches of social science appears then to arise from the fact that its special field of work gives rather larger opportunities for exact methods than any other branch. It concerns itself chiefly with those desires, aspirations and other affections of human nature, the outward manifestations of which appear as incentives to action in such a form that the force or quantity of the incentives can be estimated and measured with some approach to accuracy; and which therefore are in some degree amenable to treatment by scientific machinery . . . .

If then we wish to compare even physical gratifications, we must not do it directly, but indirectly by the incentives which they afford to action. If the desires to secure either of two pleasures will induce people in similar circumstances each to do just an hour's extra work, or will induce men in the same rank of life and with the same means to pay a shilling for it; we may then say that those pleasures are equal for our purposes, because the desires for them are equally strong incentives to action for persons under similar conditions (*Principles*, pp. 12–13).[5]

The terms which Marshall used for the intangible side of the equation included 'desires, aspirations and other affections of human nature'; 'a person's motives' (belonging both to Man's 'higher' and his/ her 'lower' nature); 'the desires for . . . pleasures'; and 'a mental state'. I should note that I have already made one leap into abstraction in generalising all of these terms within the more general category of 'human value', or 'the sense human beings have that some things matter more than others'. This is, however, only one step in an extraordinarily complex chain of abstractions which will turn out to underlie the use of money (price) as a symbol for 'the things that matter to people'.

We might define the first member of the series of abstractions as the exchange of money for things. Exchange can, on one level, be seen as a fairly simple action – a swap of *this* for *that*. In the classical examples of barter it is always pointed out that the value implication of a swap is that each participant feels that the value of what s/he will receive is at least as great as the value of what s/he gives up.

The complexities involved become clearer in the next step, where the exchange is between, on the one hand, a particular good or service, and, on the other, a sum of money. The first side of the trade now has to take into account not only the evaluation of the thing to be relinquished and the thing to be gained ('how does the value, to me, of this cow compare with the value, to me, of these magic beans?'); but an *interaction* between all that is summed up, on the one hand, in the notion of *effective demand* ('what are my total resources and my total needs?'[6]); and, on the other hand, in the costs of production. (Behind the latter are relative materials scarcities; preferences of workers; level and type of technology available; level and type of capital equipment available; etc.)

The great complexity of this symbolism may be obscured by its familiarity. We are conditioned so that, without too much questioning, we normally take wages as some measure of the 'value' of an individual's work; we speak of one painting as 'more valuable' than another in light of what each will fetch at auction; either we assume in casual conversation that there is some underlying reality that corresponds to that auction value, or else, if we feel otherwise, our different personal evaluation strikes us as worthy of note.

I am not saying that we always accept price as representing our own perceptions of value – cf. the advertising slogan, '*Price* is what something costs: *value* is what it's really worth'; or Oscar Wilde's famous definition of a cynic as 'someone who knows the price of everything, the value of nothing'. (For another example, in economics, of the recognition that 'price' and 'value' *do* have different meanings, see the quotation from Hal Varian which is in Chapter 14, n. 10, below.)

What I am saying is that we take it for granted that price represents *some* kind of evaluation, and we find it noteworthy – sometimes even surprising – when the evaluation symbolised by price differs very much from the evaluation which we generate out of our own basis values, needs and moods of the moment.

MARSHALL'S OWN USES OF THE WORD 'VALUE'   This section will analyse rather closely the various ways in which Marshall used the word 'value'. It may be summarised as follows:

> **On the stated level of meaning, Marshall usually (though not always) meant 'price' when he said 'value'. However, his strongly-held goal (on both the stated and the logical meaning levels of his work) was to use that kind of value – price – to cast light upon something else, to which I have been referring, most broadly, by the term 'human values'.**

The result of using a word which has an important common meaning as well as a special economic one, was a confusion on the logical level. Marshall sometimes worked out the logic of his level 1 meaning (value = price), but at other times, without announcing the switch, he was trying to work out a similar-looking logic, but employing the wished-for meaning which kept coming in on level 2: value as 'what matters to people'.

A   As exchange value   Quotations 2 and 3 in this chapter accord well with the idea of a mapping from an intangible to a tangible kind of value. If, however, one were to concentrate solely upon one particular selection of passages from Marshall's writing it would be possible to conclude that, in fact, he was putting forth a tautology, not a mapping; for 'value' is used in only one, not in two senses. Consider the following:

4 [Adam Smith] showed the need of analyzing the causes that determine the difficulty of attainment of various economic results; of inquiring which of them are so far uniform in their mode of action that they can be reduced to law and then made the basis of scientific measurement. [Smith's] chief work was to indicate *the manner in which value measures human motives . . . .* the best economic work which came after the *Wealth of Nations* is distinguished from that which went before, by a clearer insight into the balancing and weighing, by means of money, of the desire for the possession of a thing on the one hand, and on the other of all the various efforts and self-denials which directly or indirectly contribute towards making it ('The Present Position of Economics' (1885) in *Memorials*, p. 157; italics added).

In this relatively early passage from Marshall's writing, which lays out his basic claim for economics as a scientific endeavour, the word 'value' may simply be read as 'price'.

In *Principles* Marshall remarks that 'The notion of Value is intimately connected with that of Wealth'; and then goes on to quote Adam Smith, as having said that 'The word *value* has two different meanings, and sometimes expressed the utility of some particular object and sometimes the power of purchasing other goods which the possession of that object conveys.' (In the first three editions of *Principles* Marshall specified yet further, adding the sentence: 'The one may be called value in use, the other value in exchange' *Var.* II, p. 190.) Marshall adds to this,

5 But experience has shown that it is not well to use the word in the former sense. [i.e., as use value.] The value, that is the exchange value, of one thing in terms of another at any place and time, is the amount of that second thing which can be got there and then in exchange for the first. Thus the term is relative, and expresses the relation between two things at a particular place and time (*Principles*, p. 51).

When he said that 'value measures human motives' (quotation 4), Marshall was referring to *exchange value*. The measurement of human motives is achieved, according to that passage, because exchange-values, translated into action, become prices. But prices are the result of *all* the forces of demand and supply, *including* the 'desire for the possession of a thing', 'the efforts and self-denials', etc. Hence:

6 the general relations of supply and demand govern value [*meaning price*]. But marginal uses do not govern value; because they, together with value, are themselves governed by those general relations (*Principles*, p. 340). (See also quotation 13 in Chapter 6, above.)

Here we encounter the first, most obvious impediment to Marshall's programme: exchange values measure only *the interaction of* a myriad human motives on the purchasing side with costs, other human motives, and the other determinants of the supply function; they do not measure human motives, or human values, in any straightforward way. If what is wanted is a straightforward link by which to measure human motives on the demand side, an estimated demand curve might be a more useful tool than a set of prices. (But see below for problems with this solution.) When Marshall turned to consumer surplus as his basic tool for welfare analysis, he did, indeed, look to demand estimation for essential support. But he continued to say – perhaps as a sort of shorthand for his more complex intentions – that 'material wealth . . . is the one convenient means of measuring human motive on a large scale' (*Principles*, p. 18).

B 'Real value' and 'real cost' When he rejected Adam Smith's 'value in use' (stating that 'the notion of *Value* is intimately connected with that of Wealth') Marshall declared his intention to use the word only in its special sense, as coinciding with exchange-value, i.e., price. However he was not perfectly consistent in this. Consider the following passage; the first two uses of the word could be interpreted in several ways, but the third, which I italicise, is clearly *not* intended to mean price:

7 The main purpose of this chapter has been to inquire what classes of things are to be included under the term wealth: and the question what value is to be ascribed to any elements has been discussed only incidentally; as for instance where we had to reject from the inventory of wealth part of the value of a thing on the ground that it had been already counted, or for some other reason. For this purpose private property had been counted at its exchange value. But the *value* [italics added] of public property cannot always be so

measured. No direct estimate can be formed of the value which the Thames has for England. As we shall see presently the exchange value of a thing is a very imperfect measure of *the total real benefits* which it confers: it is an imperfect measure even with regard to commodities in the hands of private consumers; a still more imperfect measure with regard to railways, and useless with regard to such elements of national wealth as rivers and seas (*Principles*, 1st edn, pp. 114–15. This was the original conclusion to Book II, Chapter II. Quoted in *Var.* II, pp. 189–90).[7]

It is a plausible (though not verifiable) reading to say that the italicised '*value*' is '*the total real benefits which it confers*' – the meaning, I would claim, which is more frequently intended in common use of the word.[8] In common parlance, as suggested earlier, the word 'value' may often be understood to mean 'the real worth of a thing' – which only sometimes happens to coincide with its price. This meaning stands out even more sharply in the following passage:

8 But [the economist] does not ignore the mental and spiritual part of life. On the contrary, even for the narrower use of economic studies, it is important to know *whether the desires which prevail are such as will help to build a strong, righteous character.* And in the broader uses of those studies, when they are being applied to practical problems, *the economist, like everyone else, must concern himself with the ultimate aims of man*, and take account of *differences in real value* between gratifications that are equally powerful incentives to action and have therefore equal economic measures. A study of these measures is only the starting-point of economics: *but it is the starting-point* (*Principles*, p. 14; italics added).

In yet another place Marshall distinguishes between 'the term "labour-value" to express the amount of labour of a given kind that the produce will purchase; and "real value" to mean the amount of necessaries, comforts, and luxuries of life that a given amount of produce will purchase' (*Principles*, pp. 525–6). If we wish to ask: 'what is the real – that is to say, the human – value of "labour value"?' we will find that Marshall does have an answer; he puts it in terms of 'real cost . . . from the social point of view'. The following passage was motivated by his strong moral feelings regarding the effect of work upon a person's life and spiritual development. When that effect was negative, it created an added cost of production which, he implied, society should take into account:

9a The *real cost of production* of a thing is the aggregate of efforts and sacrifices which are incurred in its production. Thus the work of very young children in factories, even though paid for in money at the full market rate, is seldom worth its real cost: the satisfactions, which are derived from its contributions to production, are not worth the social cost of child life spent in grievous and depressing toil, and without an adequate education to prepare for the duties of after life (from Book II, Chapter I of *Industry and Trade*, pp. 181–96).

There was a footnote to this passage:

9b The degree of correspondence between the price paid for any particular industrial work and its real cost, though a matter of vital importance from the social point of view, is not very closely connected with the subject of this Book.

Here Marshall was dodging some of the critical issues raised in accepting exchange value (i.e., price) as a proxy for use value; in particular, the issue of the factors which intervene uniquely, in labour economics, between 'price' and 'cost' (as he had used these terms in this footnote).

In the case of all other commodities, the action of 'use' (i.e., using the commodity) resides with the buyer; in the case of labour, that action remains with the seller: it is only the secondary result of the action (the actual product, or service) that may be used by the buyer. At the same time, the labour exchange, from the point of view of the worker, includes more factors than just the consumer's considerations of 'what will I get, compared to all the other things I might purchase with the same money?' The worker's opportunity cost is, as Marshall suggested, more complicated than just the value of the leisure foregone. It includes the 'quality of the labour' (i.e., all the environmental, social and spiritual experiences sometimes referred to as 'quality of the work-place') as it is experienced *by* the worker, *after* his/her 'labour' (most properly understood as a verb, not a noun) has been sold.[9]

C The social point of view The social point of view cited by Marshall (in quotation 9b, above) clearly goes beyond a concern with exchange value; it must include a concern for the effects of work upon the worker – even the meaning of work *to* the worker; for these, along with the productive results of human labour, constitute its social value. When, in the passage quoted above, he disavowed the relevance of such social value to his book, *Industry and Trade*, Marshall made a major concession to the art of the possible, to the detriment of his scientific ambitions. The subject of labour is the one where he felt most acutely the distance between his desire to measure 'real costs' and the actual possibility of doing so. However, the social point of view was, most deeply, the basis for Marshall's interest in economics; and his most ambitious claim for the field included a pretense to measure something which, if it fell short of 'real cost', he nevertheless kept trying to push beyond 'the full market rate'.

D Total   In a discussion on the 'real worth' of salt vs. tea,[10]
value   Marshall sharpens the distinction between total versus marginal utility:

10   It is a common saying in ordinary life that the real worth of things to a man is not gauged by the price he pays for them: that though he spends for instance much more on tea than on salt, yet salt is of greater real worth to him; and that this would be clearly seen if he were entirely deprived of it. This line of argument is but thrown into precise technical form when it is said that we cannot trust the marginal utility of a commodity to indicate its total utility . . . under ordinary circumstances, the price of salt being low, everyone buys so much of it that an additional pound would bring him little additional satisfaction: the total utility of salt to him is very great indeed, and yet its marginal utility is low (*Principles*, p. 107).

Here it is clear that the total benefit to be derived from a purchase (the consumer's expectation of which may be seen as the basis of his/her evaluation of its worth) may be divided into two portions. One is the amount of benefit which would have only just justified making the purchase. The other portion is the consumer's surplus. The two together add up to total utility.

The place where real life actually goes on is, in fact, normally at the margins of the circumstances obtaining at any particular moment. We are seldom put in the position where King Lear found himself – of having to gauge the real value, or 'total utility' we would place upon salt. Lear set in train a tragic course by taking offence at Cordelia's comparing his value in her eyes to that of salt, because he evaluated the worth of salt at a margin where his immediate need for it was close to being satisfied; only when King Lear was confronted with a saltless dish was he able to understand the matter in the total, rather than the marginal, sense. How important is that total evaluation? Is it important for economists, or only for poets and philosophers?

It certainly is important that economists not be misled into thinking that, since exchange value is easy to ascertain, and since we have managed to get a neat conceptual lasso around the *idea* (not, as it will turn out, the *measurement*) of consumer's surplus, all we need to do is to add those two things together, and we can measure total value. Because of the difficulties with consumer's surplus, that addition will, unfortunately, not give us the answer to how to measure total value. Marshall was sufficiently aware of this so that he avoided overt claims to be trying to measure total value; but we will see that he was nevertheless after the measurement of something more than exchange value.

A CLOSER   **11**   We have seen that economics is, on the one side, a
LOOK AT   Science of Wealth; and, on the other, that part of
MARSHALL'S   the Social Science of man's action in society, which
PROGRAMME   deals with his Efforts to satisfy his Wants, *in so far
                           as the efforts and wants are capable of being
                           measured in terms of wealth, or its general
                           representative, i.e. money* (*Principles*, p. 41; italics
                           added).

12   Utility is taken to be correlative to Desire or Want. It has been already argued that desires cannot be measured directly, but only indirectly by the outward phenomena to which they give rise: and that in those cases with which economics is chiefly concerned the measure is found in the price which a person is willing to pay for the fulfillment or satisfaction of his desire . . . we assume that the resulting satisfaction corresponds in general fairly well to that which was anticipated when the purchase was made.*

* [Marshall's footnote] It cannot be too much insisted that to measure directly, or *per se*, either desires or the satisfactions which results from their fulfillment is impossible, if not inconceivable . . .[11] . . . we fall back on the measurement which economics supplies of the motive or moving force to action; and we make it serve, with all its faults, *both* for the desires which prompt actions and for the satisfaction which results from them (*Principles*, p. 78, from the text and from n. 1).

The hope which Marshall expressed in these representative passages appeared a splendid one. It was the hope that **money, that convenient quantifier, could be used as a proxy for enough of the things of importance to the field of economics so that economics could develop as a science, with increasing reliance upon quantitative techniques or 'exact methods'.** The salient question here is: what can and must be included in 'enough of the things of importance to economics' in order for this scientific development to take place? In the answer to that question lie some of the critical limitations of this hope. Marshall was aware of the existence of these limitations, and often expressed his concern that they could become not only binding, but strangling.

What precisely was it that Marshall hoped could be achieved when 'the economist studies mental states rather through their manifestations than in themselves'? (*Principles*, p. 14). He had in mind a particular logic when making such statements as this. He never in one place completely traced through this logic (nowadays we would call it a model), but it is easy enough to put the pieces together as follows:

- We cannot measure human values, satisfactions or motives in themselves.
- We can, however, make a scientific study of 'mental states through their manifestations' when these manifestations are both observable and measurable.
- Specifically, we can do this by looking for some regular relationship between observable, measurable actions on the one hand, and unobservable, unmeasurable motivations and/or satisfactions on the other.
- Such regular relationships may be found to exist between unobservable *motivations/satisfactions*, and measurable *expenditures*. In other words, from observing how people spend and earn money, we can deduce their preferences, and the value motivations that underlie them.
- Expenditures, whether from the point of view of the recipient or of the payer, are made on the basis of exchange values.
- The goal, then, is to measure human motivations and satisfactions in order to study their effects scientifically; and exchange-values, or prices, are the proxies that will permit this.

We might inquire whether Marshall could have accomplished some or all of what he wanted with a less ambitious plan than this. A red herring may be included here in the fact that, for Marshall, the study of human motivations/satisfactions appears, at least in some places in his writings, to be an end in itself. To someone with a more exclusively economic perspective, the goal might be to study motivations/ satisfactions only in order to measure them – not, as with Marshall, to measure them in order to study them. And if it were found that the measurement could be made well enough for economic purposes without any such study, then that might be sufficient.

However, in order to understand what human welfare really is, it is necessary to understand what it is that people value – not only in the marginal sense but in the sense of a 'total utility' whose measurement has so far escaped science. That sense of 'what people value' is, of course, what economists are supposed to be *given* in a social welfare function. Here is where it becomes relevant to return to the issue that was raised in the first section of in this chapter: is there some objective definition of 'progress'? Supposing we conclude, instead, that all of the values which assess 'better' or 'worse' states of the world are purely subjective: how, then, do we aggregate such individual, subjective, valuations into a concept of social welfare? By headcount (a solution of pure democracy)? Weighting according to the resources controlled by each individual (a solution of market capitalism)? Or by some basic needs or Rawlsian max-min approach?

Marshall, in any case, was not waiting for what has still, in the years intervening, not appeared: the definition of a fully satisfactory social welfare function. He assumed – as I would urge that social economics must do – that the economist must take some responsibility for understanding the nuances of human welfare that cannot be built into an algorithm.

The modern adoption of efficiency as *the* great promise of economics – 'Whatever you want to do, I can tell you how to do it efficiently' – implicitly assumes a social welfare function into existence. Marshall was not so willing to operate in a world where social welfare was 'presumed to be given'; he was concerned about real issues, which required that such a function (if the analysis was to depend upon it) really be produced. His hope was that, by constructing an economic science wherein the real values (or total utilities, or human values) of real people are implied in the primary data of prices, such a science could in some way generate the welfare functions that its economists were awaiting. He hoped that such a science could, then, legitimately combine analysis and prescription; for the value inputs in the analysis would allow it to give rise (when correctly used by persons with the qualities of empathy, imagination and ethical sensitivity which

Marshall called upon economists to employ), to ethically sound and socially relevant prescription: the output, 'ought', would be derived from an economic science whose input confessedly combined both 'is' and 'ought'.

THE PRACTICAL   Marshall's claim is best understood, at least in part,
APPLICATION   as a practical one. He retained through the 8th
FOR MARSHALL'S   edition of *Principles* a level 1 disclaimer: 'The
CLAIM   *measurement of motive* thus obtained is not indeed
                   perfectly accurate; for if it were, economics would
rank with the most advanced of the physical sciences; and not, as it
actually does, with the least advanced' (*Principles*, p. 21; italics added).
However, from there he went on to describe, in concrete terms, what he
expected such a measurement of motives to be able to achieve:

13 Thus, for instance, [economists] can estimate very closely the
    payment that will be required to produce an adequate supply of
    labour of any grade, from the lowest to the highest, for a new
    trade which it is proposed to start in any place . . . . And they can
    predict with tolerable certainty what rise of price will result from a
    given diminution of the supply of a certain thing, and how that
    increased price will react on the supply.
        And, starting from simple considerations of this kind,
    economists go on to analyze the causes which govern the local
    distribution of different kinds of industry, the terms on which
    people living in distant places exchange their goods with one
    another, and so on: and they can explain and predict the ways in
    which fluctuations of credit will affect foreign trade; or again the
    extent to which the burden of a tax will be shifted from those on
    whom it is levied, on to those for whose wants they cater; and so on.
        In all this they deal with man as he is: not with an abstract or
    'economic' man; but a man of flesh and blood . . . . They deal
    with man as he is: but being concerned chiefly with those aspects
    of life in which the action of motive is so regular that it can be
    predicted, and the estimate of the motor-forces can be verified by
    results, they have established their work on a scientific basis
    (*Principles*, p. 22).

    To an economist who does applied work, particularly one who is in
the position of advising any maker of economic policy, much of the
above would have a familiar ring. The second sentence, in particular,
immediately brings to mind the list of elasticities of demand and supply

which s/he would need to know in order to make the prediction vaunted here. A labour economist, looking at the first sentence, would mentally list the information about demographics (mobility and composition of the local labour force), labour supply elasticities, and available training and education opportunities, which would have to be known in order to supply Marshall's 'close estimate'. None of these are easy facts to get hold of; some have to be deduced by processes which involve, normally, a good deal of guesswork. Figures on elasticities, especially, can seldom, even when calculated, be regarded as 'facts'; and what validity they do possess tends to have a short half-life. Going on to the second paragraph, the analyses, explanations and predictions promised there suggest exponentially larger requirements for empirical knowledge.

Marshall took for granted that economics is strongly rooted in empirical knowledge. Disapproving of 'long trains of deduction', he would not have sanctioned their use in the generation of these practical analyses, explanations and predictions. But even if one possessed all the facts that might be desired, some short deductive links would still be necessary, and these, he was claiming, could be constructed upon the regularities of behaviour which allow us to use money/price as a measure of motivations/satisfactions.

The claim is bold. It implies, at the least, that economics can scientifically express (some appropriately defined version of) total value – or what I have been calling 'human value' – in terms of money. And once human value can meaningfully and consistently be expressed in any quantifiable terms (such as pounds or dollars), it would then be possible to weigh the relative costs and benefits of various courses of action, and, finally, to use economics honestly in the role which it is constantly called upon to play – as a guide to public policy.

THE BASES FOR MARSHALL'S CLAIM There are two different bases upon which Marshall rested his comparison between money and motivations/satisfactions. One, to which he referred often, was the statistical base; this has to do with the probability of finding a similar mean in two similar populations. The following will do for an example:

A Statistical

14 If we take averages sufficiently broad to cause the personal peculiarities of individuals to counterbalance one another, the money which people of equal incomes will give to obtain a benefit or avoid an injury is a good *measure of the benefit or injury*. If there are a thousand persons living in Sheffield, and another

thousand in Leeds, each with about 100 pounds a-year, and a tax
of 1 pound is levied on all of them; we may be sure that the loss of
pleasure or other injury which the tax will cause in Sheffield is of
about equal importance with that which it will cause in
Leeds . . . . This probability becomes greater still if all of them
are adult males engaged in the same trade; and therefore
presumably somewhat similar in sensibility and temperament, in
taste and education. Nor is the probability much diminished, if we
take the family as our unit, and compare the loss of pleasure that
results from diminishing by 1 pound the income of each of a
thousand families with incomes of 100 pounds a-year in the two
places . . . .

By far the greater number of the events with which economics
deals affect in about equal proportions all the different classes of
society; so that if *the money measures of the happiness* caused by
two events are equal, it is reasonable and in accordance with
common usage to regard the *amounts of the happiness* of the two
cases as equivalent (*Principles*, pp. 13–15).

B The socio- The other base upon which Marshall rested his
historical comparison between money and motivations/satisfac-
base tions was socio-historical. It depended upon the fact
that Marshall was writing at a time (the late-
nineteenth, early-twentieth centuries), and in a place (England) which
contained a large commercialised element. Marshall was aware that
contemporary economic conditions were something new in human
experience. Economic activity had come, it appeared, to be the
dominant activity in life. 'The best men in society', he noted, were
engaging their energies in the business world. Parliament was now
spending more than half its time on economic issues. This reality was at
the back of what may have been Marshall's most expansive statement
of hope for making this science a regular, definable one: the following
combines his socio-historical observations with the statistical reasoning
cited above:

15 Those actions that are governed by free enterprise and self-
regarding motives are, as we have seen, those which are most
easily reduced to law and measured; and reasonings with regard to
such actions afford the simplest types of economic theory: but they
are not the whole of it. *Wherever any motive*, whether self-
regarding or not self-regarding, whether of public or private

interest, whether based on wise judgement or on ignorant principles, *affects any considerable class of people in the same way*, then the action of that motive can often be reduced to some kind of money measure, if not directly, yet at least indirectly by comparison with other motives that can be measured directly; and then it can be brought more or less within the range of economic reasoning.

Economics is a science of human action; and economic laws, properly so-called, are laws of human action. (*Principles*, 1st edn, p. 86; the first paragraph was deleted from the 2nd edn, the second from the 5th edn. Quoted in *Var*. II, pp. 149–50. Italics added.)

As may be seen from the italicised phrases, Marshall does, at least, maintain one kind of consistency: he admits that it is only when it is assumed that there will be no income effects that his 'great working machine' can operate in all its scientific glory. The serious inconsistency occurs in his emphasis: he wavers as to whether or not he regards the narrow interpretation which neglects differences in wealth as too narrow to build a science upon.

The 'astonishing assertion' (Blaug) that 'by far the greater number of the events with which economics deals affect in about equal proportions all the different classes of society' (quotation 14, above) is implicitly denied elsewhere in *Principles*. For example, when commenting on 'the general doctrine that a position of (stable) equilibrium of demand and supply is a position also of *maximum satisfaction*', Marshall states that this doctrine is true if narrowly interpreted, but not universally true in a broad sense:

16 In the first place it assumes that all differences in wealth between the different parties concerned may be neglected, and that the satisfaction which is rated at a shilling by any one of them, may be taken as equal to one that is rated at a shilling by any other (*Principles*, pp. 389–90).

As we shall see, Marshall tended to assign to the Doctrine of Maximum Satisfaction the more extreme claims which one can find throughout his own writing. This doctrine (known to Marxians as 'commodity fetishism' or 'market fetishism') was the idea that (to paraphrase from the Mathematical Appendix): if one is to define H as the sum total of satisfactions, and V as the sum total of dissatisfactions ('efforts, sacrifices, etc.') which accrue to a community *from economic causes*, then the forces of demand and supply operate in such a way that there is a constant tendency for H minus V to be a maximum for society as a whole. Or, to summarise the conclusion of this doctrine in the words which Marshall used earlier in the book, 'the maximum satisfaction is *generally* to be attained by encouraging each individual to spend his own resources in a way that suits him best' (*Principles*, p. 393).

Marshall disagreed with this doctrine, and his strongest reason for doing so was based on 'the necessity of taking account of the variations in the amount of pleasure, or other satisfaction, represented by the same sum of money to different persons under different circumstances' (*Principles*, p. 15), especially the fact that the same amount of money generally represents a larger amount of satisfaction for a poor man than for a rich one. From this last point Marshall deduced his 'broad proposition' regarding the utility-enhancing effects of redistribution, 'voluntary or compulsory', from the rich to the poor (*Principles*, p. 391).

It is obviously within a Utilitarian framework of thought that the Doctrine of Maximum Satisfaction would have appeal, and Marshall's repudiation of this doctrine is one of the instances of his not-altogether-successful effort to distance himself from Utilitarianism. Marshall's position took account of both the equality prescription which results from combining Utilitarianism with the assumption of identical utility functions, and also the efficiency argument (though by no means in its strongest form) which was used as a defence against too radical a response to the equality prescription. However, the route which had led Marshall to this conclusion was not identical to that of the Utilitarians. In searching, as they did, for a way to compare utility functions, he did not claim that all utility functions are identical, but rather that, statistically, the effects of economic events average out the same in their effects upon individuals. This was a support for his whole argument which was so important to Marshall that he could not abandon it, even though he himself recognised the dangers in its application.

MARGINAL ANALYSIS AND INTERPERSONAL COMPARISONS   It is, of course, total utility – or total value, as I have been calling it – which is essentially impossible to measure. It was not without good reason that, as soon as the idea of marginal value was available, neoclassical economists concentrated on it as exclusively as possible. Marshall also saw the concept of marginal utility as the great solution which could make the link between the important unquantifiable subjects of economics and the useful quantitative techniques.

In quotation 15 we saw Marshall's claim that 'any motive' which 'affects any considerable class of people in the same way' (this is not an insignificant qualification) 'can often be reduced to some kind of money measure.' The quotation just preceding (14) shows how he became more cautious as time went by, and increasingly fell back upon an emphasis upon marginal values as the things to be measured; but it is important to remember that, to Marshall, *the reason for measuring marginal values was that the resulting data were to be used for the light they could shed upon the underlying total values.* An examination of Marshall's use of marginal evaluations within this endeavour shows that, while these data are more relevant for action, yet they still do not make the bridge he looked for that would span all the distance from motivations/satisfactions to the price which provides the 'money measure'.

Marshall took as his data the observable marginal willingness to pay, or to perform work for pay. These marginal willingnesses are revealed because consumers stop purchasing, and workers stop working, when the limits which they impose are reached. Near the beginning of the eighth edition of *Principles* Marshall proposed the logic of marginal analysis as a basis for what would be more thoroughly developed, in concept, as indifference maps:

17 For instance the pleasures which two persons derive from smoking cannot be directly compared: nor can even those which the same person derives from it at different times. But if we find a man in doubt whether to spend a few pence on a cigar, or a cup of tea, or on riding home instead of walking home, then we may follow ordinary usage, and say that he expects from them equal pleasures (*Principles*, p. 13).

This passage stays on relatively safe ground in that it avoids both interpersonal and intertemporal comparisons of utility. However, these avoidances only highlight what was unsatisfactory to Marshall about marginal calculation, depending, as it does, upon the exchange value of a thing which 'is the same all over a market; but the final degrees of utility to which it corresponds are not equal at any two parts' (*Principles*, p. 673).

Marshall generally accepted the fact that scientific specifications of interpersonal comparisons require highly restrictive assumptions

regarding income differences: i.e., that such income differences do not
exist; or that they average out; or that they do not matter. We have
seen examples of his numerous attempts to avoid the narrowness of
these restrictions by using, in effect, the principle of regression to the
mean; or, when all else failed, by adopting the highly questionable
assumption that, in areas of economic interest, inequality of income
would not be great enough to affect the relevant utilities. He tried to
slay the monster early on in *Principles*, with a firm (level 1) statement
that 'No one can compare and measure accurately against one another
even his own mental states at different times: and no one can measure
the mental states of another at all except indirectly and conjecturally by
their effects' (p. 13). Yet the issue of interpersonal comparison kept
coming back to haunt him, causing Pigou to observe that in Marshall's
actual work he circumvented the problem by tacitly assuming – or
writing, in some places, as though he assumed – that utilities can be
measured.

CONSUMER'S   For the times when his awareness of the differences in
SURPLUS AS   individual marginal utilities of money dampened
THE LINK   Marshall's optimism about using prices to gain direct
                      insights into human values, he had yet one card to play:
his brilliant conception of consumer's surplus. He introduced that
subject thus:

18   We may now turn to consider how far the price which is actually
     paid for a thing represents the benefit that arises from its
     possession. This is a wide subject on which economic science has
     very little to say, but that little is of some importance.
        We have already seen that the price which a person pays for a
     thing can never exceed, and seldom comes up to that which he
     would be willing to pay rather than go without it: so that the
     satisfaction which he gets from its purchase generally exceeds that
     which he gives up in paying away its price; and he thus derives
     from the purchase a surplus of satisfaction. The excess of the price
     which he would be willing to pay rather than go without the thing,
     over that which he actually does pay, is the economic measure of
     this surplus satisfaction. It may be called *consumer's surplus*
     (Principles, p. 103).

   In other words, for any individual the consumer's surplus measures
the difference between the *exchange-value* (= price) of the purchase

and its *use-value* (or total value) to him/her. The consumers' surplus (if there were a history of apostrophes, this is one whose placement would take special prominence) which is inferred from the aggregation of individual into societal utility functions has, in principle, the same meaning; but of course the aggregation problem posed here – first of all, in the requirement of a sufficient comparability between the demand curves of persons with different incomes – throws us right back into the difficulties of comparability which have already been mentioned.

In the reminiscences of Marshall set down by his nephew, C. W. Guillebaud, we find a poignant commentary on Marshall's wish to be able to measure consumer's surplus:

19 He told me on one occasion that a major disappointment in his life was the recognition, which gradually forced itself on him, that his concept of consumer's surplus was devoid of important practical application, because it was not capable of being quantified in a meaningful way. At the outset he had high hopes that it could have had practical application, and for many years he had wrestled with it, but had finally reached the conclusion that it was a theoretical but not a practical tool in the economist's workbox.[12]

Other economists held onto Marshall's hope for longer than he did. Pigou, in 1953, quoted Marshall's most optimistic remarks on the possibility that the statistics of consumption will evolve to the point of supporting reliable demand curve estimates, and went on to say,

20 strenuous efforts have been made and are being made to realize that hope . . . . The prospect of filling at least the demand compartment of one very important set of 'empty economic boxes' are [sic] being substantially advanced. With open arms Marshall would have welcomed the work that is being done in this field.[13]

As to how the matter has been perceived more recently, we may quote from an economist the beginning of whose career overlapped the end of Marshall's life, in the 1920s, and who has continued to practice actively up to the present:

21 There was some interesting [empirical] work done in the 20's and 30's when it looked as though it would be possible to estimate supply and demand curves. A competitive economy is like a big

computing machine which uses prices in its computations to solve problems, setting demand equal to supply by successive approximations. I tried estimating the presumed underlying curves, and found you can do it till you're blue in the face and not get anywhere.[14]

In these two quotations Pigou and Leontief are referring to the *inductive* approach to demand estimation. The alternative, *deductive* approach was best exemplified by Walras, who put into practice the idea of deriving demand curves from utility schedules. The work which has built on the Walrasian approach has used it increasingly as a way of constructing an abstract conceptualisation. In Chapter 17 will be found a brief examination of some modern efforts to base exact estimates of welfare measurements upon demand specifications, the latter either derived empirically and inductively, or built up deductively from concepts of utility. Before reaching that modern comparison, in the chapter following this we will reflect further on the deductive versus inductive alternatives which continue to be available in this area.

Notes

1.   *Webster's New Collegiate Dictionary* (Merriam Company, 1974).
      When we speak of a person as 'having good (or poor) values' we are broadening usage 4 into a reference system which we understand to be employed as, essentially, a basis for all subsequent 'value judgments'. ('*Value judgment n*: a judgment attributing a value (as good, evil, beautiful or desirable) to a certain thing, action or entity', Webster's).
2.   Nicholas Maxwell, 'How Can we Build a Better World? From Knowledge to Wisdom', in manuscript, p. 31.
3.   Batie, 1989, p. 20. The quotation in this passage is from J.B.Callicott, 'On the Intrinsic Value of Nonhuman Species' in *The Preservation of Species: the Value of Biological Diversity*, ed. by Bryan G.Norton (Princeton University Press, NJ, 1986) p. 140.
4.   Cf. J. S. Mill's raptures on the single, ultimate value of Utilitarianism; J. S. Mill, *Autobiography* (The Liberal Arts Press, New York, 1957) esp. pp. 42–4.
5.   The qualifying phrases used here – 'people *in similar circumstances*', 'men *in the same rank of life and with the same means*' – imply an assumption that the marginal utility of money (MUe) can be assumed to be equal among people whose circumstances are, in some relevant way, equivalent. Marshall often stressed that comparisons between rich and poor are

difficult because their MUe is probably different; he did not take such pains to spell out what emerges as his corollary assumption: that among people of 'comparable circumstances' the MUe of different individuals is probably similar enough that it is safe to assume it is the same.

Confusion may readily be introduced between this buried assumption and Marshall's references to '*constant* marginal utility of income'. In the latter case the subject was the utility of a *single individual*: when Marshall explicitly made the constant MUe assumption he was referring to a situation, or time period, in which the circumstances faced by an individual did not change so much that his/her marginal utility of money would change appreciably. (This ruled out, for example, an expenditure so major as to change the individual's sense of his/her own wealth; or any marked change in real income or wealth.) Marshall never attempted to hold the marginal utility of income constant across income classes.

6. Of course, the evaluation, 'the worth of this cow to me' also depends upon some understanding of one's total resources and one's total needs; that fact is simply less obvious in the barter case.

7. Compare another passage from the first edition:

There is another class of corrections which must be made before *the money measure of the total utility of wealth can be taken to represent the real happiness which its possession affords.* Not only does a person's happiness often depend more on his own physical, mental and moral health than on his external conditions: but even among these conditions many that are of chief importance for his real happiness are apt to be omitted from an inventory of his wealth. Some are free gifts of nature; and these might indeed be neglected without great harm if they were always the same for everybody; but in fact they vary much from place to place. More of them however are elements of collective wealth which are often omitted from the reckoning of individual wealth; but which become important when we compare different parts of the modern civilized world, and even more important when we compare our own age with earlier times (*Principles*, 1st edn, pp. 179–80; italics added).

This passage was kept throughout the eight editions, except that in the third edition the following sentence was put in – and retained thereafter – as a replacement for the first sentence of what has just been quoted: 'There remains another class of considerations which are apt to be overlooked in estimating the dependence of wellbeing upon material wealth.' It is worth noting this change, because it somewhat weakens the original claim.

8. This meaning is essentially what economists suggest by the term, 'total utility' – a concept which Marshall in general tried to avoid, but which was, obviously, of great importance to his consumer's surplus.

9. I am grateful to Mohan Rao for bringing to my attention several of the points made in this paragraph.

10. Marshall did occasionally employ the term 'real value' in its modern sense – as a contrast with *monetary* (rather than as a contrast with *exchange*) value. One of his rare references to the real versus monetary distinction

may be found, for example, in 'The Present Position of Economics' (in *Memorials*; see esp. p. 162).

11. The ten lines omitted in quoting this footnote respond, in part, to 'Some Remarks on Utility' by Pigou, *Economic Journal*, March 1903. Therein appeared an early example of the criticism invariably made by commentators regarding Marshall's conflation of motivations (i.e., 'the desires which prompt actions') with satisfactions. Marshall's stated recognition, that prices only reflect satisfactions as those are correctly anticipated in the desires which define the demand blade of the price scissors, evidently did not satisfy Pigou, who quoted critically the last sentence of the footnote in his 1953 piece on Marshall. (See quotations 2 and 3 in Chapter 15, below.) It is not clear why Marshall was determined to retain that last sentence; in any case he went on attaching price, on the demand side, sometimes to desire, sometimes to satisfaction, and sometimes to both. And he has continued to draw criticism for doing so, up to the present day. Blaug also quotes the same final sentence out of context, to criticise it with the comment:

> After citing impulse, habit, self-denial, mistaken expectation and other causes of disparities between desire and satisfaction, Marshall concluded that, given the absence of direct measurement of either desire or satisfaction, we must fall back on price and make it serve, 'with all its faults, *both* for the desires which prompt activities, and for the satisfactions that result from them!' . . .
> The tendency to draw facile welfare conclusions from utility theory, ignoring inequalities of the distribution of income and the difficulties in making meaningful interpersonal comparisons – the chief offender being Marshall himself – were largely responsible for producing a skeptical attitude toward the achievements of marginal utility analysis (Blaug, *Economic Theory in Retrospect*, pp. 353–4).

Both Biaug's and Pigou's remarks can be seen as unfair, when one concentrates solely upon Marshall's most cautious formulations – e.g., quotations 2 and 3 in this chapter. However, whether through carelessness or confusion, or (as I claim) because he was attempting to carry something illogical to its logical conclusion, there were plenty of passages in which Marshall gave ample ground for such criticism.

As I continue this analysis I shall need a term for that thing 'the measurement [of] which economics supplies', so I shall use 'motivations/ satisfactions'. (As we shall see, Pigou proposed that the word 'utilities' be used in this situation; but that only makes it more imprecise.)

12. C. W. Guillebaud, 'Some Personal Reminiscences of Alfred Marshall', in AMCA. For the reason why such measurement was so important to Marshall, see *Principles*, pp. 407–8. For his own more sober acceptance of their unattainability, see *Principles*, p. 110; also *Principles*, p. 92.

13. Pigou, 1953, p. 25.

14. Wassily Leontief, speaking at Boston University in the GEA Speakers' Series, Spring 1986. Page 25 of the Mimeo *Report on the Speakers' Series*.

15 The Problems and Why They Persist

In order to get at the 'human values' which underlie motivations or satisfactions, Marshall wished to find a measure of motivations and satisfactions. Recognising that these things could never be measured directly, his programme was to study them through their manifestations – specifically, as they might be found to have a regular relationship with a fully observable, quantifiable action, e.g., the expenditure of money.

The first, most obvious problem encountered in this programme has already been discussed: prices result from the interplay of so many things that, lacking a reliable method of holding all the rest constant, prices cannot give clear information on just one of these causal agents. This is one of the familiar difficulties which has plagued modern attempts to specify demand curves: other than in quite exceptional circumstances it is not possible to be sure whether one is observing movement along a curve, or movement of the curve itself – shifts in demand or shifts in supply, or both.

The next problems stemmed from the fall-back position which Marshall took in recognition that prices could not play, in a perfectly clear, direct fashion, the role he wished for them. He fell back on asking of prices that they give information on *marginal* utilities only; and from there, with the addition of consumer's surpluses, he hoped to build up towards what was essentially to be total utility. Here there are two difficulties: one with the interpretation of what prices actually say about marginal utilities; the other with measurement of consumer's(') surplus. A review of these questions will ultimately bring us back to the more general question of the measurability of total utility; I will start that circular journey from the issue of consumer's(') surplus.

CONSUMER'S SURPLUS AS THE DIFFERENCE BETWEEN EXCHANGE VALUE AND TOTAL VALUE

As we set out it is important to keep in mind the following points:

- The definition of consumer's(') surplus depends upon a definition of demand functions.

321

- Demand functions may be derived empirically (with consequent restrictions upon the generality with which they may be applied); this is the inductive approach.
- Or else, in the deductive approach, they may be deduced from utility functions, either direct or indirect. The need for defining something concrete in the real world is then thrown back a step to the even more difficult problem of specifying and quantifying realistic utility functions.

We all know what the triangle of consumer's surplus looks like on a graph, lying above the price line and below the individual or aggregated demand curve; we often see it shaded in, as in Figure 15.1.

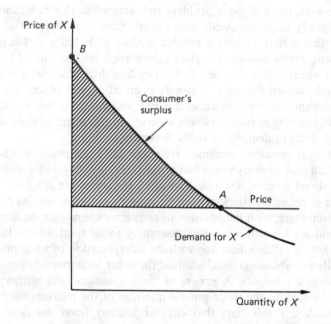

Figure 15.1 Consumer's surplus

In the case of an aggregated demand curve, the right hand point (*A*), where the demand curve intersects the price line, is the point of current operation; that is where the marginal consumer is just willing to pay the price demanded by the market. Everyone who is not a marginal consumer, and who would be willing, if necessary, to pay more for the good than its current market price, is represented on the demand curve to the left of intersection *A*. The ('ineffective') demands of all those who are not willing (or able) to pay the market price are represented on the right hand tail of the demand curve, as it continues below the price line (to the right of *A*).

The number of assumptions and simplifications built into this neat picture is not always recognised. The problems for calculating consumer's(') surplus begin with the necessity for being able to specify the whole of the demand curve above the price line. This means knowing the elasticity of demand at any point in section *AB*. As is well known, elasticities may be calculated reasonably well for points near those which have recently been observed, but the farther you go in time away from the present, or in Cartesian space away from the cluster of recent and contemporary points, the less certainty can be attached to demand elasticity estimates.

There are a couple of other factors which add to the conceptual difficulty of measuring demand. The first of these is the fact that demand – along with much else of interest to economics – is normally analysed in relation to wants, not needs. This is not because wants are more important than needs, or even more common in human experience, but because they avoid some modelling problems. If a different norm had been established and accepted, where a demand curve was assumed to refer to necessities, unless stated otherwise, we would have a greater awareness than is now common of the real, underlying difficulties.

As the price of a 'want' gets pushed higher, consumption of that item goes to zero. As the price of a 'necessity' rises, consumption of almost everything else declines; therefore realistic consideration of demand for a necessity precludes, to begin with, *ceteris paribus* conditions on other consumption. Further, in the case of necessities the identification of 'demand' with the normal concept of 'effective demand' is called into question, and A. K. Sen's idea of 'entitlements' becomes more appropriate. In the normal concept of effective demand the limit to what you can offer is the total of all you have. If the emphasis of economics were on needs instead of wants, we would anticipate that, in answer to the question, 'what would you pay rather than go without food (or water, or air)?', the economist would accept for his/her diagram, not the (effective demand) answer, 'I would pay all I own' but '. . . anything I could get my hands on'. However we are then talking of a more uncertain quantity; it is obviously not infinite (it would require an infinite lifetime to get one's hands on an infinite quantity of money), but it cannot be made determinate by simply bounding it with the total present endowment.[1]

Part of what is at issue here is the attempt to understand demand for a single commodity under *ceteris paribus* conditions. In certain cases (especially with respect to poor people) this appears to be an absurdity when considering any but the smallest price of certain necessities. Mark Blaug's commentary on the requirement that 'everything else stays constant' is relevant here, and anticipates our later discussion of Marshall's insistence upon a constant marginal utility of money:

1 Marshall was reluctant to abandon the use of the demand curve to measure the consumer's surplus from a change in price and for that reason, despite all submissions to the contrary, he retained both the additive utility function and the concept of an approximately constant MUe [marginal utility of expenditures, or of money].

   Marshall's uneasiness about the assumption of a constant MUe may account for his failure to draw up an explicit list of the restrictions placed upon the demand curve for an individual commodity x. The traditional description of *ceteris paribus*, a description derived from Edgeworth and never repudiated by Marshall, includes such items as: (1) tastes; (2) money income; (3) the prices of closely related goods; (4) the prices of unrelated goods; and (5) expectations about future prices. The logical corollary of ignoring income effects is to hold real income, not money income, constant along the demand curve. In the foregoing list, however, (2), (3) and (4) together imply that real income varies with every change in the price of x. Moreover, (3) and (4) violate the general assumption of the *Principles* that the purchasing power of money is to be kept constant; every change in the price of x unaccompanied by an opposite change in some other price alters the value of money.

   There are two ways of resolving this dilemma. One is to argue that the real-income effect of a change in the price of an 'unimportant' commodity, and the corresponding change of the purchasing power of money, is so small as to be negligible. This was Marshall's own way out of the dilemma (Blaug, *Economic Theory in Retrospect*, p. 351).[2]

What Blaug depicts as Marshall's way out of the dilemma is the solution that was described by Edgeworth in the section entitled 'Historical Context' in Chapter 13. However, as I have suggested, Marshall himself was not content with so restrictive a resolution; he kept breaking out of it without, however, replacing it with anything else that had a high degree of logical consistency.

As noted, the first, and largest, problem in measuring consumer's(') surplus is that empirical knowledge is rarely adequate for specification of the entire section *AB* of a demand curve such as the one drawn above. For a true calculation of consumer's(') surplus, whether it is to be performed algebraically or geometrically, we must know the specification of all of *AB*. Given the difficulty of arriving at such a specification empirically, the alternative is to deductively derive the demand curve which logically 'must' result from a given utility function. This alternative requires direct grappling with utility.

This is the tack taken by McKenzie and Pierce and by J. Hausman in their recent work on consumers' surplus (discussed more fully in Chapter 17.) They appear, on the face of it, to beg the difficult (if not impossible) question of how to define utility, by using indirect or quasi-indirect utility functions which they do not compute directly, but derive from the expenditure functions. However the problem has only been pushed back one step, for whether the indirect utility function is derived from the expenditure function or from the ordinary demand curve, its derivation depends partly upon maximisation of some assumed utility function.

FROM UTILITY TO DEMAND AND CONSUMER'S SURPLUS How much, after all this time, can we actually claim to know about that concept, 'utility', on which utility functions are, somehow, based? We recognise that individual indifference curves give no support to any interpersonal comparisons, or even to comparisons of a single person's tastes at distinct times. We are, however, faced with the fact that, for the aggregations which are essential for policy-making, some sort of interpersonal comparison is essential. Hence we are thrown back from *indifference maps* whose theoretical rigour includes external consistency (in that it is, theoretically, possible to construct a pretty accurate indifference map for a given individual), to *utility functions* which may be devised so as to maintain internal consistency within a theory, but which have a dubious relation to the real world.

The language of Benthamite utility calculation, or the 'felicific calculus', already sounded absurd and old-fashioned to J. M. Keynes's ears; today, every student of economics receives, early on, the information that even measurement of utility unique up to a multiplicative constant (which is possible in the Marshallian system, with its assumed constant marginal utility of money for an individual) is a chimera. Individual utilities cannot be measured in a way which permits actual (either quantitative or proportional) interpersonal or intertemporal comparisons. Without the ability to make such comparisons we cannot aggregate individual preferences into any soundly based picture of societal preferences, let alone societal welfare; we cannot step outside the snapshot portrait of the preferences of individuals, taken one by one, at a single point in time.

To be sure, we are always making at least implicit interpersonal comparisons in our own lives, or in any interactions we may have with policy. In an example we saw earlier (in Chapter 10, under 'Packed Definitions'), simply talking about cost-of-living implies interpersonal comparisons, in that any price index has had to assign weights to different goods and services whose prices have changed at different rates. These weights have to come from somewhere; ultimately they imply – even if they were not knowingly based upon – some assumptions about different people's utilities. However, the often unconscious assumptions which we make as a necessary basis for action are probably a good deal less simplified than the ones which are used for formal indexing or than those which Marshall found necessary as a basis for conscious, scientific, interpersonal comparisons of utility. Although we have no formal algorithm for doing so, we quite often intuitively manage to take into account, for example:

- the greater value of a unit of money to a poor than to a rich person; this underlies the acceptance (where it exists) of the idea of government transfer programs, of progressive taxation, etc.
- externalities in production or consumption which are not reflected in market prices (this is perhaps most commonly expressed in the non-economist's attitude of 'efficiency be damned! I don't care what the experts say – this is not worth what it does to (the environment, my health, my sanity, etc.)'; and
- needs, which have never fitted into the theory as well as wants; for example, the greater needs of a person with a disability, of a parent with young children, etc.

However, operating in our private capacity, we generally do not make overt claims – on level 1 – that our intuitive interpersonal comparisons are supported by rigorous scientific analysis. And yet, like Marshall, in our economic theories – on level 3 – we go right on drawing utility inferences from indifference maps, both individual and aggregated. The theory which claims a scientific basis for doing so supports an effective assumption, both in policy-making and in much second-rate economic theory, that it is legitimate to proceed *as if* we had a rigorous scientific basis for our interpersonal comparisons.

FANCY FOOTWORK IN ECONOMIC DEFINITIONS It is unusual nowadays to hear talk about the measurement of motivation by money; a process of abstraction has stepped back from *motivation* to *utility*, and then to systems of models wherein utility is represented (and is subjected to manipulations by arithmetic, algebra, the calculus, and linear algebra) as a *mathematical symbol*. It is hard to remember that somewhere at the beginning of this process of abstraction, real things were supposed to be represented; and it is equally hard to pull real things out of the process at the end.

Marshall was there at the beginning of this process, and the fact that he had originally tried out two very different approaches to his most wished-for set of translations from motivation to money – i.e., the deductive and the inductive approaches to demand estimation (see Chapter 16) – leaves the field with an opportunity, too often seized, to forget that we still cannot talk about demand, over any significant range of time or geography or things desired, in quantified terms.

The practice of proceeding *as if* such quantification were possible is supported by the fact that, when an economist is accused of committing the error of speaking as though quantifiable utility functions were real things from which demand schedules can be deduced, s/he can answer, 'No, I am only depending upon what is observable, in the form of prices.' But when the objection is raised that it is usually impossible to go from these observable facts to a quantified aggregate demand function, the economist is equally likely to reply, 'We all know that – that's why we deduce our demand curves from utility functions.' Such backing and filling is, obviously, not representative of the best economic work; but it nevertheless takes place with enough frequency to colour much of the character and the practice of the field.

Such a pattern of argument appears frequently enough that it deserves a name: it may be graphically described as 'fancy footwork'. Perhaps the most surprising thing about this pattern is how long economists have been getting away with it. We have seen Marshall doing it in shuffling between deductive and inductive demand specifications; we will see his heirs do exactly the same in the next two chapters.

An even commoner, related example is in the definition of utility itself. An economist may at one moment speak loosely of the concept as it was used by the early Utilitarians, to mean pure pleasure of the self. When this is challenged on empirical grounds (e.g., with examples of altruistic behaviour), the economist may shuffle over to a (perhaps sociobiologically fortified) 'interdependent utility' model, in which individuals receive personal gratification from doing good to others.[3] If it is objected that 'once a concept is defined so that it encompasses *all* the incidents that are members of a given category (in the case at hand, the motives for all human activities), it ceases to enhance one's ability to explain', then the third step is to retreat to the idea that utility is required simply as 'a formal attribute, a common denominator, according to which all specific quests for satisfaction can be ranked, a step needed to allow mathematisation . . . but with no substantive attributes'.[4]

When the emptiness of this concept proves unsatisfactory, the economist may then slip back to the first position: 'Well, self-interest rules *most* actions, and particularly those which are of interest to economics. A Benthamite-type assumption is a good enough approximation; we don't really get into the details of individual acts and individual motives, anyway.' By this time perhaps the sceptic is simply weary with the argument; at any rate, the economist who is willing to keep shuffling among these three utility definitions usually manages to get the last word.

THE PSYCHOLOGICAL SIGNIFICANCE OF MONEY   A. C. Pigou seems to have been particularly adept at recognising and challenging fancy footwork in economic texts. In the series of lectures on Marshall which he gave in 1953, he recognised Marshall's technical solution to a dilemma, as described by Edgeworth (in Chapter 13, above), but Pigou also saw that Marshall was not content with a technical solution which was to deal only with unimportant commodities. He criticised, in passing, Marshall's use of money to serve simultaneously as a measure of both desires and satisfactions – 'two things which in fact, do not always move in step' – but reserved his most severe criticism for the inconsistency wherein Marshall makes sums of money serve to measure, not only the motivating force, *outside* the individual, but also the *internal impulse* which is generated by that motivating force. 'Thus' (Pigou goes on to say,)

2 for conditions where the marginal utility of money may be regarded
as constant, [Marshall] writes: 'The excess of the price which a man
would be willing to pay rather than go without having a thing over
what he actually does pay is the economic measure of his surplus
satisfaction' (*Principles*, p. 124) – *not*, be it noted of the force
exercised by the expectation of that satisfaction. Again, he speaks
of 'the money measure of happiness' (ibid., p. 131) (Pigou, 1953,
p. 38).

Pigou notes Marshall's inconsistency in not always keeping the
marginal utility of money constant, and then continues with a
perceptive passage that brings out particularly clearly the existence of
a hidden agenda in Marshall's work:

3 Marshall's reference to the marginal utility of money brings out
straight-away a serious flaw in his procedure. Money by itself
cannot be used as a measure of desires or satisfactions unless there
is also brought in some factor indicating the psychological
significance which such and such a sum of money has for the
individual we are considering. This factor obviously cannot itself be
money. For it is impossible to measure the meaning or
psychological significance of a shilling by the number of shillings
that a man will offer for it. He will obviously offer one shilling,
neither more nor less, whatever its psychological significance may
be. If, then, we want *to make contact with psychological significance*,
we cannot do it by means of money. We are forced to postulate that
desires and satisfactions – lump them together, if you like, under
the common name utility – can in some sense be measured *per se*;
the very thing which Marshall has explicitly declared to be
impossible. It thus seems that, for once, Marshall has been
inconsistent with himself, or at least has side-tracked a difficulty.
According to his formal statement utilities are not measurable; in
his actual work he tacitly assumes that they are (ibid., p. 40; italics
added).

Note that the last sentence distinguishes between level 1 in meaning –
referred to by Pigou as Marshall's 'formal statement' – and the tacit
assumptions, on level 2, which are the *basis* for the 'actual work' on
level 3. Pigou's charge is that Marshall himself sometimes operated, on
the effective level, *as if* these assumptions were true. I point this out to
illustrate that, although the terminology may be unfamiliar, my

division of levels of meaning, and the comparison of one level with another to test for consistency, is a common sense approach which has always been available for any rigorous analysis of a text.

Demand curves and consumer's(') surplus both depend upon insufficiently observable observables, and/or upon specification of utility functions. Utility functions are simply algorithms for the value which people put upon things. And the whole process started because we cannot measure those directly. In the end, as Pigou noted, Marshall appeared, at least in some places, to jump into behaving *as if* that direct measurement were possible – since it could not be achieved by any indirect route.

'UTILITIES   If Marshall had been alive to respond to Pigou's
ARE NOT   critique, he could have pointed, as I have already
MEASURABLE'   done, to numerous places where he stays within the
                 boundaries established by his 'formal statement' that
utilities are not measurable. Many passages attest to his awareness of this brute fact; and also to his vacillation between, on the one hand, a recognition of the danger of building upon false grounds if he were to ignore it; and, on the other, the temptation to do so.

In any case, Marshall himself recognised that his hopes for economics were questionable, and successive editions of *Principles* showed a gradual retraction from the original optimism. We can see this in the types of changes he made in his successive revisions of the book. Consider, for example, the following note from the first edition:

4   It must be understood however that the separate measurement of each element of a pleasure is in practice done roughly by a sort of instinct. The only measurement with which science can directly deal is that afforded by what a person is willing to sacrifice (whether money, or some other commodity, or his own labour) in order to obtain the aggregate of pleasure anticipated from the possession of the things itself (footnote from *Principles*, 1st edn, p. 154).

That passage was replaced in the 2nd edition with the following:

5   Of course this estimate is formed by a rough instinct; and in any attempt to reduce it to numerical accuracy . . . we must recollect what has been said, in this and the preceding Section, as to the impossibility of comparing accurately pleasures or other satisfactions that do not occur at the same time: and also as to the

assumption of uniformity involved in supposing the discount of future pleasures to obey the exponential law (quoted in *Var.* II, p. 257).

Between the first and second editions Marshall abandoned – in this passage – the claim of a 'measurement with which science can *directly* deal', replacing that by a more modest 'attempt to reduce [the estimate formed by a rough instinct] to numerical accuracy'. The original 'measurement' had been of a sacrifice of one of three things; and here it is relevant to note that the use of 'his own labour' was originally put in the same category, as a measurable proxy, with 'money' or 'commodities'. In the second edition that careless lumping together of things of quite different degrees of measurability was removed, and a caveat was added on the 'impossibility' of making comparisons between different times.

HEDGING   In the final edition of *Principles* we find the same
MEASUREMENT   themes – especially the effort to sum up satisfactions
WITH   – discussed once more in the Mathematical
CONDITIONS   Appendix. There Marshall provides a most interest-
ing discussion of the difference between the method of analysis of 'the total utility of particular commodities' which he has set forth in Book III, as compared to the Doctrine of Maximum Satisfaction. The latter is described as depending upon a set of differential equations which 'will be interpreted to represent value as governed in every field of economics by the balancing of groups of utilities against groups of disutilities, or groups of satisfactions against groups of real costs' (*Principles*, p. 700). Marshall says that 'The difference between the two cases is mainly one of degree: but it is of a degree so great as practically to amount to a difference of kind':

6   For in the former case [i.e. in Marshall's own analysis] we take each commodity by itself and with reference to a particular market; and *we take careful account of the circumstances of the consumers* at the time and place under consideration. Thus we follow, though perhaps with more careful precautions, the practice of ministers of finance, and of the common man when discussing financial policy. We note that a few commodities are consumed mainly by the rich; and that in consequence their real total utilities are less than is suggested by the money measures of those utilities. But we assume, with the rest of the world, that as a rule, and in the absence of

special causes to the contrary, the *real total utility* of two
commodities that are mainly consumed by the rich stand to one
another in about *the same relation as their money measures* do: and
that the same is true of commodities the consumption of which is
divided out among rich and middle classes and poor in similar
proportions.[5]

Such estimates are but rough approximations; but each
particular difficulty, each source of possible error, is pushed into
prominence by the definiteness of our phrases: we introduce no
assumptions that are not latent in the practice of ordinary life; while
we attempt no task that is not grappled with in a rougher fashion,
but yet to good purpose, in the practice of ordinary life: we
introduce no new assumptions, and we bring into clear light those
which cannot be avoided.[6]

But though this is possible when dealing with *particular
commodities* with reference to *particular markets*, it does not seem
possible with regard to the innumerable economic elements that
come within the all-embracing net of the doctrine of Maximum
Satisfaction. The forces of supply are especially heterogeneous and
complex: they include an infinite variety of efforts and sacrifices,
direct and indirect, on the part of people in all varieties of industrial
grades: and if there were no other hindrance to giving a concrete
interpretation to the doctrine, a fatal obstacle would be found in its
latent assumption that the cost of rearing children and preparing
them for their work can be measured in the same way as the cost of
erecting a machine (ibid; italics added).

It is evident that Marshall recognised the possible objections that can
be raised to his programme, and he has attempted, in this final
Appendix to his final edition of *Principles*, to split off the 'wrong' kind
of utility measurement from the right kind, claiming the latter for his
own, and assigning the former to the proponents of the doctrine of
Maximum Satisfaction. In so doing he did not retain very much for his
own programme: in effect, the above-quoted passage reduces 'the
advantage which economics has over other branches of social science'
(see quotation 3 in Chapter 14) to the fact that, *while still relying on
common sense to make ordinary estimates of real values, or utilities,
economics at least makes clear the assumptions which underlie these
common sense approximations.*

This depressing conclusion was not wholly new to Marshall. An
awareness of the vulnerability of his position showed up in his letters

even before the publication of the first edition of *Principles*.[7] From the start Marshall had frequently glimpsed, and intended to avoid, the danger into which most commentators – myself included – feel that he fell. The interesting question is: Why, when he was so aware of these dangers, could he not avoid them?

The answer may be, in part, that he was trying out something relatively new – marginal utility analysis – and he had not, as we have, the benefit of his own and subsequent work to show him its limitations. In addition to this, however, I would speculate that, as I have noted before, Marshall was impelled by a very strong desire to establish the basis upon which economics could secure a scientific footing. This desire was born both of the wish to think highly of the discipline in which he was engaged; and also of the wish for that discipline to be as effective a tool as possible for the improvement of the human lot.

MARSHALL'S RECOGNITION OF THE FLAWS IN HIS PROGRAMME   In fact, Marshall was prepared to agree with most of the contemporary criticisms made of this aspect of his work, and he would also, I believe, have embraced most of the critical analyses which continued after his lifetime. He conceded that total utilities are not measurable; that marginal utilities of income vary at least between income classes – and that this really *does* matter. A summary of the difficulties which he saw as preventing marginal analysis from serving perfectly as the link between the important unquantifiables and the useful quantitative techniques may be laid out, briefly, as follows:

– First, while price = exchange value (which is derived, on the demand side, from the marginal utility of consumers), the marginal utility of one consumer does not necessarily equal that of another; and the same person's marginal utility at different times is incommensurable. Hence, even while the price, or exchange value, of a good remains the same, where more than one person is involved the marginal value of money cannot be calculated; therefore we cannot conclude from the willingness of two people to pay the same price that their purchases have the same meaning for them both.

– Second, demand schedules are related to utility only in an ordinal sense; the utility conclusions which may be inferred from aggregate demand schedules only hold on fairly stringent assumptions regarding the distribution of people 'of different incomes and also of different sensibilities'. These utility conclusions must be used with great caution, and with full understanding of all of the variables which determine demand – i.e. taking 'careful account of the consumers at the time and place under consideration' (quotation 6, above).

–   Third, comparisons which may be made within markets are limited thereto; the same comparisons cannot be stretched across markets.

–   Fourth, supply prices in part reflect the supply price of labour; and there the forces of supply (i.e., motives to work) are too heterogeneous to admit of valid comparisons which are supposed to reflect underlying motivations.[8]

–   Fifth, prices reflect the simultaneous cutting of the demand and supply blades of the scissors: thus the effort to trace a direct line from *price* to *demand* to *utility* suffers from one further remove.

Marginal value is a precise concept; and also a limited one. A precise statement of its meaning includes the highly relative nature of its interpretation: as we have already quoted, it simply 'expresses the relation between two things at a particular place and time'. Yet, as we have seen in a number of places, Marshall wished to capture in his measurement of human motives something broader and more permanent than the ephemeral marginal value which may be deduced from a willingness, at a particular moment, under particular circumstances, to stop working, or employing, or consuming.

MARSHALL'S LEGACY FOR SOCIAL ECONOMICS   A difference between Marshall and the modern economist is that Marshall recognised what kinds of information he would have to have if he were to be able, legitimately, to make the kind of welfare analysis in which he was interested. And then he claimed – hoping to be able to make the claim true – that economics had, or would soon acquire, access to those kinds of information. The modern economist, with the sophistication gained by a century of working over Marshall's legacy, knows that this hope will not be fulfilled; and so s/he has given up hoping it – and has forgotten, somewhere along the way (or has never learned) that indifference curves are still being sketched, tangencies found, and deductions and conclusions drawn *as if* we believed, with Marshall, that economics can supply a measurement of human value which is adequate for the welfare goals which are pressed on the discipline of economics by the exigencies of the real world.

That *as if* behaviour is more or less unrealistic depending upon how we define the needs of the field. And here is where there is a deep divide between the theoretical and the applied economist. For the *pure* theoretician, acting as such, realism is not important. The pure theoretician is fortunate in being able to ignore the questions which, because it has no better place to take them to, the world brings to the economist's doorstep. To these fortunate members of the profession it does not matter whether a utility function ever *can* be defined, but only whether it is possible to draw indifference curves which represent what the utility function might reasonably be supposed to generate, supposing it *could* be defined.

The applied economist who deals with any sort of welfare analysis (as most applied economists do) also uses indifference maps. The *reason* for using them is that they are very convenient tools for thinking about welfare issues. The *justification* for using them is that the theorists do so; for most economists, whether on the applied or the theoretical side, have received their education at the hands of academic economists who (for reasons that are probably best explained by a sociology of the profession, its reward structure, etc.) tend to lean heavily in the theoretical direction. The problem is that the techniques used in pure theory, where real people and real things are not the issue, may not always be appropriate in applied economics.

The role which I see for social economics, in this connection, is to reassess the tools which we actually use, and to define what additional tools are needed. The need, overall, is for ways by which economists may reasonably well understand and predict behaviour and abstract forces and evaluate the consequences of actions and abstract forces upon those whom they will affect.

- In this context how useful, for example, is such 'as if' behaviour as that which, two paragraphs earlier, I have ascribed to the modern economist? Can it be replaced by a more realistic behaviour which is at least equally useful?
- Similarly, the use of money-evaluations as a proxy for well-being is sometimes the best readily available method; but the pretence that that method is 'scientific' may be misleading.
- I do not advocate that social economists abandon a close study of money and prices, or their use for helping economists to assess priorities and policies; what I hope is that a more critical pressure upon the field, in assessing how well this tool does the various jobs we give it, will result in improvements in this and other tools.

Social economics cannot respond to the needs that bring policy makers and others to the field simply by citing more facts (though it should seek better ways of identifying which are the most useful facts to be sought for the response to certain types of question); or by an appeal to common sense (though there is need for a better understanding of how and where that which Marshall called 'common sense' can be taught and used). The reason to call for an alternative approach, such as social economics, is because there is a need, beyond facts or common sense, for new theories and techniques that can, among other things, employ a greater emphasis upon empiricism, and admit the usefulness of such human qualities as judgment or common sense.

Marshall, with his exceptional inclusiveness (or, as Keynes called it, 'dualism') of character, spanned both the applied and the theoretical ends of the spectrum in his thinking. His aims regarding application were laid out relatively early in his career. It is, as Marshall stated in 1897, necessary to measure, in human terms, the gains and losses that may result from practical actions:

7   It is useless to say that various gains and losses are incommensur-
    able, and cannot be weighed against one another. For they must be,
    and in fact they are, weighed against one another before any
    deliberate decision is or can be reached in any issue (A. Marshall,
    'The Old Generation of Economists and the New' in *Memorials*,
    p. 302).

In other words, however conscientious we are about retaining congruence between levels 1 and 3 (our statements and our logical processes) we may have to recognise the concessions made on level 2, where theory is used, willy-nilly, to support action.

SUMMARY OF   Marshall had boasted, 'The pure science of Ethics
THE GOAL AND   halts for lack of a system of measurement of efforts,
THE PROBLEM   sacrifices, desires, etc., fit for her wide purposes. But
               the pure science of Political Economy has found a
system that will subserve her narrower aim.' (See quotation 2 in Chapter 14.) By claiming that he had narrowed the aim of economics, as compared to that of his early interest, Ethics, Marshall could hope to achieve his goal. But had he really narrowed his aim for the *application* of his science? Do applied economists today practice a science with a narrower aim? Here again, in the interplay between applied and theoretical economics, we find a pattern of fancy footwork.

A long road has been traversed from Marshall's employment of marginal utility economics to modern welfare economics; but for any economist, who, like Marshall, believes that economics is important because it responds to questions of policy and action from the real world, the goal has not essentially changed. We continue to be inheritors of Marshall's hope (which persisted on the effective level in his thinking and writing, even after most of its specific forms had been dashed) that we can study the expenditure of money (including the expenditures which we calculate that people *would* make under hypothetical circumstances) and learn how to interpret it in such a way that we can infer the underlying *real costs* and *real values*. In any serious discussion of human welfare 'real costs' and 'real values' cannot, as concepts, be avoided.[9]

Unfortunately Marshall obscured the nature of what he was seeking when, early on, he cast his eye over Adam Smith's distinction between use-value and exchange-value, and rejected the first. We then seem to be left with a particularly unhelpful tautology; to have come this far only to say that Marshall's scientific engine uses marginal analysis to specify a regular relationship between *exchange values* and *money* would be an exercise in futility.

What, then, is the proper first term in this regularity? – Of all the versions of 'value' that we have examined, which one can be represented by money so regularly as to permit the scientific quantification which Marshall hoped to be able to impose upon motives to action? We would most like, of course, to be able to put total – or real, or human – value into the equation, but these we have long since abandoned, along with Smith's term, 'use value' (which means approximately the same thing). What Marshall had obviously hoped was to be able, somehow, to use *marginal value* in their place. However, for reasons which have been given (especially the difference in marginal utility represented by the same thing, at the same price, between a rich and a poor man) we are unable, as Pigou pointed out, to pin down marginal utility to any 'psychological significance'. By the time he found himself writing the Preface to the final edition of *Principles*, Marshall was impelled to stress the slipperiness of marginal utility over the great hopes which, in earlier editions, he had held out for it:

8 this notion of a margin is not uniform and absolute: it varies with the conditions of the problem at hand, and in particular with the period of time to which reference is being made. The rules are

universal that, (1) marginal costs do not govern price; (2) it is only at the margin that the action of those forces which do govern prices can be made to stand out in clear light; and (3) the margin, which must be studied in reference to long periods and enduring results, differs in character as well as in extent from that which must be studied in reference to short periods and passing fluctuations (*Principles*, p. xiv).

DISCOURAGING   Here, in a close examination of Marshall's develop-
CONCLUSIONS   ment of the tools of marginal analysis – which many
have considered to be the heart of his work – we have come to a critical place. It is one of the places where one may most clearly see two paths forking out of Marshall's work. Elsewhere I have noted that Marshall's ability to follow both paths made his economics a richer, more relevantly human science than that which came after him. In this case, however, the divergence is one which cannot plausibly be straddled.

The tension in the situation derives from the fact that there are, on the one hand, the list of unquantifiable 'human values' which Marshall evidently considered to be important for inclusion within the field of economics. Those unquantifiables include (to quote from passages of Marshall's which we have seen throughout Part III): 'desire for the possession of a thing'; 'efforts and self-denials'; 'human motives on a large scale'; 'benefit or injury'; 'happiness'; 'loss of pleasure'; 'the desire for pay'; 'desires, aspirations and other affections of human nature'; and 'the force of a person's motives – not the motives themselves'.

On the other hand there are 'statistics' (which deal with *particular* quantitative statements), and 'mathematical language' (which deals with *general* quantitative statements), and 'mathematical theory' which 'reasons on the basis of these statements'.[10] These tools can only operate upon quantifiable subjects.

What is a person, who believes that quantitative techniques have a particular usefulness in economics, to do when confronted with unquantifiable matters of importance?Marshall, as I have suggested, while confronting this question in some of his statements, simply continued, in general, to follow both paths.

In modern usage, price is employed as a proxy for all of the other kinds of value we have discussed in a way which implies an acceptance of just what Marshall claimed: that price can be made to stand, in some way, for the real value we assign to things. We will see in the next chapter how, for example, Milton Friedman's use of a concept such as 'the index of a consumption indifference curve' turns out to pack in much more than the words superficially suggest; when the phrase is unpacked, it appears that in fact utility has been defined in terms of utility. In such usage, the apparent simplification of equating utility with consumption conceals a circling back to the older (pre-ophelimity) meaning of utility; if consumption cannot be aggregated in terms of the material things consumed, but only with respect to the 'real values' of those things, then: WELFARE = UTILITY = CONSUMPTION = REAL VALUES can be abbreviated to: WELFARE = REAL VALUES.

Little or no progress has been made on Marshall's search for a scientific way of inserting values into a social science. His unfortunate, tautological legacy for welfare economics has been hidden, but it has not been corrected.

Notes

1. See Talcott Parsons' 'Wants and Activities in Marshall', *Quarterly Journal of Economics*, XLVI, November 1931, for evidence and discussion of Marshall's lively awareness of this problem.
2. Another way out, as we shall see in discussing the Friedman paper in Chapter 16, is to suppose an equal and opposite change in some unrelated price when the price of the good under consideration changes.
3. Sociobiology may support this with suggestions as to why evolution would have resulted in genes that promote feelings of personal gratification from the welfare of others, especially of close kin.
4. I first heard an exposition of the elusiveness of the neoclassical definition of utility from Harvey Leibenstein, in a 1982 class on 'markets, efficiency, and freedom', at Harvard University. More recently, it has been well laid out by Amitai Etzioni in *The Moral Dimension*, 1988. The two passages just quoted in the text are from that book, on pages 27 and 23.
5. Here Marshall leaves himself open to Pigou's criticisms, for he implies that there is some 'normal' 'psychological significance' which people agree is attached to a given amount of money; but that, for the rich, the significance of the same amount is less.
6. The theme here is the idea that the economist's programme of attempting precise measurement of the unmeasurable is defensible as an extension of the rough, or imprecise, guesses at measurement made in everyday life. We will find it repeated by some modern economists in the next chapter. Note, at the end of the next paragraph of the quotation, the implicit return to the idea of 'true cost'.

7. Cf. for example the letters of 26 November and 2 December 1889, written by Marshall to John Neville Keynes. Quoted in *Var.* II, p. 261.

8. Moreover – an omission which Marshall does not pick up – there is no explicit psychological theory on which to base assumptions regarding a regular relationship between *incentives*, 'the force or quantity [of which] can be estimated and measured with some approach to accuracy' and *motives*, or 'the forces of supply'; e.g., between *wages* and the *motivation to work*.

9. A modern example is the use of shadow pricing. The shadow price of a thing is its marginal value as it *would* appear at the intersection of supply and demand in a world in which all real costs and real values were assigned to, and accounted by, the gainers and losers therefrom.

10. From A. Marshall, 'The Graphic Method of Statistics' (1885) in *Memorials*, p. 180.

16 The Continuing Controversy Over Marshall's Demand Theory: Some Aspects of the Literature on Marshall's Work

The examination of Marshall's programme for demand analysis, in the two preceding chapters, noted his own perceptions of its potentials and its flaws. Here we turn to consider how that programme has fared in the subsequent development of economic theory.

A PLEA FOR RENEWED ATTENTION TO THE HISTORY OF ECONOMIC THOUGHT First, in this chapter, we will consider some elements of the discussion that has taken place in the economic literature regarding the technical problems which exist in the tools that Marshall had hoped to use for mapping the unquantifiable onto the quantifiable. We will see that the economists who commented directly on this part of Marshall's work dealt with it for the most part (Pigou is the most notable exception) on level 3, tracing through the logic to expose its gaps and contradictions, but with little awareness of the level 2 implications for what economic science seems to promise.

One reason to summarise the problems in Marshall's demand analysis which have been emphasised in the field is to respond to an assumption about the cumulative nature of economic science which has come to be quite broadly taken for granted in the field.[1] This assumption accompanies (as cause, or effect, or both) a markedly ahistorical character in neoclassical economics. Students are rarely encouraged to read literature that is more than fifteen years old; the assumption seems to be that all the earlier work that is of value is subsumed in later work.

While not every student can be expected to reexamine, let alone reinvent, every proposition of economics, the current level of ahistoricity implies too much trust. Practitioners, theorists and students need to understand not only the end results, but some of the processes that led to those results. Without such understanding it is too easy to maintain unrealistic beliefs about the nature of economic science as a field wherein all untruths are progressively shed off, and wherein all all relevant truths will ultimately be – or perhaps already are – contained in a set of mutually consistent axioms and laws which can be translated into mathematical language and operated on through quasi-mathematical manipulations to yield explanations and predictions that are valid and important with respect to the reality of human behaviour.

The economist who accepts this vision is apt to think, when economic predictions fail, that this is because the mathematical forms have not yet been worked out quite right. In part, of course, the issue of mathematical forms does take account of the crucial mapping from real world to idea; some attention is paid, e.g., to the question of whether a Cobb-Douglass function is really an adequate expression of a set of production decisions. But the mathematical form is not the beginning of the mapping; it takes for granted much uncommented-on translation from world to word or symbol.

As we saw earlier (in Chapter 10) the mapping from world to symbol necessarily involves such processes as idealisation, simplification, exaggeration, and 'isolation' (via the phrase '*ceteris paribus*'). As long as the individual who applied these processes remembers what it is that s/he has, for example, simplified *from*, the danger of these forms of unrealisticness is limited. However, when these practices are combined with a strongly ahistorical tendency, so that students accept the simplifications, idealisations and unrealistic assumptions that were made before their time, without knowing from whence they came, then the mines are laid to blow up our economic stories.

What we will see in this chapter is how the field of economics has monitored itself, and what sorts of problems are picked up in the rolling process of accumulating (for each successive present) the best of the past – a process that is supposed to catch and excise the errors of the past. Then, in Chapter 17, when we watch some modern authors building on one small area of Marshall's accomplishment (his idea of consumer's surplus), we will have a chance to assess the effectiveness of this cumulative process. In particular, we will see which kind of error has been most likely to slip through the net of standard economic criticism.

Some of the commentary considered here and in the next chapter, while exposing the technical or 'internal' inconsistencies in Marshall's programme, seems only to dig itself deeper into what I have identified as the more profound difficulties in such areas as definition, mapping, measurement, and aggregation. The kind of critical consciousness which was described and recommended in Part II will not, in itself, provide the alternative paradigm which is needed if we are to escape from these difficulties; but it should serve to make us unwilling to accept the fancy footwork and poor science of which will see examples in Chapters 16 and 17.

TWO TYPES OF PROBLEMS ON LEVEL 3   The fray of competing interpretations regarding Marshall's demand theory highlights two types of problems, *inconsistency* and *incompleteness*:

1   Marshall's statements about demand include *inconsistencies* of three types:

1a   The most famous of these is the *internal inconsistency* problem: that if as many things are held constant as Marshall, at different times, seemed to want to hold constant (i.e., all prices except Px; money income; real income; consumers tastes; technology; and the society's endowment), then no degrees of freedom remain to permit the change in Px which was to precipitate the analysis of demand or of consumer's surplus.[2]

1b   As distinct from the logical and mathematical contention that these things cannot all be held constant at once, there is also the charge that some of Marshall's procedures and assumptions are inconsistent with the realities which he claimed to be studying: e.g., his apparent neglect of the income effect upon welfare when the latter is measured by consumer's surplus (via the assumption of constant marginal utility of income); or his related assumption of the 'unimportance' of the commodities under consideration. These may be described as *external inconsistencies*, since they refer to a contradiction between, on the one hand, some element within the Marshallian system and, on the other, that reality onto which the system is supposed, in some fashion, to be mapped. The impoundment of such elements as income effects, importance of commodities, or marginal utility of income in what Marshall called the 'pound' of *ceteris paribus* is inconsistent with his statements about the specifics of the world which he claimed to be studying. The things he did not allow to vary are precisely those things whose variation his system was set up to analyse.

1c   Finally, as Pigou pointed out, there is a *methodological inconsistency* in Marshall's apparent fall-back upon assuming a direct measure of utility as a foundation for the system by which he hoped to be able to deduce measurements of utility.

2   Marshall's statements about demand are *not complete*: they lack specificity in definition and in mathematical analysis. For example, he left the way open for endless future disagreements about what, exactly, he meant by 'constant marginal utility of money';[3] about what, exactly, he intended to hold constant at any given time; about when he did and did not intend to restrict his analysis to commodities relatively unimportant within total expenditure; about whether his was a 'constant-other-prices-and-money-incomes demand curve' (what is today referred to as the 'Marshallian' or 'normal' demand curve), or rather some sort of compensated demand curve, such as the 'constant-real-income demand curve'. It is this lack of definition and of specificity which permits an inconclusive altercation of alternative interpretations.

FIVE TYPES OF   It is natural to wonder why Marshall should have left
EXPLANATIONS   his theory of demand in such ragged state. This
question arises out of more than idle curiosity, for all of the subsequent interpretations assume some answer to it, and their proponents depend upon their particular answers to this question to support suggestions as to how we should proceed from the point at which Marshall left us. Thus, if we assume that Marshall simply got the math wrong, we are free to substitute our own, correct mathematics. If we assume that Marshall's mathematics was better than our own, we have to look for what he perceived that has since been overlooked. If we assume that his intuition was his outstanding attribute, we are likely to search for reasons to show that his conclusions were correct, even while the supporting math may have been faulty. If we assume that Marshall was, above all else, consistent, then we have to find reasons to

justify ignoring certain parts of his text in relation to other parts – and so on.

One can organise the possible explanations for the contradictions and incompleteness of Marshall's demand theory into such categories as these:

1. *Mathematical incompetence in specific instances.* Marshall was inventing the applications for some of the math he used; in spite of his highly regarded abilities as a mathematician, it would, perhaps, not be surprising if he overlooked instances where pieces that he worked out separately did not fit together as a whole; or, indeed, if not all of the pieces were themselves fully worked through.

2. *Insufficient attention.* Marshall went to great lengths both to play down his own use of mathematics and to disparage their excessive use by others. If he is to be taken at his word on this subject, he did not regard mathematical analysis as having nearly the importance given to it by modern economists; hence, when the mathematics did not lead precisely to the outcome which he felt was the right outcome, he may have simply overlooked the discrepancies.

3. *Low priority given to consistency.* Although Marshall's penchant for seeing and presenting all sides of a subject is by no means the same as not caring about internal consistency, the appearance of the latter certainly may be caused by the former; and, indeed, the two may go together. Or, again, not everything can have highest priority, and the relative importance of internal consistency may be diminished when a higher importance is assigned, for example, to one or both of items 4 and 5 in this list.

4. *Desire to make economics useful.* If Marshall's image of the shape economics had to take in order to be useful conflicted with the dictates of internal consistency or mathematical completeness, he may have chosen to ignore some gaps in the latter.

5. *Desire to make economics realistic.* Modern attempts to impose consistency upon Marshall's economics of demand have led to the adoption of realistically absurd assumptions; and Marshall himself sometimes proposed assumptions which stringently limited the realistic application of his demand theory. However, the argument can be, and has been, made, that Marshall was not trying to create a theory of such generality that, in order to fit all times and places, it would have to retreat into extreme abstraction. Perhaps he gave the empirical specifics of a particular reality (i.e., 'external

consistency') higher priority than either theoretical consistency or a broader generality.[4]

My own discussion so far has emphasised category 4. I would not, however, reject any of the other explanations out of hand; indeed, in order to explain something so surprising as the apparent errors, omissions and inconsistencies with which this area of Marshall's theory is rife, one probably needs at least as many as five explanations.[5]

'THE REAL ALFRED MARSHALL' I shall not emphasise here – I have not emphasised elsewhere – an attempt to settle the question of Marshall's intentions with regard to such specifics as: *which* demand curve he meant to use; or, *with respect to what* the marginal utility of money was to be held constant. To the extent that I am trying to get at 'the real Marshall', my intention is to analyse the purposes and priorities which informed his approach to, and procedures in, the whole field of economics. The goal throughout has been to achieve some understanding of what he believed to be really important; what types of intellectual achievements attracted him; and how his personal motivations interacted with his knowledge of economic realities and his appreciation of science. My underlying belief is that such an understanding will give us a better basis from which to speculate (if we are interested in doing so) regarding Marshall's 'real' intentions with regard to demand curves, marginal utility, etc.

Such an understanding of Marshall, the man, may, however, have the effect of lessening our interest in the intentions of Marshall, the economist; and in that sense it may be felt that there is something reductionistic in the endeavour which I here pursue. I make this comment because it has been my observation that when a scientist (whether 'natural' or 'social') studies the work of another member of his/her field – in particular a great and renowned member – s/he most often proceeds from an unexamined assumption that the basis of the intellectual work being studied is purely intellectual. Such an assumption excludes reflection on the possibility that, underneath the purely cognitive actions of the scientist's mind, there are motivations, beliefs, etc., which direct the choice of which, out of the infinite possible cognitive actions, will be the ones taken. Which subjects the scientist studies, which facts s/he emphasises, what simplifying assumptions are made, what methods used – the element of choice in all of this is enormous; and the basis for such choice is not solely cognitive, but includes, clearly, motivations and beliefs occupying a mental position which may be seen as existing prior to, or 'underneath', the purely intellectual activities.

If a scientist is in the habit of looking at other scientists' work without an awareness of such other-than- or pre-intellectual aspects of thinking, then discussion of such aspects may seem reductionistic. There is the danger that, for example, a close examination, such as I am making of Marshall, will seem to direct the reader to think that Marshall's economics can be viewed as 'nothing but' the outcome of his personal motivations, pre-cognitive beliefs, moral wishes and so on. There is a tendency to regard that analysis which *integrates the cognitive and non-cognitive elements that underlie intellectual activity* as reductionistic. Is this tendency the cause, or the result, of the attempt to exclude normative elements from modern, positivistic science?

Without being able to answer to that question (in Marshallian fashion I am inclined to beg it by saying 'probably both'), I would like to return from this detour via a strong statement that I do *not* intend to imply that Marshall's economics can be well understood as 'nothing but' the outcome of his personal motivations, pre-cognitive beliefs, moral wishes and so on. My real meaning is that Marshall's economics is *more than* just an intellectual exercise; that an attempt to understand it as such is itself an act of reductionism; and that one purpose of my work in this area is to achieve a larger, more relevant picture of what Marshall was doing, as free as possible from the reductionism of contemporary thought.

THE DANGER This leads into the next point, which is that it is
OF 'PRESENT- important to maintain an awareness that certain
MINDEDNESS' modern ways of thinking may be anachronistic if
ascribed to Marshall. The sort of reductionism which (I have just claimed) has been imposed upon him is an outgrowth of increasingly positivistic trends in modern economics. Similarly, we should consider the possibility that modern economists' concepts of methodology may result in some false interpretations of Marshall's meaning. R. F. G. Alford is exceptional in his awareness of this problem. I will follow his lead in using two passages from *Principles* (including the reference numbers that Alford used, so as to be able to quote intelligibly his comments on them):

3   It should be noted that, in the discussion of consumers' surplus, we assume that the marginal utility of money to the individual purchaser is the same throughout. Strictly speaking we ought to

take account of the fact that if he spent less on tea, the marginal utility of money to him would be less than it is, and he would get an element of consumers' surplus from buying other things at prices which now yield him no such rent. But these changes in consumers' rent (being of the second order of smallness) may be neglected, on the assumption, which underlies our whole reasoning, that his expenditure on any one thing, as, for instance, tea, is only a small part of his whole expenditure (from *Principles*, 8th edn, 1920 printing, p. 842; quoted in R. F. G. Alford, 'Marshall's Demand Curve'; *Economica*, NS vol. 23, February 1956; repr. in AMCA, vol. III, p. 319).

4   It will be noted however that the demand prices of each commodity . . . assume that *other things remain equal*, while its price rises to scarcity value: . . . The substance of our argument would not be affected if we took account of the fact that, the more a person spends on anything . . . the greater is the value of money to him (in technical language every fresh expenditure increases the marginal value of money to him) . . . for there are very few practical problems, in which the corrections to be made under this head would be of any importance (in Alford, 1956, pp. 131–2.)

Alford goes on to remark that

Quotation 3 . . . makes it very clear that to Marshall assuming something did not mean postulating it, nor did it mean that the thing assumed had to hold true; indeed it meant almost the opposite, as can be seen from the contrast Marshall makes between 'assuming' and 'strictly speaking'. To Marshall assuming something in the sense in which this is used in quotation 3 meant that *deviations from the assumed condition would occur but only to a degree that could be neglected.* That this was the sense in which [MUe] was assumed constant along the demand curve is clear from quotations 3 . . . and 5.' (ibid., pp. 319–20; italics added).

Friedman adds another useful comment on the subject: 'Assumptions made in [Marshall's] analogies of consumer's surplus cannot, without additional evidence be supposed to apply to other applications of the "demand curve"' (1949, p. 188).

Perhaps the reason this eminently sensible approach is not always taken is that, because Marshall so often failed to completely specify his simplifying assumptions, commentators take the assumptions where they can find them, and apply them even when they are not specified.

Friedman also pays tribute to the idea that 'the role assigned to economic theory has altered in the course of time until today we assign a substantially different role to theory than Marshall did' (ibid., p. 196). However, almost immediately after saying this, Friedman himself falls into the error of present-mindedness by attributing to Marshall his own goals for economics: 'Economic theory, in [Marshall's] view, has two intermingled roles: to provide "systematic and organised methods of reasoning" about economic problems; to provide a body of substantive hypotheses, based on factual evidence, about the "manner of action of causes". In both roles the test of the theory is its value in explaining facts, *in predicting the consequences of changes in the economic environment*' (ibid., p. 197; italics added). The italicised half of what Friedman says about how Marshall would test, or evaluate, a theory, is a gratuitous insertion of Friedman's own vision of positive economics; Marshall himself was explicit on the folly of thinking that a social science could be used for prediction (cf. *Principles*, p. 638: 'any error made in the first step of prediction will be accumulated and intensified in the second').

Alford's perceptive remarks on Marshall's meaning with regard to *assumptions* are, I think, even more helpful when they are stretched to take in the problem of *theoretical or internal consistency*. It is plain enough, from Alford's quotations numbered 3 and 5, that Marshall recognised a conflict between (a) his logical understanding of the marginal value of money, and how it is increased by additional expenditures; (b) his intention to hold the marginal value of money constant; and (c) his depiction of a demand curve which illustrates different price-quantity combinations. Obviously, MUe (the marginal utility of money) *couldn't* remain constant along such a demand curve, given point (a).

This is not just a contradiction between reality and theoretical assumptions: it is a contradiction among the theoretical assumptions themselves. But it is one which, Marshall said, may be neglected, because the perturbation which it causes (both to the analysis and to our analytically-enhanced understanding of reality) is so small. (We may regard this argument as lending support to points 2 and 3 in the earlier catalogue, of 'types of explanations' that are available for the inconsistent nature of Marshall's demand theory.)

THE MOST BASIC PROBLEMS: METHODOLOGICAL INCONSISTENCY AND CIRCULAR REASONING It is interesting that discussions of the problems in Marshall's demand theory in the literature since his death have focused, for the most part, upon the incompleteness of his statements (the second of the 'problems' discussed at the beginning of this chapter), and upon *internal* inconsistencies – noting the external inconsistencies only in passing (with the exception of Georgescu-Roegen, who takes seriously questions of reality). It has been left almost entirely to Pigou to take any notice of the methodological inconsistency of making measurements of welfare ultimately dependent, via demand measurements, upon measurements of utility – the immeasurability of which Marshall had early accepted.

The last problem – methodological inconsistency – is the one which to me has seemed the most serious, for it may preclude any forward motion in those areas of economics (comprising a significant part of the field) which are affected by it. In the last sentence of the preceding paragraph the circularity of the problem becomes especially obvious; for, after all, what is welfare (the thing ultimately to be measured), if it is not utility – the thing on whose measurement welfare measurement depends? The most basic statement of the problem may be put thus: 'We cannot measure welfare (i.e., utility), because doing so requires us to be able to measure utility (i.e., welfare).'

A neoclassical economist might respond that that last statement, while dramatic, is not quite fair; Marshall's effort, and that of those who came after him, was not to *measure welfare*, per se, but to be able to *compare* (using only such measurements as might prove necessary for the comparison) *changes* in welfare. Does this definition break free from the circularity just depicted? One effort to make it do so recasts the problem by redefining utility.

Pareto depended upon a Walrasian utility function not too dissimilar from the one Marshall sometimes used, where utility was specified as a *sum of functions of the quantities of goods.*[6] Neither of these two economists, it should be noted, was satisfied with this. Pareto tried to replace the concept with 'ophelimity', which does not pretend, as 'utility' does, to refer to real well-being or satisfaction; it only refers to the assumption that people try to get what they think they want within their budget constraints. Marshall himself rarely if ever referred to 'utility functions' as such, recognising, I believe, that the attempt to map 'real well-being' – which was emphatically what he was interested in – onto any abstract functional form was an endeavour filled with pitfalls.

The basis for this reticence was, at bottom, totally at odds with the programme of which we have seen Marshall boast that it gave economics an advantage over all the other social sciences. It came from the side of Marshall which said: 'Wealth exists only for the benefit of mankind. It cannot be measured adequately in yards or in tons, nor even as equivalent to so many ounces of gold; its true meaning lies only in the contribution it makes to human well-being' ('Fragments', quoted in *Memorials*, p. 366). Whatever Marshall hoped to get at in 'that measurement of motives which is prominent in economic science' *(Principles*, p. 645), it was not – at least, when he wrote the above fragment (probably in the last decade of his life) – 'human well-being'. What was it, then?

WHAT IS Among more modern commentators we will, in the next
BEING chapter, see some examples of a renewed willingness to
MEASURED? confront Marshall's most boldly vaunted endeavour. A
particularly salient example will be the work of McKenzie and Pearce, whose programme will appear familiar as they take on the following 'three basic questions':

(i) What conceptually do we wish to measure?
(ii) What functions, if any, expressed in terms of parameters and variables, *observable in principle*, will measure exactly, and in a general way, that which we wish to measure?
(iii) How do we choose the best approximation to the defined formula, given that some parameters and/or variables appearing in the function, may be hard to discover in practice (G. W. McKenzie and I. F Pearce, 'Welfare Measurement – A Synthesis', *American Economic Review*, September 1982, p. 669).

These authors' answer to their second 'basic question', addressing the general issues initially raised by Marshall's consumer's(') surplus analysis, will be examined in Chapter 17. There it will be seen that what they are trying to measure is very similar to what Marshall wanted to measure, and for reasons very similar to the ones laid out in the model of his programme, as it appeared above in Chapter 14.

Among those who have directly grappled with Marshall's own work, Milton Friedman stands out for the boldness with which he is willing to use the term, 'utility', as though it had a clear, mathematical definition. At one point in his writings on Marshall, Friedman simply identifies utility with real income. The context for that identification is one where real income is in fact the variable of interest to Friedman. He expresses dissatisfaction with the solution of setting real income equal to U, 'where U is the level of utility or the index of a consumption indifference curve, so that movement from one indifference curve to another means a change in income', because 'this definition has the defect that it introduces a variable into the demand function that is not directly observable on the market.'[7] Accordingly, Friedman offers a pair of alternative specification of real income, namely two 'constant-utility' demand curves, using either base-weighted or terminal-weighted index numbers to measure purchasing power. Once again, utility (kept constant as defined by the price indexes) is the foundation for what is being measured; but, again, this is utility defined in a special way – as 'the index of a consumption indifference curve'. (This phrase will be discussed below.)

Friedman's goal, in the two papers he wrote concerning the Marshallian demand curve, was to propose a form of demand curve which would be as useful as possible to economists. He recognised that 'we can make effective use of the aggregate demand curve only if we can neglect, or handle in some crude way, the differences among individuals in the required price or income compensations.'[8] From what we have seen of Marshall's struggles, the need to neglect differences among individuals is a familiar requirement in the definition of an aggregate demand curve.[9]

M. J. Bailey's response to Friedman's original paper on the Marshallian demand curve emphasises the transition from the *individual* to the *aggregate* demand curve, taking up what Friedman admits is his own failure to deal explicitly with this problem. Friedman replies that Bailey

> regards the transition as raising especially acute difficulties for [the] definition . . . which equates income with level of utility for the individual, and especially for the variant of the associated demand curve which holds money income constant and uses changes in the price of Y to compensate for any effect on the utility level which might otherwise result from a change in the price of X. I do not believe that this is so; the difficulty only takes a somewhat different form. In principle, we can conceive of an aggregate demand curve that keeps each individual separately on the same indifference curve by means of price comparisons, the differential price compensations required for different individuals because of differences in tastes and

resources being produced by a system of excise taxes or subsidies varying from one individual to another (ibid., p. 279).

Perhaps Friedman's imagination is better than that of most people; for myself, even 'in principle' I find the attempt to conceive of such an aggregate demand curve quite mind-boggling. If we leave principle and go to practice, the idea of specifying excise taxes or subsidies that could keep the utility level of each individual constant in the face of a price change is simply absurd.

FALLOUT FROM THE AGGREGATION PROBLEM   It is worth looking back at the way that Friedman, without noting that he was doing so, casually introduced an assumption on the definition of utility into a passage just quoted: ' . . . where U is the *level of utility* or the *index of a consumption indifference curve* . . .' Here we see the (generally) unspoken assumptions of neoclassical economics: measurements of welfare depend upon measurements of utility, and utility is simply another name for level of consumption.[10] There are reasons for this elision, the most forceful one being that what Marshall had thought of as utility is – once again – not measurable. But why, one wonders, is the old language retained when the meaning is changed? *Why not simply say that we are measuring levels of consumption, and leave out the words 'welfare' and 'utility'?*

An answer to this is embedded in the dogged problem of aggregation. If we consume nothing but widgets, it will be clear that aggregate consumption falls when it changes from 2000 to 1900 widgets, and that it rises in the reverse case. If, however, we consume both widgets and ergs, and erg consumption rises from 500 to 550 at the same time as widget consumption falls from 2000 to 1900, how can we tell whether aggregate consumption is up or down? The simple solution, of course, is to use price as a proxy for some essential characteristic of consumption goods (their 'real value'?) and take the *net change in money value of consumption* as the measure of *change in consumption*.

Even before we introduce the possibility of changes in relative prices, this solution brings us to the same weighting problem which had emerged in the 'urban cost-of-living' example used in Chapter 9. If ergs cost four times as much as widgets, in the above example we will find, if we use price as the conventional system of weights, that aggregate consumption has risen; whereas if ergs and widgets have the same per unit cost, it will appear that aggregate consumption has fallen. (Suppose, similarly, that we took physical weights as the essential characteristics, and that an erg weighs twice as much as a widget: then we would conclude that aggregate consumption was unchanged.)

Remember, as we go through all this, that the point of it is that we are defining aggregate welfare in terms of aggregate consumption. In order to let this meaning stand out more plainly, let us now substitute for 'widgets' something more concrete, i.e., *food*; while letting 'ergs' stand for 'everything else'. Then let us consider the situation in which food is consumed by the whole society, but dominates the consumption of the poor (who can only purchase a minute fraction of the society's whole production of 'ergs'). In the example given, the amount of food purchased in the society has fallen by 100 units (5 per cent), and erg purchases have risen by 50 units (10 per cent). Should the government conclude that its economic policies have been a disaster? A rousing success? What kind of accounting is needed, in addition to GNP, to answer these questions?

Willy-nilly, the acceptance of price as a proxy implies an acceptance of just what Marshall claimed: that price can be made to stand, in some way, for the real value we assign to things. In that case, the apparent simplification of defining utility simply in terms of consumption conceals a circling back to the older (pre-ophelimity) meaning of utility; if consumption cannot be aggregated in terms of the material things consumed, but only with respect to the 'real values' of those things, then, denoting 'measurement of' by 'M · ':

$$M \cdot WELFARE = M \cdot UTILITY = M \cdot CONSUMPTION = M \cdot REAL\ VALUES$$

can be abbreviated to:

$$M \cdot WELFARE = M \cdot REAL\ VALUES.$$

'The index of a consumption indifference curve' turns out to pack in much more than the words superficially suggest; when the phrase is unpacked, it appears that utility is once again being defined in terms of utility.[11]

Have modern theorists, with their updated techniques for modeling 'changes in welfare', managed to escape from this circularity? That question is explored in the next chapter.

Notes

1. Such an assumption ignores the strong argument which Hicks made, that the character of the social sciences differs from the natural sciences, among other things, in its lack of cumulativeness. See 'The Scope and Status of Welfare Economics', repr. in Hicks, 1981, pp. 232–4.

2. See quotation 1, Chapter 15, from Marc Blaug; also the following summary statement:

> in all important applications of the concept of consumer's surplus, Marshall concerned himself solely with the range of normal price variations, defining the consumer's surplus from a change in prices as the area between the demand curve and the price axis within the range of the price movement . . . . It is true that the notion remains a useful one for demonstrating the fact that the price paid for an article is not a measure of the satisfaction it affords, but we cannot measure this surplus in any meaningful way. At best we can appraise the welfare effect of one price-quantity situation compared to another, provided the expenditure on the commodity in question is a small fraction of total expenditures (Blaug, *Economic Theory in Retrospect*, p. 358).

Friedman and Fouraker credit Frank Knight with being the first prominent economist to point out that it is impossible to hold all of the other significant variables constant as price varies. Fouraker states the case very simply: 'if the individual's money income is held constant, then his real income will vary inversely with the commodity's price' (L. E. Fouraker, 'Marshall's Two Concepts of Consumer Demand', *Indian Journal of Economics*, vol. 37, April 1957; quoted in AMCA, vol. III, p. 332).

Milton Friedman, in his ingenious proposal that Marshall actually intended a *compensated* demand curve (compensated either with respect to income or to a particular group of other commodities), points out that a situation where money income is held constant while real income varies is inconsistent with 'one of Marshall's basic organising principles, namely, the separation of the theory of relative prices from monetary theory, the theory of the level of prices' (Milton Friedman, 'The Marshallian Demand Curve' *Journal of Political Economy*, vol. LVII, December 1949; repr. in AMCA, vol. III, p. 184).

3. Higgins and Liebhafsky interpret Pareto's interpretation of Marshall's constancy assumption as depending upon a utility function which 'produces a case in which the marginal utility of money is a function of money income *only* and is independent of prices'. (G. Higgins and H. H. Liebhafsky, 'Pareto and the Marshallian Constancy Assumption', *Southern Economic Journal*, vol. 35, October 1968, repr. in AMCA, vol. III, p. 454. See also a letter by Pareto charmingly translated by Georgescu-Roegen; quoted in Nicholas Georgescu-Roegen, 'Revisiting Marshall's Constancy of Marginal Utility of Money'; from *The Southern Economic Journal*, vol. 35, Oct. 1968; reprinted in AMCA, vol. III, n. 1, p. 466). Such an assumption implies a homothetic indifference map such

that the income elasticity of demand for every good is equal to 1; the advantage of this strong assumption is that it solves the path dependency problem which otherwise renders exact calculation of consumer's surplus impossible. (In this context path dependency refers to the fact that the final utility level reached by progressive responses to price changes will depend upon the order in which those price changes occurred. Another solution to this problem is the use of compensated demand curves – taking us out of consumer's surplus calculation and into compensating or equivalent variations. See Chapter 17, below.)

The homothetic indifference map imposes upon indifference curves that the income-consumption paths are straight lines out of the origin. An alternative interpretation of 'constant marginal utility of money' is to plot one composite good, denoted as 'money', on the vertical axis, and to impose the requirement that the indifference curves be vertically parallel. Then the income effects on the single other good, plotted on the horizontal axis, are zero. In this case the compensated and uncompensated demand curves are identical, and the measures of consumer's surplus, compensating and equivalent variations, all give the same results.

If Pareto adopted the first of these interpretations, putting Marshall's famous constancy in terms of ophelimity, Hicks, by contrast, made the second assumption, saying:

> The demand for X is . . . independent of income. His [the consumer's] demand for any commodity is independent of income . . . . This is actually what constancy of the marginal utility of money did mean for Marshall (Hicks, 1946, pp. 39–40).

Other possible implications of constant marginal utility of money/income (or MUe) include the well-supported notion that Marshall generally assumed an additive utility function; the notion that constant MUe implies that the change in expenditures on *X* and on the aggregate of all other commodities be equal and opposite; also, Georgescu-Roegen's sensible idea that Marshall did not intend perfect constancy, but only quasi-constancy, which is consistent with the idea that *X* is an unimportant item in the consumer's total budget (see next note); or Walker's hypothesis that the chief function, for Marshall, of constant MUe was to permit him to analyse market transactions in a particular way (D. A. Walker, 'Marshall's Theory of Competitive Exchange', *Canadian Journal of Economics*, November 1969; repr. in AMCA, vol. III).

4. C.f. the following analysis by Nicholas Georgescu-Roegen:

> Marshall, I submit, may not have intended to construct a theory applicable to all *conceivable* situations. Perhaps, like almost every other great economist from Quesnay to Keynes, he only wanted to analyze the economic actuality of his own time and place. And there are good reasons in support of the view that the assumption of quasi-constancy of marginal utility of money fits an important category of incomes in that actuality, namely the middle-bracket incomes.

In almost every society, the 'middle class' individual spends a substantial part of his income on *numerous* 'mere conveniences' – magazines, cards, fancy apparel items, flowers for special occasions, a brief annual outing, etc. All these items constitute *marginal* expenditures in relation to the entire income; and being numerous, a variation in income causes one of these items either to disappear from the budget or to become a new item of expenditure. Moreover, the utility of money among such items is practically the same: the individual finds it difficult to decide whether to buy one item or the other . . .
This is, no doubt, as far as one can go in trying to vindicate Marshall (Georgescu-Roegen, 1968, p. 465).

5. Such a comment may sound facetious, but it is, in fact, intended in full seriousness. While scientists in general find it more elegant to assign to each result a single cause, and to each cause a single result (I cannot help thinking of the kind of school quiz in which the student is asked to match each of the twenty items on the right with the most appropriate one of the twenty items on the left; has our perception of reality been influenced by such experiences as this?); nevertheless the science of the human mind offers the term, 'overdetermined', as a useful, and, indeed, necessary characteristic for much of human behaviour. For instance, in considering how the unconscious mind chooses, out of all the material available to it, which details to put into a dream, Sigmund Freud suggested that only those details which are 'overdetermined' by serving a multiplicity of needs will actually turn up in dreams.

6. For comments on this interpretation of Pareto, see. E. B. Wilson, 'Pareto on Marshall's Demand Curve', *Quarterly Journal of Economics*, vol. 58, November 1943; repr. in AMCA, vol. III, p. 154; see also n. 2, above. For an example of Marshall's definition of utility along these lines, see Alford's quotation from and discussion of a passage in *Economics of Industry* where 'Marshall refers to price as measuring some final utility to the consumer, to utility as always referring to some quantity of a commodity and to some particular person (and depending on future opportunities of getting it or substitutes for it) and to demand price as depending not only on utility but also on the consumers' means.' (R. F. G. Alford, 1956, repr. in AMCA, p. 324).

7. Milton Friedman, 'A Reply' to J.M.Bailey's 'The Marshallian Demand Curve', *Journal of Political Economy*, vol. 62, January 1954; repr. in AMCA, vol. III, p. 276.

8. Friedman, ibid., p. 280. A comment on the previous page is even clearer: 'One cannot pay more than lip service to variables that are specific to individual consumers' (p. 279). Friedman suggests that the way to handle such differences is that they must be 'largely neglected or regarded as averaging out.' (p. 282).

9. Of course Friedman's use of the 'aggregate demand' concept is not identical to Marshall's; it includes, for one thing, an awareness of the Hicksian IS-LM analysis.

358 *Marshall's Legacy to Welfare Economics*

10. One could give many examples of the uncommented-upon acceptance of
     this identity. An illustrative case is all of Varian's section 7.5, 'Topics in
     Welfare Economics'. There we may find the statement that, 'to a first
     order, changes in utility are proportional to changes in income' (p.
     273), and the conclusion that 'The basic lesson is that prices do indeed serve as
     a measure of value and can be used to evaluate proposed projects' (p. 276)
     (Hal Varian, *Microeconomic Analysis*, 2nd edn, Norton, 1984). Varian's
     use, here, of 'value', to mean something apparently different from 'price',
     is noteworthy.
11. I cannot resist referring to this as the ultimate F-twist – producing
     F′utility.

17 Some Modern Solutions to Marshall's Problem: the Literature on Welfare Measurement

Chapter 16 has briefly described and discussed some of the outstanding problems which economic literature has identified in Marshall's embracing theory of demand. Now the system of critical analysis which has been developed throughout this book will be applied to some modern economic writings.

SOME FAMILIAR PROBLEMS: MEASUREMENT AND CONSISTENCY Let us turn to a consideration of some ways in which modern economists have attempted to come to terms with Marshall's measurement problems: specifically, the continuing effort to base estimates of welfare measurements upon information regarding consumer demand.

Most of this chapter will consist of a close examination of four contributions to the literature which attempts to update Marshall's endeavours to measure welfare changes. I will look at two apologies for consumers' surplus: Arnold C. Harberger's 'Three Basic Postulates for Applied Welfare economics',[1] and R. Willig's 'Consumer's Surplus Without Apology'.[2] Then I will discuss Jerry Hausman's 'Exact Consumer's Surplus and Deadweight Loss';[3] and 'Welfare Measurement – A Synthesis' by G. W. McKenzie and I. F. Pearce.[4] The reader who wishes to judge the validity of my comments (particularly with regard to what I claim is *omitted* in these articles) may wish to have them at hand as s/he proceeds.

I will look at these attempts particularly in relation to welfare economics (or policy economics), which is generally concerned with defining improvements or reductions in social welfare in such a way that proposed social policies or programs can be evaluated (ideally before being put into effect) in order to determine which actions are more, and most, desirable. A goal of welfare economics is to provide a basis for making such evaluation both *precise* and *explicit*. If we add the requirement that the basis for evaluation should also be *consistent* and *non-absurd* (with respect to what we know of the real world), we may be approaching the establishment of an impossibility theorem.[5]

We might take as an example the inconsistency of the Kaldor–Hicks welfare criterion, which can simultaneously find situation A superior to B, and B superior to A. This possibility arises because, on the one hand, a social welfare function is treated *as if* it were an individual utility function; while, on the other hand, the recognition that different individuals are involved (with different marginal valuations with respect to income) results in indifference curves that can intersect. The problem is that most people's evaluations of most things alter with changes in wealth or income; hence it is impossible to establish an unambiguous ranking of the social output without additional information on distribution and on comparative utilities. (This is the type of problem which Marshall avoided by making his 'constant marginal utility of money' assumption; see Chapter 14, n. 5.)

THE UNDERLYING METAPHORS   Other, related types of inconsistency plague the systems of measurement which we will consider below. Among them, we will see that the measure to be called EV^1 alone makes its calculations without specific reference to the new price levels. Hence this measure is able to achieve a consistent ordering among alternative proposed price policies even when P is defined to include changes in both prices and income (or in more than one price) – as opposed to other measures, which are consistent only for a single price change. (That is, for the other three measures it is possible to find cases where situation A is preferred to B, B to C, and C to D – but D is preferred to A.) However, the consistency of ordering of EV^1, as also of the other three measures, still depends upon the maintenance of a metaphorical function (see below) which fails to account for the problem of varying marginal valuation with respect to income. Interpersonal differences in this regard will continue to permit indifference curves to intersect on the social welfare map.

The problem of marginal valuations which vary with respect to income raises serious questions about the ambiguities of community indifference curves; and behind those ambiguities lie deeper questions about the validity of the social welfare concept. That concept is useful, in some cases, as a metaphor. If it were always treated carefully, e.g., by being translated into a simile and hedged round with such precautionary language as – *'let us proceed, for a while, as if all of society could be viewed as one individual, having to make choices between a range of goods and bads; and remembering that the analytical representation of individual welfare as a utility function is itself a rather clumsy metaphor . . .'* – it would have less potential to cause difficulties. In actual practice, the incorporation of layers of metaphor which are the supporting structure of social welfare analysis is too often forgotten. It is dangerous, even temporarily, to employ an imaginative extension from a simplifying and abstracting formulation of one concept (utility functions as representations of individual welfare) to an even less appropriate formulation of another even more tenuous concept (social welfare functions as representations of social well-being). When we do so, the problems which show up as inconsistencies – like those referred to in the case of the Kaldor-Hicks criterion – are only the tip of the iceberg of the real problems in this procedure. The deepest problems tend to take the form of the kind of circularity described at the end of the last chapter.

In establishing either systems of welfare measurement (consumer's(') surplus, equivalent or compensating variations), or criteria for evaluating welfare (Pareto, Kaldor–Hicks or Scitovsky), as well as in computing index numbers, we ultimately run up against the necessity of comparing a *change in welfare* with a *number*, the latter representing something like the 'change in income that would be necessary to compensate the consumer to bring him (back) to his final (initial) level of welfare'. We will see, as we go on to examine modern measures of welfare changes, that *changes in welfare* continue to be analysed with reference to *levels of welfare*; and these levels still remain to be defined. *Changes* in welfare may be handled as ordinal problems; *levels* require cardinal specificity. Hence the admission of McKenzie and Pearce (in their discussion of equivalent variation) that 'What we really want to find is some cardinal representation of the ordinal utility function for the individual' (1982, p. 669).

CONSUMER'S(') By and large, the kind of welfare analysis for which
SURPLUS IN Marshall had originally developed the consumer's(')
MODERN USE surplus measure is now performed with one of two
A Harberger alternatives – either compensating variation or
equivalent variation. Before turning to an examination of those measures, it is instructive to consider two articles which have argued for the preservation of Marshall's original measure.

Arnold Harberger stated: 'I feel, precisely because of the power and wide applicability of the consumer-surplus concept, that a recognizable degree of consensus concerning it would increase, to society's general benefit, the influence on public policy of good economic analysis' (Harberger,1971, p. 786).Like Marshall, Harberger wants economics to enhance the welfare of society, and he believes that it can do this better if it can be – or at least appear to be – scientific. For a modern reader the distance which remains between that *scientific appearance* and *reality* is more readily apparent in Harberger's paper than in much of Marshall's work, where there is so much cautious qualification and balancing of alternative views that Marshall's very subtlety may engender a tendency to latch on to the simplest statements and ignore the ponderous phrases and slightly old-fashioned language which carries the rest.

The burden of Harberger's argument is that, in order to achieve a recognisable consensus, 'three basic postulates' should 'be accepted as providing a conventional framework for applied welfare economics.' These postulates are:

    (a) the competitive demand price for a given unit measures the value of that unit to the demander;
    (b) the competitive supply price for a given unit measures the value of that unit to the supplier;
    (c) when evaluating the net benefits or costs of a given action (project, program, or policy), the costs and benefits accruing to each member of the relevant group (e.g., a nation) should normally be added without regard to the individual(s) to whom they accrue (Harberger, p. 785).

How much simpler Marshall's own task would have been if he could have brought himself to accept postulates (a) and (b): here we have a direct equation between human value (use value) and price (exchange value)! Harberger is content to support these propositions, as we have seen that Marshall would have liked to do, with the simple version of the meaning of marginal value.[6] As for postulate (c), that accomplishes the same thing as (if it is not precisely identical to) Marshall's 'astonishing assertion' that the effects of most economic events are randomly distributed among income-classes. (See Chapter 14, quotation 14.)

Harberger is aware of the problems with consumer-surplus analysis (as he calls it, obviating the apostrophe-placement problem), and he faces these frontally:

I encounter with considerable regularity colleagues who are skeptical of consumer surplus on one or more of several alleged grounds:

(i) Consumer-surplus analysis is valid only when the marginal utility of real income is constant.

(ii) Consumer-surplus analysis does not take account of changes in income distribution caused by the action(s) being analyzed.

(iii) Consumer-surplus analysis is partial-equilibrium in nature, and does not take account of the general-equilibrium consequences of the actions whose effects are being studied.

(iv) Consumer-surplus analysis, though valid for small changes, is not so for large changes.

(v) The concept of consumer-surplus analysis has been rendered obsolete by revealed-preference analysis (ibid., p. 786).

The particulars of Harberger's defence against these charges do not succeed in removing the problems which we have seen in analysing Marshall's programme. However, Harberger has one overall line of defence, which is an impressively honest statement of what may have been Marshall's final fall-back position, but which Marshall never put so forcefully and clearly. Harberger claims to be optimistic that his paper, which he refers to as 'a tract – an open letter to the profession, as it were – pleading that three basic postulates be accepted' (p. 785), will succeed in its mission; and he states thus his reasons for such optimism:

i) we already have a reasonably well-established consensus on the basic methodology of national-income measurement,

ii) it is easy to show that postulates a–c incorporate a greater degree of subtlety of economic analysis than does national-income methodology, and

iii) most of the 'objections' to consumer-surplus analysis hold *a fortiori* with respect to the measurement of national income.
. . . . Of course, economists do not truly believe that real NNP or national income is a complete measure of welfare. But it is equally true that in most of the contexts in which changes in these magnitudes, or comparisons of them across regions or countries are dealt with, the discussion often carries strong welfare connotations, often to the point where it would be meaningless if those connotations were denied (pp. 786–7).

An unfriendly view of this plea interprets it as saying, 'We should strengthen the ability of the economics profession to affect policy by closing ranks on the acceptance of three heroic simplifications; and we can suppress our qualms over thus ignoring distributional and other complications with the reflection that the measure to be supported by the proposed simplifications is no worse than another which is already widely used.'

A more sympathetic interpretation, however, would read the paper's message as follows: 'It is useless to say that competitive demand and supply prices do not measure true (human) values, for estimates of true values – i.e., of welfare – must be, and in fact they are, made before any deliberate decision can be reached on any issue. Economists using consistent postulates, with full consciousness of their limitations, are needed by society's policy-makers; and such economists will be more useful if they can enhance their credibility through consensus.'

B Willig I will leave the reader to choose for him/herself between these alternate ways of reading Harberger's article, while I turn very briefly to point out the similarities with another well-known proponent of consumer's surplus.

Robert Willig remarked that estimation of 'unobservable compensating and equivalent variations – the correct theoretical measures of the welfare impact of changes in prices and incomes on an individual' is very difficult, if not impossible; in part because these two measures depend upon Hicksian compensated demand curves, where the income parameters include compensation which varies with the price to keep the consumer at a constant level of utility. By contrast, we can come closer to observing consumer's surplus, because it is related to 'the observable Marshallian demand curve' (Willig, 1976, p. 592). Though Willig does not overtly make this point, it is evident that he is casting his lot with those who believe that the right way to approach welfare analysis is the empirical and inductive approach.

Willig, like Harberger, accepts that there are theoretical problems with consumer's surplus (henceforth *CS*). He also takes the position that compensating variations (*CV*) and equivalent variations (*EV*) are without theoretical problems. The case he makes is that the estimates obtained by use of 'observed consumer's surplus' are close enough to the estimates arising from *CV* or *EV* so that 'the error of approximation . . . . will often be overshadowed by the errors involved in estimating the demand curve.'[7] His well-known conclusion was that we should stop worrying about the accuracy of our welfare measurements and, employing consumer's surplus as our standard, get on with the business for which we want to use such measurements.

Willig's conclusion, like Harberger's, is that economic science is already so inexact (essentially because of measurement problems) that it is foolish to eschew the easiest way of defining welfare on the grounds of its inexactness. These are not conclusions to be lightly ignored or put aside; however, those who have taken them seriously have often only taken a piece of them. Subsequent references to Willig's unfortunately named 'Consumer's Surplus Without Apology' have too often implied that it has now been 'proven' that the *CS* measure needs no apology at all – i.e., that there is no fault to be found with it. However Willig's actual message was that *at the level of the individual consumer* we should not need to apologise for using a measure which is *no worse than* the data on which it depends.

Willig himself is partly to be blamed for this misreading. Although the body of his text supports the summary of his limited claims as just stated, his last sentence supports almost any interpretation the reader may care to make: 'To conclude, at the level of the individual consumer, cost-benefit welfare analysis can be performed rigorously and unapologetically by means of consumer's surplus' (Willig, 1976, p. 587). The word there which has led so many astray is 'rigorously'. It is not strictly false: as long as the analysis is performed according to the formulae laid out, with full knowledge of the supporting mathematics, the analysis can be said to be rigorous without necessarily being accurate; but the assumption is easily and too often made that where there is rigour there is accurate mapping from reality.

ALTERNATIVES TO THE CONSUMER'S(') SURPLUS MEASURE: DEFINITIONS

More modern welfare measures have largely abandoned the inductive approach.[8] Before going on to look at the claims for superiority of the deductively-based compensating and equivalent variations I will set out a brief description of these measures.

The measurement which at present claims the strongest allegiance in the profession is *equivalent variation*; this attempts to represent the change in income that would be necessary in order to bring a consumer, while remaining at his/her *original* economic circumstances, to the level of welfare that would be created by some proposed economic change.

The alternative concept, *compensating variation*, indicates what compensation would be necessary in order to make a consumer who has *already* experienced a change in some price as well off as s/he was *before* the price change; it tells what increase or decrease to current income would be necessary to buy, under a new price regime, the current utility level.

Each of these may be broken down by yet more subtle distinctions which differentiate between expenditure levels with regard to both *price* (original or new) and the *utility* of the consumer (at the original level, or at that brought about by the changed price(s)). To be more specific, I will briefly define four approaches to such measurement:[9]

Where e is expenditures, P is a price vector and U is a utility level,

$$CV^1 = e(P_0, U_0) - e(P_1, U_0)$$
$$CV^2 = e(P_1, U_1) - e(P_1, U_0)$$
$$EV^1 = e(P_0, U_1) - e(P_0, U_0)$$
$$EV^2 = e(P_0, U_1) - e(P_1, U_1)$$

A summary verbal definition, as follows, shows that:

- EV^2 compares the *new economic situation* (including possible changes in both prices and income, as well as the utility level believed to be reached through these economic variables) with the income required to reach this *new utility under the original price regime*; and
- CV^2 compares the *new economic situation* with the income required to remain at the *old utility level under the new price regime*

while

- CV^1 and EV^1, by contrast, use the *original situation* as a base against which to compare different versions of an altered economic situation.

The difference between the latter pair is that:

- CV^1 specifies the income required to put the consumer back at the *original utility level* under the *new price regime*;
- while EV^1 specifies the income required to reach the *new utility level* under the *old price regime*; that is, it measures the change in income that would be necessary in order to bring consumers who are at the original economic circumstances to the same level of welfare that would be created by the proposed economic changes.

In each case, the specification of the amount of income required in order to make consumers as well off under one price regime as under another is only made possible by imagining a 'third situation' where consumption allocations in one price regime are made *as though* the other price conditions were prevailing. The imaginary 'third situations' are captured within the parentheses with mixed subscripts: (P_1, U_0) and (P_0, U_1). The 'pure' situations, describing either the original or new situations as they 'really' are, appear as (P_0, U_0) or (P_1, U_1).

Each of the four measures is able to set up a comparison by virtue of omitting specific reference to one of the four variables (old P, new P, old U, new U). CV^1 omits reference to new U; CV^2 omits old P; EV^2 omits old U; and EV^1 omits new P. It would appear that these four variants exhaust the possibilities for measuring welfare changes in this manner.

DISCUSSION OF THE ALTERNATIVE MEASURES: A Hausman In his 1981 article, Jerry Hausman disagreed with Willig's perception of the difficulties in estimating equivalent and compensating variations, and made the case that we should not be content with the CS approximation when better ones are not, after all, so difficult to achieve. (Hausman wrote at a level of generality such that most of his conclusions apply equally to CV or EV; in fact, some actually apply to CS as well. When specifying precisely, he employed CV^1 and EV^2.)

Hausman claims to employ the inductive approach, saying, 'My approach differs from much recent work in that I begin with the observed market demand curve and then derive the unobserved indirect utility function and expenditure function. The more common approach is to start from a specification of the utility function, for example, Stone-Geary or trans-log, and then estimate the unknown parameters from the derived market demand functions' (Hausman, 1981, p. 664). This claim notwithstanding, many assumptions regarding utility are required, along with the empirical demand information, to permit the transition from observed market demand to the unobservable functions which are the basis for the estimates of welfare changes. In each case, Hausman defends his otherwise uncommented-upon introduction of an assumption about utility by stating that he is only doing what is commonly done. For instance:

> The *conventional* treatment of consumer behavior considers the maximization of a strictly quasi-concave utility function defined over n goods, $x = (x_1, \ldots, x_n)$, subject to a budget constraint (Hausman, p. 664; italics added).[10]

Separability utility functions justify specification and estimation of demand curves that have only a single price in them. An important example *often used* in empirical studies is the linear labor supply relationship . . . . Numerous other commodity demand equations are specified in this form where the wage is replaced by the price of the commodity (p. 667; italics added).

In sum, Hausman's approach is to employ an indirect utility function, *based upon some* (strictly quasi-concave) *utility function* maximised over *n* goods, along with the associated expenditure function. The partial derivative of the latter with respect to the *j*th price gives the (unobservable) Hicksian compensated demand curves. Then,

> so long as the derivatives of the compensated demand functions satisfy the properties of symmetry and negative semi-definiteness of the Slutsky matrix and the adding-up condition, the indirect utility function can be recovered by integration. In practice, many commonly used demand functions in empirical work yield explicit solutions so that exact welfare analysis is easily done (p. 667).

(Note, again, that Hausman claims for the demand functions which 'yield exact solutions' only that they are commonly used – not that they bear any particular relation to reality.[11])

Upon this basis Hausman then claims that, when properly derived according to his formulation, which 'varies across individuals by their socioeconomic characteristics and their income levels' (see n. 11), his version of either *CV* or *EV* 'give the exact measure of welfare change' (p. 669). Earlier he had admitted that 'the complete demand system usually cannot be estimated due to lack of data'. This might seem to be a deterrent to the strictly inductive approach (which, however, as we have seen, he pads out with utility assumptions and deductive reasoning erected thereupon); however, Hausman depends upon Hicks's aggregation theorem 'to demonstrate that the quasi functions which correspond to the assumptions of a two-good world would give exactly the same measure of consumer's surplus as the actual functions for a single price change.' From this he concludes that 'estimates of the uncompensated demand curve are all that is required to produce estimates which correspond to the correct theoretical magnitude' (p.664). It is relevant to note the language being used at this point: the claim is that the estimates 'correspond to the correct *theoretical* magnitude', not that they correspond in any particular way to *reality*.[12] This is less ambitious than the claim, quoted above, that either *CV* or *EV* can give 'the exact measure of welfare change'.

Unfortunately, no ladder has been constructed upon which our credulity may climb from the lesser to the greater claim. Hausman said, in effect, that he would depend *only* upon observable data to derive his estimates of unobservable magnitudes; but, in fact, the progression of equations which allows him to say that this is what he is doing is larded throughout with dependence upon conventions regarding utility. The observable data still turn out to be nowhere to be found.

McKenzie and Pearce: measurement of utility/ welfare (again) The last paper we will consider is by McKenzie and Pearce (henceforth M and P), who largely confine their discussion to what they consider to be the superior measure, equivalent variation, which they define to correspond to EV^2 (above). They make it clear that they are only talking about situations of *price* changes, not changes in income (where EV^1 is as good a measure as EV^2 [13]). These authors clarify some assumptions which are hinted at but not made definite in Hausman's article. The first of these relates to one aspect of the measurement problems upon which I have already laid emphasis.

The conclusion of M and P, 'that attempts to measure real production, real income, consumer's surplus and/or the cost of living are no more than disguised attempts to measure utility itself' (p. 673) sheds light on the meaning of the 'welfare calculations' in which Hausman claimed to be interested. The latter's goal was to compute a welfare measure which could compare welfare at two price points. Ultimately such a computation must, as M and P say, involve an attempt to measure utility. The solution taken by M and P as well as by Hausman is to use indirect (or quasi-indirect) utility functions which they do not compute directly, but derive from expenditure functions giving the minimum cost of achieving a fixed level of utility.

By and large, writers in economics of this century feel somewhat uncomfortable about having to justify *inventing* a utility function to be employed as though an equation could represent real human feelings and motivations. The possibility of doing so has come under attack from a number of quarters – from the humanistically inclined, who protest that no matter how many symbols are employed, or how intricately they are interrelated, an equation cannot be as subtle or as unpredictably changeable as a creature of mind, flesh and emotions; to the logically inclined (such as Arrow, or Luce and Raiffa) who set out the rules for well-behaved functions and then find (whether empirically or logically) that individual and/or social utility functions do not or can not comply with the rules.

Alas, the derivation of the indirect utility function from the expenditure function only pushes the responsibility back one remove; for whether it was derived from the expenditure function or from the ordinary demand curves, its derivation depended in part upon maximisation of the original utility function. Recognising this more directly than most economists do, M and P state that 'What we really want to find is some cardinal representation of the ordinal utility function for the individual'; and they go on to claim that

> We are able from present knowledge to write down in the most general way an exact representation of each individual's utility function itself so that
> – its precise form is known, and
> – all its variables and parameters can be deduced in principle from observed behavior in the market.
>
> In particular, an exact global representation of the individual's utility function may be written as a linear fixed weight combination of products of prices, the fixed weights being constructed from the first- and higher-order elasticities of demand and individual income changes, with elasticities evaluated at a base point (p. 669).

This is either proof-by-assumption or proof-by-definition; the authors define an '*individual's utility function*' as '*a linear fixed weight combination of products of prices*' and then assume that such a definition requires no further support. As far as strictly theoretical work is concerned, this may be an acceptable procedure; but the fact that the issue is welfare measurement establishes an implication that the procedure being used here should, at the end, shed some light on human welfare. Nothing in the paper supports such an implication. It is emphasised, but not substantiated, in the statement: 'The concept of steel production is only vaguely defined. The concept of utility however is precise. There is no reason to suppose that an index of utility cannot be exact' (p. 679). Such breathtaking claims call for a response like Prince Hal's to Owen Glendower, when the latter made the heroic statement, 'I can call spirits from the vasty deep'. 'An exact representation' may indeed be written as stated; but will anything in the real world answer to the description?

The 'proof-by-assumption' character of this part of the analysis is buried in a discussion which begins, 'If we wish to make use of a measurable utility index it must be the money metric. This will both order social states and provide an immediately intelligible yardstick against which nonmonetary advantages can be compared. No other utility index can do as much as this' (p. 674). This is followed by assumptions concerning, and manipulation of, L (the marginal utility of money), along with the indirect utility function, to derive the expression contained in the Taylor's expansion which is equation (6) in the paper by M and P. They then state that 'Equation (6) with all its terms *is* the utility index, not a measure of it or some approximation to it' (p. 676). At this point it is well to examine the text for clues as to what definition of utility these authors may be using. In this context 'the utility index' is apparently just what they say it is – equation (6), whose derivation we can follow in their text. It depends, once again, upon the manipulation of an indirect utility function which, in seeking to be grounded in reality, can only be traced back to that 'linear fixed weight combination of products of prices'.

M and P do recognise some difficulties, when they search for the integrating factor L in order to use it to convert an observed demand function into a utility function. So they comment that 'The marginal utility of money depends partly on behavior and partly on intensity of satisfaction', and, 'if there is one integrating factor then there are many. We do not know, nor can we ever discover, which of these is the true marginal utility of money. We can never tell, therefore, which of the corresponding utility indices is the true one. All are consistent with observed behavior. Intensity of utility can never be measured' (p. 674).

They go on to discuss the by-now-familiar problems with marginal utility of money[14] and come to a conclusion which combines Marshall's wish to 'measure' satisfaction with Harberger's and Hausman's perception that, where understanding or facts are lacking, the reasonable fallback (if economics is to be believable) is the adoption of 'some agreed and understood convention' (see n. 14). 'Fortunately', they say, there is 'only one convention regarding the measure of satisfaction that makes sense.' At this point they appeal to common sense, in the form of common knowledge:

> . . . a sum of money *at given prices* can, and always will be, translated into subjective utility, instinctively and at once, by each person, using the correct utility of money function known only to himself. No one knows how many utils he is prepared to sacrifice to

avoid the construction of a motorway near his residence, but everyone would at once know how much money at current price levels he is prepared to trade for anything, subjective or objective (p. 674).

There is a significant lack of realisticness in these statements. Many people agonise at great length about how much money they are prepared to trade for objective, let alone subjective values; and many people, having finally made such a trade, remain unsure that it was the one they wanted or want. Moreover, the difference in marginal utility of money to a rich and to a poor person is, in the end, overlooked, although the revealed monetary value of avoiding a motorway near the home of one would be vastly different than in the case of the other for this reason, and not because the subjective disutility of the poor person is necessarily less than that of the rich one.[15]

The most valid point which does arise out of these statements is only made implicitly: it is the recognition that the definition of 'what we have to evaluate' has been arrived at by convention and common sense: that we cannot ever, in fact, define the true utility function, but that use of equivalent variation will provide us with the most accessible easily-agreed-upon proxy.

At this point, M and P move to the position that 'The problem resolves itself quite simply into one of finding a way to write down the money metric in terms of observable entities' (p. 673). This may not appear to be so simple to everyone, but they assert that, 'We now know precisely what it is we have to evaluate. There is no question of approximation except the practical one of how difficult it might be actually to observe demand functions or their derivatives . . .' (p. 675).

I have already commented on how 'precisely' we have arrived at our knowledge of what it is that we are to evaluate; it remains to consider the 'practical' question of the approximation of demand curves. On this latter point, M and P set out a very helpful statement:

Truth cannot of course be deduced from ignorance. If we do not know demand functions with precision then no one can know with precision the utility function.[16] If we do know the utility function, only arithmetic is needed to calculate demand. On the other hand, an approximation to utility might, in some circumstances, be deduced from approximate demand functions.

Ignorance may come in two forms. We may have precisely defined demand functions, estimated by econometric methods, that allow us to regard the precise functions so obtained only as more or less good approximations to true demand functions. Alternatively we may have more or less accurate point estimates of demand elasticities up to a given order and no information at all about elasticities of a higher order . . . .

In the first case, the best we can do is to find the full money metric appropriate to the estimated demand equations as if they were the true equations, assuming, that is, that the estimated equations possess (as they should) all of the properties essential to the existence of a utility function. If, as is almost certain to be the case, no integrating factor is immediately deducible then the money metric . . . will serve as a directly applicable method of integration. Since all elasticities are known [by the assumption of this case] the investigator may make his own choice as to the level of accuracy desired. As long as all elasticities are finite the calculation must converge, although not necessarily uniformly . . . .

In the case of the second form of ignorance, [equation] (6) can be used only in truncated form up to the order of the known elasticities of demand (p. 677).

SUMMARY CRITIQUE OF THE MODERN SOLUTIONS We could, in fact, restate the problem with which we have been grappling by saying that much of it stems from inflated claims to (or conceptions of) 'rigour' in a social science. Measurements can be made with varying degrees of meaningfulness: for some purposes, the kind of measurement ordinarily possible is, in fact sufficient – even if it does not live up to some claims for scientific rigour.

How much of the problem could be solved by a change in terminology? By speaking, for example, of 'welfare change approximations' instead of 'welfare change measurements'? This question should be pursued in the development of social economics. In the context of this chapter, in any case, we have not seen this course pursued vigorously enough to save these authors from their worst exaggerations.

Recall what I referred to as Hausman's 'more ambitious claim' – that his calculation of *CV* or *EV* could 'give the exact measure of welfare change'. We are now in a better position to evaluate this claim: in particular, to ask what is left of the claim to be able to measure equivalent variation, when it depends upon the process of converting an observed demand function into an indirect utility function.

In their search for an integrating factor to stand in for the troublesome marginal utility of money, M and P are looking for ways to go from observed demand to unobserved utility. As compared to Hausman, they use fancier language and more extravagant claims to being scientific to disguise even more unscientific leaps. Some of these unscientific leaps may be summed up as follows:

1. Utility is identified with consumption without making any attempt either to warn the reader that this identification is being made, or to justify it.
2. M and P mention, but do not resolve, the interpersonal utility problem; and yet if, as they state, the only way to imagine a social welfare function is to base it upon individual utilities, and if there is more than one individual in the society, then this problem must be addressed. If individual utilities are to be summed together as social utility, and if the only basis for comparison across individuals is what they spend, then there must be some assumption about the meaning, to each person, of the expenditure of a dollar. The statement that 'intensity of utility can never be measured', though commendably honest, does not deal with this problem. The 'observed market demand' upon which so much depends tells us (something) about consumers' willingness to pay; we have little basis upon which to analyse the results of the fact that relative *willingness to pay* depends upon relative *ability to pay*.
3. An additional difficulty which may be listed under the familiar heading, 'aggregation problems', accompanies M and P's assumption that 'the only way to imagine a social welfare function is to base it upon individual utilities'. This is, indeed, *not* the only way to conceptualise social welfare (I will not speak for social welfare *functions*, for that is an imaginary construct of little demonstrated usefulness); 'the good of the whole society' is, of course, intimately associated with the good of each of its members; but there may be some synergy (wherein the whole is different than the sum of its parts) which cannot be captured simply by looking at individual welfare (let alone individual welfare functions.)[17]

Finally,

4. M and P in the end are driven to base a significant part of their argument upon a highly unrealistic statement about 'what everyone knows' (ie., the correct utility of money function) and

'what everyone can do' (i.e., translate anything, subjective or objective, into a money price).

M and P's most convincing suggestions are their propositions about deducing 'an approximation to utility' from 'approximate demand functions'. We see, in the last long passage quoted from these authors, various ways of predicting the types of errors into which this will lead us.[18] It is the business of common sense-type judgment (I know of no alternative system that can be used for this function) to determine how acceptable such errors are under different circumstances. The scientific base which appears to have been so carefully constructed is in fact built upon a foundation of rather scantily examined convention and common sense.

CONCLUSIONS   The difficulties encountered by modern economists as
AND CHOICES   they have elaborated the consumer's surplus measure,
                as well as the compensating and equivalent variations
alternatives, begin with the difficulties which plagued Marshall in his
original attempts to use consumers' surplus for welfare measurement.
It remains true that, *under the special circumstances assumed by
Marshall*, any of these measures can be reasonably accurate. These
special circumstances include the requirements that:

- if we are to consider a possible change in welfare for more than one consumer, the group to be considered should be homogeneous in their choices as to how to use marginal increments of wealth; otherwise inconsistencies (reflecting underlying inaccuracies) will result from the initial aggregation of consumer choices into a societal welfare function. Also,
- in most usages (e.g., Hicks's) the proposed policy measure should not alter more than one price, nor should it appreciably[19] alter real income or the price level; for this to be true, the single change to be considered must be relatively insignificant within the consumer's total budget. (Hence Marshall's requirement of small changes and/ or changes only with regard to an insignificant budget item.)

It is interesting to note that all of the above are true if income effects are zero; in that case all of the measures which we have considered yield the same results, so that it does not matter, once we have accepted these restrictive assumptions, whether we chose to employ *CS, CV,* or *EV!*

It is still not possible on the aggregate (or social welfare) level to measure the currently preferred indicator, EV, so that it will do what is sometimes claimed; i.e., precisely and accurately represent the change in income that would be necessary in order to bring consumers who are at the original economic circumstances to the same *level of welfare* that would be created by the proposed economic changes.[20] The unobservable 'level of welfare' remains beyond the grasp of any aggregated measure; even on the individual level modern attempts to realise Marshall's hope of finding an observable proxy for 'level of welfare' end up by making that proxy depend upon some equally unobservable derivative of a utility function.

Have we moved much beyond Marshall's position on these matters? There is enough substance in the subsequent literature so that anyone who cares to search through it with a logical and sceptical eye is certainly better situated to understand the intricacies of the problems than s/he would have been with only Marshall's work to depend on.[21] But such an understanding does not seem to lead, as several authors have impatiently argued that it should, to a consensus. The following appear to be the principal positions from which a would-be welfare-measurer can choose today:

1. The old-fashioned solution: Accept the conditions which Marshall accepted, restricting the circumstances in which welfare measure-ment can be applied to those where income differences and/or income effects are of negligible importance.

2. The modern set of solutions: Start by recognising, as M and P do, that, as regards *real* production, *real* income, consumer's surplus, and the cost of living (each of those terms referring to underlying 'human values', beneath the transitory measurement of price) 'Each can be correctly measured only by measuring utility' (M and P, 1982, p. 673). Given this recognition, there appear to be three ways to go:

    2(a) Conclude, with the careful mathematical economist, Eugene Silberberg, that, in this context, 'attempts to measure the unmeasurable will be unsuccessful'.[22] Abandon welfare economics as a precise science – at least if, to be such a science, it must strive for the kind of goal described earlier as the programme of Alfred Marshall.

    2(b) Accept, with Harberger, the high degree of imperfection of welfare measurement, but (on the grounds that a generally respected economics profession can better advance the public interest than one discredited by internal dispute) accept the best approach to measurement that we have, and make it look as scientific as possible. (This was part of the Marshallian approach, also.)

2(c) Claim, with M and P, that welfare measurement can be done both precisely and accurately, regardless of its dependence upon measuring what some regard as unmeasurable. In order to maintain this position it is necessary to construct a bridge between (i) the recognition of the necessity of starting with utility measurement and (ii) the conclusion that the results are precise and accurate. M and P offer us two (in my opinion) rather shaky planks to serve as such a bridge.

– One plank depends upon conventional economic assumptions as being adequate to specify mathematical functions which define utility as an identity; 'utility', by this definition, actually does not exist outside of the identity established by their formula.

– The other plank proposes that, by common sense, everyone knows what utility is; it suggests that there is some algorithm that can translate that common knowledge into usable functions.

Laid end to end, perhaps these two planks would cross the chasm; unfortunately, I cannot find where they meet.

Considering options 2(a), (b), and (c), it will be fairly evident that I find the last solution the least acceptable; it seems to me to return (with more apparent sophistication but less real understanding) to a level of logical elision and failure to face some critical truths that is no improvement on Marshall's economics. (Interestingly, the truths that are slighted by M and P do not overlap much with those that suffered at Marshall's hands; it is the *need* to ignore some piece of the truth in order to achieve the desired ends 'scientifically' or 'rigorously' that is recurrent.)

Harberger is not much of an improvement on this aspect of Marshall's work and legacy, either; if one reads Harberger as proposing that the economics profession close ranks to try to fool the rest of the world, this is a distinct step backwards, morally and scientifically, if not politically. On the other hand, he does face directly the discouraging facts about the chasm between our wishes and our abilities. Nor does he, as others have done, throw a pretend bridge over that chasm.

Solution 2(a) is the most honest and the least appealing; it is, in effect, not a solution at all; it is a statement that, to the problem as posed, there is no solution. My own preference is to accept that statement, and work at thinking how else to pose the problem so that we can honestly find a useful way to achieve at least some of the goals which have lead us to take an interest in welfare measurement.

That points the way to a very large piece of work. It is a project only the beginnings of which have been seen in this book. The enormous amount that remains to be done may be deduced by subtracting the relatively modest claims, in the next and final chapter, for what has been achieved in this book, from the broader outline that was laid out in Part I.

Notes

1. *Journal of Economic Literature*, September 1971.
2. *The American Economic Review*, September 1976.
3. Ibid, September 1981.
4. Ibid, September 1982.
5. Indeed, Ebert has shown that it is impossible to define a welfare measure which satisfies the criterion of 'circularity' (if situation 1 confers higher welfare than situation 2, and 2 is higher than 3, then the sum of the improvements from 1 to 2 and from 2 to 3 should be equal to the improvement from 1 to 3) and which simultaneously satisfies either of two other measures – the 'monetary measure' or the 'real consumption measure'. (The first of these is defined thus: 'If prices remain constant and only the consumer's income changes, the change in welfare is measured by the difference in income between the two situations'; and the second – 'If in the new situation the consumer chooses a multiple of his or her 'old' bundle of consumption, the welfare measure . . . indicates how much the consumer has gained or lost in terms of the initial bundle of commodities' [Udo Ebert, 'Exact Welfare Measures and Economic Index Numbers', *Zeitschrift fur Nationalokonomie*, vol. 44, no. 1, 1984, p. 30].) This impossibility is in the context of the measurement of the welfare of only one individual. The difficulties multiply greatly, of course, when any aggregation is involved.

   I am indebted to Pankaj Tanden for bringing this article to my attention, and also for a course he gave, which I attended as a graduate student, in which the four papers which are the focus of this chapter were discussed.

6. Essentially, postulates a and b state that when demanders (suppliers) pay (get) their demand (supply) price for each marginal unit, the balance of their indifference as between demanding (supplying) that unit and undertaking the relevant available alternative activities has just barely been tipped. In effect, demand and supply prices are measures of the alternative benefits that demanders and suppliers forego when they do what they decide to do' (Harberger, p. 793).

    Of course, the competitive assumption is essential here: under less than 'perfectly competitive' conditions, the need for shadow-pricing will return.

7. Willig, 1976, p. 589. This point was first made by John Hause in the mid-1960's (in the *Journal of Political Economy*). Willig references this article, but does not give Hause credit for this central observation.

8. Not only – or even overtly – on the grounds that is is inductive. There are plenty of technical reasons to prefer *EV* or *CV* over *CS*, such as path-dependency problems.

9. Much confusion has resulted from the fact that most authors select one or another version of *CV* and of *EV* for their discussion, without reference to the existence of the alternative pair, and generally without explaining the reasons for their choice. I am grateful to have been able to draw upon the clarifying system proposed by Pankaj Tanden in 'Welfare Measurement – A Comment' (in manuscript).

10. We are so accustomed to the maximisation of utility functions that, even when we question whether the *specification* of any utility function is justified, we often forget to inquire whether the word, '*maximisation*', describes well what human beings do – with regard to utility in general, or, indeed, much else.

    The alternative which is most often considered in economics is Herbert Simon's concept of 'satisficing'. Other sciences of thought and behaviour may yield other alternatives which should be considered for a more realistic paradigm in economics. An example is the concept of 'matching' which comes out of behavioral psychology. (See R. Herrnstein and W. Vaughan, 'Melioration and Behavioral Allocation', in J. Staddon (ed.) *Limits to Action: The Allocation of Individual Behavior*; also R. Herrenstein, 'A First Law for Behavioral Analysis' (in manuscript).

    The decision process which often underlies the composition of a stock portfolio is an excellent example of the 'matching' behaviour that Herrenstein and Vaughan observed in pigeons. Here options with a low probability of reward are selected a small percentage of the time, and high probability options are selected more frequently. This is in contrast to the simple maximising model, which would concentrate exclusively upon the single highest probability option.

11. Similarly, little comfort is to be derived from Hausman's statement that 'In empirical situations where a measure of either the compensating variation, equivalent variation, or deadweight loss is needed, economists often work with relatively simple demand specifications' (p. 673). The fact that such specifications are commonly worked with says nothing about their relation to reality.

The functions which he examines in the paper include a demand function quadratic in prices and one quadratic in both prices and income. Hausman's own most complete formulation for a system of demand equations 'varies across individuals by their socioeconomic characteristics and their income levels', and includes 'A complete specification of a system of demand equations [which] would have the general form

$$x_i = x(p,y,z,e_i); \; i = 1 \ldots . ,N$$

where p is the price vector, z is a vector of socioeconomic characteristics, and e_i is a stochastic disturbance' (p. 670). This looks like a good approach to resolving the aggregation problem, but one wonders whether this is not a rather tall order for empirical work. The salient question, of course, is what is meant by 'socioeconomic levels'.

12. In other words, at best we can hope for a system of equations which would give us the correct answer if we could load it up with the correct information: at that point we would know so much about utilities that we would hardly need the formulas!

13. It could be claimed that, by their own definition – 'To every properly framed question there can be but one correct answer, or none at all' (M and P, 1982, p. 669) – M and P have not properly framed the question, as it fails to specify the circumstances for which a measure is being sought. These authors ignore the difference between those cases where consistency of preference orderings is the most desired criterion of the welfare measure (when *EV* has a distinct superiority over *CV*); versus other circumstances where, for example, instead of using the measure to compare two potential projects, it is sought as a guide to how to compensate losers from a project which will, in any case be undertaken. A question framed to emphasise the later circumstances would find the *CV* measures to be preferable to either form of *EV*.

14. 'The marginal utility of money depends partly on behaviour and partly on intensity of satisfaction. It is not sufficient to *assume* some arbitrary intensity of satisfaction function (say $\mathbf{L} = 1$) as some writers have done. Such an assumption would ordinarily be inconsistent with behavior except for very special cases (for example, homotheticity of utility). What we must have is a general function (index) for the marginal utility of money in terms of observed behavior consistent with some agreed and understood convention regarding the "measure" of satisfaction' (p. 674).

15. Hausman passes over this same point, though in a different way; he indicates that a large part of the loss theoretically compensated in compensating variation is not of much importance because it has 'only' distributional consequences (cf. Hausman, Figure 2 and discussion, p. 673) – as compared to the deadweight burden part 'which cannot be undone'. The assumption that a loss which 'in principle could be compensated for' is less serious than one for which no compensating productivity has been generated elsewhere in the society is a normative imposition with little support in the real world – where such compensations normally, in fact, do not take place.

16. I would add that M and P have not presented convincing evidence that *even precise knowledge of the demand function* can be counted on to yield a precise specification of the utility function. The assertion, at the beginning of the article, that 'Economic welfare has no more than one dimension' (p. 669) does not constitute convincing evidence, any more than Marx's repeated assertions that the common recognition of value in various goods must derive from a single source (which can only be labour) constitutes a proof of the labour theory of value. Proof-by-assertion carries little logical weight in any system, regardless of its ideology.

    Note that the sentence preceding this footnote refers to the inductive method; the one to follow refers to the deductive method, and makes it clear that the latter requires *a priori* knowledge of utility functions.

17. This is a deep problem with all social science that has grown out of the Utilitarian tradition; even John Rawls's *Theory of Justice*, in proposing an alternative to the Utilitarian social value system, essentially accepts that system: for the 'initial position' from which he proposes that we make our value judgments behind a 'veil of ignorance' is still the position of a *single individual*. A more communitarian point of view has yet to be made a major focus of Western moral philosophy; perhaps it is unacceptable within the framework of Western individualism.

18. Following Hausman (p. 669) we could presumably calculate a standard error from one of the formulas for EV – if we are so fortunate as to have, as he says, a covariance matrix for the estimated parameters.

19. 'Appreciably' is the salient word here: in fact, any one price change will theoretically change the overall price level, unless it is offset by something like Friedman's other-price-compensations idea, or by offsetting real income changes, as in the Hicksian compensated demand curve. The latter pushes us back once more, of course, upon the need to define 'real income' according to some value other than prices; while the former can have almost no application in the real world.

20. In concluding his defence of EV^1, Tanden remarks,

    > Whether this constitutes a sufficient argument for the use of EV in cost-benefit analysis, however, continues to depend upon the extent to which we are willing to make inter-personal utility comparisons, a problem to which no adequate answer has yet been furnished in the literature (Tanden, p. 10).

21. We cannot assume that such a modern reader would necessarily understand the problems better than Marshall himself did – since we can never know to what extent he was aware of the difficulties which he apparently ignored.

22. Eugene Silberberg, *The Structure of Economics: A Mathematical Analysis* (McGraw-Hill, New York, 1978) p. 362.

Part IV
Conclusions

18 The Challenge and the Chart

The main endeavour of this book has been to present a constructive third alternative to existing systems of economic theory. Social economics is intended as a companion to, not (in most areas) as a replacement for, Marxian and neoclassical economics. At the same time, such an endeavour must be motivated at least in part by dissatisfaction with the now dominant paradigms. A subtheme of the book has been the issue of why the neoclassical system of economic theory, in particular, is not sufficient to provide all that is required from the field of economics today.

Some of what this author has felt to be the most important deficiencies of the neoclassical system are also fairly subtle ones. They are not, in fact, so difficult to perceive from a distance, but as one approaches closely to the paradigm, the outlines of these problems get blurred by a combination of realistic compromise and unrealistic pretence: a wish for the rigour of science, transformed by the art of the possible. Thus, one goal of Part III was to probe inside the cloud of science and art that neoclassical economics has thrown about itself, and to reveal some details that are not quite what they seem. Whether or not that effort has succeeded, I will now step back from it, to summarise what I see as the major areas where a companion system is needed, to do what is not done by neoclassical economics.

THE NEED FOR AN ALTERNATIVE TO THE NEOCLASSICAL CONSUMPTION ORIENTATION In one sense, it is the greatest strength of the neoclassical paradigm that is its greatest weakness. Explication has been required, however, to disentangle these aspects, because (not surprisingly) practitioners in the neoclassical system have preferred to show their strengths, and have often preferred to distract attention from the accompanying weakness.

The great strength/weakness of neoclassical economics is that *of all the sciences, it is the one which most effectively addresses the question of how to maximise the availability of goods and services for human consumption.*

On the plus side, this is a service of the first importance. If no social science existed with this special ability, most people interested in the broad field of economics would feel it appropriate to drop almost everything else and concentrate upon inventing it.

On the minus side, several points may be made:

- It is *not enough* to show how to maximise consumption. What we are really interested in is something more abstract – I have called it welfare – which depends upon consumption first, as the *sine qua non* for all of its other aspects; but consumption alone does not reach to the other aspects.

- It is also possible to have *too much* consumption (and too much production for consumption). The approach of maximising consumption possibilities must take some responsibility for ills, both ecological and psychological, which threaten the continued health of our species and our interaction with the world in which we live. For all its abjuration of ethics, neoclassical economics expresses an ethos; one which cannot persist throughout the world with the dominance it now has in developed countries, such as the USA, where social and economic behaviour is to a large extent organised and justified by a consumption-oriented economic theory.

- There has been *insufficient acknowledgment* of just what it is that neoclassical economics does, and does not do. Neoclassical economists often talk and write about 'utility', 'welfare', and 'social welfare'; about 'utility functions' and 'social welfare functions'. Exhaustive analysis of what is meant by 'utility' very often reveals that all that is being talked about is, in fact, consumption.[1] The same is true for all of the other terms just listed in quotation marks.

To drive home the last point, as the leading edge of the other two, we might try to imagine: what would a system of economic theory look like (how would it feel to be a practitioner of that system) if a ruthless acknowledgment were made of these realities? If, that is, phrases like 'maximisation of utility' and 'welfare maximisation' were replaced, whenever this is what is actually implied or specified in the model, with 'maximisation of consumption possibilities'? I suggest that such an alteration of terminology would make some very real differences. Among other things, it would engender a far greater awareness, among both users and theorists, that often what is offered by the neoclassical system of theory is not enough; and often it is too much.

It is first of all in those situations – when maximisation of consumption possibilities is not enough, or when it is too much – that an alternative system of economic theory is needed. Yet, unlike the Marxian system, the alternative needs to be one that can make use of the very great strengths of the neoclassical consumption orientation. We need consumption, and we need it, temporally, before anything else; but we need other orientations as well.

AREAS OF   The consumption emphasis of neoclassical econo-
CONTENT AND   mics has taken that system of theory in a particular
APPROACH   direction which, in retrospect, one can understand,
WHICH REQUIRE   but which does not seem to have been the only way
A NEW EMPHASIS it might have gone. It was the combination of the
consumption emphasis with particular methodological requirements which led to a close association between the concept of *efficiency* and the idea of *maximising*. Both of these, in their places, are very useful ideas. In the neoclassical system their place has expanded, I contend, beyond desirable bounds, because they have been pulled to fill up the vacuum created by the effort to do without the concept which I have called *human value*.

Growing out of the long history and tradition of political economy, neoclassical economics maintained the intention of dealing with – and it is received, on level 2, as though it can and does deal with – questions about how humans actually act on the basis of what they perceive as their wants. However, the formal theory (on both level 1 and 3) is limited to consideration of 'effective demand' – what people can and will purchase at prevailing prices – which is a much more limited concept than 'what humans perceive as their wants'.

In Chapter 15 I mentioned the 'as if' behaviour which proceeds as if we believed, with Marshall, that economics can supply a measurement of human value which is adequate for the welfare goals which are pressed on the discipline of economics by the exigencies of the real world. Similarly it was noted that the use of money-evaluations as a proxy for well-being is sometimes the best readily available method; but the pretence that that method is 'scientific' may be misleading.

At present there appear to be built into the most basic structure of neoclassical economics reasons why it can only accommodate certain concepts, certain methodologies, even certain belief structure; others simply do not exist within its framework. Areas which particularly need to be dealt with as parts of an alternative economic theory include:

- conceptions of Man's economic interactions with the total environment, including the interrelations between economic behaviour and the physical world;
- Man in society (the broad field of economics includes some of the most critical points of interaction between the individual and society); and
- Man as both worker and consumer.

Again, when we look beneath these issues we find values. The consumption orientation which I have cited as the point of view of neoclassical economics (a claim which I will attempt to substantiate in *Social Economics*, Volume 2) comes from a particular set of basis values. I have suggested, in this chapter, that the practical and ethical results of this dominant orientation are not entirely benign. It should be added here that the 'consumer's point of view' which one may find in neoclassical economics is the point of view of a manipulated consumer; *homo oeconomicus* is not some 'Natural Man', but is rather a creature who has been created to serve the profit-maximising goals of producers in the capitalist mode. (To put it another way, one might say that the neoclassical position orients to the point of view, not of *the consumer*, but of *consumption*.)

Similarly, the point of view of Marxian economics is also that of an artificial individual: a worker who is constrained to the values which Marx saw as those of the proletariat; anti-rural, anti-traditional, anti-feminist, anti-capitalist, but (like the neoclassical economic Man) a rational maximiser (though of class, not of individual, interest).

The emphasis upon values which has run through this book is intended to lead us to a rethinking of what are our true 'interests'. The ecological, futures oriented approaches that were cited in Part I provide some answers to that question; others answers will have to wait for further work. In the mean time, the alternative proposed in this book has suggested that the inputs to social economics should also include:

- human values, those of both the subjects of the analysis and the analyst (these are now, as they must be, an input to existing systems of economic theory, but their role is not overt);
- material from the other social sciences; and
- a recognition in social science analysis of intuition, judgment, and the full store of personal knowledge.

In Chapter 8 we asked whether these matters could be scientifically incorporated into a science of economics; and concluded that they probably could not, in the way that economics so far has chosen to define science. It was then stated that a major task for social economics will be to find a way to incorporate intuition, judgment and personal knowledge, along with human values, into a theoretic framework that is, to a sufficient extent, judgeable, teachable and applicable.

SCIENTIFIC STANDARDS FOR THE SOCIAL SCIENCES   The positivistic orientation of modern social science at its best is constructive: it says that we should distinguish between fact and speculation, between observation and wish, between our own values and those of other people. 'Distinguish between', I contend, does not necessarily mean throwing out one member of each pair. Neoclassicists often carry the positivist position too far, or distort it, to suggest that: knowledge implies certainty; only tangible facts can be known with certainty; if you don't know something with certainty, then you had better ignore it.[2]

Delving still deeper into the foundations of our ways of thinking, I have suggested that, as opposed to the narrow, perhaps distorted (from its best potential) version of positivism which has coloured much of neoclassical economic debate for the last half century, the philosophical position of *realism* is the most useful and appropriate one on which to build social economics. I have described (in Chapter 10) a version, 'safe realism', which I contrasted to the unwary-mole approach of those mainstream economists who depend heavily upon 'long chains of deductive reasoning', too seldom coming out of their tunnels of logic to see how their progress relates to the real world. This position is intended to be hospitable to speculation, while still distinguishing (more carefully than does positivism) among various levels of speculation and of 'fact'. Moreover, I hope that my emphasis upon *values* will also lead to a more realistic way of incorporating the best ideals of positivism; for when a large part of the range of human value has been interdicted from our formal conversation, it is more apt to go underground and appear in a more dangerous, because unrecognised, form.

I suggested, in Chapter 2, several ways in which normative, value-laden issues could be dealt with in a positive fashion. A summary statement of these would point to a positive recognition of a normative potential for economic analysis not only to respond to the known wishes of the people of today, or to the anticipated wishes of the people of the future, but for it to recognise that economic acts will change the

very wishes the response to which has been the economist's claim to
avoiding normative issues; accepting, that is, that an important source
of satisfaction is the exploration of new goals, recognition of which is
inconsistent with the assumption of all goals as given. Thus,
preferences themselves cannot finally be kept exogenous to models
intended as bases for economic action.

SOCIAL   The positivistic neoclassical economist has attempted
ECONOMICS IN   to deny the endogeneity of values by dealing with
RELATION TO   human wishes as they are reified in *revealed*
ECONOMIC   *preferences* (the idea that values are revealed in
SYSTEMS   expenditure patterns). An interesting point occurs
                      here: revealed preferences obviously have more
meaning (in the sense of coming closer to being identified with human
values) where markets more closely approximate the neoclassical ideal
of the 'perfectly free market', characterised by 'perfect competition'. In
the conditions of shortages and queues which are so often – perhaps
inevitably – associated with centrally planned economies, values may
be better revealed by asking people what they wish they could
purchase, rather than by observing what it is that they actually do
purchase.

This comparison, however, forces us to ask some searching questions
about what it is that is actually revealed in the expenditure patterns of,
say, the shopper in a US market, confused by the multiplicity of items
on the shelves, distracted by remembered snippets of (emotive, not
informative) advertisements, and manipulated by the store's own
profit-oriented decisions on what to 'push'.[3] Or what is revealed by the
patterns of automobile purchases? If you read, in the business-oriented
publications, the congratulatory articles about promotion campaigns,
you will not come away thinking that the unmanipulated values, let
alone the needs, of the consumers played much part in the 'preferences'
thus revealed.

In the next volume of *Social Economics* I will hope to investigate
further the question of how important and how meaningful such
behaviour is; perhaps, in any case, we should (if we care about values)
be focusing more on the larger allocational issues, e.g., of decisions
between food versus transportation versus recreation.

As soon as we ask ourselves, 'What are the important questions?'
('What matters?'), we may find ourselves (especially if we are
economists) wondering to what extent our questions are motivated

by a desire to respond to the needs of producers; their most overtly felt, and expressed, need being always to increase sales. What if, instead, it was consumers who came to us for advice, on how to be more effective consumers – what if it turned out that what they meant to ask was, *How can we increase our welfare without increasing our consumption*? In the context of contemporary Western (and, increasingly, global) capitalism, that very idea is heresy. We are committed to a cycle of increased production, to increase jobs, to increase purchasing power, to increase consumption, to increase production . . . . Yet there are strong reasons to believe that, if we do not embrace such a heresy, we may destroy the basis upon which we hope to sustain future standards of consumption, of well-being, and of civilisation.

This brings us back to the suggestion that was made in Chapter 4: that while we need an alternative system of theory because the two now in existence do not adequately reflect the realities of the two kinds of economic systems (capitalism and socialism) with which they are associated – we need it even more to help us understand, perhaps even to help us to plan, other economic systems which are required as alternatives to those now dominant.

Some of the elements of the needed alternatives in *economic systems* were hinted at in the discussion (during Chapters 2 to 4) of what is needed in a new system of *economic theory*. As this is written, much of Europe, in particular, is living with a level of intellectual/political questioning new to most people.

– Great issues are being reopened on the proper and desirable role of government.
– Efforts are being made to find some new balance between market and command systems which, before, had been assumed to be mutually antithetical – incapable of being balanced together.
– There is a reawakened awareness of the need to find checks and balances for the growth of bureaucracies, even while recognising and enhancing their necessary, constructive role.

Much of this is more evidently political than economic, but the thread that runs through it all (in Western as well as in Eastern Europe) is the desire to find ways of freeing markets to operate efficiently, while still fine tuning them

– to allocate costs with their associated benefits
– to balance social versus private costs and benefits;

- to incorporate into current accounting the costs and benefits that will be faced in the future
- to take into account the welfare effects of taste-creation by economic actors
- to enhance the positive values of work
- to recognise and respond to who is hurt, and who helped, in various forms of modernisation and change; and
- to minimise damage to the politically and economically powerless.

This focus upon efficient and responsive markets accompanies the recognition of a need

- to reconsider our definitions of welfare, and with them, our societal goals; and
- to pursue equity for its own sake, as well as in the service of efficiency.

This social agenda is the background for the theoretical agenda of social economics. Many of the items listed here have only been summarily touched on in this book; indeed, each of these items (and many more) deserves sustained attention on its own which should, and I hope, ultimately will, result in social economics books being written (by a variety of authors) on each individual topic.

THE　　　　　The applied, policy orientation of social economics
CONSEQUENCES　will, as just suggested, regard as relatively uninter-
OF AN APPLIED,　esting theoretical approaches to 'welfare maximisa-
POLICY　　　　tion' which have no possibility of practical
ORIENTATION　application. A discussion, in Chapter 13, of general
　　　　　　　　equilibrium analysis produced the overall conclusion
that we do not have, and are not likely to achieve, the initial distribution which will produce, via a perfect market, the optimal solution perceivable from our present state of the world. We also do not have, and are not likely to achieve, a perfect market. Therefore there is no reason to believe that the first best solution of general equilibrium analysis, to be reached via unrestricted competition, is a solution of sufficient relevance for the real world to be the basis for a useful welfare economics.

This line of thinking motivated a search for some way of levering ourselves out of the patterns of neoclassical analysis which are so deeply rooted in assumptions of equilibrium. It was proposed that the empiricist conclusions of Chapter 11, buttressed with the tools of discourse analysis of the rest of Part II, could be used to give ourselves a fresh start. They should assist us in moving towards the ability to see the world neither as equilibrium nor as disequilibrium states – not as states at all, but as processes. The idea of an equilibrium state (or, for that matter, of a disequilibrium 'state') would then appear only as a limit case, to be employed with great caution in our thinking, as being, in many contexts, discontinuous from reality.

The other tool of neoclassical analysis which was discussed as especially destructive of efforts to create a more applicable, useful, system of economic theory was 'the simplifying assumption of a static world'. A system of theory which does not employ this exceedingly convenient way of escaping the problems of accounting for complexity, change and time will have to begin much of its theorising almost from scratch, eschewing, to begin with, any technique that seems to require static assumptions, and asking how we may apprehend a world of time and change. Words, I have proposed, do this reasonably well – not perfectly, but they at least do not *deny* time and change. The careful uses of words described in the first five chapters of Part II constitute the core of the techniques which I would propose for social economics.

Another critical companion to the applied, policy approach of social economics is an emphasis upon a variety of ways of *accounting* for the things that are of importance to us. New accounting systems will need to be worked out, while more sensitivity will be needed to the ways in which different existing systems can be employed. We need to be able to adjust our standards overtly, instead of covertly, to reality: thus, for example, we need to be prepared to speak of e.g. 'welfare change approximations' instead of 'welfare change measurements'. Evaluation has to come to a more central place in our thinking, in place of measurement, which must be less frequently assumed to be meaningful.

A further idea which has been particularly emphasised here (though implementation is far from being worked out) is the need to discover how far it is possible to go in 'internalising the externalities' – to insert into the cost and profit accounting of individual or institutional actors the costs and benefits to society or to other individuals which result from their actions. This contrasts with the neoclassical approach, the latter emphasising the idea of 'compensating the losers', thus tending (in theory) towards allocating *benefits* to the actors who have borne the *costs*. Sometimes this neoclassical approach will be the more practical way to go; but in general it seems less likely actually to happen, and carries with it more problems of moral hazard, than the social economics suggestion just put forth.

In describing the applied, policy orientation of social economics, it may be helpful to relate some of the background of how I came to Marshall as the economist on whom I would most depend for the synthesis and construction of a new system of economic theory. The confluence of the subjects of this book began at a time when I had been focusing upon the subdisciplines of development and labour economics. These two, above all, are the regions where the limitations of the neoclassical paradigm most make themselves felt. Here change, cultural evolution and the complexities of human behaviour seem to make a mockery of laws and regularities. The very purpose of economic development is to escape *ceteris paribus*; while many of the motives and concerns which have to be accounted for in the study of the human activities called 'work' or 'labour' often seem to lie outside the boundaries of the neoclassical point of view. It cannot be said that Marshall directly contributed very much to what we know today as development economics *per se*;[4] however the topics of *progressive change and human well-being*, which are at the heart of the subject of development, are often more directly addressed in Marshall's economics than they are in today's formal development economics, which tries to fit them into the modern neoclassical welfare framework.

Mark Blaug has commented that

Economics began as *An Inquiry into the Causes of the Wealth of Nations* and yet 200 years later we have virtually abandoned that inquiry as unproductive and have taught ourselves to be content with smaller questions. Worse than that, static equilibrium analysis has furnished us with standards of rigor that cannot be met by the analysis of dynamic problems of entrepreneurship and the competitive process, so that discussion of these questions is met with scorn almost as soon as it is started.'[5]

I continue to find that, among streams of thought in modern economics, the areas of labour and, above all, of development, are the ones where the work is being done that is most likely to feed into social economics. As was suggested in the section on Development and Change (in Chapter 3), by viewing the economic realities of today in the context of the history of the Industrial Revolution we may stand the best chance of understanding the forceful economic processes in which (willy-nilly, whether with delight or with horror) we find ourselves swept up.

If we look to development economics for the greatest array of efforts to understand economic realities in this context, this area, which has had a marginal position in the neoclassical paradigm, should move into the centre of social economics. However, if it is to develop more successfully in the future than it has done to date, it will have to shake off the limitations imposed, as Blaug remarks, by the anti-dynamic 'standards of rigour' of neoclassical economics.

THE NEED FOR NEW WAYS TO BUILD METHODS AND TECHNIQUES, NEW FOUNDATIONS TO BUILD THEM ON, AND NEW GOALS TO BUILD THEM TOWARD The conclusion which comes from a scrutiny of the roles, in economic analysis, of measurement and evaluation, statics and dynamics, equilibrium and disequilibrium, is that all of our tools will need to be reexamined, to see which of them can accommodate to a more accurate representation of reality, and which ones pull us back towards the assumption of static equilibrium.

With regard to the techniques of social economics, the broadest proposal made in this book has been that, in putting somewhat less emphasis upon the formal techniques (such as mathematical modelling) which are so characteristic of neoclassical economics, social economics will be putting relatively more weight upon less formal characteristics of the practitioners, themselves, of this system. The radical suggestions were made that we could often do better work with *less*, rather than *more* mathematically sophisticated techniques: that in order to press forward the frontiers of knowledge, it is advisable, most of the time, to operate well inside of the frontier of known techniques.

A specific suggestion was also made regarding the approach of *axiomatisation*: this is a tidy and appealing procedure which, however, is rarely actually employed in social science, and should not be appealed to as the norm. Social economics would emphasise a use of judgment and of personal experience wherein axiomatisation would be understood to be only one of many ways of employing human powers of reasoning to advance a social science.

These proposals may be felt to point to a severe loss in rigour. To assuage such a feeling we are reminded that the ideal of developing models, theories and systems of theory as if they contained no beliefs other than the formally stated assumptions, or as if (as was said in Chapter 6) the theorist was programming a computer – this is *only* an ideal. It is not the way social scientists in actuality proceed. To abandon this ideal is to drop a pretence, not to reduce the rigour of actual procedure.

Chapter 17 provided us with a plethora of examples for the ways in which, along with various more or less sophisticated techniques, even the most technical subjects in even the most neoclassical analysis constantly call forth appeals to convention, common sense, and the recognition that, when asked to measure the unmeasurable, we simply do the best we can, falling back upon evaluation when quantification fails.

I have proposed social economics as a system of theory that would be constructed with different standards and types of rigour, emphasising verbal logic, 'deep intellectual honesty' (see Chapter 2) and a sophisticated understanding of 'communication'. The undergirding for the methodological approach of social economics needs to be a combination of self-knowledge with the ability to admit what we do not know. The social economist must also take some responsibility for understanding the nuances of human welfare that cannot be built into an algorithm.

The concept of *responsibility* is one which has not previously been given much weight in the field of economics.[6] In Chapter 2 I suggested that the social economist should assume responsibility in the following areas:

- The social economist should think about the goals of the field: what should these goals be? How should they relate to the individual economist's personal value system?
- The social economist should be prepared, whenever attempting to answer a question in a real-world situation, to take responsibility for examining that question. At the very least, the social economist should probe what it is that the questioner really wants to know: is the question, as posed, adequate to reach for the desired knowledge, or should it be reformulated?
- The social economist should be able and willing to access other information and skills than his or her own. Very often, the questions asked of economists go beyond the wisdom or knowledge of any single person. Knowing whom else to ask or to call in is often as valued as (and may be more valuable than) giving a partial answer.
- The social economist should take responsibility for knowing and understanding what, methodologically, s/he is doing when s/he 'does' economics.

The other *quality of the practitioner* that I have stressed, along with responsibility, has been the characteristic of 'judgment'. This quality takes on special relevance in the social sciences where 'meaning' is very different from 'fact', 'description' is somewhere in between the two, and 'understanding' is impossible without all three. One reason for the emphasis upon judgment, and also upon 'deep intellectual honesty', has been the hope of promoting a greater level of awareness and understanding than is now common in the social sciences, with regard to meaning, and to different levels of meanings.

The process of making such awareness and understanding widespread may look reductionist, because it will call into question many claims that are now considered necessary for upholding the rigorous scientific standards to which we think we adhere. Those standards in fact not infrequently disguise a confusion between fact and meaning, knowledge and belief, proof and persuasion.

THE TEACHING OF SOCIAL ECONOMICS Though recommending *different* standards of 'rigour' (that term has acquired, especially in economics, such specific connotations that perhaps it will be better to find a new one), I am hopeful that, given the quantity of material now being written in all the social sciences, it is not only possible but necessary to impose higher standards than ever before for what shall be culled out as the 'best' work. Those standards can and should include a requirement for writing to be as clear and direct as possible, so as to reduce the possibilities for misunderstanding and misuse. The natural ability to express oneself lucidly has always been valued. To this can be added a learned ability to recognise different levels of meaning in what one is writing, as well as in what one reads and hears, so as to avoid sending out unintended messages. Here what is being proposed has to do with how the discipline is taught as well as with its content.

A new kind of economics will require new approaches to the education both of those who go on to practice it in the real world and those who go on to develop and teach it. Developed with an openly empiricist, applied orientation, social economics will need to remain open to feedback from its users. A major goal for social economics is to create a framework within which the best applied work can find a home – a framework for generalisation about the useful real-world activities of economists – so that it will be possible to teach that kind of economics to those who wish to learn it.

Unfortunately, the training now given to many economists tends to have the effect of making them deaf to the voice of common sense, so that they learn, when operating as economists, not to attend to dissonances between the everyday assumptions upon which they otherwise operate and the assumptions which they encounter in the field. It is precisely because it is, in fact, to judgment, intuition and life-experience that applied economists now turn, that efforts should be made to enhance these things – rather than downgrading them – in the education of economists who will apply their skills and knowledge to real world problems.

WHAT HAS BEEN ACCOMPLISHED IN THIS BOOK The foregoing suggests, in broadest outline, the challenge faced by social economics. This book has not covered in detail as much as might be wished of the area that has been charted here. The methodological suggestions of Part II are proposals on how to move beyond the limits of the territory now defined as 'economics', in the direction of a more realistic, more empirical, and (it is to be hoped, for a significant range of purposes) a more useful additional system of economic theory. Those methodological suggestions may help us to get where we wish to go; they do not, unfortunately, create the place to which we are going. This book has laid out reasons to believe that there is a need for social economics; it has given a number of ideas of what we are looking for in such a system of theory, and it has proposed ways for developing it; but it has not created the finished product, social economics. Nevertheless, this concluding section will summarise what may be claimed for *Social Economics*, Volume 1.

The major accomplishment has been a mapping of the terrain. This has been done in positive space, with a delineation of the concerns of the broadly defined field of economics; in negative space, in terms of what, within that broad field, is poorly illuminated by the neoclassical and the Marxian lamps; and then again in positive space, as Chapters 2, 3 and 4, in particular, drew the outlines of the territory to be claimed by social economics.

It was stated from the outset that, in this preliminary work, those outlines could only be very rough and simple. They are suggestive of where attention needs to be paid; as further work is done they will doubtless require revision as well as filling in. But they provide a starting definition.

The map of Part I might (if we are to explore this metaphor to the fullest) be visualised as a chart outlining the *content* – the subject-matter – to be claimed by social economics; on top of this has also been laid a transparency, covering a wider area, and sketching the contours of *the goals, the methods and the approach* of this system of theory. The chart is of social economics as a part of *the field of economics*; the transparency depicts this system of theory as, more generally, a part of *the social sciences.*

Looking at the rest of the book, what has been accomplished has been to start filling in the details in a few places of this two-layered map.

The chart itself, as just mentioned, was outlined, not in complete detail, but fairly comprehensively, in Part I.

Part II concentrated almost exclusively upon the transparency: it filled in some of the areas described in Chapter 2 under III (Tools and Methods) B (Judgment), and also under III A (The Use of Assumptions).

Part III was devoted to the space on the chart that came under IIC: Values as Part of the Subject Matter of the Field. Here, too, it was important to make some studies in negative space, for if there are to be social economists who deal with 'human value' in the ways that have been proposed in this book, they will not be able simultaneously to use the term in the usually less well-defined but sometimes more specific way that it is employed in neoclassical economics. This is a place where there could be a fight over territory – but it may be amicably resolved if all economists can agree to use the term 'price' when they mean price, and reserve 'value' for something broader. The significance of this apparently small semantic concession should not be underestimated; neoclassical economists would thereby be relinquishing some territory which they have, at least tacitly, claimed for theirs.

THE The first and largest debt of social economics is to the
BACKGROUND neoclassical school, against which it is often reacting,
FOR SOCIAL but upon which, even more often, it builds. In
ECONOMICS particular it has been useful, throughout this initiatory volume, to refer to the early stages of development of neoclassical economics, in the hands of Alfred Marshall. He summarised much of the best of the classical economics tradition, and grappled with many of the great questions and the most important purposes which are at the heart of the endeavour to understand human economic systems.

Other inputs to social economics are to be found in institutionalism and in the 'humanistic' alternatives that have more recently been offered. More directly, the impetus for social economics has come from the need for policy economics which is most felt in the branch of the field dealing with economic development. That branch is the conduit through which ecological concepts have often been introduced, in the form of proposals for 'sustainable development'. The insights and the values of the field of human ecology are a major source of material, new to economics, which has cried out for incorporation into ways of thinking about economic issues.

Additional insights and values also have come to social economics from modern thinking about groups that have been in a second-class or subordinate position within their societies; theories of minority groups in general: theories of class domination and subordination; recent work on 'traditional' cultures, knowledge-bases and values; feminist thinking; and some ideas on the partially conflictual relationship, even within single individuals, between modern Man as producer and as consumer.

I suppose it may at some time seem appropriate to write a revisionist history which will point out various individuals who have been doing social economics all along, even if (like *le bourgeois gentilhomme*, being told he had been speaking prose all his life) they didn't know it. (Reality being usually more complex than we wish, and always more complex than we can describe, it is more likely that those who are so nominated will, in fact, have been doing something like social economics only *some*, not *all*, of the time.) One such is Sir John Hicks, whom I would like to quote for a final comment on the project that has been undertaken in the initiation of social economics:

> Our theories, regarded as tools of analysis, are blinkers . . . . Or it may be politer to say that they are rays of light, which illuminate a part of the target, leaving the rest in darkness. As we use them, we avert our eyes from things which may be relevant, in order that we should see more clearly what we do see. It is entirely proper that we should do this, since otherwise we should see very little. But it is obvious that a theory which is to perform this function satisfactorily must be well chosen; otherwise it will illumine the wrong things. Further, since it is a changing world that we are studying, a theory which illumines the right things at one time may illumine the wrong things at another. This may happen because of changes in the world (the things neglected may have gained in importance relatively to the things considered) or because of changes in ourselves (the things in which we are interested may have changed). There is, there can be, no economic theory which will do for us everything we want all the time (Hicks, 1981, pp. 232–3).

In this book, social economics has been built upon the work of thinkers from many disciplines, but most of all from a myriad economists, most of them operating somewhere in the tradition of Alfred Marshall, whether they have called themselves neoclassical, or institutionalist, or something else. It is to be hoped that more and better work in the development of social economics lies ahead, and that it will receive assistance from many people with knowledge in many fields.

Notes

1. An uneasy exception is in labour economics, where the worker's utility has to be dealt with. Too often, however, this is modeled as composed primarily of the results of earnings, defined as the ability to 'consume' leisure and to pay for goods and services to be consumed during leisure. There is some acknowledgment of negative utility gained from dirty, dangerous or distasteful jobs; the opposite – jobs which have something desirable in them (e.g., which may make a person willing to accept a lower wage to play in a symphony orchestra rather than be a garbage collector) – fits into the neoclassical paradigm as 'consumption on the job'.
2. Examples of this sort of positivism in other fields include the extreme assumptions sometimes made by positivist psychology that only actions, not emotions, are 'real' because only the former can be directly observed; or, in ethology, the attitude that prevailed for so long: that, since we have no proof for 'consciousness' in animals, we should assume *that it does not exist*. The alternative (of assuming that we don't know whether or not it exists – both answers are possible) was, for a long time, unacceptable. (See Donald Griffen, *The Question of Animal Awareness* (Rockefeller University Press, New York, 1976).)
3. The decision of many department stores to put cosmetics and perfumes in the most prominent location (by the entrance, on the ground floor) does not reflect anything about consumer preferences; it reflects the fact that these are the items which can be sold with the largest mark-up – hence which are most profitable to the retailer.
4. The most direct comments which can be gleaned from *The Principles of Economics* on anything that could be called development economics are in IV, xiii. Marshall's other major works, *Industry and Trade* and *Money, Credit and Commerce*, contain a few additional references to topics currently included in development economics; however, nowhere does he deal with the subject as a field, or sub-field, in itself.
5. Mark Blaug, *Economic History and the History of Economics* (New York University Press, 1985) p. xviii.
6. The social science field wherein it seems to have been most emphasised has been anthropology, where debate has never really been stilled over whether the profession's responsibility to the subjects of his/her observation was, passively, to leave them undisturbed; actively to

prevent their disturbance by other outside influences (e.g., modernism); or actively to help them to adapt, as constructively as possible, to outside influences.

Bibliography

Abbreviations

AMCA: see Wood (ed.), *Alfred Marshall, Critical Assessments*.
Memorials: see Pigou (ed.), *Memorials of Alfred Marshall*.
Principles: see Marshall, *Principles of Economics*, 8th edn.
Var. I and *Var.* II: see volumes I and II of Marshall, *Principles of Economics*, 9th (Variorum) edn.

YUSUF AHMEN, SALAH EL SERAFY and ERNST LUTZ (eds), *Environmental Accounting for Sustainable Development* (World Bank, Washington, DC, 1989).

R. F. G. ALFORD, 'Marshall's Demand Curve', *Economica*, NS 23 (February 1956) (in AMCA).

KENNETH J. ARROW, 'An Extension of the Basic Theorems of Classical Welfare Economics', in J. Neyman (ed.), *Proceedings of the Second Berkeley Symposium on Mathematical Statistics and Probability* (University of California Press, Berkeley, 1951).

KENNETH J. ARROW, 'The Organization of Economic Activity: Issues Pertinent to the Choice of Market Versus Nonmarket Allocation', in the *91st Congress, 1st Session, Joint Committee Report*, 'The Analysis and Evaluation of Public Expenditures: the PPB System', A Compendium of Papers Submitted to the Subcommittee on Economy in Government (US Government Printing Office, Washington, DC, 1969).

M. J. BAILEY, 'The Marshallian Demand Curve', *Journal of Political Economy*, 62 (January 1954) (in AMCA).

EDWARD B. BARBIER, *Economics, Natural-Resource Scarcity and Development: Conventional and Alternative Views* (Earthscan, London, 1989).

SANDRA S. BATIE, 'Agriculture as the Problem: New Agendas and New Opportunities', *Southern Journal of Agricultural Economics* (July 1988).

SANDRA S. BATIE, 'Sustainable Development: Challenges to the Profession of Agricultural Economics', Presidential Address, AAEA Summer Meeting (Baton Rouge, LA, 1989).

GARY S. BECKER, *The Economic Approach to Human Behaviour* (Chicago University Press, Chicago, 1976).

DANIEL BELL, *The Cultural Contradictions of Capitalism* (Basic Books, New York, 1976).

DANIEL BELL and IRVING KRISTOL (eds), *The Crisis in Economic Theory* (Basic Books, New York, 1981).

ROBERT BISHOP, *Lectures on Microeconomics*, in mimeo (MIT, 1960).

MARK BLAUG, *Economic History and the History of Economics* (New York University Press, 1985).

MARK BLAUG, *Economic Theory in Retrospect*, 4th edn (Cambridge University Press, 1985; first printed 1962).

403

LAWRENCE BOLAND, 'A Critique of Friedman's Critics', *Journal of Economic Literature*, 17, pp. 503-22.

HELEN BOSANQUET, *The Strength of the People* (first pub. 1902, repr. 1980, Garland, New York).

KENNETH BOULDING, 'Economics as a Moral Science', *American Economic Review*, 59(1) (1969).

BRUCE CALDWELL, 'A Critique of Friedman's Methodological Instrumentalism', *Southern Economic Journal*, 47 (1980), pp. 366–74.

NAPOLEON A. CHAGNON and WILLIAM IRONS, (eds), *Evolutionary Biology and Human Social Behavior* (Duxbury Press, North Scituate, Mass. 1979).

JOHN MAURICE CLARK, *Preface to Social Economics* (Farrar & Rinehart, New York, 1936).

ROBERT COOTER and PETER RAPPAPORT, 'Were the Ordinalists Wrong about Welfare Economics?', *Journal of Economic Literature*, 22 (June 1984).

CUTLER J. CLEVELAND, 'Biophysical Economics: Historical Perspective and Current Research Trends', in *Ecological Modelling*, 38 (1987) pp. 47–73 (Elsevier, Amsterdam).

CUTLER J. CLEVELAND, ROBERT COSTANZA, CHARLES A. S. HALL and ROBERT KAUFMANN, 'Energy and the U.S. Economy: A Biophysical Perspective', in *Science*, 225, 31 August 1984, pp. 890–7.

HERMAN DALY, 'The Economic Growth Debate: What Some Economists Have Learned But Many Have Not', *Journal of Environmental Economics and Management*, 14 (1987).

HERMAN DALY and JOHN COBB, *For the Common Good: Redirecting the Economy toward Community, the Environment, and a Sustainable Future* (Beacon Press, Boston, MA, 1990).

PHILIP J. DAVIS and REUBEN HERSH, *The Mathematical Experience* (Birkhäuser, Boston, 1981).

RICHARD DAWKINS, *The Selfish Gene* (Oxford University Press, 1976).

PETER B. DOERINGER, 'Internal Labor Markets and Noncompeting Groups', *American Economic Review* (May 1986).

PETER B. DOERINGER and MICHEAL J. PIORE, *Internal Labor Markets and Manpower Analysis* (D. C. Heath, Lexington, Mass., 1971).

RONALD DORE, 'Goodwill and the Spirit of Market Capitalism', *British Journal of Sociology*, 34 (1983).

UDO EBERT, 'Exact Welfare Measures and Economic Index Numbers', *Zeitschrift fur Nationalokonomie*, 44, (1) (1984).

PAUL EKINS (ed.), *The Living Economy* (Routledge & Kegan Paul, London, 1986).

RICHARD ESTES, *The Social Progress of Nations* (Praeger, New York, 1984).

AMITAI ETZIONI, *The Moral Dimension: Towards a New Economics* (The Free Press; Macmillan, New York, 1988).

R. FLOOD and M. LOCKWOOD, (eds), *The Nature of Time* (Basil Blackwell, London, 1986).

L. E. FOURAKER, 'Marshall's Two Concepts of Consumer Demand', *Indian Journal of Economics*, 37 (April 1957) (in AMCA).

WILLIAM FRAZER JR and LAWRENCE BOLAND, 'An Essay on the Foundations of Friedman's Methodology', *American Economic Review*, 73 (1983), pp. 129–44.

MILTON FRIEDMAN, 'The Marshallian Demand Curve', *The Journal of Political Economy*, LVII (December 1949) (in AMCA).

MILTON FRIEDMAN, 'A Reply' to J. M. Bailey's 'The Marshallian Demand Curve', *Journal of Political Economy*, 62 (January 1954) (in AMCA).

MILTON FRIEDMAN, *Essays on Positive Economics* (University of Chicago Press, 1953).

RALPH GENTILE and HARVEY LEIBENSTEIN, 'Microeconomics, X-Efficiency Theory and Policy: Cleaning the Lens', *Man, Environment, Space and Time*, 1 (1) (Autumn 1979).

NICHOLAS GEORGESCU-ROEGEN, 'Revisiting Marshall's Constancy of Marginal Utility of Money', *Southern Economic Journal*, 35 (October 1968) (in AMCA).

BRUCE GLASSBURNER, 'Alfred Marshall on Economic History and Historical Development', *Quarterly Journal of Economics* (November 1955).

NEVA GOODWIN, *Back to the Fork: What We Have Derived from Marshallian Economics, and What We Might Have Derived*, unpublished doctoral dissertation, Boston University (1988) (no. 8724711, University Microfilms International Dissertation Information Service, Ann Arbor, Mich.).

NEVA GOODWIN (ed) *Global Commons: Site of Danger, Source of Hope* (a special issue of *World Development*, Forthcoming, 1991).

NEVA GOODWIN and BRUCE MAZLISH, 'The Wealth of Adam Smith', *Harvard Business Review* (July–August 1963).

DONALD GRIFFIN, *The Question of Animal Awareness*, 1st. edn. (Rockefeller University Press, New York, 1976).

WILLIAM B. GRIFFITH and ROBERT S. GOLDFARB, 'Amending the Economist's "Rational Egoist" Model to Include Norms', in manuscript (George Washington University, 1989).

ARNOLD C. HARBERGER, 'Three Basic Postulates for Applied Welfare Economics', *Journal of Economic Literature* (September 1971) pp. 784–97.

JOHN C. HAUSE and GUNNAR DU RIETZ, 'Entry, Industry Growth, and the Microdynamics of Industry Supply', *Journal of Political Economy*, 92 (August 1984) pp. 733–57.

JERRY HAUSMAN, 'Exact Consumer's Surplus and Deadweight Loss', *American Economic Review* (September 1981).

RICHARD HERRNSTEIN, 'A First Law for Behavioral Analysis', in manuscript (1980).

R. HERRNSTEIN and W. VAUGHAN, 'Melioration and Behavioral Allocation' in J. Staddon (ed.), *Limits to Action: The Allocation of Individual Behavior* (Academic Press, New York, 1980).

JOHN HICKS, *Value and Capital: an inquiry into some fundamental principles of economic theory*, 2nd edn (Oxford University Press, 1946).

JOHN HICKS, *Wealth and Welfare: Collected Essays on Economic Theory: vol. 1* (Harvard University Press, Cambridge, Mass., 1981).

G. HIGGINS and H. H. LIEBHAFSKY, 'Pareto and the Marshallian Constancy Assumption', *The Southern Economic Journal*, 35 (October 1968) (in AMCA).

ABRAHAM HIRSCH and NEIL DE MARCHI, 'Making a Case when Theory is Unfalsifiable: Friedman's Monetary History', *Economics and Philosophy*, 2 (1986), pp. 1–22.

ALBERT O. HIRSCHMAN, 'Against Parsimony: Three Easy Ways of Complicating Some Categories of Economic Discourse' *American Economic Review*, 74 (1984).

ROEFIE HUETING, *New Scarcity and Economic Growth: More Welfare Through Less Production?* tr. Trevor Preston (North-Holland Publishing Company, Amsterdam, 1980).

T. W. HUTCHISON, *A Review of Economic Doctrines 1870–1924* (Clarendon Press, Oxford University Press, 1953).

D. KAHNEMAN, P. SLOVIK, and A. TVERSKY, *Judgment under Uncertainty: Heuristics and Biases* (Cambridge University Press, 1982).

ANDREW M. KAMARK, *Economics In the Real World* (University of Philadelphia Press, PA, 1983).

J. M. KEYNES, *Essays in Persuasion* (Norton, New York, 1963).

ARJO KLAMER, *Conversations with Economists* (Rowman and Allanheld, Totowa, N.J., 1984).

JÁNOS KORNAI, *Anti-Equilibrium* (North-Holland, Amsterdam, 1971).

THOMAS KUHN, *The Structure of Scientific Revolutions*, 2nd edn (University of Chicago Press, 1970).

T. R. LAKSHMANAN, 'Knowledge Technologies and the Evolution of the Economic Landscape', paper presented at the International Workshop on Technical Change at the Center for Energy and Environmental Studies, Boston University (11–12 October 1988).

WASSILY LEONTIEF, *Essays in Economics* (first pub. 1966, Transaction Books, New Brunswick, 1985).

HARVEY LEIBENSTEIN, *Beyond Economic Man* (Harvard University Press, Cambridge, Mass., 1976).

HARVEY LEIBENSTEIN, 'A Branch of Economics is Missing: Micro–Micro Theory', *Journal of Economic Literature* (June 1979).

CHARLES E. LINDBLOM, *Politics and Markets* (Basic Books, New York, 1977).

R. DUNCAN LUCE and HOWARD RAIFFA, *Games and Decisions* (Wiley, New York, 1957).

ERNST LUTZ and SALAH EL SERAFY, *Environmental and Resource Accounting: An Overview*, World Bank Policy Planning and Research Staff, Environmental Department Working Paper 6 (June 1988).

M. LUTZ and K. L. LUX, *The Challenge of Humanistic Economics* (Benjamin Cummings, Menlo Park, Calif., 1979).

ALASDAIR MacINTYRE, 'Utilitarianism and Cost-Benefit Analysis, An Essay on the Relevance of Moral Philosophy to Bureaucratic Theory', in Kenneth Sayre (ed.), *Values in the Electric Power Industry* (University of Notre Dame Press, Indiana, 1977).

J. L. MACKIE, 'Newcomb's Paradox and the Direction of Causation', *Canadian Journal of Philosophy*, 7 (1977).

USKALI MÄKI, 'Friedman and Realism', in *Research in the History of Economic Thought and Methodology*, 8 (1990).

USKALI MÄKI, 'How to Combine Rhetoric and Realism', *Economics and Philosophy*, 4 (1988).

USKALI MÄKI, 'On the Problem of Realism in Economics', *Ricerche Economiche* (special issue on 'Epistemology and Economic Theory') (March 1989).

USKALI MÄKI, 'Rhetoric at the Expense of Coherence: A Reinterpretation of Milton Friedman's Methodology', in *Research in the History of Economic Thought and Methodology*, 4 (1986) pp. 127–43.

USKALI MÄKI, 'Types of Unrealisticness in Economics: The Case of J. H. von Thünen's Isolated State', paper prepared for presentation at the Annual Meeting of the History of Economics Society in Richmond, Virginia (10–13 June 1989); preliminary draft.

JOHN MALONEY, *Marshall, Orthodoxy and the Professionalisation of Economics* (Cambridge University Press, 1985).

ALFRED MARSHALL and MARY PALEY MARSHALL, *Economics of Industry* (Macmillan, London, 1879).

ALFRED MARSHALL, *Money, Credit, and Commerce* (Macmillan, London, 1923).

ALFRED MARSHALL, *Principles of Economics*, 8th edn (first publ. in 1920, repr. by Porcupine Press, Philadelphia, 1982).

This edition is referred to in the text as '*Principles*'

ALFRED MARSHALL, *Principles of Economics*, 9th (Variorum) edn, C. W. Guillebaud (ed.) (Macmillan, London, 1961).

This edition is referred to in the text as '*Var.*'.

BRUCE MAZLISH, *Toward a New Science: the Breakdown of Connections and the Birth of Sociology* (Oxford University Press, 1989).

BRUCE MAZLISH, *James and John Stuart Mill: Father and Son in the Nineteenth Century* (Basic Books, New York, 1975; paperback edn with new intro., Transaction Press, New Brunswick, NJ, 1988.)

DONALD N. McCLOSKEY, *The Rhetoric of Economics* (University of Wisconsin Press, Madison, 1985).

G. W. McKENZIE and I. F. PEARCE, 'Welfare Measurement – A Synthesis', *American Economic Review* (September 1982).

M. S. McPHERSON, 'Mill's Moral Theory and the Problem of Preference Change', *Ethics*, 92 (1982).

M. S. McPHERSON, 'Economics: On Hirschman, Schelling and Sen', *Partisan Review*, 41 (1984).

MARY MIDGLEY, *Beast and Man: The Roots of Human Nature* (Cornell University Press, New York, 1979).

PHILIP MIROWSKI, 'The Probabilistic Counter-revolution, or How Stochastic Concepts Came to Neoclassical Economic Theory', *Oxford Economic Papers*, 41 (1989) pp. 217–35).

PHILIP MIROWSKI, *More Heat than Light* (Cambridge University Press, 1989).

GUNNAR MYRDAL, *The Political Element in the Development of Economic Theory*, Paul Streeten (ed.) (International Library of Sociology, London, 1953).

GUNNAR MYRDAL, *Value in Social Theory*, intro. by Paul Streeten (Allen & Unwin, London, 1958).

R. R. NELSON and S. G. WINTER, *An Evolutionary Theory of Economic Change* (Harvard University Press, Cambridge, Mass., 1982).

RICHARD B. NORGAARD, 'Environmental Economics: An Evolutionary Critique and a Plea for Pluralism', *Journal of Environmental Economics and Management*, 12 (1985).

ROBERT NOZICK, 'Newcomb's Problem and Two Principles of Choice', in *Essays in Honor of Carl G. Hempel*, N. Rescher *et al.* (eds) (Reidel, Dordrecht, 1969).

ARTHUR OKUN, *Equality and Efficiency: The Big Tradeoff* (Brookings Institution, Washington, DC, 1975).

TALBOT PAGE, 'Equitable Use of the Resource Base' Reprint # 144, Resources For the Future (Washington, D.C., 1977).

TALCOTT PARSONS, 'Wants and Activities in Marshall', *Quarterly Journal of Economics*, XLVI (November 1931).

TALCOTT PARSONS, *The Structure of Social Action: A Study of Social Theory with Special Reference to a Group of Recent European Writers* (Free Press of Glencoe, New York, 1961).

TALCOTT PARSONS, 'Economics and Sociology: Marshall in Relation to the Thought of his Time', *Quarterly Journal of Economics* (February 1932).

DAVID PEARCE, 'Foundations of An Ecological Economics', *Ecological Modelling*, 38 (1978).

HENRY M. PESKIN, 'A National Accounting Framework for Environmental Assessments', *Journal of Environmental Economics and Management*, 2 (1976).

A. C. PIGOU, *Alfred Marshall and Current Thought* (Macmillan, London, 1953).

A. C. PIGOU (ed.), *Memorials of Alfred Marshall* (Kelley & Millman, New York, 1956).
Referred to in the text as *Memorials*.

THOMAS MICHAEL POWER, *The Economic Pursuit of Quality* (M. E. Sharpe, Armonk, New York and London, 1988).

ROBERT REPETTO, 'Natural Resource Accounting for Countries with Natural Resource-Based Economics', paper presented at the World Resources Institute, Washington DC (3 October 1986).

ROBERT REPETTO (ed.), *The Global Possible: Resources Development and the New Century* (Yale University Press, New Haven, 1985).

ROBERT REPETTO, WILLIAM MAGRATH, MICHAEL WELLS, CHRISTINE BEER and FABRIZIO ROSSINI, *Wasting Assets: Natural Resources in the National Income Accounts*, World Resources Institute Report (Washington DC, 1989).

LIONEL ROBBINS, *An Essay on the Nature and Significance of Economic Science*, 2nd. edn (Macmillan, London, 1948).

VERNON N. RUTTAN, 'Sustainability is not Enough', *Journal of Alternative Agriculture*, 3 (Spring/Summer) (1988).

WESLEY C. SALMON, (ed.), *Zeno's Paradoxes* (Bobbs-Merrill, Indianapolis, 1970).

PAUL A. SAMUELSON and WILLIAM D. NORDHAUS, *Economics*, 12th edn (McGraw-Hill, New York, 1985).

PAUL A. SAMUELSON, 'Modes of Thought in Economics and Biology', *American Economics Association* (May 1985).

TIBOR SCITOVSKY, 'How to Bring Psychology Back into Economics', in manuscript (1987).

TIBOR SCITOVSKY, *Human Desires and Economic Satisfaction: Essays on the Frontiers of Economics* (Wheatsheaf Books, Brighton, Sussex, 1986).

TIBOR SCITOVSKY, *The Joyless Economy* (Oxford University Press, 1976).

DAVID SECKLER, *Thorstein Veblen and the Institutionalists: A Study in the Social Philosophy of Economics* (Colorado Associated University Press, Boulder, CO, 1975).

A. K. SEN, 'Rational Fools: A Critique of the Behavioral Foundations of Economic Theory', *Philosophy and Public Affairs*, 6 (1977).

A. K. SEN, 'Goals, Commitment and Identity' *Journal of Law, Economics and Organization*, 1 (1985).

A. K. SEN, 'Social Choice Theory', in K. J. Arrow and M. Intriligator (eds), *Handbook of Mathematical Economics*, III (North-Hollands, Amsterdam, 1986).

A. K. SEN, 'Prediction and Economic Theory', *Proceedings of the Royal Society, London*, A407 (1986).

EUGENE SILBERBERG, *The Structure of Economics: A Mathematical Analysis* (McGraw-Hill, New York, 1978).

LEONARD SILK, *Economics in the Real World: How Political Decisions Affect the Economy* (Simon and Schuster, New York, 1984).

GEORG SIMMEL, *The Philosophy of Money*, trans. Tom Bottomore and David Frisby (Routledge & Kegan Paul, London, 1978).

HERBERT S. SIMON, *Models of Man* (Wiley, New York, 1957).

ADAM SMITH, *The Wealth of Nations*, Liberty Classics edn (Oxford University Press, 1976).

ADAM SMITH, *The Theory of Moral Sentiments*, Liberty Classics edn (Oxford University Press, 1974).

GARETH STEDMAN JONES, *Outcast London* (Penguin Books, 1984: first pub. in 1971).

CHARLES L. STEVENSON, *Ethics and Language* (paperback edn 1960; first publ. 1944; Yale University Press).

PAUL P. STREETEN, *First Things First: Meeting Basic Human Needs in Developing Countries* (Oxford University Press, for the World Bank, 1981).

PAUL P. STREETEN, *The Frontiers of Development Studies* (Macmillan, London, 1972; repub. 1979).

PAUL P. STREETEN (ed.), *Unfashionable Economics*, (Macmillan, London, 1970).

PAUL P. STREETEN, *What Price Food?* (Macmillan, London, 1987).

PANKAJ TANDEN, 'Welfare Measurement – A Comment', in manuscript (1982).

STEPHEN TOULMIN, *Cosmopolis: The Hidden Agenda of Modernity* (Free Press, Glencoe, Ill, 1990).

D. A. WALKER, 'Marshall's Theory of Competitive Exchange', *Canadian Journal of Economics* (November 1969).

J. K. WHITAKER (ed.), *The Early Economic Writings of Alfred Marshall 1867–1890* (Macmillan, London, 1975).

P. WILES and G. ROUTH (eds), *Economics in Disarray* (Blackwell, Oxford, 1984).

ROBERT WILLIG, 'Consumer's Surplus Without Apology', *American Economic Review* (September 1976).

E. B. WILSON, 'Pareto on Marshall's Demand Curve', *Quarterly Journal of Economics*, 58 (November 1943).(in AMCA)

H. K. H. WOO, *What's Wrong with Formalization in Economics?* (Victoria Press, Newark, Calif., 1986).

JOHN C. WOOD (ed.), *Alfred Marshall, Critical Assessments* (Croom Helm, London, 1982).

This reference is listed in the text as 'AMCA'

HAL VARIAN, *Microeconomic Analysis*, 2nd edn (Norton, New York, 1984).

Indexes

Note: readers may also refer to index #2, ALFRED MARSHALL; index #3, NEOCLASSICAL ECONOMICS; or index #4, INDEX OF NAMES

1. SUBJECT INDEX

2. ALFRED MARSHALL INDEX

3. NEOCLASSICAL ECONOMICS INDEX

4. INDEX OF NAMES